American

CORNBALL

A Laffopedic Guide to the
Formerly Funny

CHRISTOPHER MILLER

HARPER

NEW YORK ▪ LONDON ▪ TORONTO ▪ SYDNEY

Also by Christopher Miller

FICTION

The Cardboard Universe
Sudden Noises from Inanimate Objects
Simon Silber: Works for Solo Piano

For Sarah Pogell

HarperCollins books may be purchased for educational, business, or sales promotional use. For information please e-mail the Special Markets Department at SPsales@harpercollins .com.

FIRST HARPER PAPERBACK EDITION PUBLISHED 2015.

Designed by Kate Nichols

Library of Congress Cataloging-in-Publication Data
Miller, Christopher, 1961-
  American cornball : a laffopedic guide to the formerly funny / by Christopher Miller. — First edition.
    pages cm
  ISBN 978-0-06-222517-7 (hardcover) — ISBN 978-0-06-222519-1 (epub) 1. American wit and humor. I. Title.
  PN6165.A49 2014
    818'.602—dc23
                                  201303214
                  ISBN 978-0-06-222518-4 (pbk.)
        15 16 17 18 19 ID6/RRD 10 9 8 7 6 5 4 3 2 1

Contents

Introduction

*A ham is funny, a sausage is positively uproarious, and fishballs
are sort of laughable; but veal stew is regarded as possessing few, if
any, of the true elements of humor. Soup is still funny, but not as
funny as it was a few years back. Hash is immensely humorous, but
a croquette is not.*
                                        —IRVIN S. COBB, 1911

THIS BOOK IS a guide to things that used
to make Americans laugh. Some are still
good for a laugh, but few are as funny as
they used to be, and the most laughable thing about
many is that people did once find them funny. This is
a book, in other words, about anvils, backseat drivers, castor oil, dishwashing husbands, efficiency experts, flappers, gold
diggers, hangovers, icemen, just-marrieds, kissing booths, ladies' clubs,
mothers-in-law, next-door neighbors, old maids, pie fights, rolling pins,
stenographers, traveling salesmen, ulcers, women drivers, yes-men, zealots, and many other acres of corn gone to seed, or paved over by modernity, or depleted by imprudent overplanting.

Most of these things ceased to be funny long ago—long enough that
few of us alive today have ever laughed at them, but recently enough that
we still encounter traces of their former glory, reminders that they *were*
once funny. Those reminders—novelty postcards, novelty songs, cocktail
napkins, old show tunes, old movies, old-time radio programs, early sitcoms, gag gifts, light verse, comic prose, comic strips, dirty jokes, and
so on—are the data from which I draw my conclusions. I see myself as
an archaeologist digging into the enormous trash heap of pop culture,

down to artifacts that, though still easy to unearth, have been buried long enough to be worth another look.

Specifically, and arbitrarily, I'm defining "long enough ago but not *too* long ago" as the first two-thirds of the twentieth century. Sometimes I dig a bit deeper into the dung heap for precedents and prefigurations, since often the best way to understand an old joke is by revisiting even older ones. (No one can *really* understand the whoopee cushion without going back centuries before its official introduction in the 1930s.)

Humor is not only famously subjective but also famously unstable. Every era is deaf to some of the notes that elicited a laugh in previous eras. I'd be surprised if any reader agreed with all of humorist Irvin Cobb's pronouncements above; I myself find croquettes *funnier* than hash (because of their pretensions, their shameless social climbing). Certain targets, though, do have a timeless appeal. There is no evidence of a time when drunkenness, for instance, didn't strike people as funny. Or baldness: my favorite moment in the Old Testament is when God sends two she-bears out of the woods to maul the children who have laughed at Elisha's bald head. Aside from fads like panty raids, flagpole sitting, and phone-booth stuffing, few jokes can be confined to a single generation. In choosing what to include in this guide, I have favored jokes that died out, peaked, or assumed a distinctive form in the early or mid-twentieth century.

"How can you have an entry on X and not even mention the moment in Y where A and B attempt to C and hilarity ensues?" It's a fair question, and one that every reader will ask at some point or other. The answer is that there's a limit to how much of his or her life one author should waste on this stuff. And there's a limit to how much any book—no matter how densely and cunningly packed—can accommodate. Even if I knew everything there is to know about rusty rib-ticklers, dusty gut-busters, rancid knee-slappers, fusty side-splitters, moldy monkeyshines, geriatric japes, and liver-spotted laffs—and I'm ashamed of knowing as much as I do—there's no way a single volume could do justice to the range of American humor in the first two-thirds of the last century. Li'l Abner alone could sustain a book as long as this one.

American
CORNBALL

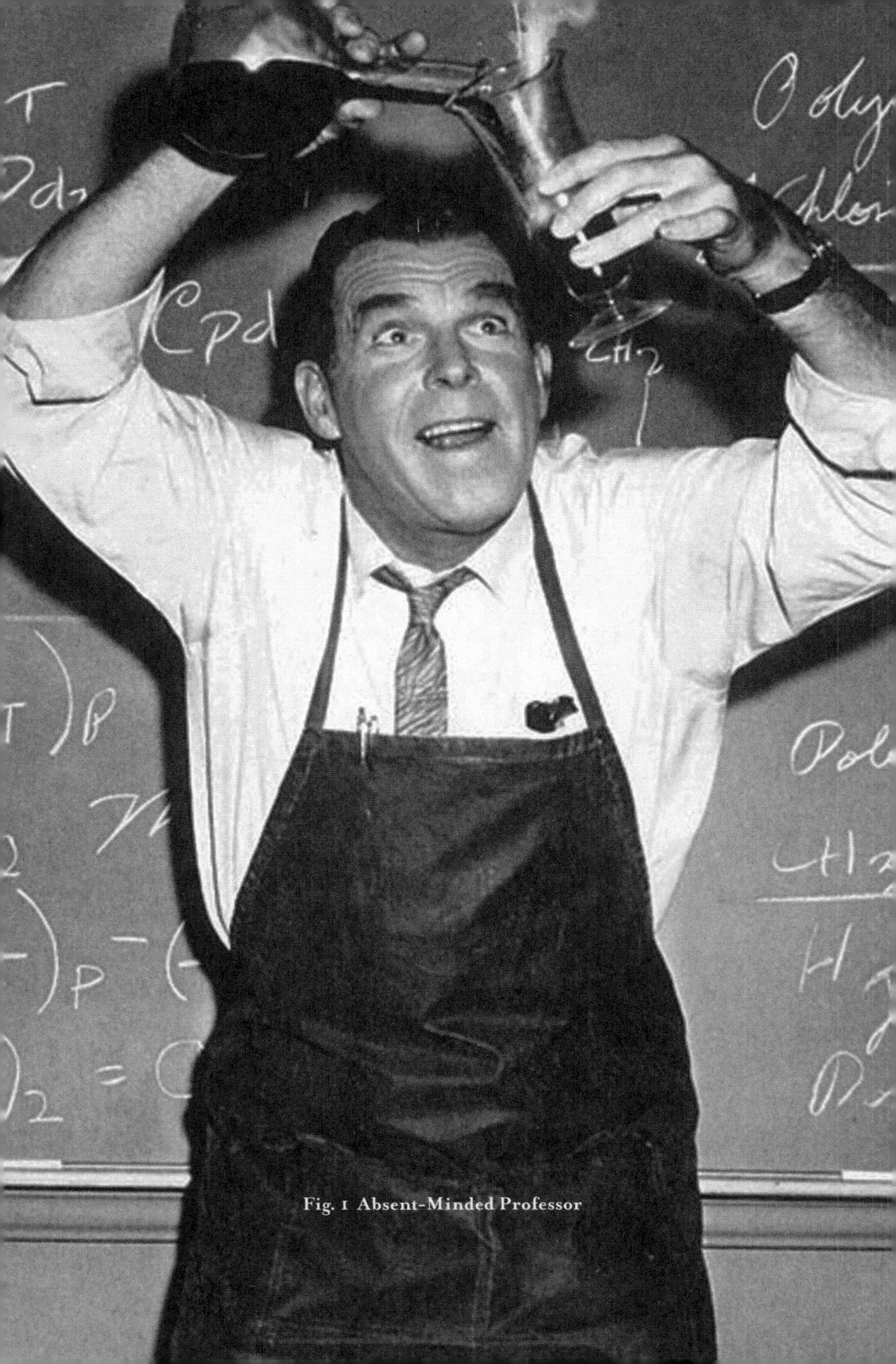

Fig. 1 Absent-Minded Professor

Absentminded Professors

Have you heard? Professor Munch
Ate his wife and divorced his lunch.
—COLE PORTER,
"WELL, DID YOU EVAH?" (1939)

I N *THE ABSENT-MINDED Professor*, a Disney film from 1961 **(Fig. 1)**, Fred MacMurray's nerdily all-consuming passion for chemistry causes him to miss his own wedding three times in a row. When his thrice-jilted bride gives him a chance to explain why he flaked out once again, all he can do is babble about meta-stable compounds and molecular configurations. And yet his fiancée forgives him, and we forgive him, too. In comic narratives, the absentminded are almost always lovable as well as laughable, and the laughter they inspire is notably gentler—more indulgent, less malicious—than the laughter provoked, for example, by BLOWHARDS, TIGHTWADS, or YES-MEN.[1] We think of absentmindedness as nothing but a deficit—an absence—and so we exempt it from the condemnation reserved for character defects like boastfulness, stinginess, or sycophancy.

Of course, some of the most mean-spirited laughter has always been reserved for physical infirmities and accidents of birth, rather than voluntary behaviors for which in theory laughter might serve as a corrective. (Though only in theory: the "correctional" account of humor has never amounted to more than wishful thinking on the part of satirists—and sometimes out-

---

[1] **SMALL CAPS** indicate cross-references to other entries.

right dishonesty—as to their true motives.) But in the case of the fat, the old, the ugly, the stupid, the bald, we can usually find other reasons to dislike them, traits that may have no connection to their infirmities but still make it tempting to target those obvious weak points. What makes it hard to feel malice toward absentminded professors is their saintlike lack of ego: they are so absorbed in their studies that there's not much personality left to ridicule or hate.

Disney wasn't taking any chances, though, in *The Absent-Minded Professor*, and Fred MacMurray is ideally miscast as the title character. True, he has a laboratory full of bubbling glassware and a chalkboard covered with abstruse EQUATIONS, but otherwise he's nothing like the stereotype. He's all-American instead of European, Christian instead of Jewish, and never wears glasses except to glance at his lab notes. He looks more like a coach than a professor. These precautions were necessary because, in the 1950s and '60s, America was deeply ambivalent toward its scientists. At best they were a necessary evil: they might discover something useful to the Pentagon or General Motors, but they couldn't be trusted. And it wasn't only narrow-minded lowbrows who mistrusted them. The example of émigrés like Wernher von Braun reminded America that the eerie selflessness and Faustian curiosity of the most brilliant scientists entailed a sort of moral idiocy—a perception memorably expressed in such works of the time as *Naked Lunch* (1959), *Cat's Cradle* (1963), and *Dr. Strangelove* (1964).

Professor Lucifer Gorgonzola Butts—Rube Goldberg's mad INVENTOR—has no personality at all, so his inventions can hardly be seen as expressions of their inventor's nature, the way we think of poems and symphonies and paintings. No, they are merely so many symptoms of HEAD INJURIES and other insults to the brain. In the course of a long career, Professor Butts "puts his head in a nutcracker and squeezes out an idea" for a golf-ball locator; "chokes on a fish bone and coughs up an idea" for a self-lowering awning; invents a painless tooth extractor "while in a state of scientific delirium"; trips on a rug and ("while looking at the stars") invents a more complicated way to slice bread; falls on his head and ("while still groggy") invents a new can opener; takes "a swig of Goofy Oil" and invents a self-sharpening razor blade; "gets caught in a revolving door and becomes dizzy enough" to invent a bulky apparatus that reminds its wearer to mail his wife's letter; "dives into an empty swimming pool and finds an idea" for an automatic radio duster, and so on.

Since as a rule it is science that the absentminded professor professes, he is not always easy to tell from his evil twin, the mad scientist. As a rule, the latter is distinguished by some passion more sordid or unholy than the sheer quest for knowledge: a lust for power, say, or wealth, or sexual irresistibility. When a thirst for omniscience becomes a wish to play God, as with Dr. Moreau or Dr. Frankenstein, it's safe to say your scientist has passed from absentminded to mad. Our culture's anti-intellectualism ensures that mad scientists are always more glamorous than absentminded professors, since nothing is nerdier than an all-consuming love of knowledge for its own sake. By that criterion, the book you're holding is supremely nerdy, since the odds of it earning its author anything much in the way of money, power, love, or godlike exaltation are vanishingly small.

Alley Cats

THE ARCHETYPAL CARTOON CAT is scrawny, disheveled, and black, though (except for anonymous bit players whose sole function is to bring bad luck) not *entirely* black, but black with white jowls **(Fig. 2)**. That's how Rube Goldberg drew cats. It's how Ernie Bushmiller drew them, to say nothing of George McManus (*Bringing Up Father*), F. Opper (*Happy Hooligan*), Fred Willard (*Moon Mullins*), Milt Gross (*Dave's Delicatessen*), C. L. Sherman (*Pete*), and C. D. Small (*Salesman Sam*), to name a few. It's the color scheme of Krazy Kat, Felix the Cat, the Cat in the Hat, and Tweety's nemesis, Sylvester, though Sylvester has a white belly, too. So does Penelope Pussycat, the unwilling object of Pepé Le Pew's attentions, but the white patch that gets her in trouble is the misleading streak on her back. Some

Fig. 2

cats also have white paws—or, in the case of high-functioning, near-human cartoon critters like Dr. Seuss's Cat in the Hat, four-fingered white gloves.

At night, the alley cat makes a point of singing below bedroom windows. He is most often found atop a wooden fence—sitting with his head raised and belting out an aria. Alley cats were such a staple of the funnies, once upon a time, that in a series of 1915 panels called "How to Be a Cartoonist," Frank King, the future creator of *Gasoline Alley*, devoted lesson six to the cartoon depiction of "Feline Infelicity": "Place quarreling cats between the reader and the moon. Picture them as about to be hit by that universal and handy weapon, the bootjack." Maybe the early cartoonists so often made their cats black to contrast better with the moon behind them. (Or is it that, at night, *all* cats are black?) And black cats are unlucky, and bad luck is much funnier than good. As for why King recommends a bootjack instead of a boot, it must be that all the boots have already been thrown, rendering the bootjack useless now for any other purpose.

As a rule, the archetypal cartoon cat remains oblivious to the missiles flung at him by angry sleepers. If I use male pronouns, by the way, maybe it's because cartoon sleepers throw the same assortment of objects at noisy cats that wives throw at drunken or delinquent husbands: not just boots and bootjacks, but rolling pins, milk bottles, flatirons, and crockery.

But *some* of those cats must be female, because some are clearly—even if never explicitly—in heat. Cats *don't* sing, after all, so what sound are the cartoonists actually evoking? The sound of cats squaring off for a fight? Sometimes, yes; and then we see two identical black tomcats on their fence top, silhouetted against a big full moon, arching their backs and baring their claws. Not that cats always fight when they meet; sometimes there will be a convivial quartet, sloppy drunk and singing "SWEET ADELINE" or "How Dry I Am." More often, though, the recital is a solo. The sound that awakened so many comic-strip sleepers, and induced them to part with so many old shoes, was a sound that must have been all too common in the days before universal spaying, and especially in the warmer months when people would've wanted to sleep with windows open: the sound of she-cats in heat. (Since at least the 1920s, *alley cat* has been slang for a sexually promiscuous person, especially a female, as well as a verb for sleeping around.) To late Victorian ears—to the ears of people who covered the legs of pianos because those legs reminded them of human legs, and thus of loins—the sound of cats in heat would have been not just annoying but disturbing, an unignorable reminder of female lust.

In old comics, cat-song is a much commoner nuisance than barking. A Martian whose knowledge of our fauna derived from those comics would conclude that cats are bigger noise polluters than dogs. (Just as he'd assume that most cats are black with white jowls, when in fact such cats are uncommon—have they been hunted to extinction by shoe-throwing louts?) Unlike dogs, cats seldom appear as fully owned pets. They are gypsies, squatters, strays, which may account for their constant outrageous mistreatment at the hands of cartoonists. The differences between cats and dogs—or between popular attitudes toward the two species—is played out fascinatingly in the funny papers and in Saturday morning cartoons, where the color-coding of cats and dogs used to be as flagrant as the black and white hats in old Westerns. Cats, as I say, are always black, and dogs are almost always white (and almost always bulldogs with spiked collars). Dogs exist to maul cats and occasionally humans. Cats have two main functions: make noise and chase mice.

Classic cartoons, because they usually side with the prey and not the predator, tend to be pro-mouse and anti-cat. We do sometimes encounter kittens heartwarmingly—or stomach-turningly—befriended by big white bulldogs with names like Butch and Spike, who get them out of one scrape after another. (In our time, the closest thing to those cartoons may be live-action films like *Kindergarten Cop*, in which Arnold Schwarzenegger goes undercover as a kindergarten teacher.) But full-grown cats are never portrayed as cute. They are notably absent from the menagerie of classic Disney characters. It's as if the sinister predatory instincts for which cats are infamous were an adult trait, when in fact even a tiny puffy kitten will gladly torture, maim, and kill any living creature smaller than itself. That may be one reason why so many people hate cats—even cat lovers like me are sometimes appalled by our pets' hardwired cruelty to harmless chickadees and field mice—and why in real life cats are a favorite target of sadists. You don't hear half as many stories of people burning, strangling, drowning, or microwaving puppies.

Comic strips are slightly more cat-friendly, maybe because animals in comic strips are more likely to speak, or at least to think in words. Nonetheless, our Martian zoologist would probably conclude, from a stack of old comics, that on this planet cats are vermin, closer in caste to roaches and rats than to dogs. Ambrose Bierce was trying to be shocking when he defined "cat," in his *Devil's Dictionary* (1906), as "A soft, indestructible automaton provided by nature to be kicked when things go wrong in the domestic circle," but he can't have shocked the comics readers of his era.

Comics, thankfully, are not a reliable guide to real behavior. But you do have to wonder about our great-grandfathers when, in a 1916 comic strip, the hero sees a cat on a fence, observes "There's an old saying that you can't miss a cat with a spud," and proceeds to test the saying with the potato he happens to be holding. Were people once so fond of throwing things at cats that there were old sayings about what to throw? And speaking of ammunition, it is not uncommon in zany strips like *Mutt and Jeff* for people to use cats themselves, alive or dead, as missiles, throwing them as casually as they throw BRICKS. Alternatively, dead cats may be thrown *away*—unsentimentally and unsanitarily—like any other nonreturnable containers once emptied of their contents. Dead cats are often pictured in comic-strip trash heaps, among the broken bottles, tin cans, and banana peels. You won't find any dead dogs on those trash heaps. Cartoonists have always been kinder to dogs. But they clearly find cats funnier.

Alum

ALUM—ALUMINUM POTASSIUM SULFATE—is an astringent used in styptic pencils, baking powders, antiperspirants, and pickling recipes. Presumably that last function accounts for its presence in so many cartoon pantries, in a jar carefully shelved beside the sugar jar to maximize the chances of confusion between the two white powders. Unlike CASTOR OIL, another famously unpalatable substance, alum wasn't a big source of humor even in its heyday, but it appeared often enough in animated cartoons—and even in live-action comedies—to merit an entry in this guide.

It first came to my attention via "Long Haired Hare," the 1949 Bugs Bunny cartoon in which Bugs retaliates so mercilessly against the OPERA singer who smashed a banjo over his head that you finally wind up feeling sorry for the guy. At one point, Bugs puts an alum solution into a spritzer, and when the singer uses it to moisten his vocal cords, his head shrinks to the size of a pea as his voice rises several octaves: "Figaro! Figaro! Figaro!" **(Fig. 3)**. Another operatic loudmouth is silenced by chemistry in "Back Alley Oproar": when Sylvester the ALLEY CAT insists on inflicting his arias on a would-be-sleeping Elmer Fudd, Elmer puts alum in Sylvester's milk, shrinking his head and shutting him up. The gang at Looney Tunes was clearly fond of alum, and Sylvester was its usual victim. In two of his out-

ings with Tweety, "I Taw a Putty Tat" and "Birds Anonymous," a mouth-puckering dose of the stuff prevents Sylvester from gobbling the bird; in both cases he tries instead to suck up Tweety through a drinking straw.

What does alum taste like? In one Three Stooges episode ("No Census, No Feeling," 1940), when Curly ruins a snooty bridge party by accidentally adding alum to the lemonade instead of sugar—causing clothes to shrink as well as lips to pucker—Moe remarks that his drink is "a little heavy on the angora bitters. In fact, I think the goat walked right through it." Curly himself puts it differently: "Roses are red and how do you do? Drink four of these and woo-woo-woo-woo!!"

Fig. 3 "Long-Haired Hare," 1949

Amnesia

IN OLD SITCOMS, the cause of amnesia is almost always a blow to the head, and the cure is usually another blow. Amnesia is too rare in real life for there to be any folk wisdom as to its treatment; the TV remedy was probably inspired by the do-it-yourself method of fixing malfunctioning radios and TV sets by whacking them on the side. Like transistors and capacitors, brains are mysterious mechanisms that—even in our age of MRIs and CAT scans—defy simple examination. (Some would say that psychiatric drugs are the pharmaceutical equivalent of smacking the TV and hoping for a better picture.)

Considering that HEAD INJURIES have always been a favorite sight gag in comic strips, slapstick movies, and animated cartoons, it's surprising that amnesia isn't more common in those genres—surprising that someone as battered as Krazy Kat or Curly or Wile E. Coyote remembers anything at all. In Funnyland, apparently, you must have a predisposition to amnesia as well as a proximate cause. Different characters, moreover, have different tolerances for the routine wear and tear of knockabout comedy. In the *I Dream of Jeannie* episode entitled "I'll Never Forget What's Her Name," all it takes to deprive Tony of his memory is a falling vase; but in order for sturdy Herman to lose it in the *Munsters* episode called "John Doe Munster," a three-hundred-pound safe has to fall on his head. (As for Superman, it takes a meteor to knock *him* silly.) For Mr. Ed, who fits somewhere between Herman Munster and Tony Nelson on the scale of hardheadedness, a falling bucket of carrots does the trick.

Sometimes it's the character who falls, headfirst—that's how Mary Ann becomes convinced she's Ginger in *Gilligan's Island*. On another episode of the same sitcom, the castaways' Hope of the Week is thwarted when Duke, the surfer who washed up on their island two weeks earlier, heads back to Hawaii on his surfboard, promising to get a rescue vessel, but wipes out en route and forgets all about them.

These sitcom examples all date from the early and mid-1960s, which seems to have been the heyday of funny amnesia. A professor of media studies might argue that the theme had special resonance for a nation slowly emerging from the amnesiac slumber of the 1950s, but a simpler explanation would be that the amnesia plot is a natural for character-based comedy. According to the now-prevailing theory, the very essence of humor is incongruity—and what could be more incongruous than a sudden drastic personality change in a character famed for his or her distinctive personality?

Because of course when you suffer from sitcom amnesia, the funniest thing is not your lack of certain basic information (that your spouse is your spouse, your job your job, your house your house), but the way your personality changes when you no longer know what kind of person you are. When Fred Flintstone accidentally beans himself with an empty bottle, his boorish personality flips to its polar opposite, an excessively well-mannered fop named Frederick. When Lisa on *Green Acres* loses her memory after she's accidentally hit on the head with a hammer, she magically becomes a good cook instead of the notoriously bad one she's been until then: instead of her usual rock-hard and rock-heavy muffins, suddenly she's making muffins as light as feathers.

Most of the classic 1960s sitcoms had an amnesia episode, though seldom in the first season, and never in the pilot. All kinds of things can happen in a pilot episode, but the interesting thing about sitcom amnesia is the sudden strangeness of a familiar character. If there weren't already a running joke on *Green Acres* about Lisa's bad cooking, there'd be nothing funny about her sudden transformation into a good cook.

That's why it's almost always a main character who gets hit in the head: no one cares if Joe Rockhead or Herb Woodley undergoes a sudden personality change or forgets a past we never knew about in the first place. On the other hand, King Tut, one of the lesser villains on the '60s *Batman* series, toggles back and forth, à la Jekyll and Hyde, between supercriminal and bookish Yale professor—of Egyptology, to be sure—whenever he's hit in the head. One of his crime sprees is triggered by a falling flowerpot, another by a brick thrown during a love-in. (*Batman* is one of the few exceptions I've made to my ironclad 1966 cutoff date; the show ran till 1968 but feels to me—due to its ongoing unavailability on video?—as much a part of the vanished past as *The Honeymooners*.)

Amnesia has never been a popular premise for short comic films, except in cases where the actors tend to play the same role in every outing. When Stan Laurel, in *A Chump at Oxford*, gets hit on the head by a falling window sash and acquires the accent and manner of well-bred Britisher, his new self is funny not just because it contrasts with his pre-amnesiac self in the same film but also because it contrasts with the recurring character that Laurel had established in earlier films. Note, by the way, that if you suffer an identity-effacing head injury in England, you are likely to become a proper British snob with a proper British accent. In a 1937 *Li'l Abner* sequence—one of the fish-out-of-water story lines Al Capp used in order to give himself, his readers, and his heroes a vacation from Dogpatch—Abner hurts his head on a trip to England, and becomes a well-mannered highbrow wrestler called the Monocled Menace.

Ankles

In olden days a glimpse of stocking
Was looked on as something shocking
—COLE PORTER, "ANYTHING GOES," 1934

If there is one thing I admire,
it's a girl with a shapely ankle.
—*SOME LIKE IT HOT,* 1959

A HUNDRED YEARS AGO, voyeurs and oglers didn't hang out at the beach, but in the city, and they preferred bad weather to good. The best spot was a busy intersection on a rainy day, with puddles in the gutters, so that stylish young ladies, no matter how modest, were obliged to lift their skirts a little to keep the hems from getting wet. A well-placed lecher might see any number of shapely ankles, and even an occasional calf.

It's hard for us now to imagine a world where women's lower legs were as fetishized and sexually charged as BREASTS are now—easier to imagine a future (though I trust I won't be there to see it) where bared breasts will be as humdrum as ankles are now. Lust doesn't *feel* culturally contingent, but our sense of taboo and transgression clearly is, and clearly plays a part in determining what we find exciting. Who can doubt that, if women in our society routinely went around naked except for oven mitts because hands were private, men would fantasize about women's hands, find ways to steal glimpses of them, and cherish pornographic images of naked hands?

As with any body part whose exhibition modesty forbids, some women were more modest about their ankles than others. The sauciest women—ones who, a century later, would have opted for those butt-revealing hyper-miniskirts, since the tide of immodesty rises ever higher—probably made a point of running errands in the rain, and no doubt hiked their hems a little farther, on reaching a puddle, than strictly necessary. One such woman is pictured in the act in a 1910 greeting card above the following verses addressed "To the Rainy-Day Girl" **(Fig. 4)**:

TO THE RAINY-DAY GIRL

You're the queen of rainy-daisies;
At my ribs my fond heart knocks;
The alarm clocks on your stockings
Can be heard for blocks and blocks.

Fig. 4

In a series of 1908 postcards featuring advice to the lovesick from Doc Cupid—a winged and bare-assed specialist with a top hat, tailcoat, and doctor's bag—one card shows a man fainting on encountering a woman who has lifted her dress and petticoat slightly, exposing a black-stockinged calf. Doc Cupid's advice: "Stay inside when it rains. A shock may prove fatal. $10.00, please."

Not all men were as easily shocked, though, and some men sought out the very sight Doc Cupid warned against. Just how common (or at least—more important for the archaeologist of humor—how infamous) the practice was can be inferred from a 1907 episode of *The Outbursts of Everett True*, a popular two-panel comic strip by A. D. Condo that ran from 1905 to 1927. Everett is a vigilante, some would say a psychopath, who keeps seeing people doing things he disapproves of— slurping their soup, for example, or failing to shovel their sidewalks— and reacts by clobbering them while delivering a little sermon calling their attention to the error of their ways. In the first panel of the strip in question, he sees a young man standing on a rainy street corner and leering at a passing ankle. In the next panel, the young man sits rubbing his head, in the gutter—in the very puddle that caused the lady to lift her hem. Everett is still shaking a fist (and, in his other hand, an umbrella; it isn't clear which weapon he just used): "I'd like to meet about two dozen of you windy corner rubber-necks every day! I'll bet I'd soon break up the practice! You ought to have thirty days in the workhouse on bread and water, you contemptible pup!!!!" A young newsboy looks on delightedly, to show that the world at large approves of Everett's rough justice, and maybe also to remind us that the ogler's obsession is a depravity consequent on puberty. (I remember very clearly a time when I was not yet interested in breasts but had gathered that older males were; though I found their preoccupation ludicrous, I sadly and rightly surmised that it would one day be mine, too.)

Note that Everett mentions *windy* corners, though in the cartoon it is clearly the rain that leads to the exposure of an ankle. On days without rain, the ankle-gazer's best bet was a windy corner where the breeze might lift an occasional hem. In old New York, there was no better corner than Fifth Avenue and Twenty-third Street, where the Flatiron Building still stands

I am seeing great things.

Fig. 5

(**Fig. 5**). Of the several rival derivations of "Twenty-three Skidoo"—the most popular catchphrase of the early twentieth century—my favorite is that it originally referred to that street corner, to the lechers the corner attracted, and to the policemen who kept telling them to skedaddle or skidoo. That would explain why the phrase, though interchangeable in almost any context with "get lost," was especially used to rebuff unwanted sexual attentions.

As for the association with leg-ogling in particular, that is demonstrated by a very short film from 1901 called "What Happened on Twenty-Third Street, New York City" (assuming the street wasn't chosen just because, in those days, TWENTY-THREE was the funniest number). What happens doesn't happen in front of the Flatiron Building, but on top of a subway grate: after some footage of random pedestrians, a careless woman steps on the grate and a gust of subterranean air blows her dress up to her knees, causing onlookers to laugh and jeer and the victim to grab and adjust her hem in alarm. The scene anticipates both the famous shot of Marilyn Monroe in *The Seven Year Itch* (1955) and the more recent fetish for hidden-camera "upskirt" porn featuring candid or ostensibly candid shots up the dresses and down the blouses of ostensibly unsuspecting women.

Nowadays, although the wind still whips around the corner of Twenty-third and Fifth, voyeurs gather elsewhere, because ankles are no longer concealed and therefore no longer exciting. Indeed, on the evidence of old movies, and in part because of them, ankles and even calves had been devalued by the 1920s. To interest the girl-watchers and rubberneckers, a woman of that decade had to show some upper leg (or some cleavage, of course). In the hitchhiking scene from *It Happened One Night*, Claudette Colbert hikes her skirt well up her thigh in order to stop a passing car after Clark Gable's thumb has failed.

Like decommissioned nuclear reactors, former taboos—though no longer capable of producing the chain reaction of lust—are forever changed and charged by irradiation. As you'd expect from a once-naughty body part, ankles remain a little funnier than they would be otherwise. As recently as the 1940s, *ankle* was slang for "young woman"—a much more gallant synecdoche than, say, *piece of ass*. Yes, the thrill is gone. But a residual charge remains, because the detritus of a not-so-distant era reminds us that men once did get off on ankles, and that will always be a funny fact.

Anvils

THOUGH WE THINK of them as the quintessential animated gag, falling anvils were rare in cartoons until the late 1940s. The joke's great era was the '50s, when it occurred, with all sorts of ingenious variations and embellishments, in at least half a dozen Road Runner cartoons, as well as in many other classic Looney Tunes shorts: Chuck Jones had an anvil fetish. Or maybe a GRAVITY fetish: anvils (along with grand PIANOS, office SAFES, and big black trapezoidal twenty-ton weights) are an especially instructive way of illustrating gravity—of *staining* it, as biologists stain specimens, for easy observation.

Fig. 6 "Going! Going! Gosh!," 1952

In "Going! Going! Gosh!" (1952), Wile E. Coyote rigs up a flying machine consisting of a weather balloon, a table fan, and a sanitation cart—but we know he's planning as always to put these peaceable instruments to warlike use, thanks to the anvil dangling from the cart **(Fig. 6)**. Sure enough, when he spots the Road Runner far below, he releases the anvil, which causes his aircraft to shoot upward. Then the balloon deflates and the Coyote and his garbage cart plunge groundward, passing the anvil on the way down (because, as the Ninth Law of Cartoon Physics mandates, "Everything falls faster than an anvil"). Then he hits the ground, and then the anvil hits him on the head.

It would be a pleasure to describe a dozen other anvil-centric cartoons, but I'll confine myself to one: "Duck Amuck" (1953), one of the most celebrated toons of all time, which climaxes with an anvil gag. Near the very end, just before we discover that the sadistic animator making life so difficult for Daffy Duck is none other than Bugs Bunny, that animator draws Daffy in a World War II fighter plane, then draws a mountain for the plane to collide with. He waits for Daffy to deploy his parachute, then erases it and substitutes an anvil. We don't see them hit the ground, but cut to a shot of Daffy, dazed and reeling, standing by the anvil hitting it with a hammer and reciting "The Village Blacksmith." Our animator replaces the anvil with an artillery shell, which the hammer detonates, and that's when it finally occurs to Daffy to demand the identity of his malevolent creator.

It's interesting to compare those cartoony anvils to the much earlier one in "A Tale of Two Kitties" (1942), the first of the Tweety Bird cartoons. At that point, Tweety still lived in the wild, with no Granny to protect him, and not surprisingly he's less cute and more sadistic—more resourceful, too—than he would become under her civilizing influence. He started out, indeed, as a sort of tiny avian Bugs Bunny, complete with Bugs's schadenfreude and his magical ability to whisk clubs and mallets and sticks of dynamite out of thin air. When he escalates to an anvil—perhaps the first one ever featured in a Looney Tunes cartoon—it appears in close-up for several seconds, looking distinctly less cartoonish than its surroundings (and much less cartoonish than the anvils the Coyote orders from Acme); the animator, Bob Clampett, even rendered the four bolt holes by which the anvil would be bolted to the blacksmith's bench, if a cartoon anvil were ever allowed to stay put on its bench.

B b

Bachelors

> *No man is genuinely happy, married, who has to drink*
> *worse whiskey than he used to drink when he was single.*
> —H. L. MENCKEN

> *The notion of the single man began in the 1950s. The idea*
> *of the bachelor as a separate life was new and obscure.*
> —HUGH HEFNER

"WHICH IS IT to be?" asks a turn-of-the-century valentine. "A loving heart with a dear little wife, / Or a selfish, lonely bachelor life?" The first option is illustrated by a naked Cupid holding a big red heart; the second—selfish, lonely—option, by a lamp, a wineglass, a ceramic jug, a plate, and two pieces of fruit. The note of desperation or exasperation is one that persists to this day. So do the two reasons offered for shunning the bachelor life: it is selfish, and it is unhappy. Granted that most selfish people *are* unhappy, the two reasons tend to cancel rather than to reinforce each other, as always when someone appeals openly to both our ethical sense and our self-interest.

Jokes about bachelors reflect much more ambivalence than jokes about OLD MAIDS, who are almost always portrayed as horny, homely, dotty wretches. No one portrays old maids as selfish, or feels the need to convince them that they are unhappy. No one envies the old maid and her choice, if choice it was, of the road less taken. No married woman, however unhappy,

WANTED
A WIFE
WHO CAN SEW
THAT'S ALL!

Fig. 7

needs to keep convincing herself that marriage is better than spinsterhood. But married men do envy bachelors, and they spend considerable energy persuading themselves that the biggest decision of their life—the decision to marry at all, as distinct from their choice of wife—wasn't a huge mistake. And women, naturally, have a vested interest in persuading married men they're better off that way, and persuading single men that sooner or later they too must tie the knot.

One way of ensuring that men will marry in spite of their better judgment is to make sex difficult to obtain outside of marriage. Another is to emphasize what single men are missing—for instance, to convince them and their married counterparts that men can't cook, and need to marry if they want to eat well. (The bachelor played by Jack Lemmon in *The Apartment* [1960] uses a tennis racket to strain spaghetti.) What makes barbecuing "manly" is not just that it involves the hacking up and burning of dead animals in ways that would be intelligible to our Neanderthal forebears, but also that it is a ritual or demonstration—though one that usually misfires—of male self-sufficiency.

How *does* the bachelor's lifestyle compare to the husband's? Clearly a man on a fixed income will have more to spend on himself if he opts for the selfish lonely life—that's the point of the wineglass and the fruit in the aforementioned valentine. You'd think that the money he saves on anniversary gifts, tricycles, college tuition, and so on would also allow him an ample budget for hosiery, but think again: a bachelor constantly darns his own socks. Long ago it was decided that just as washing dishes is the emblem of the married man's reluctant domestication, mending socks exemplifies the squalor and sadness of bachelor life **(Fig. 7)**. In the words of another snarky valentine, this one from 1906, "The Bachelor frequently 'knocks' / Matrimony, and very oft flocks / To his club in the eve, / For pleasure, we believe, / But how about mending his socks?" The Bachelor, a china figurine made in England in 1963 by Doulton & Company, shows a graying, balding bachelor primly engaged in the task. In the same era, on our side of the Atlantic, a brand of socks named Bachelors' Friend was widely advertised, and did as much as Gordon's larder to form my childhood impression of the bachelor life as a sad and unglamorous one, though I myself seem to have chosen—if choice it is—to remain a bachelor.

Contrary to Hef's assertion, "the idea of the bachelor as a separate life" has been around forever. A century ago there were already comic strips, valentines, postcards, and songs stating in G-rated terms (and sometimes PG or even PG-13) the case for bachelor life: freedom to carouse as much as you like, come home as late as you like, date all the cuties you like; freedom to fish, smoke, and gamble to your heart's content; and freedom from the nagging wife, the rolling pin, the mother-in-law, the squalling babies, the brawling kids, the roller skate on the landing, the aproned DISHWASHING.

What did change in the 1950s is that single men—and many humorists have been single men, or multiply divorced ones—became less furtive and more boastful about what they themselves considered the single best reason for staying that way. Li'l Abner had been fleeing marriage since his strip's inception in 1934, but Abner's embrace of the single life was always comically sexless; unlike his creator, Al Capp, Abner had no interest in chasing women—he just wanted them to stop chasing him. The men who subscribed to *Playboy*, though—or to *Playboy* imitations with names like *Escapade* and *Rogue*—made no secret of the fact that, for them, staying single meant sexual promiscuity. There was even a magazine called *Bachelor*, launched in 1957 and featuring articles like "10 Ribald Commandments for the Single Man," "20 Evil Ways to Make a Woman Crumble," "A New Case for Polygamy," and "How to Be a Bachelor Though Married." But of course, if you're married, you *can't* be a bachelor; for the anguish and hilarity that will ensue if you try, see DO-MESTIC VIOLENCE, HEAD INJURIES, MARRIAGE COUNSELORS, MISSILES,

MOTHERS-IN-LAW, ROLLING PINS, and SPOUSE-KILLING.

Backseat Drivers

EVERY NEW TECHNOLOGY breeds new pests, and backseat drivers seem to have been around as long as cars themselves. In a 1919 feature for *Motor Life* magazine called "Everybody Drives but the Driver," the cartoonist John Held Jr. proposed several comical inventions to deal with the nuisance. One is "a simple and efficient muffler having a flexible tube that connects with the exhaust line." The purpose of this muffler is not to asphyxiate the fretful wife in the backseat, but just to reroute her nags ("Now John, be careful—oh!"), so that they emerge from the exhaust pipe with the fumes. (Speaking of fumes, it is surely no accident that the muffler looks like a gas mask. World War I had just ended, and humorists had already adjusted to the horror of chemical warfare and started making jokes about it. A 1916 postcard shows a bossy housewife telling off her mousy husband above the caption: "A 'GAS' VICTIM.")

Another of Held's inventions—this one for wealthy couples whose interference keeps causing their chauffeurs to quit—is a set of dummy controls in the backseat. My favorite device, though, is a wind turbine designed to harness the hot air produced by nagging passengers and relay its power directly to the rear wheels. In this case the backseat drivers shouting so windily ("At-aboy . . . Watch it! . . . Step on her . . . Careful! . . . Advance your spark") are not wives but young men like the driver himself.

I point that out because in the decades—almost a century now—since Held's cartoon, most comic backseat drivers have been wives, partly because, for most of that period, husbands did most of the driving. And especially in the early days of motoring—before the advent of self-starters, automatic transmission, electric turn signals, cruise control, and so on—driving itself was more difficult and fraught with performance anxieties, and constant second-guessing from the back of the car must have seemed like a perfect emblem of a sour marriage. That's why "The Secret Life of Walter Mitty," Thurber's famous story, begins in a car, with Walter's wife

Fig. 8

finding fault with his driving: it's a quick way to suggest the conjugal hell that drives Walter to seek refuge in fantasies of manly heroism.

If drivers must be licensed, shouldn't backseat drivers also be? A quick check on eBay just now turned up eight different Back Seat Driver's licenses issued between 1956 and 1968 **(Fig. 8)**. The world of laffs—of risqué postcards, raunchy pamphlets, dime-store gags, and mail-order novelties—is a lawless one where copyrights and patents haven't got much force; all the later backseat driver's licenses are basically clones of the first (assuming it too wasn't cloned from some even older common ancestor), with its official-looking license number in the top right corner and the joke beneath it ("The commissioner already has your NUMBER, but we've assigned this one to you anyway"), the stipulation running up the left side ("BACK SEAT DRIVER MUST CARRY THIS LICENSE IN PERSON. OTHERWISE MUST KEEP QUIET WHILE VEHICLE IS IN MOTION"), the official purpose of the license set down in comic legalese ("This is to certify that the person herein named has passed all tests for nervousness and has been licensed to irritate, annoy, criticize, and otherwise disturb the operator of the car"), and the signature of the commissioner with the funny name and funny title, in this case "G. I. M. Nervous, Commissioner of Nervous Wrecks, Dept. of Interior Confusion." Subsequent licenses alter the wording here and there, but for the most part their originality is confined to the name of the commissioner: R. U. Kidding, U. Doitwrong, I. M. N. Idiott, I. B. Reckless, I. M. Nervy, Hugo Blow, I. C. Allsorts.

Baldness

> *You soak your skull in lotions until your brain*
> *softens and your hat-band gets moldy from the damp,*
> *but your hair keeps right on going.*
> —IRVIN S. COBB

OLD METAPHORS CAN BE as baffling as old jokes. According to the dictionary, *pilgarlic*, meaning "a bald man," is a contraction of "pyllyd garleke," and the origin of the term is a "fancied resemblance of bald head to a peeled garlic bulb." Well, my mind's eye is bleary from picturing bald heads and garlic bulbs and trying to see the resemblance. Clearly, though, *pilgarlic* was never a flattering term. People have been making fun of baldness since the days of the prophet Elisha, an Old Testament pilgarlic whose juvenile mockers were eaten by bears. (Mencken called God "a comedian whose audience is afraid to laugh," but who can blame that audience?[2])

Opinions differ as to whether Charlie Brown is really bald or merely drawn that way, if the distinction makes any sense with a cartoon character. Bald eight-year-olds are rare outside of cancer units, but there is a long tradition of representing born losers as bald or balding—think of Ziggy, Elmer Fudd, or Caspar Milquetoast. Baldness often serves to

---

[2] Eaten by bears: see 2 Kings 2:23–25. Is laughter a sin? The biblical case against it is stronger than that against onanism. Cf. Ecclesiastes 2:2: "I said of laughter, It is mad: and of mirth, What doeth it?" Ecclesiastes 7:6: "For as the crackling of thorns under a pot, so is the laughter of a fool: now this also is vanity."

make a character seem ineffectual and pathetic. In the 1920s, the Johnson Smith novelty company sold no fewer than eleven different "bald pate" wigs, including several with receding headlines especially recommended—it isn't clear why—for making fun of Dutch and Irish people, one with prayer locks for impersonating an Orthodox Jew, a baldpated Chinaman Wig with a ponytail, and an "Uncle Tom Wig . . . suitable for all elderly Negro characters" **(Figs. 9)**.

Many early sitcoms devoted an episode to a character's fear of encroaching baldness. *I Love Lucy* had an episode called "Ricky Thinks He's Going Bald." *Mr. Ed* had an episode in which Ed himself thinks he's going bald. *The Dick Van Dyke Show* had one episode ("I'd Rather Be a Bald Man than Have No Head at All") in which Rob thinks he's going bald, and another ("Coast-to-Coast Big Mouth") in which Laura reveals on national TV that Alan wears a toupee. Nor did *Gilligan's Island* miss the boat on this one: in "Hair Today, Gone Tomorrow," Gilligan wakes one morning to find that his hair has gone white overnight. When Mrs. Howell tries to dye it brown the following night, Gilligan wakes up bald the next day. In an episode of *Petticoat Junction*, Uncle Joe tries to market goat milk as a miracle cure for baldness.

Scalps, like bottoms, are not meant to be bared, or to be seen when bared, and indeed bald heads remind some people of bared buttocks. Knocking off a man's toupee is a bit like yanking down his pants. The Three Stooges were forever humiliating one stuffed shirt or another by accidentally knocking off (and sometimes, as in "Disorder in the Court," destroying) his toupee—even better than knocking off his hat. Curly himself was bald, of course— "ideally bald," as Nabokov says of Professor Pnin—and Larry was well on the way.

Figs. 9

Fig. 10

His receding hairline and relatively high brow (even among lowbrows, some brows are lower than others) made him an even better candidate than Curly for Moe's forehead slaps.

Perfect baldness is less poignant and less funny than partial or encroaching baldness: not even Curly ever looked as ludicrous as Bozo the Clown. "If only about two-thirds of it is gone your head looks like a great auk's egg in a snug nest," wrote Irvin S. Cobb, speaking from painful firsthand experience, "but if most of it goes there is something about you that suggests the Glacial Period, with an icy barren peak rising high above the vegetation line, where a thin line of heroic strands still cling to the slopes."

As someone who has so far been spared that particular affliction, I've always been puzzled by how doggedly balding men fight the inevitable. Once enough ground has been lost, the remaining hair makes the missing hair more conspicuously absent. And besides, as Cobb implies, those vestiges are *ugly*—uglier, to my eye, than a completely bald head. Complete baldness looks unnatural, however, because that's not how hair loss really happens. From Mr. Clean to Lex Luthor to Captain Picard, someone without a single strand of hair looks a little inhuman.

Even one hair can make a difference: it shows that its owner is still waging a comically doomed and all-too-human struggle with the inevitable. As a perfect blue sky seems even bluer with a single puffy white cloud, a bald head looks balder with a single hair. There are old sight gags about single-haired men getting haircuts, but the single hair emerging from that shiny dome is itself a sight gag, suggesting that the fewer hairs a man still possesses, the more he treasures each.

Bananas and Banana Peels

Just slip on a banana peel
The world's at your feet
—"MAKE 'EM LAUGH," 1952

N 1954, when *Atlantic* editor Charles W. Morton wanted to denounce the tendency of certain journalists to use silly paraphrases for second references—like "the ubiquitous white pills" for aspirin or "the numbered spheroids" for billiard balls—he called his article "The Elongated Yellow Fruit" and named the trend he was denouncing "the elongated-yellow-fruit school of writing." Many of his other examples— all taken from respected periodicals—were just as outrageous, but Morton picked bananas because bananas are funnier than aspirin or billiard balls.

We'll never know how much of its funniness is due to its name and how much to its shape, but the banana is by common acclaim the funniest fruit, and your grandparents thought so, too. There are few sentences that couldn't be improved, with regard to Laff Potential, by replacing a noun with *banana*. ("Hasty banana"—jocular for "hasta manana"—was a fad phrase in 1949.) Indeed, the very word seems to suggest itself to people who are forced to replace another word; as Paul Dickson observed, "When Albert Kahn, President Carter's resourceful inflation fighter, was reprimanded by the White House for using the word *recession*, he substituted the word *banana*."

In vaudeville, *banana* meant "comedian": in two-man acts, the star was Top Banana and the hapless straight man Second Banana. A more recent, more explicit synonym for "top banana" is "big swinging dick," and it makes sense to associate the two expressions, since *banana* has long been a slang term for "penis." A bawdy poem from 1889 concludes: "And thus the tawdry hussy his ripe banana peeled." The banana-penis equation was commonplace in the 1940s, to judge by all the limericks of that era that use the one word to mean the other, as in these shocking lines from 1941:

> *There was a young man from Savannah*
> *Met his end in a curious manner:*
> *He diddled a hole*
> *In a telephone pole*
> *And electrified his banana.*

So wherever we encounter them outside the produce department—in slang, in comic strips, on T-shirts or record sleeves—we should regard bananas, and *banana*, as suspiciously as Freud deciphering the dreams of an OLD MAID. "Banana oil" was a 1920s way of saying "bullshit" or "PHOOEY," as well as the title and invariable punch line of a 1920s comic strip by Milt Gross in which a wide variety of hifalutin bullshitters were exposed as such. As with *horsefeathers*, another 1920s term with roughly the same application, the joke was in the incongruity of the compound's two components, but it was the fruit's intrinsic funniness and latent obscenity that made people say "banana oil" instead of "apple oil" or "watermelon oil." In every era, some people have dirtier minds—that is, are more alert to potential metaphors—than others, and at least a few must have thought of semen when they said or heard or read "banana oil."

There may even have been people who associated slippery banana peels with slimy used condoms, which would help explain the perennial comic power of those peels. In any case, they are even funnier than bananas themselves. One of the earliest surviving comedy records, an Edison cylinder from 1906, features a vaudeville monologue by Cal Stewart, who presents himself as a sort of living comic-strip character:

> I don't think much of a man what throws a bananer peelin' on the sidewalk, and I don't think much of a bananer what throws a man on the sidewalk, neither. . . . My foot hit that bananer peelin' and I went up in the air, and come down ker-plunk, and fer about a minnit I seen all the stars what 'stronomy tells about, and some that hain't been discovered yit.

The sensible and civic-minded Mr. Bloom reflects on their danger in the "Wandering Rocks" chapter of James Joyce's *Ulysses*: "While he waited

I think I've made a lovely start
To come and offer you my heart
And ask you if you will be mine
And say I'll be your Valentine.

R.F. Outcault

Fig. 11

in Temple bar M'Coy dodged a banana peel with gentle pushes of his toe from the path to the gutter. Fellow might damn easy get a nasty fall there coming along tight in the dark." In the big football game at the end of *Horse Feathers*, Harpo "blocks" for a ball-carrying teammate by running behind and dropping banana peels that the pursuing players slip on.

The sixty-nine-year-old title character of Samuel Beckett's *Krapp's Last Tape* is addicted to bananas, though he has known for decades that they exacerbate his constipation. The play begins with Krapp painstakingly tottering, not once but twice, to the locked cabinet where he keeps his bananas. We watch him peel and eat two, and slip on the peel of the first, before we hear a single word. The first words we do hear are a tape recording of Krapp's voice he made thirty years earlier (it turns out he makes one yearly, on his birthday), and almost the first thing it says is "Have just eaten I regret to say three bananas and only with difficulty refrained from a fourth. Fatal things for a man in my condition. Cut 'em out!" Like most Beckett characters, Krapp is stripped of everything that convinces humans of their superiority to one another and to other species. Though he turns out to be quite intelligent, he has nothing to show for it but a bunch of old tapes, and the sparseness of his condition combined with the bananas makes him seem like a caged ape.

I've never seen anyone slip on a banana peel, or—as far as I recall—seen a peel lying in a spot where anyone was likely to step on it. The accident is rarer nowadays—not that people have stopped littering (a banana peel is a wrapper, after all), but bananas have been surpassed as a popular peripatetic snack by at least a hundred other foods. If you live in a big city, you constantly see people eating while walking or standing, but how often do you see someone walking down the street and eating a banana? You're more likely to slip on a slice of pizza that has fallen facedown, making it not only inedible but treacherous in the same way as a pulp-side-down banana peel.

But people still do slip and fall on banana peels. (A fifty-eight-year-old California woman recently sued a discount store where she slipped on a peel and suffered a herniated disk.) And in Cartoonland, of course, it was for many decades the leading source of PRATFALLS (with stray roller skates a distant second). It may be the leading source even now, just because it's a quick way of indicating a certain kind of accident. Without the peel, we'd be distracted from the character's funny misfortune by puzzlement as to just why he or she fell. The cartoonist can establish that the sidewalk is icy, of course, or oily, but a banana peel is funnier.

Barrels

FOR ALMOST TWO THOUSAND YEARS—until well into the twentieth century—barrels were the favored containers for shipping and storage. Bags and crates were cheaper, but less sturdy and harder to handle. Most of the things that come in cardboard boxes now would have come in barrels in the first decades of the last century. Not surprisingly, barrels were everywhere, just as cardboard boxes would be now if they weren't so much flimsier, so much easier to get rid of.

And barrels are everywhere in old comic strips, too. Once you start watching for them, you see them on page after page. Comics are not reliable historical documents—you could read through thousands of strips and see no evidence of indoor plumbing—but barrels are well represented, probably because they're fun to draw, fun to drop on characters or send rolling up behind them.

The most famous barrel gag, though, is the pauper's barrel, sometimes known as the taxpayer's barrel thanks to an editorial cartoonist named Will B. Johnstone (1883–1944) and his popular cartoons about impoverished taxpayers. In Johnstone's hands, the barrel was originally a dwelling rather than a garment—the ancestor of the big cardboard box used by homeless people in our own time. A barrel dwelling is not as funny as a barrel garment, but Johnstone was a political cartoonist, and no one expects *them* to be funny.

Fig.12 Barrel.
See also UNDERWEAR.

As for the garment (frequently hung by suspenders, like a pair of overalls, from the shoulders of its pantsless wearer), the image is so ludicrous that it feels heavy-handed to analyze the humor, but let's do it anyhow. According to Henri Bergson, for whom the essence of humor was "the mechanical encrusted on the living," what makes a garment funny is "some rigidity . . . applied to the mobility of life, in an awkward attempt to follow its lines and counterfeit its suppleness." Bergson claimed that all garments—even those woven from natural fibers, presumably—are potentially comic, if it occurs to us "to contrast the inert rigidity of the covering with the living suppleness of the object covered."

Bergson's example is a top hat, and he could also have cited zoot suits, sandwich boards, or bustles, but surely the best illustration of his point is the wearable barrel. Some clothes are praised for fitting like a second skin, but a barrel—so bulky, so heavy, so rigid, so lifeless—is as far as clothes can get from a second skin.

When worn by a pauper in a comic strip, the barrel is basically a fig leaf. It gives no protection from the elements, and as sturdy as it is, it doesn't protect the head—the body part that's always being injured in old comics. A barrel is much funnier than a fig leaf, though, because it's such a cumbersome way of screening the genitals from public view. When the barrel's original contents are specified, incidentally, more often than not it's a pickle barrel, maybe because PICKLES—those warty, phallic, sour, shrunken dainties—are funny. Even the word is funny, though not as funny as *gherkin*.

Though Johnstone is usually credited with inventing the guy-in-a-barrel shtick, the expressions "barrel jacket" and "barrel shirt" predate the Civil War. Here's an 1858 example cited in J. E. Lighter's *Historical Dictionary of American Slang*: " . . . sentenced to wear a 'barrel jacket' every day, an old flour barrel with a hole cut out of the top for his head . . . and a pair of holes for his arms." Sounds familiar, though "*in* the barrel," meaning out of money, dates back only to the 1930s: the wearable barrel was a punishment, a portable pillory, long before it became a symbol of poverty.

But comic-strip characters have been hiding in or under barrels since the infancy of the medium. As for when exactly they started using barrels to cope with wardrobe malfunctions, that's harder to say, but I've found several borderline examples from before 1905. It is permissible to substitute some other large, unwieldy container—a crate, a burlap bag, a bottomless tin bucket (worn upside down, as a skirt)—only when no barrel is handy. In old comics, though, a barrel is almost always handy.

Baths and Ablutophobia

> *I test my bath before I sit,*
> *And I'm always moved to wonderment*
> *That what chills the finger not a bit*
> *Is so frigid upon the fundament.*
> —OGDEN NASH

> *Pigpen: I have affixed to me the dust and dirt*
> *of countless ages . . . who am I to disturb history?*
> —PEANUTS, 1955

IN HIS ABSURDIST ESSAY on "Carnival Week in Sunny Las Los," Robert Benchley explains that "the simple, childish people" of that little-known Spanish province abhor rain because of its tendency

Fig. 13

to cleanse; according to their proverb, "clean things, dead things." Like many Benchley jokes it doesn't make much sense, but it's funny anyhow, in part because people who don't bathe are funny—to think about if not to smell.

HOBOES in old comics are not only work-shy but also bath-shy, as likely to flee from a tub of hot water, or a bar of soap, as from the sort of housewife who makes them beat rugs in exchange for a sandwich. Town eccentrics—not all of them paupers—are also liable, in comics, to neglect the finer points of personal hygiene. J. Pierpont "Bathless" Groggins was a favorite character in the long-running strip *Abbie an' Slats*. B. O. Plenty, a slovenly dirt farmer, debuted in *Dick Tracy* in 1947 and was noted for his musky odor, though that didn't keep him from siring Sparkle Plenty, the tulip-on-a-dungheap beauty who went on to marry Dick Tracy's adopted son Junior. B.O. might have been more comfortable, though, in some other comic strip, such as *Li'l Abner*. It's safe to say that many of the denizens of Dogpatch, from Ole Man Mose to Lonesome Polecat, qualify as menaces by the old rule of thumb: "Bathe twice a day to be really clean, once a day to be passably clean, once a week to avoid being a public menace." According to Moonbeam McSwine, "Nobody in Dogpatch *nevah* takes no baths."

Cartoon tykes from Hans and Fritz through Dennis the Menace, Pigpen **(Fig. 13)**, and Calvin have fought the prospect of bathing. In *Tidy Teddy* (1903–1904), the hero gets so dirty in the course of every strip that the daily punch line is not a spanking but a bath. For a kid, a bath often *feels* like a punishment, as well as an end to playtime, and a prelude to pajamas, prayers, and bed. Some of us never outgrow that infantile association of bathtubs with obedience: on the rare occasions when I take a bath instead of a shower, part of the fun is a sense of Being Good.

Fig. 14 Moonbeam McSwine, *Li'l Abner.*

When comic-strip children do bathe, their ablutions tend to be per-functory. Mothers are forever reminding little boys to wash behind their ears. Why *behind the ears*? Maybe the joke is that children have their own standards of cleanliness and are unlikely to clean those body parts that are visible only to others, and only to grownups. Or it may be that the area behind the ears, which is in fact a minor site of body odor, stands euphemistically for all the smelly body parts that no one sees, and which even Mother must take on faith that her son is washing.

It is much rarer for little girls in old comics to fall short in the hygiene department—so much rarer that the difference can't wholly be explained by the scarcity of girls themselves in those comics. The comic strip was a late-Victorian invention, and never really outgrew its Victorian prim-ness about little girls, to say nothing of big ones. There's still something shocking and sexually disturbing about Moonbeam McSwine, the lus-cious but filthy farmer's daughter in *Li'l Abner* who prefers hogs to men and is often portrayed as a poster child for bad hygiene **(Fig. 14)**.

No wonder Al Capp's longtime fans were bewildered by his violent hatred of hippies. For decades Capp had lovingly depicted his hairy, smelly, freakish, lazy, nonconformist hillbillies and hicks, but then along came the Summer of Love, and suddenly Capp was more outraged by the bad grooming habits of contemporary students than by anything else going on in the real world—napalm in Vietnam, political assassinations, brutal suppression of civil rights protests—or by any of the ugly passions he'd once satirized so brilliantly. (At one time or another Capp had tar-geted each and every component of rabid hippie-phobia: bigotry, prurience, sexual envy, belligerent conformism, obsession with appearances, insistence on proprieties.) A cartoonist who hates hippies more than he hates napalm is not a social critic but at best an irascible geezer. In his last decade, the man John Steinbeck had called "our greatest satirist since Swift" had less in common with Swift than with Spiro Agnew, who in fact became a good friend of Capp's. And yet *Li'l Abner* may well have manured the ground on which some of those hated flower children blossomed, since a child growing up in the conformist 1950s would have encountered few more vivid or idyllic visions of a counterculture than Dogpatch.

Beans

I N OUR TIME, most jokes about beans refer to the FLATULENCE they cause. The causation is so obvious that we should expect to find jokes about it in any era that jokes about flatulence at all, but because the subject was bizarrely tabooed during the era on which this guide focuses, the mainstream humor of that era barely acknowledged the funniest thing about beans. In a rare exception from the 1950s, the heyday of silly gag gifts, someone or other manufactured a fart joke for drunks to give one another at office parties. It came in—or consisted of—a box the size of a small matchbox. On the cover were the words WORLD'S SMALLEST WIND INSTRUMENT and a picture of a horn and some scattered musical notes. Inside was a dried lima bean glued to a card decorated with more free-floating quarter- and eighth-notes—which, since they aren't regimented on staffs, don't indicate pitch but only duration, and suggest a staccato series of very terse farts.

But beans are funny for other reasons, too. In an admiring article on Charlie Chaplin published in *The Atlantic*, Al Capp (whose real name was Caplin, incidentally) discusses the two-reeler where the Tramp, famished as always, finds a silver dollar in the street and goes into a tough restaurant to order a plate of beans, only to find out too late that his coin is a counterfeit—and to witness a huge and terrifying waiter beating the shit out of a fellow diner who's a nickel short when the bill arrives. Here is Capp's unimprovable description of the greatest "bean" sequence in all of comedy:

> The poor bum knows now that, if he ever finishes that plate of beans, his fate will be a thousandfold bloodier. Studiously averting the waiter's impatient eye, he makes an elaborate and pitiful ceremony of each bean. First he carefully selects one, after much thought (a lovely bit, because no two things look more alike, or taste more alike, or have less individual personality, than beans from the same plate). Having thoughtfully selected from the thousand the one bean which at that moment seemed most to suit his mood, he doesn't eat it. He peels it. He slices it. He seasons each half of each bean. He tastes one half, puts it back, tastes the other. He thinks about the taste, as a gourmet would ponder over rare wines. . . .

One reason Capp's description is unimprovable is that it corresponds to no known Chaplin film. Capp misidentifies the film in question as *The Tramp*—which has no beans or restaurants or waiters whatsoever—but is clearly thinking of *The Immigrant*, where the Tramp does indeed find a coin, orders a plate of beans, and then discovers that the coin is fake. And, to be sure, he daintily eats the first five beans one by one with a fork before losing patience and scooping up a big mouthful—but that all happens *before* he realizes that he can't pay. As far as I can tell, the picky-eater scene as Capp describes it is a figment of the great cartoonist's imagination. Certainly it appears in no version of the film I've been able to track down.

Capp's article appeared in 1950, back in the dark age before DVDs or even VCRs, and it's understandable that in recalling a film he'd seen decades earlier, and maybe only once, he got some details wrong. The striking thing is what his imagination did to the film he remembered. It's already funny that the Tramp should order himself a plate of beans instead of a steak, and that the apparent stroke of good fortune that brought him those beans should prove a mirage: only in a Chaplin film could a plate of beans be too good to be true. But Capp unconsciously, or perhaps deliberately (his readers were in no position to check the accuracy of his synopsis), modified the sequence to make it funny in the same way *Li'l Abner* was funny. The paragraph quoted above is nothing less than one great comedian's embellishment of another great comedian's Ode to Beans.

We know that Capp himself found beans funny. In one of the most memorably idiotic episodes of *Fearless Fosdick*, Li'l Abner's favorite comic strip, the dim-witted flatfoot learns that a poisoned can of beans is at large, and does his best to avert a poisoning by blowing out the brains of anyone—children, parents, law-

abiding burghers, and finally his own aunt—whom he sees eating beans. Soon no one dares to eat them in public, so gangsters open "bean-easies."

In old jokes about cheap food, HASH and beans were often interchangeable. In old slang as well, many facetious terms involving *hash*, such as *hashery, hash house, hash foundry* (all terms for a cheap restaurant), and *hash-slinger*, had leguminous counterparts: *beanery, bean house* (in the Civil War, there was also *Bean Hotel*, army slang for the cookhouse), *bean foundry, bean-slinger*. It should be noted, though, that a *bean wagon* (a cheap diner made from a converted dining car) is not the same as a *hash wagon* (an ambulance). A *bean sheet* was a union card used to secure food or lodging, and a waiter was a *bean jockey*.

What beans and hash had in common was their overuse—their contempt-inducing familiarity—as a cheap substitute for meat. (During World War II, peanut butter often served the same purpose for civilians, as Spam did for soldiers; and in the Civil War, peanuts themselves served the protein needs of many Confederate troops, who called them *goober peas*.) Why, though, in their heyday, did overuse make them *funny*? Because **PREDICTABILITY** per se is funny? Maybe. Or maybe because humor is, among other things—so many others that this Laffopedia can do no more than hint at humor's countless forms and functions—a condiment for foods that sheer habituation would otherwise render inedible.

Beatniks

IT'S NOT CLEAR whether the term itself, coined in 1958 (by Herb Caen, a San Francisco journalist) on the model of *Sputnik*, was a cause or an effect of the mass media's belated obsession with a subculture that by that point had been around for almost a decade. By that point, some of the hipper outlets of mass culture, like *Mad* magazine, had been joking about beatniks for years, though of course without calling them that. In 1956, *Mad* ran an article advising readers to grow goatees, show up at parties naked, and decorate their homes with abstract paintings, arty coffee tables, and books by the likes of Schopenhauer and Kant; it's basically a primer on how to be a beatnik, but since that label hadn't yet been coined, the title is "How to Be Smart"—that is, how to make the grade as a nonconforming pseudo-intellectual.

As any epidemiologist will tell you, naming a syndrome makes it much easier to recognize. The big blip in media interest in beatniks occurred

BEATNIK DISGUISE
REAL GONE, MAN!
Set consists of genuine French beret, long cigarette holder, beatnik beard that would make a real beatnik green with envy. Easily applied or removed.

☐ 4831.   Set, Postpaid $2.75

Fig. 16 From the Johnson-Smith novelty catalog

between 1958 and 1960, in highbrow as well as lowbrow publications; in that period *The New Yorker*
published no fewer than eighteen
cartoons about the subculture. *Mad*
itself continued to make fun of
beatniks. The September 1960 issue
featured a fake magazine-within-a-
magazine called *Beatnik*; its cover
shows a beatnik party, complete
with bongos, beards, berets, dark
glasses, an Abstract Expressionist
painting, a bottle of Chianti, and
even a hipster reading a book about
Zen. The cover text promises a feature on "18 New Ways to Rebel
Against Society."

Fig. 17 Maynard G. Krebs

With one notable exception, it was years before sitcoms got on the
bandwagon: 1963 in the case of *Petticoat Junction* (with an episode called
"Bobbie Jo and the Beatnik"), 1964 in the case of *The Addams Family*
("The Addams Family Meets a Beatnik"), 1965 for *The Munsters* ("Far
Out Munsters") and *The Beverly Hillbillies* ("Cool School Is Out" and
"Big Daddy Jed"), and not till 1966 for *Green Acres* ("Uncle Ollie," in
which Oliver's long-haired, work-shy hepcat nephew roars into Hooter-
ville on his motorcycle). By the time sitcoms notice a subculture and start
featuring it in episodes, that subculture usually is stone dead.

The exception to this rule, in the case of beatniks, is *The Many Loves
of Dobie Gillis*, which aired on CBS from 1959 to 1963 and featured, as
the teenaged hero's sidekick, a spacy, lazy, goateed beatnik named Maynard G. Krebs, played by Bob Denver (later to play Gilligan) **(Fig. 17)**.
Krebs is said to have been the inspiration for Shaggy on *Scooby Doo*, and
also to have done more than any other fictional character to shape middle
America's concept of a typical beatnik.

Beatniks were frequently suspected of pseudo-intellectualism. Their
berets and facial hair, like their unverifiable enthusiasm for modern jazz,

free verse, and abstract art, was seen as a way for ordinary schmucks to look smarter and deeper than they were. And there must have been some truth to that. Certainly Alfred E. Neuman never looked as intelligent as on the cover of the 1960 paperback collection *Like, Mad*, in goatee, beret, horn-rimmed glasses, and turtleneck sweater. He actually looks like a stoned intellectual, rather than a MORON trick-or-treating as a hipster. Maynard G. Krebs, to be sure, was neither intelligent nor pseudo-intelligent—was, indeed, as dim as Gilligan—but that's because he wasn't just a one-shot character but Dobie's best friend, and therefore, like all sitcom teenagers of that era, had to be lovably nonthreatening.

Belches and Burps

> Barbara Slater: Do you rhumba?
> Curly Howard: Only when I take bicarbonate.
> —THREE SMART SAPS, 1942

> Fred Allen: You couldn't ad-lib a belch at a Hungarian dinner.
> Jack Benny: You wouldn't dare talk to me that way
> if my writers were here!

IN OUR GRANDPARENTS' DAY, *burp* was the common euphemism for *belch*, though considering the nature of the sound in question, it's odd that the more imitative of the two words was the polite one. *Eructate* never caught on (though it has the rare—unique?—distinction of being both Latinate *and* onomatopoetic), not even among people who perspire instead of sweating. Maybe that's because commercials don't have occasion to talk about belches as much as they do about sweat, and it's Madison Avenue that usually helps such genteelisms reach the heartland.

Speaking of Madison Avenue, marketing consultant J. Colossal McGenius, a minor character in *Li'l Abner*, is so good at his job that he charges ten thousand dollars for every word he utters, and for each of his

HICCUPS and belches, too. And what with his addiction to soft drinks like Eleven-Urp and Burpsi-Booma, he belches a lot. He may have inspired (literally, "filled with gas") the character of Poptop Jones, a one-shot character in *Dick Tracy* whose addiction to soda pop led to constant belching.

Belches are more common in old comic strips than in old movies or radio programs, because the noise itself, like that of flatulence, was virtually taboo till recently. I still remember how thrillingly disgusting (and unprecedented, in my moviegoing experience) the sound was in the original *Willy Wonka and the Chocolate Factory* (1971), in the scene where Charlie and his grandpa drink too much of Willy's levitating soda pop, and only by belching repeatedly can save themselves from being sucked up into a huge exhaust fan. Ingestion is a funny business, sometimes unspeakably so. From the instant it enters the mouth, or at least the instant it passes the esophagus, everything we eat and drink becomes unfit for polite society, and so do its sometimes noisy misadventures during its transformation into urine and feces.

Bigamy

> Mrs. Teasdale: "This is a gala day for you."
> Rufus T. Firefly: "Well, a gal a day is enough for me.
> I don't think I could handle any more."
> —*DUCK SOUP*, 1933

> One at a time is love. Two is promiscuous.
> With three it's sexual independence,
> and beyond that, research.
> —SAM LEVENSON

FOR TWO WEEKS in the summer of 1963, "Surf City" was a number-one hit for Jan and Dean, who had help from Brian Wilson with the lyrics. The only part of those lyrics that I can ever remember is the refrain:

We're goin' to Surf City, 'cause it's two to one,
We're goin' to Surf City, gonna have some fun,
Two girls for every boy!

I just looked up the rest of the words. Aside from a more precise description of the girls in question ("two swingin' honeys for every guy") and tips on how to woo them ("all you gotta do is just wink your eye"), the highlight for me is when the singer wonders what he'll do "if my woody breaks down on me somewhere on the surf route," which if it meant what it sounds like would be a bitter irony indeed, like that famous episode of *Twilight Zone* where a harried bookworm finds that he's the only person alive and looks forward to all the reading he'll be able to do now, but then accidentally breaks his reading glasses. Slang has changed since 1963, though, and the "woody" in question is just an old wood-paneled station wagon.

"Woman wants monogamy; / Man delights in novelty," begins a Dorothy Parker poem entitled "General Review of the Sex Situation." Though that basic incompatibility has been the basis for a lot of humor (and, of course, a lot of grief), surprisingly little has involved bigamy in the usual sense, maybe because—less surprisingly—few men have chosen to satisfy their craving for variety by taking multiple wives. But also because the topic is one that mainstream humor finds harder to handle than adultery.

There are exceptions. The Marx Brothers loved to joke about polygamy—most memorably in the scene from *Animal Crackers* where Groucho, as big-game hunter Captain Spaulding, speed-dates, sweet-talks, and proposes simultaneously to two women (in each other's presence), a cute one played by Margaret Irving and a DOWAGER played, as always, by Margaret Dumont:

> You two girls have everything—you're tall and short and slim and stout and blonde and brunette. And that's just the kind of a girl I crave. We three would make an ideal couple. Why you've got beauty! Charm! Money! [To Margaret Dumont] You *have* got money, haven't you?

After a Strange Interlude spoofing Eugene O'Neill, Groucho pops the question: "Well what do you say, girls? What do you say? Are we all going to get married?" And though the cuter Margaret exclaims "That's bigamy!" (to set up Groucho's line "Yes, and it's big of me, too"), neither woman seems especially shocked or repelled by the idea, or by Groucho's hint that in his case, two women may not be enough: "Think of the honeymoon—strictly private. I wouldn't let another woman in on this. Well, maybe one or two. But no men!"

It's one of those scenes where Groucho says one outrageous thing after another to dull-normals who remain impossibly unruffled. (When the Marx Brothers do provoke other characters to anger—think of Edgar Kennedy's famous "slow burn" in the lemonade scene from *Duck Soup*—it is almost always through actions rather than words. You can watch their movies with the sound off and still make sense of nearly all the major mood swings.)

Groucho's honeymoon comments suggests another reason that bigamy humor isn't more common: few men are content to daydream about two girls when they could be daydreaming about three or four or five. The dual-proposal scene in *Animal Crackers* ends, in fact, with five giggling young beauties in bathing suits walking by, and Groucho joining them "to sow a couple of wild oats."

Robert Benchley wrote a facetious essay on bigamy shortly after World War I: "In the United States during the years 1918–1919 there were 4,956,673 weddings. 2,485,845 of these were church weddings, strongly against the wishes of the bridegrooms concerned. In these weddings 10,489,392 silver olive-forks were received as gifts." Wars seem to get us thinking about bigamy because they get us thinking about the "Enoch Arden" situation, where a woman remarries in the mistaken belief that her first husband is dead.

At least, that's how I explain the fact that there were two Hollywood comedies about polygamy in 1940 (*Too Many Husbands* and *My Favorite Wife*) and another in 1941 (*Tom, Dick and Harry*). In *Too Many Husbands* (advertised with such taglines as "TWO'S COMPANY . . . THREE'S ILLEGAL!" and "HOW HAPPY SHE COULD BE WITH EITHER . . . IF THE OTHER WOULD JUST GO AWAY!"), it is the wife who is spoiled for choice when her first husband returns from the presumed-dead after she has remarried. Both husbands have always taken her for granted, but now they must vie for her favor.

In *My Favorite Wife*, Cary Grant plays Nick Arden, who must choose between a first wife he thought dead (Irene Dunne, who as it turns out was merely marooned for seven years on a desert island) and the second wife he's just married. His first wife reappears at the moment of optimum funniness—between wedding and wedding night—and Grant's refusal to consummate his marriage, during the interval when *he* knows but his second wife doesn't yet that his first is still alive, upsets his bride so much that she enlists the aid of a PSYCHIATRIST. In *Tom, Dick and Harry* (remade in 1957 as *The Girl Most Likely*, a musical), Ginger Rogers isn't actually married to anyone, but she must choose among three suitors, and there is a racy fantasy sequence where she refuses to choose: all three men undress in her presence, and she seems to like the prospect of taking them all on at once.

You'd think the bigamy theme would have been common in bawdy men's magazines or on risqué postcards, but it never was, maybe because it doesn't lend itself well to single-panel humor. Or maybe the idea made readers uncomfortable, even readers of porn magazines. That would explain why, when you do see a bigamy cartoon, it's almost always set in some remote and exotic place, rather than in the cities and suburbs where most cartoons are set. Specifically, such hanky-panky is confined to DESERT ISLANDS and the harems of sultans. Even in *Playboy*, more often than not the "harem" cartoons were no more than polygamous versions—orchestrations, as it were—of conventional marriage clichés. A 1960 cartoon from a book called *Just Married* shows a sultan and his eight or nine wives in the office of a marriage counselor who asks, "Now, what seems to be the problem?" A 1948 cartoon by Hank Ketcham—future father of *Dennis the Menace*—shows four sultans gathered around a hookah and singing "I want some girls just like the girls that married dear old dad." A Whitney Darrow cartoon from the same era shows two Arabs leaving a movie theater with Arabic on its marquee. Says one guy to the other: "Same old stuff—boy meets girls, boy loses girls, boy gets girls."

Since the desert island is a—*the*—classic male fantasy, as well as the single most overused gag situation in magazine cartoons, it is not surprising that male cartoonists (and till recently, that was almost a redundancy) have elaborated the cliché in much the way the male imagination elaborates sex fantasies. If it would be fun to be shipwrecked on a desert island with a beautiful woman and no male competition, wouldn't it be *twice* as fun to be shipwrecked with two? Or why not three or five or ten? Like our fantasies, though, the cartoons tend to fixate on possible trouble in paradise: grownups are complicated people, incapable of simple wish-fulfillment even in their daydreams, needing all their pleasures spiced with pain. In an unsigned cartoon I found in *Big Dame Hunters*, a 1962 collection of bawdy cartoons that first appeared in *Bluebook, Whisper, Man's Conquest, Man's Illustrated, Real Adventure*, and *Conquest*, three sexy women on a desert island watch a man approach their shores. "We'll have to set up a schedule," says one cutie to the other two. "We don't want to kill him."

Bindlesticks

IF YOU'RE A HOBO on the road, or a mischievous runaway kid, you probably don't own anything as fancy as a knapsack, but you don't need a knapsack for your few belongings. One thing you do own is a handkerchief, and by wrapping the other things inside it and tying the ends of the hanky to a stick, you can make a handy cartoon carryall. Of course, the hanky is probably less than immaculate, since you're a rambunctious kid or a devil-may-care hobo, and you now have nothing but your sleeve to blow your nose on, but as a comic-strip vagrant you have to expect some hardships.

Such, I'm guessing, is the joke—almost inscrutably archaic in the age of Kleenex—behind the cartoon bindlestick **(Fig.18)**. And—like the bimbo bursting out of the enormous cake, or the little cask of brandy tied round the neck of the trusty St. Bernard—the bindlestick is something we know *only* from cartoons. Most of us would feel a sense of unreality if we ever did lay eyes on one in real life, as if we'd somehow strayed into

Fig. 18

Cartoonland. There, though, bindle-sticks are—or were—a common sight. Little Orphan Annie uses a polka-dotted hanky for her bindlestick when she runs off to Cosmic City. Sluggo, when he hits the road in 1939 after quarreling with Nancy, also opts for polka dots. Li'l Abner's bindle, in a 1947 adventure, is yellow with green dots.

What's with all the polka dots? Is that really the best pattern to command re-spect from the riffraff, roughnecks, and tough customers a runaway is likely to encounter? Maybe not, but polka dots are funny, and an easy way for the cartoonist to indicate cloth; otherwise, it might as well be a hornet's nest hanging from the stick. Like most cli-chés of cartoon iconography, in other words, the polka-dotted bindlestick obeys the two great comic-strip imperatives: the need to be funny and the need to make the object represented recognizable even at comic-strip resolution.

As for the stick itself, was that ever really the easiest and most comfortable way for runaways and hoboes to carry their belongings? Couldn't they have rigged up some kind of rudimentary backpack? No doubt. But the stick was the whole point: like a walking stick in certain hands, the bindlestick, if it was ever used in real life, must have been a pretext to carry a weapon—to ward off angry dogs, fellow vagrants, hos-tile locals, and the like. The polka-dotted bundle dangling from the end makes it look less menacing—probably another reason for those polka dots—but neither they nor our romanticized notions of HOBOES should blind us to the fact that the hobo life was more often ugly than pictur-esque, the closest thing in peacetime to the state of nature as described by Hobbes: "continual fear and danger of violent death, and the life of man solitary, poor, nasty, brutish, and short." And in that state it pays to carry a big stick.

Black People

AMOS 'N' ANDY was a hugely popular radio sitcom that aired nightly from 1928 to 1943, and then weekly until 1955. The show concerned the exploits of black characters played by white voice actors (most notably its creators, Freeman Gosden and Charles Correll), but there was also a television sitcom with black actors that aired from 1951 to 1953 (and then in reruns all the way to 1966). Many of the radio episodes can be heard online; they are still funny, and—considering the rate at which they were cranked out—impressively well written and well acted. People who have never heard the show think of it as pure racism, but in fact its representation of blacks was distinctly less offensive than average for most of its era. Still, it is undeniably a product of that era. It reflects attitudes we now find unacceptable and—if we are white—highly embarrassing. I'm glad that an archive of the show exists online, but no one would want the show rebroadcast now, and if some rogue NPR programmer started airing old episodes, some of the loudest voices raised in protest would be white ones.

For white Americans, the temptation to bowdlerize the more glaringly racist parts of the past can be overwhelming. I succumb to it myself sometimes. I would never vote to ban or burn *Huckleberry Finn*, and have nothing but contempt for the well-meaning philistine who recently produced a sanitized version of the book with every instance of *nigger* replaced by *slave*. But a few years ago, while photocopying excerpts from an old Johnson Smith mail-order catalog in preparation for a college course on American humor, I found myself censoring the ad for the Jolly Nigger Puzzle ("The grinning nigger clings on to the

Darkey in a Watermelon

Upon opening the watermelon, which is made of papier mache, is found a little pickaninny, southern darky with cloth diaper fastened with a miniature safety pin and a small nursing bottle. His white eyes flash and the whole face indicates perfect happiness.
No. 5776. **Darkey in Watermelon** 15c
3 for 40c., or $1.35 per doz. postpaid.

Fig. 19

Fig. 20

brightly polished steel ball in his mouth in a way that is most provoking").

Racist humor is a huge and sickening topic. The role of humorists in constructing and perpetuating ethnic stereotypes is a subject that demands—and has received—whole books.[3] Here I just want to say a little about the gradual ebbing of that tide in the first two thirds of the twentieth century. As you'd expect, it ebbed from different shores at different times. Flagrant stereotyping of African Americans, of the sort you still find in the stupidest Hollywood movies, was already a no-no in *The New Yorker* when the magazine debuted in 1925, though cartoons about near-naked cannibals continued to appear in its pages well into the 1950s, usually courtesy of Charles Addams.

---

[3] See, for example, *The Rhetoric of Racist Humour*, by Simon Weaver; *Sambo: The Rise and Demise of an American Jester*, by Joseph Boskin; *Toms, Coons, Mulattoes, Mammies, and Bucks: An Interpretive History of Blacks in American Films*, by Donald Bogle; *That's Enough, Folks: Black Images in Animated Cartoons, 1900–1960*, by Henry T. Sampson; *Black Like You: Blackface, Whiteface, Insult & Imitation in American Popular Culture*, by John Strausbaugh; *African American Viewers and the Black Situation Comedy: Situating Racial Humor*, by Robin R. Means Coleman.

Other magazines took longer to outgrow the taste for racist humor, and some, like *Captain Billy's Whiz Bang*, never did. That publication—a lowbrow humor magazine edited by Wilford H. Fawcett, who went on to found Fawcett Books—had two regular features devoted to darkie jokes: Whizbang Blackouts and Burnt Corkers. In 1926, Cap'n Billy offered a five-dollar prize for "the best colored joke," since in those days it was common knowledge that "there is no other form of humor in the whole wide world that explodes into laughter as easily as that supplied by the colored folk."

So our sense of the state of racist humor at a given time in America's past (or at present) depends on which artifacts we are consulting. At one extreme, you have those in which our culture was putting its best foot forward: *The New Yorker*, the leading newspapers, the big ambitious movies and novels of Oscar- and Pulitzer-hungry auteurs. At the other extreme, the more hateful scribbles in the stalls of public toilets[4] (scribbles left, I've always suspected, by the same people who make a point of not flushing the toilet, and for the same reason: to publicize precisely what is most unlovely about themselves). In between is everything else that makes up our culture.

I hasten to add that it isn't a question of highbrow and lowbrow. The literary writers of the early twentieth century expressed more racial hatred than Cap'n Billy ever did. Think of *The Great Gatsby*: not Tom Buchanan's alarmist endorsement of *The Rise of the Colored Peoples* (Tom is a bully and a BLOWHARD, and his semi-articulate spouting of white-supremacist views serves rather to discredit him than to promote those views), but the narrator's own casual racism, as when, out for a drive, he notices some blacks in another vehicle: "[A] limousine passed us, driven by a white chauffeur, in which sat three modish Negroes, two bucks and a girl. I laughed aloud as the yolks of their eyeballs rolled toward us in haughty rivalry."

Even more than "the yolks of their eyes," what really makes us wince is the word *bucks*, with its mixture of dehumanizing contempt and sexual

---

[4] Beginning in 1926, Captain Fawcett also published a similar magazine called *Smokehouse Monthly*; *smokehouse* was his favored synonym for *outhouse*.

envy. Vachel Lindsay's comic poem "The Congo" (1915), subtitled "A Study of the Negro Race," begins:

> I. THEIR BASIC SAVAGERY
> *Fat black bucks in a wine-barrel room,*
> *Barrel-house kings, with feet unstable,*
> *Sagged and reeled and pounded on the table,*
> *Beat an empty barrel with the handle of a broom,*
> *Hard as they were able,*
> *Boom, boom, BOOM, . . .*

But it is misleading to single out Lindsay or Fitzgerald when so many other authors of the time were doing the same thing. And in today's self-righteous cultural climate it's important to remember that, unless we happen to be saints, ugly sentiments are a big part of our psyches. Serious writers try to tell the full truth about themselves; if a writer *never* sounds more like a shithouse wall than like a campaign speech carefully worded for optimal and omnidirectional inoffensiveness, it's safe to say that he or she is dishonest. When writers are afraid to express any feelings that wouldn't pass muster with St. Peter, the result is not reform, but insipid and sanctimonious writing.

On the other hand, there's something frighteningly wrong with anyone for whom the shithouse wall is *enough*—anyone who feels no need to counterbalance the ugliest possible sentiments on any subject with other possible sentiments. Such is the implied reader of the Johnson Smith catalog. The Jolly Nigger Puzzle was offered in the 1929 edition. That same year, the company also offered Nigger Make-Up (listed as such in the catalog index), an Uncle Tom wig, an Uncle Tom mask, three other Negro masks, the Alabama Coon Jigger (a windup toy), a pair of Performing Coon dolls, the Whistling Coon ("Press the bulb and the Coon rolls his eyes, pokes out his tongue and whistles in a very life-like manner"), a book of Darkey Jokes and two books of Coon Jokes, a book of "comic lectures and Negro sermons" called *Brudder Gardner's Stump Speeches*, and a book called *The Minstrel Show, or Burnt-Cork Comicalities*. I should also mention the ad on page three for live chameleons: "If ah

Fig. 21 Swizzle sticks, c. 1960

could [change colors] like dat chameleon," exclaims a comic darkie with giant lips and big white eyes, "I'd go lie down on a sheet!"

If we leap ahead to 1942, we find that the company no longer offers the Jolly Nigger Puzzle, unless I missed it in my increasingly blear-eyed perusal of the catalog's 620 pages. The Whistling Coon seems to be gone as well. Nigger Make-Up has been renamed Negro Make-Up, but the product description is unchanged: "a black stockingette mask, odd eyes, buck teeth, and imitation plantation straw hat." And the catalog still offers the Performing Coons, the books of coon jokes, minstrel sketches, and comic Negro sermons, and the various masks and wigs, along with some new ones: a Topsy wig and a Ubangi mask pictured right next to the Hitler mask. Other new additions include three different china statuettes of black children defecating. There was also an ashtray featuring a black boy eating a big slice of watermelon. With the benefit of hindsight, I think I see a depressingly gradual trend away from the overt racism of the 1929 catalog, but I'm not sure even of that. Another item added since 1929 is the black bisque statuette of Three Wise Niggers ("You have often seen 'Three Wise Monkeys,' but here's a new one. . . .") hearing, seeing, and speaking no evil.

Of course, no one would expect a catalog that also offered stink bombs and fake VOMIT to be at the forefront of social enlightenment. And Johnson Smith was in good company. Hollywood wasn't terribly enlightened either, in those days, tending to portray blacks as superstitious, childlike, and above all lazy. Lincoln Perry made a career with his character Stepin Fetchit, The Laziest Man in the World, though Perry himself was anything but lazy, acting in fifty-four films and pursuing a second career as a journalist. Willie Best evolved a similarly feckless character billed in several films simply as "Sleep 'n' Eat"; on *Amos 'n' Andy*, the slow-moving, slow-witted "Lightning" was another Fetchit clone.

When open mockery of black people went out of fashion, Hollywood largely forgot about them, since it had never known how else to deal with them. Why doesn't Quincy Adams Wagstaff, the philandering college president played by Groucho Marx in *Horse Feathers* (1932), show any interest in Thelma Todd's beautiful black maid (Theresa Harris)? It was a missed opportunity for interracial romance, and one of the last such onscreen opportunities for decades, since the Motion Picture Production Code—adopted in 1930 but not put into effect till 1934—forbade portrayals of miscegenation.

Nowadays, most of us are familiar with golden-age Hollywood racism by way of cartoons. Animation buffs speak in hushed tones of the Censored Eleven—eleven Looney Tunes and Merry Melodies cartoons, dating from 1931 to 1944, that haven't been broadcast since 1968 because of their pervasive stereotyping of blacks. (Many other old cartoons are edited when broadcast nowadays, but the Eleven are too relentlessly racist for editing to remedy.) Though frequently repellent, they are notably more mirthful than another batch of cartoons that are seldom aired nowadays: the wartime anti-German and anti-Japanese cartoons enlisting the likes of Daffy Duck ("Daffy the Commando") and Bugs Bunny ("Bugs Bunny Nips the Nips") in the propaganda effort: habitual and unexamined contempt makes for better humor than sudden hatred.

Defenders of the Censored Eleven insist that those cartoons are no more than typical of the attitudes of their time, and that, as chain-smoking parents used to tell their emulous teenagers, back in those days nobody knew any better. Not true. The NAACP protested at least one of the cartoons (1943's "Coal Black and de Sebben Dwarfs"), and tried unsuccessfully to persuade Warner Bros. not to release it. Warner Bros. knew perfectly well that some people would find the film insulting, but the studio didn't care because it also knew that those same people were a minority in no position to make much of a fuss. It took the civil rights movement and a decade of social unrest to change that.

Blondes

> *Bertrand married a tall Blonde who knew that*
> *Columbus discovered America, and which kind of*
> *Massage Cream to buy, and let it go at that.*
> —GEORGE ADE

> *It was a blonde. A blonde to make a bishop*
> *kick a hole in a stained-glass window.*
> —RAYMOND CHANDLER

THE MOST FAMOUS GOLD DIGGER in movie history may be Lorelei Lee, the blonde bombshell heroine of *Gentlemen Prefer Blondes*. Most people know that story in one or more of its screen adaptations, though it started life, in 1925, as a brilliant comic novel by Anita Loos. In Lorelei's lexicon, a gentleman is any male with a lot of money, and what those gentlemen really prefer is venal, vapid, and sexually licentious young women; hair color is a secondary consideration.

Marilyn Monroe deserves much of the credit, or blame, for the Hollywood's "dumb blonde" stereotype. Think of films like *The Seven Year Itch* (where, in hot weather, she keeps her underwear in the refrigerator) or *How to Marry a Millionaire* (where she plays a helplessly nearsighted airhead who'd rather stumble through life like Mrs. Magoo than wear glasses), or

Fig. 22
Gentlemen Prefer Blondes,
1953

of course the 1953 adaptation of *Gentlemen Prefer Blondes* **(Fig. 22)** (where, with her immortal question—"Excuse me, but what is the way to Europe, France?"—she typifies the dumb American as well as the dumb blonde).

Because true blondes are rare outside of Scandinavia, blondes are also suspected of vanity and deceit. In his exhaustingly arch but purportedly factual history of the world, *The Decline and Fall of Practically Everybody* (1950), Will Cuppy attributes both deceit and vanity to Lucrezia Borgia, as if her rap sheet weren't long enough already:

> She also had bright yellow hair, which she washed once a week with a mixture of saffron, box shavings, wood ash, barley straw, madder, cumin seed, and one thing and another to bring out the hidden glints and restore its natural color. You left it on your head for twenty-four hours and washed it off with lye made from cabbage stalks, the only hazard of which was the second-degree burn. If your hair remained on the scalp, you were a blonde.

There was a lot more humor about "bottle blondes" in the time of our grandfathers and great-grandfathers, possibly because their wives and daughters didn't have access to the high-end hair dyes available now to wannabe blondes, but more likely because, in an era of breast augmentation and penis enlargement, of Botox and collagen and colored contact lenses, dyeing your hair barely even counts as a fashion statement, let alone a form of deceit. But it was funny once. In *2000 Insults for All Occasions* (1965), Louis A. Safian compiled a daunting catalog of stale jokes, including at least a dozen about bottle blondes: "They call her 'Kitty' because she has dyed nine times"; "As a blonde, she's chemistry's greatest contribution to the world"; "Some women are blonde on their mother's side, some on their father's side, but she's blonde on the peroxide," and so on. Most of these put-downs were already old when, in *I, the Jury* (1947), Mickey Spillane's hard-boiled detective Mike Hammer finally saw Charlotte Manning naked and scandalized readers by dryly observing: "All that was left were the transparent panties. And she was a real blonde." (Question: *Why* did readers get so exercised about such a coy reference to something everybody knows anyhow? Maybe because the crime fiction genre has always fetishized blondes, and men don't like the suggestion that their obsession with women's hair color is partly an obsession with pubic hair.)

The comic-strip character Blondie **(Fig. 23)** started life—way back in 1930—as a fun-loving, gold-digging FLAPPER, and Dagwood as a rich man's son whose determination to marry the little blonde chippie led to his disinheritance and committed him to the life of a wage slave. "What time does the twelve fifteen train leave?" asks Blondie in an early strip, but her marriage to Dagwood two months later, and the ensuing evaporation of her sex drive, leaves her saner and wiser, especially by comparison to Dagwood. As for Blondie's predecessor Dumb Dora (star of an earlier flapper strip by the same cartoonist, Chic Young), she had *black* hair. In general, the "dumb blonde" stereotype never really established itself in the funnies. The two cuties in Archie Andrews's

Fig. 23

life, Betty and Veronica, are notable neither for brains or brainlessness, but blonde Betty is sweeter and less materialistic than dark-haired Veronica. The fact is that, while cartoonists have always prided themselves on an ability to draw pretty girls, most know how to draw only one. Hair color (and hairstyle) is the easiest way to differentiate otherwise-identical beauties, and blonde hair often serves as a female equivalent of the good guy's white hat. In addition to Betty and Veronica, think of Daisy Mae Yokum and Moonbeam McSwine, or even *Scooby-Doo*'s Daphne (the pretty blonde) and Velma (the mousy brunette).

One reason for the "dumb blonde" stereotype is that, when women are identified by hair color, they are almost always cast as sex objects. If there had been a single serviceable word meaning "a sexy woman with big breasts," at least half the movies with *blonde* in their title might have used that other word instead, and blondes would be less imposed on to represent what—and only what—is physically attractive about their gender. (*Beauty* wouldn't do, since only little girls find the word a selling point in titles; to grownups of both genders it connotes snootiness and even frigidity.)

As it is, Hollywood's fascination with the hair color can be inferred from the dozens if not hundreds of movies with *blonde* in the title. From the 1940s alone, we have (to name a few) *My Favorite Blonde*, *Blonde Alibi*, *What a Blonde*, *Hold That Blonde*, *Follow That Blonde*, *Blonde for a Day*, *The Beautiful Blonde from Bashful Bend*, *Blonde and Groom*, *The Blonde Stayed On*, *Free, Blonde and 21*, *Blonde Fever*, and *The Uninvited Blonde*. I should also mention 1937's *Smart Blonde*, which concerns a female reporter—an ex-showgirl—and suggests that by the 1930s the "dumb blonde" stereotype was already common enough to merit subversion.

The fad for "blonde jokes" came along too late for an entry in this guide to grandparental humor, but we can still ask *why* they didn't come along sooner. After all, the sexy-but-dimwitted cutie has been a laughingstock throughout the era this guide does cover; in magazine cartoons, from the heights of *The New Yorker* to the depths of *Gags 'n' Gals*, those cuties were by a wide margin the *favorite* laughingstock from the 1920s through the 1960s. But in fact, blonde jokes aren't later incarnations of the bimbo jokes in men's magazines, but of the more infantile and sexually innocent jokes that were once called MORON jokes and were later repackaged as Polack jokes. Like redneck jokes, they reflect a change in our society's thinking as to which groups are okay to laugh at.

Blowhards

> *He who tooteth not his own horn,*
> *the same shall not be tooted.*
>
> —DAMON RUNYON

THOUGH NO ONE KNOWS what state *Li'l Abner*'s Dogpatch belongs to, we know it's represented in the U.S. Senate by Senator Jack S. Phogbound ("Thar's no Jack S. like our Jack S.!"), a corrupt and blustering politico so full of hot air that when he can't make it to Dogpatch for a campaign appearance, he sends a gas bag made up to look like him, and no one notices the substitution.

With their penchant for filibusters, senators are often portrayed as blowhards. The best-known cartoon blowhard, Foghorn Leghorn—that big blustering rooster with the southern accent—was based on a blustering character named Senator Beauregard Claghorn, who debuted in 1945 on Fred Allen's radio show (he was voiced by Allen's announcer, Kenny Delmar) and was usually the highlight of the "Allen's Alley" segment, in which Allen went around the neighborhood asking its colorful denizens for their opinion on some current issue. Claghorn is such a die-hard southerner that he refuses to wear a Union suit and takes umbrage at such things as Northern Spy apples; he also tends, likes many radio characters of his era, to laugh at his own jokes.

The golden age of funny blowhards coincided with the golden age of radio, when writers discovered that certain stock characters worked especially well as pure voices. No character type worked better than the blowhard, who is *all* talk, as we say, and uses talk to compensate for everything he isn't. With a gifted voice actor to animate his lines, a radio blowhard could be a thing of beauty—as in the case of Fibber McGee, or his windbag next-door neighbor, Throckmorton P. Gildersleeve (the "P." stood for "Philharmonic"), who made such a hit, and so much noise,

Fig. 24 Suitable for framing

that in 1941 he got his own show, *The Great Gildersleeve*—one of the first spinoffs in broadcast history. Less abrasive and more unctuous than the average blowhard, but every bit as phony, Gildersleeve was sponsored, fittingly, by Parkay margarine.

As for Foghorn Leghorn, he made his first cartoon ("Walky Talky Hawky") in 1946. His catchphrase, "That's a joke, son," was borrowed from Claghorn, but the rooster's name, like its personality, was not so much a borrowing as an inspired transcription into a barnyard key. If you're going to create a cartoon animal to embody the male traits of arrogance, bluster, and audible self-satisfaction, what better animal than a big strutting rooster? Leghorn is usually pitted against some feisty little bird—a baby chicken hawk or rooster—who relates to the big blowhard as a pin to a balloon. ("Balloon juice" was a slang expression, by the way, a century ago, for nonsense; to be full of balloon juice was to be full of hot air.)

In the funny pages, the champion blowhard was Gene Ahern's inexhaustible windbag, Major Hoople, star of *Our Boarding House* (1921–84), parasitic husband of its landlady, and so much funnier than the other tenants that the strip itself was often referred to by his name rather than its own. A fat work-shy self-righteous long-winded blustering grandiose feckless confabulating braggart, Hoople is forever boasting of shooting elephants, overpowering octopi, advising heads of state, and so on. Even more than later blowhards like Ralph Kramden and Fred Flintstone, Hoople takes a pathetic pride in belonging to a SECRET SOCIETY, and often wears its special headgear—a fez—around the house. His favorite interjections are "Harrumf!" and "Egad!" and many of his speeches are in fact no more than elaborate egads and harrumfs.

Hoople's bluster is met with derision by his long-suffering wife and the wisecracking boarders, which gives him something else to bluster about. When chided for his laziness, he replies "Egad—just because I am not exerting physical force, you get the impression that I am a sluggard, eh? Hmf. M'lad, in comparison of energy, my brain is equal to the action of a shop of skilled mechanics." To a lodger who observes that Hoople's bout of gout coincided suspiciously well with his wife's spring cleaning, Hoople replies "Sir! You have the effrontery to imputate me of deceitfully incapacitating myself in order to gain exemption from taking part in domestic tasks? Indeed, sir, retract that accusation, or I will . . . um-m-m . . . fuff-f-f-f . . ."

Even when the jeers are provoked by obvious lies, Hoople responds with honest indignation, and sometimes we get a sense, beyond all that is lovably silly or maddeningly shameless about him, of the spookiness of the pathological liar—the sense that there's nobody *there*. What kind of person not only wants to be admired for things he knows he hasn't done, but also craves that admiration as an end in itself? Popeye's friend Wimpy is also an ingenious and long-winded liar, but Wimpy lies as a means to an end: as long as he can feed his hamburger habit, he doesn't care what people think of him.

Aside from shameless imitations like Judge Puffle and Colonel Gilfeather, the closest thing to Major Hoople in the comics would be the more boastful denizens of Okefenokee Swamp—not Pogo or Porkypine, of course, but the likes of Howland Owl, Beauregard Bugleboy, or Albert the Alligator. Where the humor of Hoople's lies is inextricable from his personality, *Pogo*'s Walt Kelly was so fond of tall tales, fish stories, Irish bulls, and such that even minor characters are likely to spout them.

Most of what makes blowhards funny is verbal, and they were as common in old-time radio comedy as they are unthinkable in silent movies. (Silent movies can portray simple *windbags*, since you don't need sound to show someone yakking away, but the special pathology of the blowhard is too subtle to portray via pantomime and intertitles.) Fibber McGee was a shining example, with his blustering opinions, his joblessness, and his compulsion to embellish his account of any exploit he isn't inventing altogether. (And, like Major Hoople, he is not merely an exaggerator and confabulator but an INVENTOR in the Edisonian sense as well.)

At first glance, Ralph Kramden seems very different: a working stiff whose many faults don't include laziness, and whose surly working-class manners contrast so sharply with Hoople's grandiloquence as almost to give credence to the latter's silly aristocratic pretensions. But it's more illuminating to consider the points they have in common: both are fatsos, both are loudmouths, both are braggarts, both are dreamers, both waste a lot of time on GET-RICH-QUICK SCHEMES, and both are full of shit. One explanation for these similarities could be that Ralph Kramden is modeled on Hoople or Gildersleeve, just as Fred Flintstone is modeled on Ralph. Another could be that all four of them—as well as W. C. Fields in many of his roles, and Bob Hope in his "blustering coward" mode (blowhards are usually COWARDS, and vice versa), and Ignatius J. Reilly in *A Confederacy of Dunces*—descend from Falstaff, who himself descends from the braggart figures in Greek and Roman comedy.

In any case, there's something uniquely satisfying about the syndrome in question—about the specific combination of seemingly distinct traits shared by all those funny, boastful, grandiose fat men, so much so that the absence of any one of the traits is enough, in my book, to exclude a character from the Blowhard Hall of Fame. There should probably be a separate entry on Tinhorns or Pipsqueaks—skinny, reedy, whiny, extraunimpressive blowhards such as Barney Fife who pipe instead of booming. Over on *Green Acres*, you sometimes heard a fife and drum playing "Yankee Doodle" during Oliver's windier orations.

It's often said, especially with regard to fiction, that verbal humor is inferior to nonverbal humor, to character-based humor, but that's a false dichotomy. There are many funny characters, from Matthew Bramble to

Miss Jean Brodie, whose funniest behavior is not their actions but their use of language (in dialogue, letters, in first-person narration). Think of Ignatius J. Reilly, one of the funniest characters in all of American fiction. His actions are funny enough, but his words are even funnier, and whenever he opens his mouth, we get character humor and verbal humor together. That's the case with each and every one of the other blowhards mentioned above—and the reason that blowhards tend to be roughly twice as funny as other comic figures.

B.O.

> *Just once I'd like to have a tall dark stranger look at me*
> *like I wasn't on the sixth day of a five-day deodorant pad.*
> —ERMA BOMBECK, *AT WIT'S END*, 1965

> *I must find out what zis "pew" means every time I appear.*
> —PEPÉ LE PEW

LIKE CONSTIPATION and halitosis, B.O. has always been an affliction more openly acknowledged by ads—in print, on radio, on TV—than by the programs and articles they sponsor. The abbreviation "B.O." was introduced in 1919 in ads for a women's deodorant called Odo-Ro-No, but really came into its own in the age of radio in ads for Lifebuoy soap, singing commercials that simulated a foghorn on reaching "B.O.," thus brilliantly implying that body odor is a sort of dense fog around the offending body, and also—since foghorns sound so flatulent—a kind of constant or ongoing dermal fart. Who wouldn't have run out and bought a bar of Lifebuoy?

"B.O."—like "B.M.," "V.D.," "B.U.,"[5] and "W.C."—is what linguists call a *eusystolism*, a euphemistic use of initials for words we'd prefer not to utter or spell out. Unlike "W.C.," it can also be justified as a time-saver, allowing one to refer to body odor in two syllables instead of four. Like "B.M.," however, it is one of those euphemisms that wind up being more

---

[5] A semi-jocular 1930s abbreviation for "biological urge"—in other words, lust.

Fig. 25 From the golden age of odor anxiety

disgusting than the indelicate terms they replace. In the case of "B.O.," that effect was surely intentional: the abbreviation makes the affliction sound as unspeakable as venereal disease.

For much of the twentieth century, armpits were both unspeakable—hence the silly euphemism *underarm*—and unpicturable. In TV commercials for deodorant, the actress would apply the product—euphemistically, or metonymically, but in any case absurdly—to her forearm, one of the least odoriferous parts of the body.

Not surprisingly, we find fewer B.O. jokes in the mainstream of popular culture than in the backwaters and swamplands. The Three Stooges liked to joke about it:

> "How's your cold?"
> "Oh, pretty good. But I still don't smell so good."
> "I'll say." (1941)

> "Listen to me spout Shakespeare: 'A rose by any other name would smell—'"
> "And so do you!" (1950)

> "Eureka!"
> "You don't smell so good, either!" (1951)

Such jokes are rare, however, in any form of humor more mature or civilized than Stooges shorts. Our culture is amazingly neurotic about smells—or not so amazingly, when you recall Freud's argument, in *Civilization and Its Discontents*, that the suppression of the sense of smell is a key part of the sexual repression that civilization entails and enforces. How else can we explain why the smelly are ostracized more than the noisy or unsightly? For that matter, why do Pepé Le Pew cartoons all have coy titles like "Heaven Scent," "For Scent-imental Reasons," "Two Scents Worth," "Past Perfumance," and "Who Scent You?" Did Eddie Seltzer—a producer at Warner Bros. who reportedly hated the amorous skunk—forbid Chuck Jones to use words like *stench* or *stink*?

Pepé Le Pew, by the way, is not quite the only animated cartoon character with body odor. At the beginning of "Hare Ribbin'" (1944), a stupid bloodhound sniffs along the ground until he comes to Bugs Bunny leaning against a tree by one raised arm. Without seeing him— though he's specifically hunting for rabbits—the bloodhound sniffs up and down Bugs's right side several times, from toes to white-gloved fingertips, before pausing at the armpit, wincing, and turning to the audience to say, in Lifebuoy's famous foghorn voice, "B.O.!" But such jokes are rare in old cartoons—considerably rarer than jokes about SUICIDE, for instance.

References to body odor are also uncommon in old comics— surprisingly, given all the BUMS and HOBOES in the funny pages. Bob Oscar ("B.O.") Plenty first appeared in *Dick Tracy* in 1947. His initials are no accident—he trails a musky scent the way Joe Btfsplk trails a little black storm cloud—but in the comics he's a rarity. And though another segment of the cartoon population—the little-boy segment—is equally afflicted with ablutophobia (the fancy word for fear of bathing), children are never depicted as smelly, not even by Al Capp, whose *Washable Jones*, a Sunday "topper" strip for *Li'l Abner*, was also set in Dogpatch and starred a dirty but goodhearted and unscented ragamuffin. More recently, "Pig-Pen" was voted the fifth-most beloved *Peanuts* character, and one secret of his lovability is surely that, unlike any filthy person in real life—and unlike any real pigpen—he isn't smelly but *dusty*. Can you recall a single reference to his body odor? He has less in common with a sweaty vagrant than with an old rug being beaten in a sunbeam. Children, of course, don't foster the bacteria responsible for the most characteristic form of adult body odor, but—as we all recall from our grade school days—kids who seldom bathe or change their clothes *do* stink.

Over in Dogpatch, many if not most of the characters stink. (The luscious Moonbeam McSwine prefers the company of hogs to men, and is never seen without a retinue of flies.) But that doesn't stop them from leading full and happy hillbilly lives—or from ostracizing Big Barnsmell, the Inside Man at the Skunk Works and the only bachelor who doesn't run for his life on Sadie Hawkins Day: he *wants* a wife, but not even the most desperate of Dogpatch virgins will settle for *him*.

I've often wondered why there are no scratch 'n' sniff comic strips. If any form of narrative would benefit from an olfactory track, it's got to be the funnies. Imagine not only seeing but *smelling* Jiggs's corned beef, Blondie's perfume, Pogo's Brunswick stew. As for Daddy Warbucks's cigars—or B. O. Plenty's musk—well, we wouldn't have to scratch or sniff *those* panels. But we might just choose to anyhow. The comics are all about enjoying things you wouldn't like in real life.

Boardinghouses

WHETHER YOU PREFER Frost's definition of home as "the place where, when you go there, they have to let you in," or Auden's definition, "a place where no tax is levied for being there," a boardinghouse is at best a parody of home. It features all the amenities and nuisances of home—communal meals, shared bathrooms, daily frictions, moralizing elders, lack of privacy—but only for a price. The landlady is a surrogate mother, and if you want to eat, you eat what she serves, when she serves it.

Boardinghouse humor was common in the first decades of the twentieth century, when boardinghouses themselves were common. Like the artificial shared-living situations of MTV's *Real World* series, the boardinghouse brought together a motley bunch of strangers in circumstances that ensured mutual annoyance and schadenfreude. An apartment building, by virtue of its emphasis on apartness, can never be as good a Petri dish for the humor of close quarters, though Milt Gross had some success in *Nize Baby* (1925) and *Dunt Esk* (1927) with his Lower East Side tenement and its shouted conversations between housewives on different floors whose gossip traveled vertically instead of back and forth across a picket fence.

In a boardinghouse, the boarders were forced to endure one another's company at least once a day, at dinner. We still joke about the "boardinghouse reach," and the joke is a remnant of a time when all sorts of bad manners were associated with boardinghouses—slurping your soup, blowing your nose in your napkin, taking more than your share. Granted that the Cabots and the Lowells seldom dined there, the point of such jokes wasn't that boarders were necessarily boors, but that when people from different regions and social strata eat their meals together, the lack of any standard code of table manners guarantees that some diners will be appalled by others. The same must have been true in the humbler restaurants of the era, but at least at restaurants you don't have to eat with the same people every evening—and some of the most annoying manners reach their full annoyance potential only after repeated exposures.

In a 1910 collection called *Literary Lapses*, the now-almost-forgotten Stephen Leacock published a pseudo-scholarly paper on "Boarding-House Geometry," outlining the uncertainties of boardinghouse existence in the reassuringly certain language of Euclid:

> All boarding-houses are the same boarding-house.
>
> Boarders on the same boarding-house . . . are equal to one another.
>
> A single room is one which has no parts and no magnitude.
>
> The landlady of a boarding-house is a parallelogram—that is, an oblong angular figure, which cannot be described, but which is equal to anything. . . .
>
> All other rooms being taken, a single room is said to be a double room. . . .
>
> Any two meals at a boarding-house are together less than two square meals. . . .

THE BOARDING HOUSE MISTRESS

Here's the lady who hustles our hash,
Five per week, in advance, strictly cash,
To keep her in order.

Fig. 26 Board, optional. Hash, obligatory.

And so on—and on, and on, until you see the justice of Samuel Butler's verdict on Canadian humor: "When I was there I found their jokes like their roads—very long and not very good, leading to a little tin point of a spire which has been remorselessly obvious for miles without seeming to get any nearer."

Boarders weren't confined to boardinghouses, though. In *Everything but Money*, a 1966 memoir of growing up in an East Harlem tenement, Sam Levenson recalls that "the letter boxes downstairs rarely listed only the family name": as crowded as most of those apartments would have been with family only, money was even scarcer than space, so the occupants made room for strangers. Levenson recalls that the typical boarder, "who might stay from a week to forty years," had the sort of nondescript face one sees in composite sketches of suspects; that he walked around the apartment in his underwear but was still referred respectfully as Mister; that he had first dibs on the bathroom in the morning; that he was sometimes the only member of the household with a job; that the lady of the house tended to feel sorry for him; and that he inspired all kinds of rumors:

> There were some facts we were sure of: he slept in a long night-gown; he was tattooed, he kept raw eggs in his dresser; he bought razor blades a thousand for nineteen cents; he sent poems to newspapers and read political pamphlets. The rest was rumor: he was a deserter from the Kaiser's army; he wore a money belt; he had two wives in Passaic, New Jersey; he was inventing a substitute for plaster.

Though nowadays we picture boardinghouses through a haze of nostalgia, as if picturing a Norman Rockwell painting, it isn't hard to see why in their heyday they were considered so funny. If you've ever lived in a small apartment building, just imagine what life would have been like if you'd also eaten all your meals there with the building's other tenants at a communal table. Imagine, further, that instead of choosing from a menu, you had no choice but to eat whatever the landlady felt like making for that meal—and since you were paying a set weekly fee for those meals, she fed you as cheaply as possible, relying heavily on poverty foods such as BEANS, HASH, and SOUP. You'd also be sharing a single bathroom with the other lodgers (which meant a lot of waiting in line in a drafty hallway in your bathrobe and slippers), and if you spent much time in the common living room, you'd soon be all too aware of their personalities, and have a pretty good sense of *why* certain lodgers were still single, and why they were reduced to living with strangers rather than with relatives. In reality, boardinghouse life must often have been closer to a Kafka novel than a Rockwell painting.

In comic narratives, the boardinghouse is usually ruled by a stern, dumpy middle-aged landlady, often a widow for whom the boarders serve as surrogate children as well as sources of income. Even if she's married, her husband tends to be as irrelevant as Major Hoople, who, as the star of *Our Boarding House* (see BLOWHARDS) and do-nothing spouse of its landlady, is treated with no more respect by the wisecracking boarders than if he too were a paying guest and not a freeloading husband.

As with other comic stereotypes that are constantly confronted and corrected by reality, the landlady stereotype, in its heyday, allowed for a lot of variation. At one extreme there were vengeful harridans like the one described by Langston Hughes in his story "Landladies," a witch who refers to Simple (Hughes's Everyman) as Third Floor Rear and plasters his surroundings with signs like GUEST TOWELS—ROOMERS DO NOT USE and TURN OUT LIGHT—COSTS MONEY and WASH FACE ONLY IN BOWL—NO SOX. At the other end of the spectrum you get Martha Hoople, the long-suffering and almost motherly landlady of *Our Boarding House.*

Around 1905, a postcard manufacturer published a line of cards illustrating at least five different types of MOTHER-IN-LAW: Jolly, Contented, Harmless, Suspicious, and Threatening. Nothing is more eloquent of how landladies were perceived back then than the fact that those same cards were recycled years later, with the same adjectives and illustrations, in a series of postcards about different types of *landlady.* Like a mother-in-law, a landlady is—at least at her funniest—a nightmare travesty of a mother, or even of a wife.

The main reason boardinghouse humor disappeared is that boarding-houses themselves did, though as always it took lesser humorists a while to notice the change. From 1957 to 1972, Frank Roberge drew a lame boardinghouse strip called *Mrs. Fitz's Flats*. By 1957, boardinghouses were already on the way out, and by 1972 they were pretty much a thing of the past, like the army as portrayed in *Beetle Bailey*, but no one claims that comic strips are a reliable barometer of the times. The comics page is less a weather gauge than a time capsule.

Indeed—to end this entry with a digression—many long-running strips survive not because they are any good, much less because they reflect our changing world, but precisely because they refuse to change or to acknowledge change. Now that the sports section is as engorged with scandal as the athletes with steroids, the funnies are the one place left in the newspaper where readers can forget the real world and its problems. Many comic strips—*The Lockhorns, Blondie, Marmaduke*—have achieved the status of living fossils, and seem positively dorky when they do ac-knowledge recent inventions or current events. Magazine cartoons are a little different: in their search for new gags, magazine cartoonists do pay attention to new technology, and even to current headlines. But no one wants to see Dagwood texting Blondie, or Mary Worth googling herself.

Bores and Babbitts

I N 1906, OLIVER Herford published *A Little Book of Bores*, an im-pressive typology of the pest as it was known a hundred years ago. He distinguishes twenty-six subspecies, one for each letter of the alphabet, and allots a limerick to each:

> *M's a Methodical Man*
> *Who prates with precision and plan*
> *Beware, how you balk*
> *The stream of his talk,*
> *Lest he go back to where he began.*

Or, to cite one of the breeds I sometimes fear I belong to:

> *Q is a Quoter who'll cite*
> *His favourite authors all night.*
> *Tho' teeming with Thought,*
> *Like the Moon he is naught*
> *But a second-hand dealer in Light.*

Other types include the "Decadent Dreary / Whose Works are depressing and eerie," the "Frankly Familiar Friend / Who loves free advice to extend," the "Grumbler Gruff / Whom everything puts in a huff," the "Intensely Intense / Who dilates on the Whither and Whence," the "Optimist glad / Who doesn't know how to be sad," and the "Well-informed Wight / Who aims to set every one right."

"Bores bore each other too," wrote Don Marquis, "but it never seems to teach them anything." Their obtusity is the very thing that makes them so unbearable in real life, and so ripe for ridicule. Like people with loud voices—and there's a lot of overlap between the two groups—bores can be unbelievably oblivious to social feedback. (Maybe because, *pace* Marquis, the most boring people *aren't* themselves bored; like Typhoid Mary, they are *carriers*.) And since, as Bergson wrote, "a comic character is generally comic in proportion to his ignorance of himself," bores will always be funny, at least when you have the option of changing the channel or turning the page: few human types are as flagrantly unaware of how they look, or sound, to others.

The first decade of the last century was especially aware of, and amused by, bores. It's easy to feel, while reading the humor of that era, that if not for the nick-of-time arrival of World War I, the world would have lapsed into an irreversible coma. In 1906, the same year that Herford published his field guide to bores, *The Smart Set* published an essay by Gelett Burgess called "Are You a Bromide? or The Sulphitic Theory, Expounded and Exemplified According to the Most Recent Researches in the Psychology of Boredom." Burgess used terms from the pharmacology of his day to distinguish stimulating people (Sulphites) from people who put you to sleep (Bromides):

The Bromide does his thinking by syndicate. He follows the main traveled roads, he goes with the crowd. In a word, they all think and talk alike—one may predicate their opinion upon any given subject. They have their hair cut every month and their minds keep regular office hours. . . . The Bromide conforms to everything sanctioned by the majority, and may be depended upon to be trite, banal and arbitrary.

But the hallmark of the Bromide (and the reason the term survives to our day as a synonym for *platitude*) is the stock response, and more specifically the conversational reflex, a consequence or symptom of "the accepted bromidic belief that each of the ordinary acts of life is, and necessarily must be, accompanied by its own especial remark or opinion." Burgess lists some fifty such reflexive remarks, and many are still with us a century later:

> "That dog understands every word I say."
> "Of course if you leave your umbrella at home it's sure to rain!"
> "After I've shampooed my hair I can't do a thing with it!"
> "If you'd only come yesterday, this room was in perfect order."
> "I thought I loved him at the time, but of course it wasn't really love."

In 1922, Sinclair Lewis published a novel about an ideally smug and conformist American businessman named George F. Babbitt, who gets "his opinions and his polysyllables" from the editorial page. For decades thereafter, "Babbitt" meant an all-American, Rotarian, Republican bore—a Bromide, in short, or at least someone who speaks the same language, as Ira Gershwin pointed out in "The Babbitt and the Bromide," a 1927 song that imagines those two archetypes in conversation:

> *Hello! How are you?*
> *Howza folks? What's new?*

I'm great! That's good!
Ha! Ha! Knock wood!
Well! Well! What say?
Howya been? Nice day!
How's tricks? What's new?
That's fine! How are you?
Nice weather we are having but it gives me such a pain:
I've taken my umbrella so of course it doesn't rain. . . .

The art of dullness hasn't changed much since the days of Burgess and Herford, though the past century saw the emergence of some especially virulent strains of bore, like the Telephonic Talkathoner,[6] the Super-8 Sadist who forces his guests to pay for their suppers by watching home movies, and the Nattering Neurotic, who in countless gag cartoons from the 1950s bores his analyst to tears or yawns or snores. I've never seen a cartoon about a long-winded sinner boring the bejesus out of his or her confessor, but surely such a type exists as one that priests complain about, and joke about, among themselves: the Prating Penitent.

[6] "Every improvement in communication makes the bore more terrible," wrote Frank Moore Colby more than a hundred years ago—a strikingly prescient remark, considering that Colby wrote before the advent of radio, television, email, chat rooms, blogs, Twitter, or texting, or everyday telephony.

Born Losers

There is much to be said for failure.
It is more interesting than success.
—MAX BEERBOHM

Sing of human unsuccess / In a rapture of distress.
—W. H. AUDEN

WHEN I REVIEW old lists of comic types, I'm always struck by how clear-cut the gender roles used to be in comedy. In Louis A. Safian's *2000 Insults for All Occasions* (1965), the chapter on "Failures" contains some hundred insults, and they all refer to men. Ditto with the chapter on "Sad Sacks"—and for that matter the chapters on "Big-Heads," "Boozers," "Bores," "Chiselers," "Fair-Weather Friends," "Idlers," "Liars," "Meanies," "Screwballs," "Tightwads," and many other types with no obvious reason to be attributed to just one of the sexes. Only a few types are exclusively female, like "Fallen Angels," "Playgirls," and "Wives," but not, surprisingly, "Gossips," which—like "Chatterboxes," "Dumbbells," "Hypochondriacs," and "Snobs"—is unisex. There is a sort of gallantry in exempting women from most of the two thousand insults (as we still tend to exempt them, for no other reason, from the favorite all-purpose insult of our era, *asshole*), though like all gallantry toward women, it reflects their subjugation. Till recently, it wasn't *possible* for a woman to be a failure in the sense that men are called failures. She could be a slut, a spinster, or a wife ("Wives" is one of the longest chapters in Safian's book), but not simply a born loser like the Born Loser, or a sad sack like Ziggy or Sad Sack (short for "sad sack of shit," an old bit of army slang).

Ziggy, Sad Sack, the Born Loser: they are among the least vivid of all long-running comic-strip characters, and the least funny. Bad luck can be funny, but it isn't enough in itself to define a funny character. When we laugh at a character in a comic strip (or sitcom, or movie, or book), part of what we're laughing at is the causal connection between the kind of person that character is and the kind of treatment he or she receives from the world. Character is destiny, and funny character defects are funny partly because they provoke funny retribution. When a character's ongoing misfortunes have nothing to do with his or her behavior, those misfortunes can be funny only in the dumb way that the sight of an innocent stranger falling in a mud puddle is funny.

An interesting exception to that rule is Charlie Brown, though it's worth noting that he never "carried" *Peanuts* the way Dennis the Menace, for example, carried *his* strip. Charles Schulz wisely surrounded Charlie with sharply defined characters like Lucy and Linus, like spicy condiments for a bland main dish. It's also worth noting that fairly early in the strip's fifty-year run, Snoopy eclipsed his owner as the star: a born loser can't compete for laughs with a daydreaming beagle.[7]

In general, the funniest losers are defined by other qualities—by character defects we love to hate—and their repeated failures are well-deserved comeuppances. I'm thinking of BLOWHARDS like Ralph Kramden, schemers like Lucy Ricardo, control freaks like Homer Bedloe, snobs like Mrs. Drysdale, snoops like Gladys Kravitz. They all fail week after week, and their failure is funny, but it isn't the main attraction.

On the other hand, chronic loserdom is a precondition for our laughter at the antics of Keaton and Chaplin: the knowledge that, even when a film ends happily for the protagonist—ends at a moment when things are momentarily going well for him—he'll be back in hapless nebbish mode in the next film. Bad things happen to good people, and sometimes so many befall the same innocent victim that we do come to think of him or her as a born loser—as someone who suffers as naturally as ice melts or iron rusts. If anyone can face that sad fact, surely humorists can.

---

[7] Strictly speaking, Charlie Brown wasn't a *born* loser: for the first year or two of the strip, he was more often portrayed as a mischievous kid like Calvin of *Calvin and Hobbes*. Nor did he initially wear a striped sweater.

Bosoms and Breasts

1

*"Who was the confounded idiot?" she spurted,
her magnificent bosom heaving in accordance with the laws
governing the upheaval of magnificent bosoms.*
—S. J. PERELMAN

IN THE MOVIES, in the funnies, in the comic imagination at large, women can be sorted into two great armies: those with breasts and those with bosoms. If you're not sure which is which, just do the math: if there's two of them, they're breasts, since no one is allotted more than a single bosom. Bosoms are both more and less than breasts. Their appeal—insofar as they appeal to anyone—is utterly different, and so are the jokes they inspire. The higher your weight, your social standing, and (up to a point) your age, the better the odds that you possess a bosom; it is as crucial a component of the comic dowager's uniform as the lorgnette and the upturned nose. The endearingly dim-witted matrons in

Fig. 27 The original bosom buddies

Helen Hokinson's classic *New Yorker* cartoons—those well-upholstered middle-aged club women saying clueless things about modern art or current affairs—were almost always bosomy. The magic moment when a pair of breasts become a single bosom may be impossible to pinpoint even for the owner, and is certainly more disputable than the moment when a pair of bushy eyebrows may be said to have merged into a single unibrow. Sometimes—as with the difference between poetry and prose, or fiction and nonfiction, or comedy and drama—it's a packaging decision.

When a woman is commended for a "magnificent bosom"—and Perelman wouldn't have used the phrase facetiously if it hadn't been overused sincerely—she isn't being praised for an especially alluring secondary sex characteristic, but rather for a status symbol, a sign of worldly success in nonsexual terms (though sex may well have laid the groundwork for that success). Bosoms always make me think of Oscar Wilde's aphorism: "Twenty years of passion make a woman look like a ruin; twenty years of marriage make her look like a public building" (perhaps the kind of public building with a balcony, since *balcony* is a synonym for *bosom*).

The word has been around, meaning what it does, for more than a millennium, but really came into its own in the nineteenth century, when self-righteous prudes on both sides of the Atlantic effected a reform of the English language—a purge of undesirable words and a visitation of hazy euphemisms—even more extensive than that achieved in our time by the forces of political correctness. According to Hugh Rawson's very entertaining *Dictionary of Euphemisms and Other Doubletalk*, the Victorians were so serious about the *bosom* versus *breasts* distinction that as well as turning *breast knots* into *bosom knots* and *breast pins* into *bosom pins*, they even took to referring to the part of a plow once known as the *breast* as the *bosom* instead.

One reason for the enmity between real writers and self-righteous euphemizers is that euphemistic language is—by design, not just from ineptitude—the polar opposite of good writing: purposely abstract instead of concrete (as with *bosom*, euphemisms are often chosen for their way of clouding the mind's eye), purposely vague instead of precise (as when the *New York Times*, needing to report a newsworthy use of the word *bullshit*, referred to it as *a barnyard epithet*), and purposely lacking the wealth of connotations that make a word evocative (as with *blind* versus *seeing impaired*). Of course, even the most blameless euphemism will *acquire* connotations if it's used enough; that's why euphemisms need to be replaced periodically, like air filters.

But maybe it's unfair to call this particular word imprecise: since prudery affects the way we dress even more drastically than it does the way we speak, the triumph of *bosom* corresponded to the triumph of actual bosoms. In any prudish era, women's outfits will crowd their breasts closer to the bosomy end of the spectrum—and what I've been describing as a binary opposition, bosom or breasts, is really of course a continuum. The "Sweater Girl" of the 1940s and '50s was a reaction to the prudery of the Motion Picture Production Code, which forbade the sort of gratuitous cleavage you find in pre-Code movies, and yet permitted—in one of those paradoxes of censorship—even the bustiest of starlets to wear the tightest of sweaters. Simple adjustments inside the sweater enabled its wearer to change her place on the aforementioned continuum—as it were, to trim her sails to the prevailing winds of modesty or raciness.

One benefit of all that euphemism and repression—a legacy from the Victorian era that even our prodigal and porn-happy age hasn't quite exhausted—is that you can get a laugh, or at least a laff, just by reminding us that women do have breasts. In our grandfathers' day, many low-brow cartoons did no more than that, just as many comic postcards did no more than insist on the fact that women have RUMPS. "Oops, pardon me!" says a man to a large but elegant middle-aged woman, in a cartoon from the 1930s: they are playing tiddlywinks, and he has just winked one into her décolletage. In a cartoon from a 1957 issue of *Showgirls*, a bosomy DOWAGER at a cocktail party aims a jet of seltzer down the front of her low-cut dress and angrily addresses another partygoer: "Do be careful where you flip your cigarettes, young man!"

And before leaving the subject of heaving bosoms, I should mention *balumpatron*, Mort Walker's handy word for "the short curve lines used [by cartoonists] to indicate a bouncing bottom, bosom, or belly." It is also good to know that in the nineteenth century, falsies were referred to as *palpitators*, *palpitating bosoms*, or *patent heavers*—terms that make them sound mechanical, maybe even battery-powered, like something from an old novelty catalog. In reality, the wearer herself had to do the palpitating; the prostheses merely made it more noticeable, brought it an inch or two closer to the viewer.

2

B is for Breasts
Of which ladies have two;
Once prized for the function,
Now for the view.
—ROBERT PAUL SMITH

BREAST JOKES HAVE always been a relatively tame way of joking about sex in general, and in our grandfathers' day there was even more breast humor than nowadays. Breasts were funny partly because men don't have them, and men of course were the standard of normality. The same mind-set that found something laughable in the very notion of a lady athlete or a lady driver—the same mind-set that saw nothing wrong with such constructions as "If a student hopes to be a great writer, he should study the classics"—found women's torsos screamingly funny just because they weren't like male torsos. Thus a cartoon in the 1953 collection *More Over Sexteen* shows a pilgrim standing outdoors with his wrists in a pair of stocks labeled MEN; nearby is another pair, this one labeled WOMEN, with the usual wristholes but also a second pair of holes, higher up and larger.

Breasts have always been a big part of what Hollywood has to offer—Russ Meyer called them the cheapest of all special effects—though bare ones were rare even before the adoption of the Production Code in the early 1930s, and then nonexistent until that puritanical code lapsed in the late 1960s. Even draped breasts could get a film in trouble with the censors, if they received too much attention from the camera, or from the publicist. *The Outlaw*, a 1943 western starring Jane Russell in a bra reputedly designed by Howard Hughes, wasn't released until 1946 due to its chest-thumping ad campaign; posters for the New York City premiere read "The Music Hall gets the Big Ones. What are the two great reasons

for Jane Russell's rise to stardom?"

In the pulpy, small-
format, low-budget men's
magazines of the 1940s and
'50s—magazines with names
like *Gaze, Jest, Breezy, Joker,
Stare, Snappy, Gee-Whiz!,
Nifty, Blush,* and *Wham*—it
is often the breasts that
leap when the doctor taps a
woman on the kneecap with
the little hammer. There are
also many gags about short
men dancing—often making
a point of dancing—with tall
women in low-cut gowns.
There are gags about men
recognizing women—never
their wives, of course—by the
breasts alone. From the shade
of a beach umbrella, a middle-
aged man at the seaside catches

Fig. 28 Dan DeCarlo, 1950s

a neck-down glimpse of a big-breasted gal in a bikini and exclaims,
"Why, if it isn't Miss Pringle from Accounting!" A clown-suited man at a
masquerade party leers at the breasts of a woman in a skimpy grass skirt,
matching top, and Polynesian mask and says, "I'm glad to see you came
to the party after all, Mary!" Such cartoons must confirm women's worst
fears about men and our tendency to fixate on selected body parts instead
of on the whole person.

Some breast jokes are lower than others. At the very bottom of the
barrel are the ones where breasts remind a guy of something else (or vice
versa), or are mistaken for something else. On a 1950s postcard, a grocer
is wrapping a pair of grapefruit when a busty customer enters his shop (in
a bright yellow blouse, naturally). "Why, good morning, Miss Jones," he

says. "I was just thinking about you!" On another postcard set in a sporting goods store, a man with a bag of golf clubs says to an almost flat-chested young lady behind the counter, "Oh yes, I almost forgot . . . two golf balls."

Jokes about breasts, like jokes about PENISES or RUMPS, are almost always the work of men. It's hard to find much evidence that women joked about breasts in the era this book is concerned with, though no doubt they did. Certainly they joked about the moronic behavior that those glands inspire in men. Their best jokes were off the record, though, surviving only anecdotally. Of the much-hyped sex appeal of Clara Bow, the well-endowed actress who became known as the "It Girl," Dorothy Parker quipped "*It*, hell—she had *those*." Judy Holliday, who seems to have been as witty offscreen as on, once dealt with an aggressively amorous casting director by removing the foam-rubber falsies from her bra and handing them to him, saying, "Here, I believe it's these you're after."

Bowling

THERE ISN'T NEARLY as much bowling humor as GOLF humor (partly because humorists are much more likely to be avid golfers than avid bowlers), but there's enough to enable me to say that the two are very different, and part of the difference is due to the relative social standings of the two sports. In *Class*, his book on social status in America, Paul Fussell observed that as a rule, the larger the ball, the lowlier the sport. In America, at least, bowling is the proletarian sport par excellence. Not that proles never play golf; they do, of course, even on old sitcoms, but there the joke is on their social climbing, or on the class anxieties that complicate the normal performance anxieties of the weekend athlete. Golf, like OPERA, is a bit absurd to anyone who hasn't grown up with it, and when a baboon like Ralph Kramden plays eighteen holes, the incongruity is almost as great as when a three-hundred-pound diva in a steel brassiere wails at the top of her lungs to embody romantic love. Ralph was clearly meant to hurl heavy balls, not to trudge around after tiny ones; at the bowling alley we see him in his element.

Fig. 29 *The Flintstones*

Who else bowls? Ozzie Nelson. Fibber McGee—who, like Ozzie, seems to have no job, leaving him plenty of time for the game, and who in one episode gets his thumb caught in a bowling ball. Fred Flintstone **(Fig. 29)**—even more than his model Ralph Kramden, since Fred was conceived not just as an animated version but as a dumbed-down caricature of Ralph In one episode Barney drops a bowling ball on Fred's foot (a bowling ball being one of the funniest things that can fall on a foot), and Fred hops around in pain exclaiming "Yabba-dabba-dy-yi-yi-yi!," inspiring a new dance among impressionable Bedrock teenagers.

Sitcom bowlers tend to be **BLOWHARDS**, and after a comically bad frame they bust out the comically lame excuses. Here are a few beefs and bellyaches transcribed from jokey crying towels that heartless macho types give one another to ridicule any efforts to save face after an embarrassing frame: LOUSY ALLEY! . . . PIN BOY'S FAULT . . . IT'S MY SHOES—THEY'RE TOO BIG! . . . FOUL LINE MOVED . . . TOO MUCH YELLING . . . MY FINGER SLIPPED! . . . SORE THUMB . . . SOMEBODY SWITCHED BALLS ON ME! . . . LOPSIDED BALL . . . THESE PINS MUST BE GLUED DOWN! . . . HAD INDIGESTION . . . THE ALLEY IS TOO LONG! . . . DIDN'T GET ENOUGH SLEEP . . . THEY FORGOT TO SWEEP THE ALLEY!

Brainy Girls

Men seldom make passes
At girls who wear glasses.
—DOROTHY PARKER

Brains are an asset, if you hide them.
—MAE WEST

I N 1962, PALL MALL cigarettes ran a series of full-page magazine ads about the art of girl-watching and the various species of girls to watch. One ad focused on the White-Coated Lab-Loon, a busty but bespectacled type with a lab coat, a clipboard, and a no-nonsense manner. "Don't let this girl's costume fool you," advises the text, explaining that although the girl "has to prove that she has a brain," she "really doesn't want to compete with men. In her heart, she wants to *attract* men and, eventually, marry one." And though she herself may seem prouder of her mind, that shouldn't stop you from ogling her body: "If the girl is watchable, she should be watched, no matter what her motives or ambitions may be."

Since young women in pop culture are first and foremost sex objects, pop culture has had to come to terms with young women who claim to prefer things of the mind to the raptures of the heart. Often those women are portrayed as homely, and the audience is left to gather—when it isn't spelled out for us—that the woman's intellectual ambitions are a sad compensation, a consolation prize for someone who can't get a date. Alternatively, it can be implied that the bookish girl simply doesn't know what she's missing because she's never been kissed. In *Funny Face*, all it takes for the lovely Audrey Hepburn, a mousy intellectual in a Greenwich Village bookshop, to question her high-minded celibacy ("My philosophic search / Has left me in the lurch") is a peck on the cheek from a character played by Fred Astaire. Not Cary Grant or Gary Cooper: Fred Astaire. Well, he has as much right to play a chick magnet as she has to play an existentialist, but when she falls for him she hasn't even seen him dance; she's only seen him trash her bookstore. And from the moment he steals a kiss—as evidently none of the Village hipsters has ever tried to do—Audrey is imprinted on him.

"Love never went to college," says Lorenz Hart (who clearly did), and that may explain why college girls have a hard time with Love. According to the typology of comic figures in the Famous Artists Cartooning Course (1965), the Studious Co-ed is "Slim, almost gaunt, vitally interested in classical studies." She is "uninterested in men, except biology professors." However, "she might be persuaded to take off the glasses and wow 'em in an evening gown," which of course is still what happens in "makeover movies," where the Ugly Girl is a beautiful actress in dowdy clothes and horn-rimmed glasses.

Still, the idea that women are allotted either brains or sex appeal (or of course neither), but never both, is sufficiently entrenched that exceptions—slutty bookworms, bookish sluts—are automatically funny. Ira Gershwin's "Saga of Jenny" praises her proficiency with languages, though not unreservedly: "But at seventeen, to Vassar, it was quite a blow / That in twenty-seven languages she couldn't say no." Conversely, in "Zip," a Lorenz Hart song from *Pal Joey* (1940), we eavesdrop on the thoughts of highbrow stripper Gypsy Rose Lee on the job:

> *Zip! Walter Lippmann wasn't brilliant today.*
> *Zip! Will Saroyan ever write a great play?*
> *Zip! I was reading Schopenhauer last night.*
> *Zip! And I think that Schopenhauer was right.*[8]

---

[8] There's something close to a consensus that Schopenhauer is the funniest philosopher—the best name to use in cases like this, where *any* philosopher's name would be funny. (At one point he had his own entry in this guide.) In Ira Gershwin's "Isn't It a Pity?", two infatuated lovebirds lament that they didn't meet sooner:

> (He) Isn't it a pity we never met before?
> Imagine all the lonely years we've wasted . . .
> You reading Heine, me somewhere in China. . . .
> (She) What joys untasted,
> My nights were sour
> Spent with Schopenhauer. . . .

Bricks

I'm tickled silly
When there is a scene
Where a chap gets a rap
On the bean;
When, willy-nilly,
A brick or a pie
Comes to rest on his chest
Or his eye.
—IRA GERSHWIN, "SLAPSTICK," 1921

SOMETIMES HALF THE HUMOR of a Robert Benchley piece was in his decision to write about a subject that he plainly neither knew nor cared a bit about, as in the case of his 1920 review of a book, by a certain Stewart Scrimshaw, called *Bricklaying in Modern Practice*.[9] After informing us that the first American brick was made in New Haven, Connecticut, in 1650, Benchley adds that "Mr. Scrimshaw does not say what it was made for, but a conjecture would be that it was the handiwork of Yale students for tactical use in the Harvard game." And it's a fair conjecture (except that, as Benchley concedes in the next sentence, Yale hadn't been founded in 1650), given that humorists seldom notice bricks at all except as funny objects for funny characters to throw at one another's heads.

In a 1918 comic strip, Jack Farr imagined Shakespeare being shown around Hollywood. Highlights of the tour include the seltzer factory, the brickyard, and a bakery that produces four thousand custard pies a day. "A scream in every one of 'em—can't write a comedy without 'em," observes the guide (a movie mogul who finds Shakespeare's own comedies hopelessly passé). We know about custard pies and seltzer bottles, but *bricks*? Who besides George Herriman relied on bricks for laughs?

The short answer is everyone, or almost everyone, in early comedies and comics. "My grandfather said, 'A comic-strip character should get

[9] The book and its author are real.

hit on the head with a brick at least once a week,'" recalls the title character of the meta-comic *Sam's Strip* in 1962, fondly recalling what might
be termed the Golden Age of Imitable Violence. In the first decades of its
existence, the comics section gave the message that everyone was throwing bricks, and that it was all in good fun. Like animated cartoons, where
even a shotgun blast in the face results in nothing more than powder
burns, singed eyebrows, and perhaps a crisscross bandage or two, old
comics imply that being pelted in the head with a brick is about the same
as being squirted in the face with seltzer, or struck with a custard pie: an
indignity and an annoyance, to be sure, but nothing more.

In the collective memory of our own era, the brick is associated with
Herriman's *Krazy Kat*—not only the greatest comic strip of all time, but
also the most brick-intensive: nearly every installment involved the efforts of Ignatz, the psychopathic mouse, to bean lovestruck Krazy Kat,
the androgynous character who insisted on misconstruing those bricks as
signs of affection **(Fig. 30)**.

But Herriman wasn't the inventor or even the popularizer of the funny
brick. (Nor is Krazy the only cartoon cat with an odd reaction to brickbats.
In "Felix Doubles for Darwin," a 1924 animated cartoon by Otto Messmer,
Felix is hit in the back of the head with a brick not once but twice, and each
time he reacts by laughing, though he isn't
otherwise portrayed as masochistic or
insensitive to pain.) Ever since the
advent of the comic strip as we
know it, it's been raining bricks
in Cartoonland. Sometimes
literally: in a 1915 cartoon
by Frank King, a downpour
of bricks from the heavens is
labeled a "Shower of Cubist
Confetti." Though Ignatz is
content most days to throw a
single brick, many cartoonists

Fig. 30 *Krazy Kat*

prefer to draw showers or salvos. Sometimes fun-loving urchins in the Katzenjammer tradition will dump a whole load of bricks from a coal scuttle onto the head of a passing authority figure.

Like BARRELS, bricks are everywhere in old comics, littering alleys and vacant lots like fruit in an orchard. (According to the *Historical Dictionary of American Slang*, an *alley apple* was 1920s slang for "a rock, stone, or brickbat, as thrown in a street brawl.") It's hard to spend a day poring over vintage strips without concluding that, once upon a time, no one was more than an arm's length away from a nice red throwable brick, and that only the social contract—so seldom obeyed or enforced in the comics—would have prevented your neighbor from beaning you with one. In a 1926 one-panel strip called *Newspaper Bromides*, which involved comically literal misinterpretations of well-known expressions (a joke revived by *Mad* magazine with its "Horrifying Clichés"), a drawing captioned "He Took the Stand in His Defense" is illustrated by a frightened man clutching a three-legged table to shield himself from two of the objects most often thrown in comic strips: a brick and a ROLLING PIN. In *Mutt and Jeff*, people are so fond of expressing their feeling with bricks that they seem to keep them around the house for ready use; at least, when someone throws an assortment of heavy objects out a window or a doorway at the title characters, the salvo will often include a brick or two.

Briffits and Dustups

BRIFFIT IS MORT WALKER'S TERM for the dust cloud that comic-strip characters and their vehicles leave behind when they go fast, whether they're motoring down a dusty road or sprinting through a rain forest. Since the history of the comic strip is roughly coextensive with the history of the motorcar—a *Hogan's Alley* strip from 1897 shows the Yellow Kid himself giving a bunch of his fellow urchins a ride in his new "horseless carriage"—there may be no way to test my hunch that the original joke with briffits was not just that comic-strip characters kick up a lot of dust when they run, but that they emit a cloud of exhaust, just like those newfangled automobiles that in

Fig. 31 *Count Screwloose*

1897 were by far the fastest thing going. That would account for briffits in circumstances inimical to dust. "Briffits are permissible," says Walker, "even if the floor is marble and highly polished."

An exhaustive field guide to comic-strip cloudage would have to include the tiny black personal storm cloud that hovers over certain unhappy or unlucky characters (most notably *Li'l Abner*'s Joe Btfsplk), and the puffy thought balloons used to indicate that the words inside are merely thought and not spoken. But the most notable clouds in the funny pages are the ones used to indicate brawls.

It doesn't take much to annoy Andy Capp, and if you have the nerve to do so in the confines of his comic strip, the last panel will usually feature a punch-up instead of a punch line. February 14, 1961—Valentine's Day—

was the first of Andy's fights to take place in a cloud of glory. The cloud in question is a thing of beauty, billowy and plump, and casts a little shadow on the ground because the fight takes place in midair. Andy is mugging a stranger to get a bouquet for Flo, but as often as not it's Flo he brawls with, in a cloud of marital strife. Not since *Bringing Up Father*, with its rolling pins, has a comic strip made domestic violence so fun to look at.

Though these days we associate the fight cloud with *Andy Capp*, it was far from the first strip to adopt the convention. There was never a time when cartoonists *didn't* have the cloud at their disposal, though the earliest example I've tracked down, an 1896 *Yellow Kid* cartoon—thus from the second year of what some consider the first real comic strip—is less a cloud than a wheel of multiple exposures, lacking the three-dimensionality of a modern fight cloud and looking more like a time-lapse illustration of a handspring, as if Duchamp's celebrated nude had cartwheeled down her staircase rather than primly "descending."

This proto-cloud has the virtue of illustrating the Sixth Law of Cartoon Physics, as propounded by mirthologist Mark O'Donnell in a celebrated 1980 monograph: "As speed increases, objects can be in several places at once. This is particularly true of tooth-and-claw fights, in which a character's head may be glimpsed emerging from the cloud of altercation at several places simultaneously." O'Donnell calls this a "cloud of altercation"; I call it a "fight cloud," and I've also seen it called the "big ball of violence."

Whatever you call it, it was most often used, in early comic strips, to represent fights between different species—between a dog and cat, say, or a dog and a man (to name the two most common interspecies matchups). Many early fight clouds look more like dances than dustups; the unnatural frontality of the brawlers—facing us instead of each other—would make their brawl hard to recognize as such if encountered out of context. By World War I, though, most cartoonists who used the clouds at all had arrived at something like the modern way of drawing them.

Since then, cartoonists have found all kinds of ingenious variations and refinements on the basic fight cloud. I'd be remiss not to mention the cloud of *fornication*, or big ball of sex, that pornographic comics sometimes use in preference to a tedious play-by-play. Like other gaseous bodies, the cloud of altercation can expand to fill the shape of its container, the rectangle of a comic-strip panel. And has anyone pointed out the resemblance between the fight cloud and another hoary comic-strip cliché, the Human Snowball?

Not that the cloud is strictly a comic-strip phenomenon; if anything, it's even commoner in animated cartoons, probably because it's even harder to draw a whole slugfest in blow-by-blow detail than to convey the gist of the fight in a single panel. There's a fight cloud in "Popeye the Sailor," the very first Popeye cartoon. In "Porky in Wackyland," Porky Pig observes a fight that appears to involve a cat and a dog, but when the fighters pause for breath and the dust settles, we see they are two halves of the same two-headed creature, a cat-dog.

So why do we associate the cloud of altercation specifically with *Andy Capp*? Probably because Reg Smythe, the strip's creator, was the last major newspaper cartoonist to continue using the cloud on a regular basis. Given how *often* he used it, the wonder is how long it took Smythe to start using the cloud. For the first three years of *Andy Capp*'s existence, the strip's shutter speed was fast enough to show fighters clearly, rather than just a cloud of commotion with here and there a body part protruding. In strips from the late 1950s, Smythe sometimes drew Andy slugging Flo in the jaw or kicking her in the rump. By modern standards, the unflinching depiction of wife-battering in those early strips is jarring. Smythe must have felt so, too, in 1961, and realized he'd have to change the way he represented violence, since the alternative would have been to reform the drunken thug who'd made him rich and famous.

Brothers-in-Law

> *My brother-in-law has an allergy. He's allergic to work.*
> —HENNY YOUNGMAN

IT'S OFTEN SAID that when you marry someone, you marry a whole family. That's the point of half the jokes about horrible MOTHERS-IN-LAW. Sometimes, though, a spouse's brother is even worse than the mother. If a comedy marriage is supposed to be comically awful, one way to heighten the awfulness and thus the comedy is to give the harpy wife a deadbeat brother.

Edgar Kennedy, the actor who played the beleaguered lemonade vendor in *Duck Soup*, was most famous for his "slow burn"—his funny way of gradually losing his temper and finally blowing his top. In order to give him more occasions to smolder, he was often saddled in his short films not only with a shrewish wife and her shrewish live-in mother, but also with a feckless live-in brother-in-law, Jack. In "Host to a Ghost" (1947), for example, Jack sells the house out from under Edgar so that Edgar has to buy another house, from Jack. In "You Drive Me Crazy" (1945), Jack borrows Edgar's car, then phones him when the car breaks down. Edgar borrows a neighbor's car to fetch his own, but promptly wrecks it; he buys another car to give his neighbor, but before he can deliver it he gets into a head-on collision with his own car, which Jack has finally managed to start.

The lazy, mooching, good-for-nothing brother-in-law was something of a stock character in old-time radio comedy. Chester Riley on *The Life of Riley* was afflicted with one. So was Kingfish on *Amos 'n' Andy*. Jane Ace's sponging brother on *Easy Aces* defended his perpetual unemployment by explaining that he was waiting for the dollar to stabilize before finding a job. Danny Thomas played a perpetually unemployed ne'er-do-well brother-in-law on *The Bickersons*, one of the darkest of all classic radio sitcoms, and Frances Langford played Blanche, the sister who refused to hear a word against him. The sister of such a man is in a difficult position, and what she winds up doing on a sitcom, as a rule, is to enable her worthless brother and defend him to her angry husband. Blanche had a way of lending her husband John's prized possessions to her brother; in one episode, she lends him John's new car so he can go to the race track, though it means that John (Don Ameche) will have to take the train to work until he gets his car back.

For the same reason that comically maddening MOTHERS-IN-LAW were almost always the *wives'* mothers, comically maddening brothers-in-law were usually the wives' brothers (Uncle Fester on *The Addams Family* is a notable exception): in the era in question, it was mostly men who decided what was funny, or produced the artifacts that enable us now to deduce what was funny back then.

Buck Teeth

"MIGHTY LIKE A Moose," a short silent comic film from 1926, describes itself as "[a] story of homely people—A wife with a face that would stop a clock—And her husband with a face that would start it again," though in fact, as in so many later "makeover" movies, the homely people are played by notably good-looking actors (Vivien Oakland and Charley Chase). Each, however, is afflicted with a single disfiguring flaw—in her case, a big nose; in his, buck teeth. (When urchins see him coming, they use Chiclets to simulate giant incisors.) Each has secretly been saving for cosmetic surgery, and on the same day, at the same hour, in the same medical building, each, unbeknownst to the other, has the flaw corrected and suddenly becomes not just attractive but unrecognizable, like Clark Kent when he removes his glasses. Emerging from their ordeals at the same time, they strike up an acquaintance in the lobby when they both pause to get their shoes shined. Giddy with new possibilities, they embark on the preliminaries of what both improbably believe to be not a second honeymoon but an extramarital fling.

In those days, then, buck teeth could be a deal-breaker. In most bucktoothed humor of the era, though, the afflicted are too stupid even to notice their affliction. Buck teeth were once the standard way of signaling that a character was especially stupid, though as Mort Walker points out, "doctors have never determined a direct relationship between acumen and malocclusion." Walker cites Goofy, Lucky Eddie (from *Hagar the Horrible*), and *Beetle Bailey*'s own Private Zero as typical bucktoothed dummies. He might have added Mortimer Snerd (Edgar Bergen's dumber dummy), Bertie (the submissive half of the Hubie and Bertie duo—the one who keeps saying "Yeah, yeah, sure, sure, boss!"), Elmer (a supporting character in the *Nancy* universe), and Oscar, the dim-witted sailor who, in one early episode of *Thimble Theatre*, tries to help Popeye crush a mutiny by drilling a hole in the hull of the ship in order to drown the mutineers. In "Little Rural Riding Hood," Tex Avery's cartoon retelling of the fairy tale, both the heroine and the Big Bad Wolf have big buck teeth, and both are flagrant idiots, presumably because of backwoods inbreeding. It's also true, of course, that the regions and the people with the least access to orthodontia also have least access to good schooling. In any case, the association is strong enough that even today an overbite—especially in combination with a weak chin (or its extreme form, exemplified by Lucky Eddie: a missing lower jaw)—simply makes its owner "look stupid."

A different effect can be obtained by adding Coke-bottle glasses and other nerd appurtenances: the geek instead of the dolt. Think of Jerry Lewis's Nutty Professor, or more recently *The Simpsons'* Professor Frink. (In the 1960s, the mad scientist on the cherry-flavored Fizzies packet had huge buck teeth and white hair, though no glasses.) Even in these cases, though, another kind of stupidity is implied: a lack of savoir faire as opposed to mere book learning.

(It must mean something, incidentally, that the stereotypical nerd with his overbite and thick eyeglasses looks so much like the stereotypical Nip of 1940s propaganda, a racist cliché that persisted as late as 1961, when *Breakfast at Tiffany's* featured Mickey Rooney in the role of Holly Golightly's bucktoothed, bespectacled neighbor, Mr. Yunioshi.)

As for the equation of buck teeth with stupidity, *that* stereotype was still alive and well in the 1970s, at least in the art department at Topps (whose employees at the time included Art Spiegelman). In 1973–74, mental defectives were depicted with buck teeth (and often, too, with googly eyes and propeller beanies) on at least nine Wacky Package stickers: Ajerx cleanser, Hungry Jerk pancake mix, Blue Beanie margarine, Head and Boulders shampoo ("For People with Rocks in Their Heads!"), Chumps candy, Play-Dumb clay ("Favorite of Dopes, Jerks and Dummies"), What-Man's Simple candy ("Special Half-Pound for Half Wits"), Jerkens Wild soap, and DimWit Dots ("Sugar Cubes for Dummies"). Buck teeth were also used, by the Wacky Package artists, in depictions of hillbillies (Moonshine Wheeze-It crackers); lunatics (Krazy crackers, "Packed in Strait Jackets"; HaHa crackers, "Made on the Funny Farm"; and Goonman's Looney noodles); and, in a jarring revival of a vintage racist stereotype, Asian gangsters (Hawaiian Punks fruit drink).

The Bum's Rush

He's been thrown out of so many bars, he now wears nothing but gray, so his suits will match the sidewalk.
—LOUIS A. SAFIAN,
2000 INSULTS FOR ALL OCCASIONS, 1965

THOUGH SOBER PEOPLE are as essential to the humor of drunkenness as straight men are to funnymen, humorists usually side with the drunks; the function of the sober, as of the sane and respectable in Marx Brothers movies, is to act stuffy and get comically indignant. There's only one stock gag that sides with the sober: the one where a no-nonsense bartender or bouncer literally tosses a drunk out the front door of a bar, as matter-of-factly as if taking out the trash. Often the bouncer isn't even pictured, just the bounce—the troublemaker forcibly propelled out through the entrance by other muscles than his own (and the recipient of this treatment is almost invariably male).

This gag is more common in single-panel magazine cartoons—even in well-bred publications like *The New Yorker*—than in newspaper comic strips, though you'd think the target audience for newspaper funnies is more likely to frequent the kind of dives where the bouncer would do a lot of heavy lifting and heaving. But maybe that's the point: the image of a drunk being tossed out of a rough bar is especially funny to people who never set foot in rough bars, only hasten past, and for whom the drunks tossed out the door suggest the unimaginable rowdiness within.

In our well-fed era, the gag usually involves ejection from bars, but in the cartoons and silent films of the early twentieth century, it was at least as common for characters to be tossed out of restaurants, and not of course for drunkenness but for pennilessness. (In the films of Chaplin, which so often deal with hunger, the headwaiters are almost as fearsome

Fig. 32 *Crazy Charlie*, 1904

as the **COPS**.) That's why it's called "the bum's rush" (when it isn't called "the old heave-ho"): bums are often drunk, but what makes someone a bum isn't drunkenness but inability to pay.

Bums

ACCORDING TO the usual distinction, **HOBOES** travel and bums stay put, remaining at rest like the inanimate objects they sometimes resemble. The distinction isn't always observed—in "Hallelujah, I'm a Bum" (1933), Lorenz Hart uses the two words interchangeably—but it's worth preserving because the two types, or stereotypes, inspire different kinds of humor. Bums are lowlier, and before Chaplin no one had really romanticized them as so many have romanticized those footloose hoboes.

Ernie Bushmiller knew the difference. In 1930, or long before he struck it rich with Nancy, he illustrated *The Milk and Honey Route: A Handbook for Hobos*, by a former hobo named Dean Stiff, who naturally ranks hoboes above bums. So would Nancy, when the time came: she's always glad to give a handout to the scruffy strangers who come to the door asking for food, but she has no patience for the vagrants who settle in her town to stay. Sometimes you wonder how she knows the difference, since Bushmiller's hoboes look exactly like his bums—battered hats, patched coats and pants, and heavy stubble (though never full beards)—except that a bum doesn't carry the regulation BINDLESTICK that in Cartoonland signifies "Just passing through."

More to the point, bums sleep in public and in daylight. And that annoys Nancy no end. Hunger gets her sympathy, but sloth just gets her goat, although (or because?) her best friend Sluggo is a bum in training. In a strip from 1959, she enters a public bomb shelter for no particular reason, sees two bums sleeping, and changes the sign to BUM SHEL-TER. (Have the semioticians gotten their claws into Nancy? No other cartoon character is half as compulsive about revising signs to better suit their referents.) In a strip from 1941, she and Sluggo find a bum sleeping on their favorite park bench and report him to a cop (who chases the bum off but then promptly falls asleep on the bench himself). In another strip from the same year, she sees another bum, or possibly the same one, dozing on another park bench in the vicinity of a flowering bush and a big freestanding sign that says CIVIC PRIDE WEEK—HELP BEAUTIFY YOUR CITY! "Seeing more of that bush . . . and less of this bench might help," says resourceful Nancy, moving the sign to conceal the human eyesore.

Nancy hasn't understood that the park bench is a bum's natural habitat, at least in Funnyland. *The New Yorker*, which in recent years has published compilations of GOLF Cartoons, Cat Cartoons, Business Cartoons, PSYCHIATRIST Cartoons, and so on, could easily compile a volume of Benchwarming Bum Cartoons, assuming they haven't already.

The main difference between these bums and Nancy's is that instead of sleeping they talk. Sometimes a bum says something wistful to another bum, sometimes to a squeamish or indignant businessman who happens to be sitting on the same bench.

In most of his "little tramp" films, Chaplin is a bum and not a hobo. He is content to stay and suffer wherever he happens to be instead of riding the rails and starting fresh somewhere else, probably because he knows that things would be the same anywhere he went: the same hunger, gamins, PRATFALLS, and police harassment. Chaplin was a major influence on Beckett, whose characters do tend to roam, but only after forcible eviction from their dens. At heart, they are quintessential bums: if it had been up to them, they would never even have set foot outside the womb.

C c

Cabbage

*An idealist is one who, on noticing that a rose smells better
than a cabbage, concludes that it will also make better soup.*
—H. L. MENCKEN

CABBAGE IS NOT just a homely and funny-smelling vegetable;
it is also an emblem of all that is useful but unglamorous, as
roses are emblems of romance. Somewhere William Gass writes
of "smelly cabbage-and-meatpie prose," and indeed no vegetable is more
prosaic. It must have different associations in China, where they know
how to cook it, but in America, where it is traditionally boiled to a glu-
tinous and almost colorless mush—flavorless, too, since Americans don't
stop cooking cabbage till it surrenders all its savor to the ill-ventilated
rooms where it's generally cooked—we find it associated with poverty
and the proletariat, with flatulence, with nagging spouses and persistent
cooking smells, with clinical depression, and in general with the unbeau-
tified life. To those of us who never touch the stuff, entering a house
where a head of cabbage has recently been boiled to deliquescence can
have the force of an epiphany—an epiphany of squalor and quiet desperation.

Of course, to those who boil it habitually, cabbage loses those associations and can be given others:

> *He boiled first my cabbage,*
> *And he made it awful hot.*
> *He boiled first my cabbage,*

And he made it awful hot.
When he put in the bacon,
It overflowed the pot.
—BESSIE SMITH, "EMPTY BED BLUES," 1928

It can even serve as a term of endearment ("Mon petite chou"), though seldom as a term of praise. When we compare something to a cabbage, we are almost always putting that thing down, as Mark Twain did when he said that "cauliflower is nothing but cabbage with a college education." In those days, *cabbage* also meant *idiot* or *simpleton* (Twain himself used the word in that sense in "The Watch," a tale from 1870: "All this human cabbage could see was the watch was four minutes slow"), as did *cabbage-head*. During World War II, one of the many derisive terms for Germans was *cabbage-eaters*. The word *boche* also has cruciferous origins (it's short for the French portmanteau *alboche*—from *Allemand* + *caboche*), and so of course does *kraut*.

Canoes

SIGHT GAGS ARE hard to copyright, and we may never know who first came up with one of the best: a pint-sized man is trying to take his big fat girlfriend or wife for a canoe or rowboat ride, but she's so heavy that she tips his end up so that his oars can't even reach

Fig. 33 Canoe humor. See also FAT WOMEN.

the water **(Fig. 33)**. Unlike the two BUMS on the park bench, or the ship-wrecked couple on the DESERT ISLAND, or the boss chasing the SECRETARY around his desk, the canoe gag is not a genre of cartoon, no matter how narrow, but a single joke, always the same joke, because that original joke is unimprovable. I own four different postcards (the earliest from 1939, the latest from 1956) with that joke. In two of them, the woman admonishes the man to "keep up" his end, suggesting to me that even when the boat angles upward as steeply as an erect PENIS, the joke has something to do with impotence as well as with fatness: the man's failure as a gondolier symbolizes another failure, and maybe one with the same cause.

Career Girls and Poor Working Girls

I N A 1946 MAGAZINE AD, a pretty young woman with an arm-load of books stands with one foot on the ground and one on the bottom rung of a library ladder (symbolizing whatever academic or professional heights she hopes to scale), and explains to the naked Cupid hovering nearby that she is "too interested in [her] career" to fuss about primping and preening. "Applesauce!" says Cupid. "You'd like to make *marriage* your career. So set the scene." He proceeds to tell her how to do so with the aid of Cashmere Bouquet talcum powder: how to Keep Fresh, Feel Smooth, and, above all, Stay Dainty (since Cashmere Bouquet "sets your daintiness[10] to high with its flower-fresh scent—the fragrance men love").

---

[10] The word *dainty*, which derives from the same Latin ancestor as *dignity*, was widely used for several decades, but especially in the 1950s, as a code word for feminine hygiene. It would be interesting to know how Madison Avenue hit on that specific bit of coyness, that euphemism for the then-unspeakable. None of the definitions in *Webster's* quite accounts for the word's mid-century association with douching, though I do like 2b, "attractively prepared and prettily served to or as if to stimulate a jaded, finicky, or very slight appetite" (the sense in which the word is used in the nursery rhyme about a blackbird pie: "Wasn't that a dainty dish to set before the king?"), since the same advertisers who urged women to douche with Lysol ("Leaves you wonderfully fresh and sweet") also tried to persuade them that they would thereby revive their husbands' waning appetites for MARRIED SEX.

Cupid is only doing his job, which is to pierce the hide of any mortal rash enough to care about anything other than sex. What interests me is the ad's assumption that women who identify with the bookish young lady would admit so readily that their intellectual or professional pursuits are just a way of marking time till Mr. Right comes along. The ad—like the male establishment it speaks for—refuses, in other words, to acknowledge that there is such a thing as a career girl, as opposed to her less threatening sister, the Poor Working Girl, who of course has been around forever. She was celebrated in a hit song from 1909:

> *You are going far away,*
> *But remember what I say,*
> *When you are in the city's giddy whirl,*
> *From temptations, crimes and follies,*
> *Villains, taxicabs and trolleys,*
> *Oh! Heaven will protect the working girl.*

She was also celebrated, less memorably, by Hallmark Cards, which between the early 1940s and the early '60s produced at least ten different greeting cards featuring the phrase "Poor Working Girl" (or sometimes "Poor Woiking Goil" or "Pore Working Gal") along with a picture of one. She was usually blonde, invariably young and cute, and as a rule expressed one of two sentiments:

1. I'd like to send you a nicer card, but I'm only a PWG.
2. A PWG is continually swamped (or "slaving away").

This second sentiment is always accompanied by a picture of the PWG, never mopping floors or waiting tables, but always at a desk job, typing or answering phones—or neglecting her work to relax, put her feet up, and sip a bottle of soda. She is never shown primping, though, much less flirting with or being fondled by her boss. The cards are interesting for their record of how these proto-career girls liked—or were encouraged—to think of themselves in those days: plucky, stylish, sexy but virtuous, slightly heroic, slightly poignant, but deeply adorable and sure to be rescued soon by Mr.

Right. Not an especially enlightened self-image, but one that differed tellingly from the now-century-old male stereotype of female SECRETARIES, STENOGRAPHERS, AND TYPISTS as vain, incompetent sexpots. But as long as their ambition was to marry their way out of the workforce, working girls never inspired the same sort of male hostility and insecurity as the later career girls who planned to keep working and to compete with men for better jobs.

Castor Oil

IN "BABY PUSS," a 1943 Tom and Jerry cartoon, Tom is tormented by a horrible little girl who wants to play mommy and so insists on his wearing a diaper and staying in a cradle. When she catches him out of the cradle, she threatens, "If you get out one more time I will hold your little nose and I will pour castor oil in your mouth, and it will taste awful bad." In the end she does just that, pouring a big spoonful of viscous greenish goo and forcing Tom to swallow it (after Jerry gets him to open his mouth in a scream by crunching his tail with lobster tongs). Tom makes a face, claps his hands to his mouth, and sprints to an open window to VOMIT, since castor oil, though principally a laxative, is also an emetic. As Jerry laughs uproariously, a blob of castor oil drips into his mouth and sends him to the window, too. The cartoon shows how familiar, and how dreaded, castor oil was in those days.[11] Animated cartoons are full of sight gags about hot sauce, strong drinks, or ALUM, and the funny reactions of those who unwittingly or involuntarily ingest them, but as far as I know none of those gags ever served as the climax of a whole cartoon, maybe because the taste sensations involved were insufficiently universal. In 1943, though, everyone had been in Tom's position.

For one thing, children weren't the only ones back then who took and

---

[11] In the mid-twentieth century, castor oil was used not only as a medicine but as a punishment. Mussolini was using it as such when "Baby Puss" was made; he force-fed it to dissidents in quantities large enough to cause severe and sometimes lethal diarrhea. He reportedly got the idea from Gabriele d'Annunzio—another reminder that poets should never, ever have a hand in politics.

YOU NEED A

AND YOU KNOW IT

Fig.34 Postmarked 1911

hated castor oil. In his 1934 essay on "Coffee vs. Gin," Robert Benchley (a proponent of the latter) complains that "the same people who tell you that a cup of black coffee will put you 'on your feet' are also the ones who go around recommending a 'good dose of castor oil' for a broken leg." He goes on to wonder, "Why must it always be a good dose of castor oil? There is no such thing as a 'good' dose of castor oil." By the way, the original star of *Thimble Theatre* (the Popeye comic strip) wasn't Popeye or Wimpy but Castor Oyl, Olive's grumpy pint-sized brother.

But most castor-oil humor, like most SPINACH humor, features children, both because castor oil was something adults would more readily inflict on their offspring than on themselves, and because children's resistance to unfamiliar flavors—and ability to be traumatized by them—is greater than adults'. One of the many beatings sustained by little Isidore in *Nize Baby* comes after he refuses to take his castor oil. When children in old comedies drew up a list of grievances against the grown-up world, castor oil was near the top: "Never be cross or cruel; Never give us castor oil or gruel," sings Jane to her prospective governess in *Mary Poppins*.

Chamber Pots

IN 1957, YOU could buy a fur-lined miniature chamber pot in a gift box that pictured, on its lid, a beaming suburban couple wearing crowns and sitting on thrones below the words "For Those Who Deserve the *Very Best*." I like to think that the gag was inspired by Max Ernst's fur-lined dinner plate, but maybe the gagster just tried to imagine the most luxurious possible version of the lowliest object in the house. By

1957, few houses still contained a chamber pot; if the first thing people did on having indoor plumbing installed was to test the almost-too-good-to-be-true technology by repeatedly flushing, the second must have been to banish the chamber pot from the house forever.

For those of us fortunate enough to have lived our whole lives in the era of modern plumbing, some old-timer has written a useful poem on "The Passing of the Pot." From this poem, we learn that these pots stank, probably even when empty:

> *The special one for company*
> *Was decorated well,*
> *But just the same it rendered*
> *That old familiar smell.*

That may be why some chamber pots—though kept under the bed for ready access during the night—spent the day outdoors like certain dogs, since in the daytime everybody used the OUTHOUSE:

> *To bring it in an evening*
> *Was bad enough, no doubt,*
> *But heaven help the person*
> *Who had to tote it out.*

Pots came in different sizes:

> *Our big one was enormous*
> *And would accommodate*
> *A watermelon party*
> *Composed of six or eight.*

Though the poem shrinks from saying much about defecation, chamber pots were used for that as well (the poem does mention how, "On icy winter mornings / The cold rim seemed to burn"). Indeed, most comic images of chamber pots show a child seated on one; more often than not the child is male.

And black: even more than OUTHOUSE humor, chamber-pot humor has a racist strain. I've seen eleven different American postcards featuring children and chamber pots, and on seven the child is black. One features a rear view of a bare-bottomed black girl on the pot above the caption: "I is busy / 'Scuse de view / When Is'e thru / I'll write to you"(Fig. 35). Another shows a front view of another bare-bottomed black child either pissing or quietly farting, to judge by the "si-si-si-si" sound emerging from between the pot and her bottom, and the card says "You'll be hearin' from me." A third card shows three young black boys shooting craps; one sits bare-assed on a chamber pot and has just rolled a seven, and the card says "'Pot' Luck." The fourth shows a naked black child racing to the chamber pot while dripping from the bathtub: "I's goin' right to pot sho' nuf if yoo doesn't write soon." Another shows the child sitting on the pot and the pot on a scale beneath the words "It's not a secret any more—I'm giving it 'a weigh' now." On another, the defecating child is naked except for a top hat; the caption reads: "You're invited here for the . . . BIG BLOW OUT!"

I is busy
'scuse de view

When I'se thru
I'll write to you.

Fig. 35 On the go

The most telling card of all, though, dates from World War II and shows a white recruit drilling and sweating in the hot sun, while a circular inset shows a black man straining and sweating on a chamber pot. The bizarre juxtaposition is only half-explained by the punning message: "On the WHOLE, army life agrees with me!" A full explanation would need to say why the guy on the chamber pot had to be black, as if the sheer humiliation of shitting caused white people briefly to turn into black people.

In any case, the image of a black person embarrassed on the pot was so entertaining to certain white people in the middle of the last century that there were all sorts of three-dimensional versions of the same gag. The 1942 Johnson Smith catalog featured three different china statuettes of black children defecating. Two of the statues were novelty ashtrays, the third a bit of mantelpiece kitsch featuring a pair of pickaninnies and an outhouse; the larger boy has just impatiently yanked open the door to reveal the smaller boy moving his bowels. Around the same time, you could also buy a little wooden outhouse with a hinged door that opened to reveal a cartoon drawing of a fat black woman, with big lips and big white eyes, sitting with her back to us on a giant chamber pot and looking anxiously back over her shoulder: the words above her head say "Quit Yo' Peakin'." On eBay, such items are classified by euphemistic sellers as "Black Americana," and the prices they fetch are strikingly, consistently, depressingly higher than similar comic depictions of white people.

Chatterboxes

I admit that my wife is outspoken, but by whom?
—SAM LEVENSON

Can she talk! She was in Miami, and when she got home, her tongue was sunburned.
—HENNY YOUNGMAN

THE 1920S WAS the heyday of wacky marathons: endurance contests in dancing, gum chewing, flagpole sitting, and so on. In 1928, in a Manhattan armory, a certain Milton Crandall staged a talkathon he billed as "a noun and verb rodeo, the world's championship gabfest." The thirty-six competitors included a hermit named Captain Smoke, a woman named May Shaw who attempted to read the whole Bible aloud, an Indian chief (or "Indian chief") who accompanied his talk with dirty drawings, and a Mexican girl who sang instead of talking.

When the contest ended after eighty-one hours and forty-five minutes, Crandall pronounced a draw between two veterans of other kinds of contests: a flagpole sitter named Howard Williams and a swimmer named Betty Wilson.

I'm glad that a man and a woman split the thousand-dollar prize for biggest windbag, since one myth of sexist humor[12] is that women talk more than men. "My wife has a slight impediment in her speech," said Jimmy Durante. "Every now and then she stops to breathe." In a cartoon that appeared in *Look* magazine in the 1950s, two male weathermen at the National Weather Bureau look at a secretary gabbing with two other secretaries. "It's remarkable," says one guy to the other. "She talks 130 words per minute, with gusts up to 175." In a 1963 cartoon from the *Saturday Evening Post*—always a reliable barometer of American humor at its corniest—we see a pair of phone booths, both occupied. The five men waiting their turn for a phone have all lined up in front of the same booth, because there's a woman in the other.

Rube Goldberg's Chatter-Box Eliminator (1929) is actuated by "hot air from wife's chatter" ("And I says . . . and she says . . . and I says . . . and . . ."), which sets off a chain of causation involving a mirror, a dwarf, a faucet, a hose, a woolen sweater, and a pair of pliers that clamp a pair of earmuffs over the ears of the afflicted husband, enabling him to read his NEWSPAPER in peace. And speaking of inventions, let's not forget chattering teeth, the windup plastic kind set in bright red plastic gums. That laff-getter was invented in 1949, and as of this writing its inventor, Eddy Goldfarb, is still alive.

---

[12] And of sexism in general. "No woman has ever set foot in Little America, the most silent and peaceful place in the world," observed Richard Byrd on returning from Antarctica in 1955.

College Professors

The really damned not only like Hell, they feel loyal to it.
—RANDALL JARRELL,
PICTURES FROM AN INSTITUTION, 1954

I N *BALL OF FIRE*, Gary Cooper plays a young scholar improbably heading a team of eight professors at work on an ambitious encyclopedia of all knowledge. Distinctly taller than the rest of them, Cooper reminds (and was meant to remind) us of Snow White with the seven dwarves, especially since the other professors are all one-note characters, and more childish than wise. Still, these scholarly dwarves remain distinctly lovable—a sure sign that the screenwriter hadn't spent much time with actual professors.

Our stereotype of college professors was much more benign back in the days when those doing the stereotyping—screenwriters, songwriters, novelists, and such—lived and worked outside of academia, and neither knew nor cared much about the strange fauna inhabiting the groves of academe. Hence all the ABSENTMINDED PROFESSORS discussed in that entry, whose distinguishing trait is an endearing lack of ego—not because there's any shortage of big egos in academia, but because for those without much up-close experience of college professors, it's easier to imagine their personalities as utterly subsumed in a nerdy quest for knowledge. In our time, when so many creative types pay the bills by preaching what they practice (as John Barth says of himself), the stereotype has changed enough to merit a separate entry.

Or maybe there are now two coexisting stereotypes, one for the sciences and one—the one we are concerned with here—for the humanities. Absentminded professors are usually science professors, and have more in common (if not in reality, at least in fiction) with mad scientists than with their underfunded colleagues in the liberal arts. They, the history and classics and English and social science professors, are notable both in fiction and in reality less for absentmindedness than for touchiness and self-importance.

They also tend to be judgmental, and to rate their own judgments more highly than most of the things they judge. The professorial narrator of *Let Me Count the Ways*, a 1965 novel by Peter De Vries, is so accustomed to passing judgment on his students' work that he finds himself grading everything else, too. In one scene he scolds God for the inadequacy of His sunsets:

> The straightforward romanticism at which You persist is by now basically uncongenial to the modern temper, which aims rather at implication and understress, as I have told You before . . . while the sun centered so exactly between Your banks of cloud (suffused with rose yet!) is quite contrived. This kind of sentimentalization of nature is simply unpalatable to contemporary taste. . . . The trees in the foreground are nicely executed, though of course reminiscent of Renoir. C–.

As a rule, the more seriously people take themselves, the less patience they have with humor in general. And that's unfortunate for the pathologically solemn or pompous, because of course pomposity is *funny*. Solemnity is funny. That's why most comedians keep a straight face, and why most comedies, on stage or screen or printed page, include at least one unsmiling Malvolio, sick with self-love. The main reason professors are funny is that they tend to be so humorless: for every Toby Belch in academia, there are five Malvolios.

That's true even of those professors—most of them philosophers or psychologists—who have theorized about humor and laughter. Kant argued humorlessly that laughter itself (and not the humor that provokes it) is the origin of our pleasure—a theory so crazy it forces the conclusion that Kant's only knowledge of humor came from watching other people laughing. He also insisted—sounding for all the world like one of Gulliver's supremely rational but maddeningly blinkered Houyhnhnms—that the incongruity involved in a joke can't possibly be a source of mental pleasure. He should have been content to say that he himself got no pleasure from incongruity, but he refused to consider that there might be certain worthwhile mental processes of which his own brain was incapable.

Still, there are *some* Toby Belches—and Falstaffs, and Benedicts and Beatrices—in academia, and we have them to thank for the most devastating humor about the world they inhabit. The best humor at the expense of college professors is self-inflicted. The spate of "college novels" since the 1950s is an example—some would say a tragic one—of novelists Writing What They Know. At least some of those writers would have produced better books if they'd known more about townies and less about gownies, but if there must be novels about academia, they might as well be written by people familiar with the milieu.

It is possible, of course, to be *too* familiar with a milieu to be alive to its comedic possibilities. The most amusing college novels have been written by people who were writers first and academics second, people who knew academia from the inside, but hadn't been in there so long as to take its absurdities for granted—people like Mary McCarthy, Randall Jarrell, Bernard Malamud, John Barth, or, on the other side of the Atlantic, Kingsley Amis and Malcolm Bradbury.

As for the caricatures of college professors in mass culture—in Three Stooges shorts, or sitcoms, or drunken-frat-boy movies—they tend to be too broad, and too lacking in true animosity. If your only firsthand knowledge of higher education is from your undergraduate years, you're probably nostalgic about even the stuffiest professors. Insofar as you noticed them at all: when a precocious novelist writes a campus novel while the experience is fresh or still in progress, the faculty barely appears except as an ignorable drone in the background, like the blather of offscreen adults in the animated Peanuts specials. Look at Donna Tartt's first novel, or Bret Easton Ellis's second: both books were inspired by their authors' student years at the same college where I taught for eight (and often felt, among my colleagues, like Alice among the comically solemn and easily angered inhabitants of Wonderland). But Tartt and Ellis barely register the professors and their vanities and rancors—the horrors and hilarities I'd focus on myself if, God forbid, I ever wrote a college novel.

George Meredith, in his essay on comedy, might have been discussing modern academia when he explained why the court of Louis XIV was such a boon to Molière:

He had that lively quicksilver world of the animalcule passions, the huge pretensions, the placid absurdities, under his eyes in full activity; vociferous quacks and snapping dupes, hypocrites, posturers, extravagants, pedants, rose-pink ladies and mad grammarians, sonneteering marquises, high-flying mistresses, plain-minded maids, inter-threading as in a loom, noisy as at a fair.

So it may be just as well for those who like a good laugh—if not for those who like a good education—that writers in our time tend to moonlight as professors.

Cops and Nightsticks

IN THE FIRST PANEL of a large two-panel 1898 strip by R. F. Outcault, originator of *The Yellow Kid* (and some say the comic strip per se), a gang of street urchins hides behind a big wooden fence, waiting to ambush an approaching policeman. In the second panel, one of the urchins has knocked off the policeman's helmet just in time for his bald head to feel the full effect of the load of BRICKS that another urchin is dumping on him from a coal scuttle. To add insult to injury, a third urchin, mounted on the shoulders of a fourth, is SQUIRT-ING Officer Dooley (who has dropped his own nightstick) in the face with a regulation seltzer bottle, while down below, a regulation cartoon bulldog has its teeth in the poor man's calf. Another urchin waits with a big ax, though as far as I know not even Outcault went so far in the name of fun as to show the actual decapitation of an authority figure. Still, it's sobering to realize that this kind of humor was selling newspapers nearly a century before Ice-T caused such a kerfuffle with "Cop Killer."

Humor, according to Max Eastman, is "the instinct for taking pain playfully," and he was certainly right about comics. In their early days, the comics were all about *funny pain*: sadistic pranks, outrageous mishaps, disproportionate reprisals. Head injuries were especially popular, whether inflicted by a hurled brick, a well-aimed ROLLING PIN, an elaborate PRATFALL, or—as so often—a cop. One of the many modern refinements absent from old comics was our attitude toward police brutality. Police are always brutal, and the thud of nightstick against skull provides not just the soundtrack but the punch line for thousands of last panels. The single most frequent image in old comics is not an ALLEY CAT singing on a fence or a goat munching a TIN CAN, but a policeman brandishing a nightstick (or *headache stick*, as it was

Fig. 36 Cop with a nightstick, 1905.
See also BUMS.

sometimes called in the 1920s). The second most frequent image is a policeman clubbing someone on the head with that stick. Unless we count SPANKING, clubbing is by far the most common form of violence in early comics, and policemen the most insanely aggro of funny-page inhabitants.

Seldom can those policemen be classed as either Good Guys or Bad Guys. In early comics, humanity is more often divided into Wise Guys and Schmucks, or sometimes Nuisances and Chastisers. On occasion, of course, the cops are the agents of a well-deserved comeuppance, of gratifyingly rapid—if rough—justice, but at least as often they clobber the meek and well-intentioned. Their nightsticks are a force of nature, a type of bad weather of which at any moment the chances are high, and almost 100 percent in last panels of certain strips. No character in the history of comics was brained as often as the goodhearted and sweet-tempered Happy Hooligan. The first Samuel Butler might have had Happy and not Hudibras in mind when he wrote:

> *Some have been beaten till they know*
> *What wood a cudgel's of by the blow,*
> *Some kicked, till they can feel whether*
> *A shoe be Spanish or neat's leather.*

Hudibras was inspired by *Don Quixote*, which Nabokov called "a crude and cruel old book," in complaining of the thrashings and other random violence that Cervantes expects us to laugh at. That violence, of course, is seldom *entirely* random; Don Quixote is not a bad man, but he's certainly a fool, and in old comedies the penalty for folly is frequently a beating. Up to a point, pain is funnier—except to readers cruder and crueler than even *Don Quixote*'s—when meted out as punishment. The *third* most frequent image in old comics is the mother spanking the naughty little boy—a rain of blows as certain in the final panel of *The Katzenjammer Kids* and its many imitations as the hail of nightsticks in *Happy Hooligan*.

In that sense, a germ of conventional morality—of a Moral Vision, even—exists in even the most hectic early comics, though the representatives of that morality aren't always the official authority figures on the scene. The violence inflicted on hapless Officer Dooley is horrifying—even Tarantino might hesitate to film such an assault—but as the urchins see it, their victim is a thug who abuses his power (and also an IRISH-MAN, as cops so often were in those days—another reason for the hostility against them), just as the dogcatcher they savage in another episode is a ghoul who cruelly kidnaps their beloved pets.

At the low end of the slapstick-justice spectrum, you get Rube Goldberg's *Mike and Ike* ("They Look Alike") sucker-punching an innocent stranger because he looks doggone so dandified and dude-ified. Higher up the scale is A. D. Condo's unforgettable *Everett True* (1905–27), a fat vigilante with a hair-trigger rage reflex, whose daily response to the irritations of everyday life is also the sucker punch, but almost always accompanied with an edifying sermon. These self-righteous assaults could almost be called citizen's arrests, if clouting a malefactor were the same as arresting one.

When the clouting is done by the police—the official upholders of the law and of the morality it encodes—we might seem to have climbed another step in the scale of ethical sophistication. But maybe not, because the cops in old comics tend to bust heads as reflexively as a junkyard dog bites; unlike Everett True, they don't even explain what infringement has moved them to violence.

Nowhere is one more strongly reminded of the largely lumpen and immigrant audience for the earliest comic strips and silent films than in their constant portrayal of police as authorized bullies and thugs, and their patent glee in the cops' discomfiture. Even in films where we root for those cops to catch the criminal, and applaud when they do, we are almost always treated first to scenes that make the police look inept, non-threatening, and laughable, because the underclass of a century ago felt the same way about police that the underclass of today does. The anti-cop sentiments of gangsta rap are nothing new. In "I'm Tickled Silly," a 1921 paean to slapstick, Ira Gershwin confesses:

> *I'm tickled silly . . .*
> *When, willy-nilly,*
> *A club or a mop*
> *Finds a home on the dome*
> *Of a cop.*

Martians trying to get a sense of our species by watching old movies or reading old funnies would rightly surmise, from all this brandishing of giant rigid phalluses,[13] that we are warlike animals—that not much has changed, in that regard, from the days of *Homo erectus*. Married women brandish rolling pins; maiden aunts favor umbrellas. Men not authorized to carry regulation nightsticks make do with whatever is handy—which often proves to be one of those big caveman clubs that look like giant chicken drumsticks, or pterodactyl femurs. (Those clubs have been striking people as funny since at least the dawn of recorded humor, in ancient Greece. Dionysus carries one in the first scene of *The Frogs*, where he appears disguised as Hercules, complete with lion skin.) Where does one acquire such a weapon? Some have clearly been fashioned from tree limbs and still have twigs growing from them, always in the wrong direction,

---

[13] A limerick from 1941:

A bobby of Nottingham Junction
Whose organ had long ceased to function
Deceived his good wife
For the rest of her life
With the aid of his constable's truncheon.

toward the thicker end, as if branches increased in circumference—like Popeye's arms, or all four of Alley Oop's limbs—the farther they got from the trunk.

Why is the club-swinging cop so much commoner in comics than in any other forum for humor? Not even slapstick comedy comes close, despite the best efforts of Mack Sennett. Maybe it's too hard in other arts to portray the police as an impersonal force of nature—too hard to show them busting heads without getting into social commentary. And social commentary isn't funny. Look at *Little Orphan Annie*, which debuted in 1924, when newspaper comics were already moving away from the humor of physical pain toward the humor of cute kids. In *Annie*, most of the blows are dealt to villains who so richly deserve to be hurt that their comeuppance—however satisfying to one's inner child's Romper Room morality—isn't funny. What does it say about humor, that the more civilized the funnies become, and the more deserved the drubbings, the less funny they are?

Couches and Courtship

> *The man who invented the couch became rich—*
> *millions were "made" on it.*
> —*ARE YOU UNDER SEXTY?* (1957)

> *Out in public she's meek and mild,*
> *But in the parlor—Mother dear, come and save your child!*
> —"IF YOU KNEW SUSIE," 1925

COUCHES ARE an interesting example of something that we don't usually think of as funny but that functions as an active ingredient in many things we do. And they *are* a little funny in themselves, maybe because they aren't chairs, and aren't nearly as common as chairs, but bear enough of a resemblance to seem like comically defective or grandiose chairs. One of the comedian Gallagher's many wacky props is a trampoline built to look like a couch.

Fig. 37 Is she wincing or winking?

I could cite the high incidence of couches on domestic sitcoms as evidence of their intrinsic funniness (the couches'—not the sitcoms'), but it may be the other way around: one reason we think couches are funny is that they're so common on sitcoms, and one reason they're so common is that those sitcoms are not only for, but often *about* couch potatoes, even if some prefer armchairs. Couches portray the family—or household—as one big lump or tangle, a point *The Simpsons* has been making with its "couch gags" for more than twenty years now. The armchair, on the other hand, is the pathetic throne of the would-be paterfamilias—think Archie Bunker.

Part of the humor of couches derives from their hybridity or ambiguity. Like the El Camino—that cross between a normal car and a pickup truck—the couch is famously two things at once: on the one hand, a respectable piece of furniture, even office furniture; on the other, a bed substitute. It doesn't have to be the convertible kind that unfolds into a bed, though there is a whole subclass of jokes about those, as in the 1950s *Playboy* cartoon by Erich Sokol that shows a sexy young woman telling another about her new sofa: "And it converts into a full-size bed when

Fig. 38 From *Winnie Winkle*, 1927

Arthur presses me in the right place." *Any* couch is potentially a bed. Jokes about couch-surfing, casting couches, psychiatrists' couches, teenagers making out on couches—all exploit the fact that a couch is a sort of bed. Would PSYCHIATRISTS be as funny, or as creepy, if their offices weren't potential bedrooms?

Social historians say that by the 1930s, automobiles—thanks to their increasing affordability and availability—had replaced the girl's living-room couch as the favorite venue for premarital shenanigans. If so, nobody told Charles Preston, editor of *Let's Go to Bedlam*. The book, a 1957 collection of cartoons by various hands about courtship and marriage, is divided into four sections: "Sound of Hunting," "Engaged to be Harried," "Niagravation Bound," and "Bedlam!" Of the twenty-eight cartoons in the first section, seven feature couples on living room COUCHES, and another shows the lovebirds on a porch swing. Only two cartoons show a couple in a car, though the 1950s was the heyday of PARKING AND PETTING. In Preston's defense, it should be said that humorists have always preferred the living room couch, for the same reason that young men have not: those menacing dads and clock-watching moms and pesky kid brothers mean that more funny things can happen on the couch, even as they ensure that fornication won't.

The couch is the setting of choice for two perennial gag situations, the marriage proposal and the petting session, and that's another sense in which couches are amusingly ambiguous. When a suitor and his sweetheart are sitting side by side in her parents' living room, things can go two different ways. The boy can drop to a knee and propose marriage (and sometimes that possibility is the only reason Dad puts up with him in the first place) or he can just keep canoodling, going as far as she'll let him—stealing milk instead of buying the cow.

It is an axiom of Cartoonland that when a young man and woman sit together on a COUCH, and the man *isn't* yet ready to propose, he will try to make out with the woman. Even if the woman doesn't want to, she'll be vexed and disgusted if he doesn't at least try. No matter how fresh he gets, nothing he might do would be as outrageous as not doing anything, and there are many cartoons set on couches (or, sometimes, in out-of-gas cars) where the joke is the guy's failure to get fresh. In a cartoon that first appeared in *See* magazine and was reprinted in *Best Cartoons of 1945*, a sailor has fallen asleep on a love seat next to a sexy and scantily clad blonde who is indignantly reporting the unbelievable event by phone to Robert Ripley.

Indeed, the role of the couch as make-out pit was such common knowledge that the surest way to show that a guy is too much of a NINCOMPOOP to seize a sexual opportunity is to show him seated on a couch with a cute girl but keeping his hands to himself—as in the Peter Arno cartoon where a man sits in front of a TV set, staring raptly at the screen and musing to the pretty woman sitting moodily at the end of the same sofa, "It's hard to imagine what people used to do before television, isn't it?" When the gal-shy Li'l Abner finally agrees to pay a visit to Daisy Mae—to "set" with her—she prepares for his visit by removing all chairs from the setting room, leaving only the couch: that way, she gloats, "Li'l Abner wil hafta set h'yar wif me. It'll be a tight squeeze, but after all these y'ars, a reckon ah deserves one."

Cowards and Scaredy-Cats

> *Bing Crosby: We must storm the place.*
> *Bob Hope: You storm. I'll stay here and drizzle.*
> —*ROAD TO MOROCCO*, 1942

COWARDICE IS an oddly endearing vice: never admirable, but often the hallmark of characters we love to hate instead of merely hating. Sometimes it's even a character's main selling point. On the spoof-western series *Maverick* (1957–62), Beauregard, the patriarch of the Maverick clan, instilled cowardice in his sons as the highest virtue; when his nephew and namesake accidentally did something heroic, young Beau was banished to England in disgrace, as "the white sheep of the family."

Maverick, though, was a fluke. More often, cowards are portrayed as intellectuals, and not just in America with its ingrained hatred of the intellect. Shakespeare's Falstaff is the archetype of the brilliantly loquacious but cowardly braggart—the man who is all talk—just as the even more articulate Hamlet, though not exactly a coward, is the archetype of a man whose unrivaled powers of thought and expression have sapped the power to act, a man in whom, as he says, "the native hue of resolution is sicklied over by the pale cast of thought." Whatever the truth of these stereotypes, they are with us still.

Dr. Zachary Smith on *Lost in Space* is a typical example of Cold War America's idea of a funny coward, and (not coincidentally) of an intellectual: brimming with book learning and able to talk like a book, but devious, self-serving, devoid of common sense, completely full of shit, and utterly lacking in physical courage or normal self-respect. When faced with danger he hides behind a child, the sturdy Will Robinson. And rightly so, since *Lost in Space* would have lost much less by the death of young Will than by the death of Dr. Smith, who was more charismatic than any of the Robinsons, for all their Boy Scout virtues. Cowards top the list of comic villains we look forward to watching week after week.

A lack of villainy is one reason the Cowardly Lion in *The Wizard of Oz* is not a very interesting character. Another is his lack of complexity: a figment in a child's dream, he embodies cowardice in something close to its pure state, as opposed to the fascinating compounds in which it occurs in real life. It's fitting that he be a lion, since in comedy a coward without bluster or bravado is barely a coward at all, but rather a MILQUETOAST. But the Cowardly Lion doesn't bluster enough, though he gets one good oration: "What makes the elephant charge his tusk in the misty mist, or the dusky dusk? What makes the muskrat guard his musk? Courage!" And so on. He concludes "What makes the Hottentot so hot? What puts the ape in ape-ricot? What have they got that I ain't got?" and the others chorus "Courage!" The Cowardly Lion agrees all too promptly. Some people consider his panicked flight from the Wizard and ensuing de-fenestration the comic highlight of the film, but maybe those people have been watching too many cartoons. In animated cartoons, exhibitions of cowardice often serve as demonstrations of the Third Law of Cartoon Physics: "Any body passing through solid matter will leave a perforation conforming to its perimeter. . . . The threat of SKUNKS or matrimony often catalyzes this reaction."

Cowardice is funniest as a form of *incongruity* (the mainspring of humor in general, according to some thinkers), and specifically as part of a hypocrite's psyche. Unipolar cowardice is boring. To be funny for long, the coward needs to keep reverting to bravado—needs to keep re-inflating so his bubble can be burst again. In *The Court Jester* (1956), the cowardly and clumsy jester played by Danny Kaye is hypnotized, in preparation for his duel with the evil Ravenhurst, to be a fearless master swordsman. The sound of snapping fingers toggles Kaye between his two personae, the fearless and the craven, and in the course of the climactic duel he switches back and forth repeatedly as he and Ravenhurst snap their fingers to punctuate their boasts. His coward mode is funnier than his fearless mode, but neither is as funny in itself as the oscillation between the two.

Crybabies and Whiners

CRYING IS FUNNIER in certain eras than in others. *Tristram Shandy* is one of the greatest comic novels in the language, but it was written during a fad among cultured gentlemen for crying as a sign of tenderheartedness, and so as a rule the tears flow only when Sterne's sense of humor briefly dries up and gives way to sentimentality. Similarly, in the 1950s and early 1960s, the spate of hit songs about crying, by men ("Cry," "Crying," "Cry Me a River," "96 Tears") as well as women ("It's My Party and I'll Cry if I Want To," "Judy's Turn to Cry"), attested to a sentimental era that took self-pity seriously.[14]

But there were dissidents even then. The 1950s was the heyday of the crying towel, defined by *The New Partridge Dictionary of Slang and Unconventional English* as "a notional linen given to someone who is a chronic complainer." The word *notional* suggests that the crying towel began as a figure of speech, and was only later reified by enterprising manufacturers. Either that or Partridge, moving in the highbrow circles in which even unconventional lexicographers move, was unaware that, since the 1940s, dozens of different crying towels have really been made and sold, mostly to bowlers, golfers, fishermen, and hunters. Whether anyone actually used such a towel to cry into is more doubtful. It's hard enough to believe that anyone ever laughed at crying-towel humor.

With the exception of those for housewives or moms (usually emblazoned with a picture of a rolling pin and slogans such as "MOTHER NEVER TOLD ME!" and "I HAVEN'T A THING TO WEAR!"), crying towels were almost always meant for men, and usually offered facetious consolation for failure at some traditionally male pastime. If you can imagine Fred Flintstone or Ralph Kramden partaking of an activity on a night out with the boys, or weekend trip with them, chances are there's an assortment of crying towels dedicated to the activity.

---

[14] Was that era touched off by "I'm So Lonesome I Could Cry," written and recorded by Hank Williams in 1949?

A good crying towel is a two-staged joke. The main joke is that the recipient is such a complainer that he needs a special towel to stanch his tears. It would be sufficient to give him a plain white tea towel in a box marked CRYING TOWEL, but as a rule crying towels go further in their cruelty, listing classic excuses of the unsuccessful sportsman. A characteristically male form of humor: boys don't cry, so it's funny when they do. "Never complain, never explain," said Katharine

Fig. 39

Hepburn (or Disraeli, or John Wayne), and what better way to penalize a whiny fellow fisherman ("ONLY THING BITING TODAY ARE MOSQUITOS") or bowler ("THEY FORGOT TO SWEEP THE ALLEY!") than with a towel that anticipates and so discredits all his favorite complaints and explanations?

Bowling, fishing, and golf comprise the holy trinity of corny lowbrow mid-twentieth-century sportsman humor. Lawrence Lariar, the Palgrave of cartoon anthologists, had a book of cartoons devoted to each. This guide has an entry devoted to each. And each has inspired many, many different crying towels. There have also been towels, though, for all sorts of other whiners: baseball players ("THE BLOND [sic] IN THE THIRD BOX DISTRACTED ME!"); photographers (though the captions that accompany the funny illustrations on this 1952 laffgetter are not excuses but needlessly underlined puns: "I LEICA YOU VERY MUCH," "LET'S GO IN THE DARKROOM AND SEE WHAT DEVELOPS"); dads ("I'M JUST THE GUY WHO BRINGS HOME THE DOUGH THAT SHE KNEADS!"); horse players ("SO YOU WANT TO FIND A BOOKIE? JUST FOLLOW THE MAN

WITH THE PATCH ON HIS PANTS"); even curlers ("IF YOU CAN'T SWEEP, DON'T WEEP"). After Truman upset Dewey in the 1948 election, the Democrats allowed themselves a bit of sore-winner gloating with a Republican Crying Towel.

One of the oldest crying towels I've seen—at least, it looks to date from the 1930s, and its slang carbon-dates to that decade—is an all-purpose towel, for all-round malcontents: "BALONEY!"; "NUTS!"; "I ALWAYS GET THE BAD BREAKS"; "I SHOULDA STOOD IN BED."

As much as we all like to kvetch, none of us likes to think of him- or herself as a sourpuss, a whiner, or a noodge. In popular culture, people who content themselves with complaining verbally are seldom shown in as flattering a light as those who take the law into their own hands, like the unseen vigilante in a 1948 cartoon by Otto Soglow that shows the Complaint Department clerk lying dead on the floor behind his counter with a dagger in his chest.

The complaint department is of course a venerable cartoon cliché, and what's interesting is how seldom our sympathies are meant to be with the complainant and not with the employee paid to listen, just as in cartoons about nagging wives, we are usually meant to side with the husband, not to wonder whether his spouse's grievances are legitimate. (In a clever combination of the two clichés that appeared in a 1960s magazine called *Zowie*, a complaint-department clerk being scolded by his wife exclaims "Oh shut up, Martha! Can't you see I'm on duty now?")

There are exceptions, like the would-be-gallant clerk in a Peter Arno cartoon who asks the pretty young woman, "Aside from the toaster, how's life been treating you?" But as a rule we side with the clerk. In another Arno cartoon, the man at the counter is younger, and the customer an outraged DOWAGER: "Young man, I was complaining about things in this store before you were born!" In a Charles Addams cartoon from 1955, in the age of Better Living Through Chemistry, a scowling matron stands in line waiting to lodge her complaint, the nature of which we can surmise from the fact that in one hand she holds a chemistry set and in the other the invisible hand of an invisible little boy wearing ordinary shoes, pants, coat, and baseball cap, but with no hands at the end of his sleeves and no head under the cap.

D d

Desert Islands

FUNNY THINGS CAN HAPPEN on a desert island. A man can mope because he's washed up with a sexy mermaid and not a sexy normal woman forked below the waist. A man marooned with a beautiful woman can scowl and hold a gun to his head as the woman spots another, older, plumper woman drifting toward the island on a piece of flotsam and joyfully cries, "Mother!" Another, pluckier male, marooned not with one willing beauty but *four* (and so with four times the incentive to fight for his current way of life), can swing a big stick angrily at the approaching rescue party, causing a sailor to ask the captain: "Do you get the feeling, sir, that he doesn't want to be rescued?" A castaway can shock a mermaid by offering her a tin of sardines. A luckless dog can be stranded on a tiny treeless islet just a few yards away from an islet with a tree, but with sharks patrolling the intervening waters.

Unlike some of the funny things considered in this guide, desert islands have appealed to great writers as well as to third-rate cartoonists. Shakespeare's final play, *The Tempest*, takes place on a desert island (though a larger one than in gag cartoons, and one that becomes a lot less deserted in the course of the play). A little over a century later, Daniel Defoe chose a desert island as the setting for *Robinson Crusoe*, the first great English novel.

If we still associate desert islands with magazine cartoons, that's because the desert island is far and away the most popular setting for such cartoons, whether in *The New Yorker* or *Playboy* or anywhere in between. The idea of being marooned on an island with an attractive woman is, I once read, the all-time favorite male fantasy. At its root it's probably a

Fig. 40

RAPE fantasy, though that's never alluded to in cartoons, not even the ones in pornographic magazines. There are plenty of cartoons about horny bosses chasing secretaries around the executive desk, but none, as far as I know, about horny castaways chasing lady castaways around the palm tree: in Cartoonland, a woman alone with a man is safer on a desert island than in a deserted office building.

Many cartoons do involve the man's exasperated efforts to convince the woman that rules of civilization no longer apply, since that's the whole point of the fantasy. In a 1947 *New Yorker* cartoon, a young couple are joined on their tiny island by a third party, a freshly shipwrecked preacher whose arrival visibly pleases the young woman and alarms the young man. (No one, incidentally, ever seems to fantasize about being stranded on a desert island with his wife, though that would seem an obvious metaphor for marriage—both the heaven and the hell of it.)

Cartoonists find their imaginations washing up on the shores of the cliché again and again. Dana Fradon's *Breaking the Laugh Barrier* (1961) is a book of lowbrow and usually racy cartoons pertaining to air travel— still sexy enough in those days to serve as the theme for such a collection.

But apparently not sexy enough by itself to sustain a full book: Fradon includes no fewer than seven run-of-the-mill desert island cartoons, each with the tail fins of a plane protruding from the water in the background, barely justifying the cartoon's inclusion in the book, and in no way contributing to the gag.

That was fifty years ago, but you still see desert island gags in magazines. You'd think that by now no good cartoonist would touch the cliché, any more than any self-respecting poet would rhyme *moon* and *June*, but the cartoon genre is uniquely hospitable to clichés. When a cartoon is set on a desert island *now*—and this was already the case half a century ago—the *first* joke is that a cartoonist has dared to do it again. Like an in-joke among friends, the gag owes some of its funniness to its artificially prolonged longevity.

Dishwashing Husbands

THE CLASSIC HOUSEHUSBAND activity is washing dishes—not because it's a more humiliating chore, in itself, than changing diapers or laundering the wife's undies (as Leopold Bloom—househusband par excellence—does in *Ulysses*), but because it's the only one entailing an apron. That apron is invariably frilly, to emphasize the femininity of the job. In a compilation of insults published in 1966 (though many clearly date from decades earlier), my favorite in the chapter on HENPECKED HUSBANDS is "He wears the pants in the house—under his apron." Except perhaps while barbecuing, wearing the apron in a household is the exact opposite of wearing the pants.[15] Unsurprisingly, the chapter contains two other jokes about men in aprons,

[15] The novelty barbecue aprons of the mid-twentieth century—with messages like "Kiss the Chef" and comic illustrations—were mainly aimed at males, like the crying towels of that era (see CRYBABIES AND WHINERS), and like crying towels they reflected male anxieties about effeminacy. They belonged to the same school of corny, never-funny comic art as the towels, or the jokey cocktail napkins produced in such abundance in the 1950s that they still clutter liquor cabinets everywhere. The aprons had to be facetious because Real Men Don't Cook, just as real men don't cry.

and five about men doing or helping with the dishes. ("They had a big difference of opinion about getting a dishwasher. She says he doesn't need one.")

Left to their own devices, few men would think to put on an apron at all before approaching the kitchen sink (or the barbecue pit), but where clothes were concerned, many women used to do—as some still do— the thinking for their spouses. So the "aproned husband" joke is related to the one about the little boy forced by his mother to dress like a sissy. *That* joke occurs repeatedly in Little Rascals episodes and was a favorite of down-home cartoonists like J. R. Williams and H. T. Webster. In old humor, little boys as well as henpecked husbands are routinely humiliated by women.

Because in those days men controlled the channels through which comedic stereotypes were created and maintained, the usual joke about dishes is the one about the domestication of husbands. Few humorists bothered to ask *why* wives were so eager to get their husband to help with the dishes, and not with the cooking, say, or the laundry. Now and then a cartoonist showed an aproned hubby dusting, but dishwashing has always—and by a wide margin—been the quintessential humiliating chore. Why? Because men hate it more than they hate mopping or cooking? No—because women do.

Washing dishes is depressing in the same way as cleaning up after a party. No matter how good the dinner has been, the dirty dishes are unappetizing, and relate to the meal as a hangover to a night of drunken revelry. More to the point: for a happily married couple, especially a childless one, the evening meal should be the climax of the day. The wife has gotten the unglamorous drudgery of housework out of the way while her spouse was at work, and now she would like to feel like a romantic being rather than a hausfrau. She'd also like to feel like an equal partner in the marriage, or at any rate, not to feel that her husband takes her for granted. All these feelings converge to make dishwashing a sore point. One of the first jokes recounted and discussed in Gershon Legman's massive *Rationale of the Dirty Joke*— the joke that inspired him to write the book, in fact—concerns dirty dishes. Legman heard it in Scranton, Pennsylvania, in 1936 from "a

Fig. 41 *The Lovebyrds,* 1935

very respectable Jewish woman of middle age" whose marriage was "gruelingly unhappy." (Like Freud discussing dreams, and for the same reasons, Legman often provided biographical information about the teller of a joke, when he hadn't just transcribed it from the wall of a public restroom.)

> A man goes to his rabbi and says he wants to divorce his wife because she has such filthy habits.
>
> "What are these habits?" asks the rabbi.
>
> "Oh, I can't tell you," says the man. "It's too filthy to describe."
>
> The rabbi refuses, without hearing more information, to grant the man the divorce.
>
> "Well, if I must, I must," says the man. "Every time I go to relieve myself in the sink, it's always full of dirty dishes."

Legman, who maintained that "A person's favorite joke is the key to that person's character," had this to say about the dishes joke:

Other than the obvious level of self-unveiling here, of the woman's unhappiness with her brutal and egoistic husband, there is perhaps a further level, even better concealed, in which the joke complains of women's woes concerning the household chores that make her too tired and unready to enjoy her sexual life, here alluded to in almost infantile terms as her husband's "pissing in the sink."

Elsewhere, Legman recounts a joke he heard in Washington, D.C., in 1946: "A bride, when asked what she thought of married life, replied, 'Between the douches and the dishes, I'm in hot water all the time.'"

While the dishwashing husband is a HENPECKED HUSBAND, the husband who dries while his wife washes is viewed more romantically. When, after months of buildup, Blondie and Dagwood are finally wed, the first thing she says to him is "You'll help me with the dishes, won't you, darling?" In "Okay, Toots" (1934), a Gus Kahn song about a happy young couple, the husband's undying affection is embodied by his readiness to share that most contentious of all household chores: "If you wash dishes, I dry dishes."

Why, when they share the chore, does the wife always wash and the husband always dry? Because washing is the dirty job? Maybe so, but the division of labor also seems to reflect gender stereotypes. Women are moist, hot, emotional beings, forever leaking tears and milk and blood; men are dry, cold, rational, forever calming down their helpmeets and drying their tears.

Do-Gooders

EARLY IN THE TWENTIETH CENTURY, there were half a dozen one-note comic strips about would-be good Samaritans: strips with names like *Mister Makepeace*, *Mr. Butt-in*, *Mr. and Mrs. Butt-In*, *H. E. Butzin*, *The Interfering Idiot*, and *Oliver Meddle*. The humor at the expense of these meddlers was surprisingly rough; even an action as well-intentioned as reporting an apparent burglary or trying to fix a child's broken toy (and breaking it further) could be punished by a savage beating at the hands of the whole neighborhood.

Comics started out as a distinctly proletarian art form—as lowbrow as tractor pulls or big-time wrestling in our own day—and the anti-do-gooder strips reflected a lot of class resentment. As a rule, the butt-in was a middle-class man, probably college-educated, and in any case convinced that he knew more than blue-collar workers about their own jobs and lives. He had a clear idea of how the world should be run, but no tact, no sense of how his well-meaning advice might offend the people he sought to correct. Collectively, the strips express a sane if narrow-minded idea of the proper limits of altruistic behavior: Don't help strangers unless they ask, or unless you're absolutely sure you understand the problem. (In *Mister Makepeace*, which began and ended in 1906, the title character was hard-of-hearing as well as intrusive, and so—like Mr. Magoo more recently—kept responding to situations he misunderstood.) The chronic butt-in was so addicted to saving the day that he saw emergencies where none existed.

There were also strips about hapless souls forever being press-ganged into helping others with disastrous results, such as *Mr. Fallguy*, a strip that ran between 1913 and 1915, and was perhaps a fable, on the eve of World War I, about the dangers of interventionism. Then there was Happy Hooligan, whose readers laughed at his mishaps without *gloating* at them. Happy, though, was less of a do-gooder than a fuckup. Where the typical comic-strip do-gooder was, as I say, a middle-class figure whose mishaps served to gratify the class resentment of the working-class audience, Happy was a tramp, and both his good heart and his constant beatings serve to reassure the same working-class audience about menacing outcasts.

All the aforementioned strips date from before America's entry into World War I, though their eclipse had less to do with that geopolitical intervention than with the steady gentrification of the funny pages. Mid-century America invented another, gentler joke about Good Samaritans: the single-panel magazine cartoon about the Boy Scout hell-bent on doing his daily good deed. My favorite variation on the theme, which appeared in *The National Enquirer* in 1957, shows a frightened Scout sprinting away from an intersection where a crowd is already forming around an old lady—we see only her legs and cane—lying in front of a truck. Even in cases like that, though, Boy Scouts never inspire the hatred incurred by the turn-of-the-century altruist. For one thing, their motives are different: not a conviction that they *know* better, but an allegiance to an organization that imposes its dorky ethics on them along with its dorky uniform. There's something endearingly funny, too, about *needing* to do a good deed, whether or not there's any call for one. And of course the standard beneficiary of the scout's do-gooding—an old lady—is herself a favorite laughingstock.

Domestic Violence

IN HIS *LADIES' AND GENTLEMEN'S Guide to Modern English Usage*, James Thurber begins the chapter on "The Split Infinitive" this way:

> Word has somehow got around that a split infinitive is always wrong. This is of a piece with the sentimental and outworn notion that it is always wrong to strike a lady. Everybody will recall at least one woman of his acquaintance whom, at one time, or another, he has had to punch or slap.

Thurber goes on for another page to talk about when and how to hit a woman, and then about food fights at formal dinner parties. Toward the end of the chapter, to be sure, he does return to its stated subject, even quoting Fowler, but then digresses again.

One man who agreed with Thurber on the occasional, regrettable necessity of hitting women was Popeye the Sailor—unsurprisingly, perhaps, since he was always a two-fisted type, but it's still jarring when he hits Olive Oyl because he's so muscular and she's so anorexic. Popeye is too gallant to strike a woman in anger, but in a Sunday strip from 1932, he dozes off while sitting with Olive on her couch, dreams of a mutiny, and acting out his dream, beats the shit out of poor Olive in a spasm of somnambulistic violence. In a

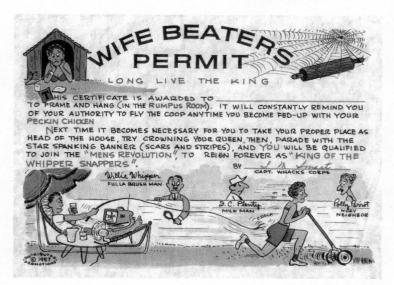

Fig. 42 Gag gift, 1957

strip from the following year, Popeye finds himself irresistibly compelled not only to dance when Wimpy plays the violin, but also to interpret the music as he goes, with the result that when Olive makes the mistake of approaching him during the "Song of War," Popeye knocks her down. His creator, E. C. Segar, stops short of endorsing violence against women, but he must have wanted to show it, or thought his audience wanted to see it. Otherwise he wouldn't have kept finding excuses for Popeye to whale on Olive. Her sadistic and sometimes misogynistic maltreatment carries over to the animated cartoons, where she's always getting twisted, stretched, and knocked about.

Another famous comic strip did endorse wife-beating at least once. In a series of *Li'l Abner* strips from 1966, Daisy Mae suffers one of those HEAD INJURIES that in comedy tend to cause drastic personality changes. Sure enough, the model wife and mother morphs into a selfish, angry vixen who leaves her husband and child in order to dance in a nightclub. We are given a neurological explanation involving a little-known part of the brain, a sort of toggle switch: "Like any wife, Daisy Mae had a fine upstandin' home-maker gland—but a accidental bop reversed it into the home-*wrecker* position—reversin' her character." So says Abner, who sets out—with the cartoonist's clear approval—to clobber Daisy Mae and so return her to her senses.

Though we think of it now as strictly a lowbrow gag, there were several cartoons about domestic violence in the early years of *The New Yorker*, before that magazine made up its mind as to just what note it wanted to strike. In a cartoon from 1925, the year the magazine was founded, a comically contorted husband lies on the floor of a room that looks to have been hit by a hurricane. His elegant wife stands in a dramatic contrapposto and says, "I'm not angry, I'm only terribly hurt!" A 1929 cartoon shows a scowling housewife wielding a rolling pin and chasing her husband around an already-trashed living room in whose center sits a bewildered baby. "For Gawd's sake stop, woman," begs her husband, "baby is getting dizzy." In another cartoon from 1929, the roles are reversed, the woman cowering on the floor of an elegant room amid the wreckage of a major tantrum, the man looming over her with fists still clenched, demanding, "What do you mean I'm disagreeable?" Such cartoons soon vanished from the magazine for good, though later Charles Addams was allowed to draw all sorts of cartoons about SPOUSE-

Fig. 43 *Nize Baby*, 1926

KILLING, with the violence implied instead of pictured: a more civilized joke, just as detective novels are more civilized than crime fiction.

The main venue for jokes about wives assaulting husbands is the comic strip (closely followed by the slapstick comedy). For more on such assaults, see ROLLING PINS—but while I'm on the subject, let me mention that the archetypal cartoon provocation for that archetypal cartoon reprisal is the husband coming home drunk and past his curfew. E. C. Segar also drew a comic strip called *Sappo*, as a Sunday "topper" or companion strip to *Thimble Theatre* (the Popeye strip). The tiny bald hero is married to a woman twice his size who makes a point of throwing a rolling pin at him—sometimes hitting, sometimes missing—any time he comes home late from a poker game. In one strip, Sappo cancels his plans to play poker when his wife shows him a rolling pin she's enhanced with a tail feather so that she can throw with more accuracy. In another strip, Sappo turns the tables on his wife when *she* stays out late ("What's sauce for the goose is pea soup for the gander"), waiting up for her with not one but two rolling pins, and several other MISSILES—but *still* gets the worst of the fight.

"I'd face a lion in his cage," boasts a red-nosed, top-hatted DRUNK as he leans against a lamppost in a comic drawing from the 1920s, "but I won't go home." In a 1946 magazine cartoon, a husband returning from a long night of carousing has just opened the front door with his shoes in his hand—clearly hoping to sneak in—only to find his living room roped off like a boxing ring, and sitting in one corner his large, angry wife wearing boxing gloves. If you're going to stay out late, you may as well misbehave while you're at it, because your spouse is going to assume you're misbehaving, and is going to clobber you when you do get home.

Doomsday Prophets

THE SIDEWALK PROPHET holding a big sign is an irresistible subject for gag cartoonists, since it merges words and images in a way no merely captioned cartoon ever can. And in a way that movies no longer do, since the advent of talkies: when wild-eyed, wild-haired prophets appear in movies (or on television), the emphasis is never on their signs, when they even have signs, but on their words, their body language, their dishevelment.

Gag cartoons involving this cliché are more likely to be funny than ones involving DESERT ISLANDS, say, or MARRIAGE COUNSELORS. My favorite prophet cartoon appeared in *Blue Book* in 1956 and shows a bearded, robed, and sandaled prophet picketing a strip club with a sign that reads BEWARE THIS DEN OF SINFUL PLEASURE, and under that, in smaller print, Never a Cover Charge. Another good one appeared in 1963 in a magazine called *Insurance Salesman*. It shows a standoff between two kindred but hostile cartoon archetypes, a doomsday prophet and a top-hatted sandwich man whose sandwich board reads "BIMBELS—Giant Sale starts Friday." The prophet's sign announces that the world ends on Thursday.

Like sandwich men, prophets are funny partly because they have turned themselves into human kiosks—one in the name of Mammon, one in the name of God—and thus into something less than human. The prophets don't mind this humiliation as much as the sandwich men do, because prophets are used to thinking of themselves as mere conduits for God's message. Cartoonists seem to see them a bit differently, as picketers boycotting everyday life, or protesting the continuation of life as we know it. They are like hippies without the drugs or sex—though a 1963 cartoon from *Argosy* shows a bearded prophet asleep in bed, his REPENT sign propped against the wall and a thought balloon over his head revealing that he's dreaming about a naked lady prophet also holding a REPENT sign.

Door-to-Door Salesmen

IN A *TIMID SOUL* cartoon from 1951, a new chain on his front door enables Caspar Milquetoast, for the first time ever, to face down a pushy salesman: "I'm sorry, but my interest in a patent combination corkscrew, bottle-opener, and potato-peeler is at an all-time low," he says—in words of almost unprecedented confidence—through a crack too narrow for his caller to get a foot in the door.

The '50s was an era of useless gadgets, and in the humor of the era, door-to-door salesmen often hawked such items, though not as often as they hawked newfangled vacuum cleaners. Earlier in the twentieth century, they were likely to be hawking encyclopedias.

In 1901, the Edison Company's film catalog described "A Wringing Good Joke" as "a remarkably pleasing picture that will appeal to both young and old, for it is the sort of trick that every boy might play on a grandparent." In addition to prankster and victim, the cast of the short comic film includes "a stout jolly wash-woman from the Emerald Isle" and "the ubiquitous book agent," who enters the house uninvited and sticks around to laugh with the boy at Grandpa's discomfiture.

Ubiquitous? Yes. A book agent was a door-to-door salesman specializing in books, especially encyclopedias and other sets. These agents were common pests in the first decades of the last century, even more than vacuum cleaner salesmen would later be.

Back then, indeed, *pest* was practically a synonym for "book agent." *Mr. Pest, Book Agent* was a short-lived (1905) comic strip. "The Pest," a short comic film from 1922, stars Stan Laurel as a book agent. Another Laurel film from the same year, *Mixed Nuts*, was made by recutting *Nuts in May* (1917) and adding scenes and outtakes from *The Pest*. In *Nuts in May*, Laurel played a lunatic with Napoleonic delusions living in a Home for the Weak-Minded; in *Mixed Nuts*, he plays a book agent selling a book about Napoleon.

These salesmen were still common enough in 1950 to feature in the very first episode of *The George Burns and Gracie Allen Show*. Any viewers not already familiar with Gracie from radio would have formed their first impression of her lovably stupid, proto–Edith Bunker comedic persona from the scene in which her well-meaning ditziness proves more than a match for an unctuous encyclopedia salesman.

It now seems odd that for much of the twentieth century, encyclopedias in particular were peddled door-to-door. The rationale for selling cleaning supplies door-to-door was presumably that the salesman would appear as a Prince Charming to rescue the housewife from the vexations of housework with magically effective new brushes and vacuums and (in the case of Amway) cleansers. But why *encyclopedias*? Maybe because

Americans believe on some level—or used to—that knowledge is power. Parents were guilt-tripped into thinking that unless they bought a set of encyclopedias, they weren't giving their children a shot at success.

It's hard to say exactly when vacuum cleaners replaced encyclopedias as the favorite items for comically pushy strangers to knock on your door and bully you into buying, but as so often, World War II is a good rough demarcation. The long-running radio sitcom *Fibber McGee and Molly* had an episode in 1936 about an encyclopedia salesman and an episode in 1954 about a vacuum cleaner salesman.

So somewhere in the 1940s, maybe. In a Charles Addams cartoon from that decade, a vacuum salesman pauses at the gates of a grand estate on seeing another vacuum salesman—still clutching his demonstrator—strung up from one of the trees. The 1949 volume of *Best Cartoons of the Year* had *two* cartoons about vacuum salesmen. In one, set in an apartment building, the salesman has plugged his product into a handy hallway outlet and used the nozzle to doff his hat to the skeptical housewife, who has just opened her door. In the other, the salesman is peddling an electric *broom*—an ordinary broom with an electric cord emerging from its handle ("Curious?" he asks the housewife at whose door we find him), as if in a last-ditch effort by a superseded technology to compete with its replacement.

In "So You Want to Be a Salesman" (1947), one in a series of sixty-three short comic "how-to" films all featuring a hapless man named Joe McDoakes, the hero gets a job selling Atom Smasher vacuums door to door, but can't sell a single one, not even to his wife. In general, when a comic narrative about a salesman is experienced from the salesman's own viewpoint, he is almost always unsuccessful: failure is funny, and effective salesmen, be they bullies or seducers, make a living by imposing their will on others, and so are unsympathetic. Because unsuccessful salesmen usually quit—or are fired—and find something else to fail at, the brief disastrous attempt at door-to-door selling is a perfect premise for a single sitcom episode. Between 1961 and 2009, no fewer than eleven television series—including *McHale's Navy, The Many Loves of Dobie Gillis, The Bob Newhart Show,* and *The Adventures of Sonic the Hedgehog*—had an episode called "Birth of a Salesman."

In "Sales Resistance," a 1953 *I Love Lucy* episode that fans of the series rank among its highlights, Lucy buys a Handy Dandy vacuum cleaner. When Ricky demands she return it, she decides to resell it instead, going door-to-door with it just like a full-time salesman, only to return in defeat, more dead than alive, with the vacuum but minus a shoe: "I was kicked down stairs, bitten by a dog, and chased three blocks by a policeman who wanted to see my peddler's license. One more hour, they'd have reported the death of another salesman." At one point Lucy throws mud on a prospective customer's floor to demonstrate the Handy Dandy's wonder-working suction, only to be told that the woman's electricity has been shut off for nonpayment.

Door-to-door salesmen were a favorite gag of cartoonist Ernie Bushmiller. Among the many to call at the house of Nancy and Aunt Fritzi were one whose fingers were heavily bandaged from using the combination can opener, potato peeler, and radish parer he's selling; one who bangs on the door at 3 A.M. hawking Snoozo sleeping pills; one selling mousetraps who gives up in mid-pitch when he sees all the neighborhood cats; one who uses the "new super door-stop" he's selling to prevent Nancy from slamming the door in his face; one selling karate lessons who accidentally punches a hole through the front door in attempting to knock; one who hypnotizes Nancy through the peephole viewer when she refuses to open the door and look at the HYPNOTISM book he's selling; and one who uses the alarm clock he's selling to ring at Nancy's door on finding the doorbell out of order. In the course of a single Sunday strip from 1951, so many different salesmen show up (hawking brooms, brushes, saucepans, medicine, and can openers) that Nancy, who is trying to nap on the couch, finally rolls up a bunch of newspapers and places them on the front porch, to make it look like the house's occupants are on vacation. In a strip from 1959, two vacuum salesmen show up at the same time and duel in Nancy's front yard with the pipes of their identical products. Most of the salesman strips seem to date from the 1950s and early 1960s, though that was already past the heyday of door-to-door selling, and *Nancy* started back in 1938. But such megatrends take a while to register on the funny pages, especially in neighborhoods like Nancy's. (Most of Bushmiller's gags about hippies date from the mid-1970s.)

Simon Bronner may have been thinking of *Nancy* when he suggested, in *American Children's Folklore*, that knock-knock jokes exist in order to teach children how to deal with door-to-door salesmen and other dubious callers: "In a mobile, urban society, one encounters more strangers than ever before. Children are especially vulnerable, and are reminded to be cautious. The object of the knock-knock routine is essentially a reminder to press strangers for their identity."

I'm glad that an intelligent man like Bronner is willing to take children's jokes seriously, and to ask why some have proven more enduring than others, but he's wrong about knock-knock jokes. Neither as a child nor as an adult have I ever, while telling or hearing a knock-knock joke, pictured a door with a caller on one side and a dweller on the other. Does anyone? If you want to teach your kids to beware salesmen and other callers, you'll do better to show them "Big Business," the 1929 Laurel and Hardy short in which the two play door-to-door Christmas tree salesmen and wind up destroying a man's house.

Certain types of kid jokes (such as elephant jokes or grosser-than-gross jokes) do depend for their effect on making the hearer envision something, but knock-knock jokes are all about wordplay, not evocation. If they teach us anything, it is to be wary of bad puns—we brace ourselves for one as soon as we hear the words "Knock! Knock!" The simple explanation for the popularity of those jokes is that children are much fonder than grownups of puns; they can get more pleasure from a bad pun than most grownups allow themselves to take in a good one.

Also, Bronner's theory presupposes a benign conspiracy of indoctrination on the part of parents and teachers consciously bombarding children with didactic jokes, when in fact the striking thing about children's oral culture is its independence from grownups and our agendas. And whatever age the audience, humor seldom has an "object," though it often serves a function. Even if children's taste for knock-knock jokes—like grownups' taste for door-to-door-salesman jokes—does reflect anxiety and curiosity about the strangers who come knocking, that isn't the "object" of the joke. It's hard enough to be funny without trying to teach at the same time.

Dowagers

DOWAGERS ARE FUNNIEST when they get indignant, and in comedy they always do. A lot of dowager humor involves the old gal raising her eyebrows and heaving her bosom in mortal indignation. If we think of bad emotions as pains, then indignation is an especially funny type of pain. And to that type of pain, dowagers are famously hypersensitive. Not even a COLLEGE PROFESSOR can rival a good dowager for sheer disgusted hauteur.[16]

That's why anything is funnier when it happens to a dowager—anything undignified, like getting hit in the face by a pie Moe intended for Larry. You don't need to have encountered a real dowager to get the humor and pathos of the ones in old movies and TV shows. At the height of my Three Stooges obsession, when I was maybe ten, I'd never met anyone remotely like the massive, haughty, BOSOM-heaving society ladies who serve as such perfect foils for the Stooges' buffoonery. But I already got the joke: these rich ladies thought they were better than other people—not just better than Larry, Curly, and Moe, but better than me and everyone I knew—when in fact they were just fat old ladies. Every ten-year-old has been instructed by pop culture (and high culture will repeat the same lesson—think of Lady Bracknell, Charlotte Haze, or Madame Verdurin) that the only women who matter are pretty girls and loving mothers. Pop culture reflects the lower class's attitude—part incredulity, part outrage, and part mirth—toward the snobbery of the rich. The average hod carrier may not be convinced, in his heart of hearts, that he's just as good as the owner of the Hod Works, but he never doubts that he's better than the owner's plump, supercilious, OPERA-going wife. It would be tempting to see the portrayals of rich menopausal ladies in

---

[16] A *dowager* college professor is also possible, of course, and I know for a fact that the creature exists. Sadly it cannot be here discussed: an academic dowager encountering the infra dig is such a fearsome sight that not even laughter-lovers, if they know what's good for them, will set *her* bosom to heaving.

Three Stooges shorts and Marx Brothers movies as expressions of class-consciousness, but they are mainly expressions of sexism. Not counting mothers, women in pop culture matter only as objects of desire, so those with any other claims to fame are ridiculed—not only rich women, but CAREER GIRLS, BRAINY GIRLS, and culture vultures like the ones in Helen Hokinson's cartoons.

Drunks and Drunkenness

> *Drinking makes such fools of people, and people are such fools*
> *to begin with, that it's compounding a felony.*
> —ROBERT BENCHLEY

> *You're not drunk if you can lie on the floor without holding on.*
> —DEAN MARTIN

IN THE CLASSIC first-season *I Love Lucy* episode "Lucy Does a TV Commercial," Lucy stars in a commercial for a health tonic called Vitameatavegamin and fortified with all kinds of good things, including alcohol. At first, before she swallows any of the stuff, Lucy is nervous, overeager, and strident, but in full possession of her faculties. After a spoonful, she relaxes a bit, and her smile seems less forced. By the third take, she starts ad-libbing, forgetting her lines, and laughing when she says something that strikes her as clever. Before she's through, she's grinning idiotically, swigging straight from the bottle, and belching. Even after almost sixty years, the performance holds up as a funny and convincing time-lapse portrayal of the stages of intoxication.

Lucy's famous sketch was prefigured by Red Skelton in *Ziegfeld Follies* (1946), in a sketch called "When Television Comes" **(Fig. 45)**. As the announcer for the Guzzler's Gin Program, Skelton—like Lucy—is required not only to plug the sponsor's product at regular intervals, but also to take a slug of it each time, just to show how "smoooooooth" it is. Skelton already seems a little addled when he begins, and he gets a lot more addled as the sketch goes on (after one drink, he is already staggering and slurring), though he never manages to anesthetize himself to the point where he can drink the stuff he's plugging without the sort of elaborate comic recoil that cartoon characters produce after accidentally drinking a bottle of Tabasco. (Lucy also winces after her first tablespoon of Vitameatavegamin, but soon learns to like it.)

To watch the two scenes in succession is to appreciate the subtlety of Lucille Ball's acting even in farcical situations. She never forgets that she is playing a character who desperately wants to be on television, even if only as the Vitameatavegamin girl, and though her determination to do a good job in that capacity finally loses out to the intoxicating properties of the health tonic she's plugging, the battle is valiantly fought. Skelton's announcer, on the other hand, puts up no resistance at all as intoxication invades his brain and central nervous system. Of course, he's taking bigger gulps of stronger stuff, but that doesn't really account for the much broader humor of his sketch. Part of the difference is that "Lucy," by that point, was a fully realized character with twenty-nine episodes of backstory behind her, whereas Skelton's announcer was a one-off with none of the depth that makes a comic character lastingly funny.

The real difference, though, is that unlike Lucille Ball, whose simulation of drunkenness leaves no doubt that she herself has been drunk more than once, and knows exactly how it feels as well as how it looks, Skelton (though himself a notable souse) enacts a broad stereotype of drunkenness, the one held by people who don't themselves get drunk, don't associate much with people who do, and don't notice drunkenness except in its most extreme manifestations—the wino reeling down the street, pissing in the alley, puking in the gutter.

I'm not under the Affluence of Incohol though many thinkle may peep I am!

Fig. 44

But some viewers would probably disagree about the relative funniness of the two sketches. Some people might find Skelton's funnier simply because he acts drunker

Fig. 45 Red Skelton

sooner—and for many people, nothing is funnier than drunkenness per se. Witness the insane oversupply of slang terms for "drunk." Paul Dickson, in a lexicographical labor of love entitled *Drunk*, lists three thousand synonyms, including *bosky*, *cross-eyed*, *zipped*, *extinguished*, and *Count Drunkula*. And the number of slang expressions for a thing is a good rough-and-ready index of how funny it is. (Though hardly a foolproof test: some things have inspired lots of slang simply because they loom large in the lives of slang-happy groups like teenagers, criminals, or soldiers.) Most slang expressions, after all, are jokes. No sitcom about zany doctors can give you as vivid a sense of the irreverence of that profession toward patients and diseases as a simple list of medical slang.

Stereotypical drunks have red NOSES, see double, HICCUP, weave as they walk, hang on to lampposts for support, and when not belligerent wear big dopey grins like those of cartoon husbands ogling bathing beauties, except that the drunks' eyes are squinched together (or represented, in cartoons, by a pair of X's like the ones on the liquor bottles). They slur their words, saying "yesh" instead of "yes" and "shay" instead of "say." They are also prone to spoonerisms ("tee martoonies"; "I'm not as drunk as thinkle peep I am").

Often, though, the drunkard's stagger gets more laughs than his garbled speech, maybe because many people are insecure about their speech, while almost everyone walks like a pro. We learn to walk before we learn to talk. In "It Must Be the Milk," a poem from 1936, Ogden Nash reflects on the similarity of toddlers to drunks:

When you see your little dumpling set sail across the nursery
   floor,
Can you conscientiously deny the resemblance to somebody who
   is leaving a tavern after having tried to leave it a dozen
   times and each time turned back for just one more?

Nash concludes that "the only way you can tell them apart is to wait till next day, and the infant is the one that feels all right when it wakes up."

In the mid-twentieth century, the paraphernalia of drinking—coasters, tumblers, bar towels, ashtrays, and especially cocktail napkins—served as a favorite venue for corny humor, often but not always concerning booze. There were dozens of sets of paper napkins printed with strikingly stupid cartoons about happy drunks, horny men, scantily clad bimbos, and so on. It's interesting to compare that fad with the mid-century fad for humorous barbecue aprons: in each case, an everyday object suddenly struck a lot of people as a venue for dumb jokes. Was it anxieties about alcoholism and associated sins that provoked so much lame humor? Or was it that cocktails are what uptight businessmen drank to lose their inhibitions and "get stupid"—and moronic cocktail napkins aided the stupefying process?

People have more in common when drunk than when sober, but alcohol seldom dissolves altogether the traits that make one personality different from another. William Steig's typology of drunks—as it appeared in a 1933 *New Yorker* cartoon—identified such varieties as the Insistent Drunk, the Pugnacious Drunk, the Unreasonable Drunk, the Oratorical Drunk, the Gallant Drunk, the Problem Drunk, the Pain-in-the-Neck Drunk, and the Intellectual Trying to Act Sober. The urge to classify, distinguish, and discriminate is irresistible because no matter how often you drink or how early you start, sometimes you're bound to encounter people drunker than you, and to notice how annoying they are.

But the joke isn't always on the drunk. Sometimes we are invited to feel superior to those who know less about booze than we do, as if they were hicks gaping at skyscrapers. There could probably be a whole volume of *New Yorker* cartoons about plump, well-heeled middle-aged ladies asking clueless questions ("What would you suggest for a small group of ladies who meet every Tuesday to do needlepoint?") of clerks in liquor stores.

The comedy of intoxication has always included the disapproval of the sober. "Dost thou think, because thou art virtuous, there shall be no more cakes and ale?" says Sir Toby Belch to Malvolio. The real humor of the scene is not that Belch is drunk, but that the killjoy Malvolio is priggishly indignant about it.

Indeed, when the drunk and the sober are shown interacting, the real joke is often on the sober. In an old *New Yorker* cartoon by Richard Taylor, we see an alcoholic getting quietly smashed at a picnic—a company picnic, perhaps. He sprawls alone at a picnic table, surrounded by empties, minding his business and feeling no pain, but a perky woman has just found him and exhorts him, "All out for the sack race, Mr. McQuade!" Now, what is it that makes this cartoon funny—funny enough that Taylor entitled a 1945 collection *All Out for the Sack Race*? Is it the image of a falling-down drunk trying to hop along at top speed with his legs in a sack? No: if *that* were the joke, the cartoonist would have drawn the actual sack race and not just its herald. Is it that the obnoxiously chipper woman is too oblivious to see that at the moment Mr. McQuade is in no condition for a sack race? Sort of. The real joke is the jarring contrast between two ideas of fun, or at least two ways of enduring a company picnic: the solitary drinker's sad but sincere and oddly dignified pursuit of oblivion, and the artificial zaniness whereby solid citizens chase in vain after a natural high and succeed only in looking like dorks.

Ducks and Chickens

SOMETIMES, ALL TOO SELDOM, we can establish the absolute funniness of a funny thing—or calibrate the relative funniness of several things—with scientific certainty. Ducks are a case in point. Joe Penner had been a struggling and deservedly obscure vaudeville comedian for years when, in 1933, he had the one true inspiration of his career and substituted the word *duck* for *hippopotamus* in the routine where he tried to sell something to his straight man. "Wanna buy a duck?" he asked, and within months he had his own hit radio show; in 1934, he was voted Radio's Outstanding Comedian, though recordings make it clear that aside from his famous catchphrase (and a few supplementary catchphrases like "You naaaasty man!" and "Don't ever *do* that!"), Penner had absolutely nothing going for him but a spastic manner that makes Pee-Wee Herman sound like a BBC announcer.

Why did a duck get more laughs than a hippopotamus, an animal Penner had been doing his pitiable best to make even funnier by mispronouncing "hippopotamamanous"? Someone should have asked the Marx Brothers. They were famously fond of ducks, and are in fact portrayed as ducks in the opening credits to their masterpiece, *Duck Soup*. In *Horse Feathers*, when Groucho goes boating with the college widow (who naturally does all the rowing), a duck follows their rowboat and interrupts Groucho's love song. In their first film, *Cocoanuts*, Chico keeps misunderstanding "viaduct" as "Why a duck?" and keeps trying to answer the question. Chico's main contribution to the Marx Brothers' mayhem was an ear that confused every other word he heard for some comically incongruous word that sounded a bit like it in Chico's farcical Italian accent (as when, in the contract-negotiation scene in *A Night at the Opera*, he mixes up "sanity clause" and "Santa Claus"), so it's worth asking why of all his punning misunderstandings, this one remains the most famous. (*Why a Duck?* is the title of a 1971 volume of images and dialogue from the Marx Brothers' films.)

Many people consider the duck the funniest of animals. (Another candidate is the duck-billed platypus.) Why a duck? Is it because they'd rather swim than fly, and have a way of mooning the observer when they dive? Or because ducks are fat? Because their quacks sound more flatulent than any other birdsong? Because they sound *irate*? Cartoon ducks are notable for their irascibility—no Disney character can throw a better tantrum than Donald, and no Looney Tunes character, not even Yosemite Sam, is as funny when angry as Daffy. I'd go so far as to argue that Daffy is the funniest of all classic cartoon characters (if you disagree, watch "Book Revue" or rewatch "Duck Amuck"), though it may be that just as your favorite Beatle depends on your own personality, so with your favorite cartoon character. There may even be some viewers who like Tweety best.

Or Foghorn Leghorn. If ducks are the funniest bird, chickens are the second-funniest. They are especially funny in the Borscht Belt, and no knockabout comedian is fully equipped without a rubber chicken, a simulacrum of the bird at its most laughable, dead and denuded of feathers and perfect for whacking second bananas over the head with. But they're funny everywhere, though they don't *taste* funny: when we want to assure someone that some unfamiliar meat, like frog legs, tastes okay, we say it "tastes just like chicken."

Chickens are funny because they're dimmer and more fretful than most barnyard animals; because their cheeping and clucking and crowing is unmusical compared to the song of the nightingale, say; because their digestive systems work so fast, transforming chicken feed into chicken shit in less time than it takes to eat a box of Milk Duds; because roosters perfectly embody male pride and cockiness at its most ridiculous; because hens get so excited and self-congratulatory every time they accomplish an egg.

Mostly, though, chickens are funny because, of all the birds, they are the ones we are most likely to know in their less ethereal moments—not soaring and singing and inspiring poets to raptures of trans-species envy, but pecking and pooping and squabbling . . . or dead and plucked and slimy on the cutting board, with their inner organs wrapped and reinserted. "Chicken ain't nothing but a bird," according to an African-American saying, and for most of us, a chicken is something less than a bird.

Easy Girls and Loose Women

> *Remember you're fighting for this woman's honor,*
> *which is probably more than she ever did.*
> —GROUCHO MARX, *DUCK SOUP*, 1933

> *Sometimes a girl can attract a man by her mind,*
> *but more often she can attract him by what she doesn't mind.*
> —HENNY YOUNGMAN,
> *400 TRAVELING SALESMEN'S JOKES*, 1967

THE INDOOR BIRD-WATCHER'S MANUAL is a witty book from 1950 that caricatures dozens of human types as if they were birds: the Blue-Nosed Killjoy, the Duck-Billed Platitude, the Great Bald Ego, and so on. One of my favorites is the Full-Breasted Pushover, *Easihadiensis Communita Chesta*. The notes on this species (appearing below a drawing of a chesty bird blithely removing her corset) give a good idea of the "easy girl" stereotype at mid-century:

> Female, comportment jolly, plumage gaudy, inclined to molt completely at slightest suggestion, roundness noted in heel area, extremely loyal to large flocks, conventions, Army, Navy, etc., migrates commonly along bars . . .
>
> CALL: Yes! Yes! Yes! (On a rising and falling pitch.)

The Indoor Bird-Watcher's Manual was written by two women, but "I Cain't Say No" was by a man, as were most of the era's jokes about women of easy virtue. In *2000 Insults for All Occasions* (1965), a man named Louis A. Safian included more than forty insults about Fallen Angels, such as "At school she was voted the girl most likely to concede" and "Her grammar is awful—she can't decline." It's easy to see why virtuous women, in the dark age before the sexual revolution, felt impelled to shun and shame those members of their sex who threatened the whole order of society by enabling men to get laid without first getting wed. It's harder to understand why *men* were so fond of ridiculing a genus of female they were constantly hoping to encounter, or why there's so much more mid-century humor at the expense of easy women than at the expense of prudes, who don't even merit an entry in this guide.

The explanation, I think, is that sexual humor often has less to do with ridiculing than with salivating over the target of the joke. This fact is usually ignored by those who theorize about such humor, but it is obvious to anyone who pages through a magazine of raunchy cartoons. In the oft-repeated gag about the male doctor who makes the pretty lady take off all her clothes when her only problem is a sore throat or an earache, the joke is neither on the horny doctor nor on the biddable patient. There *isn't* any joke to speak of, just a throb of lechery.

In short, men joke about easy girls for the same reason they joke about FISHING or GOLF: it's something they like to think about. A lot. Much of the mainstream fascination with such sub- and countercultures as FLAPPERS, BEATNIKS, and hippies was due to the perceived promiscuity of women associated with those cultures. (According to a Prohibition-era flapper joke from *Captain Billy's Whiz Bang*, "Asking the modern flapper for a kiss is like sneaking into a speakeasy and asking for a Coca-Cola.")

At what point does an easy girl become a loose woman? Maybe when her promiscuity no longer makes a thrilling contrast with her youth or innocence. For most men, easy girls are both funnier and sexier than their elder sisters because of the incongruity between their girlishness and their sexual readiness. Prostitutes are not especially funny, because there's seldom any contradiction between their appearance and their debauchery. Mae West's characters were seldom funny per se, though some of her witticisms were, and in her day it was hilariously naughty for many moviegoers that Hollywood was dealing so openly with sin.

Before the easy girl loses her bloom and becomes a simple hussy, she is likely to put in a stint as an unwed mother, if only so she can appear in cartoons where her puritanical father spurns her and her baby from his doorstep, casting her out into the cold with an imperious gesture while her own mother weeps in the background. Like the damsel tied to the railroad tracks by the top-hatted cad, the wayward girl with the unforgiving father is a melodramatic cliché that some cartoonists have found strangely irresistible. Sam Cobean must have drawn a dozen variations on the theme for *The New Yorker*, and Phil Interlandi drew half a dozen for a single 1958 issue of *Playboy*. In my favorite, the parents dwell in an apartment, the daughter stands in the corridor beside an elevator, and the heartless father gestures downward rather than outward.

As for the easy girl's male counterpart, he is not the Casanova but the asexual NINCOMPOOP—like the easy girl, a violation of the natural order of things as codified by popular culture, which ordains that men should constantly pressure for sex and women should constantly resist.

Efficiency Experts

TOWARD THE END of "Spain," a great poem he later disowned, W. H. Auden listed hopeful trends that, while not as urgent at the time (1937) as the Spanish Civil War, would be priorities once the war was over:

> *Tomorrow the research on fatigue*
> *And the movements of packers; the gradual exploring of all the*
> *Octaves of radiation;*
> *Tomorrow the enlarging of consciousness by diet and*
> *breathing.*

By "the research on fatigue / And the movements of packers," Auden meant the research conducted by industrial efficiency experts like Frank Gilbreth, later to be the subject of *Cheaper by the Dozen*—both the 1948 book and the 1950 movie. Gilbreth and his wife, Lillian, pioneered the motion study, a technique for simplifying and expediting the work of manual laborers by classifying all possible hand motions into seventeen basic ones. Gilbreth called these *therbligs*, reversing the letters of his name as much as English phonetics allowed, and thereby revealing either an endearing sense of humor or a degree of self-importance especially unfortunate in a technocrat whose ideas would affect many lives.

Either way, the celebrated book about him—written by two of his children—must have been intended partly as a corrective to the mainstream perception of efficiency experts, who by 1948 had been widely portrayed by pop culture as villains for more than a decade. (Also as nerds. In *The Rationale of the Dirty Joke*, Gershon Legman recounts a joke he heard in Minneapolis in 1944 about an efficiency expert who "compulsively counts the number of cows in a herd, as seen from a moving train, by counting their teats and dividing by four.") Like repo men—and, some would say, state troopers—efficiency experts are hateful by the very nature of their job. They are paid to stick their nose in other people's business, to find fault with the status quo, with business as usual, and to find certain employees—sometimes long-term employees—expendable. Often they do things the boss could do just as well, but part of what they are paid for is to take the blame for unpopular decisions.

At least two episodes of *Fibber McGee*, from 1938 and 1955, involved efficiency experts. So did episodes of *Amos 'n' Andy*, *Our Miss Brooks*, and *My Little Margie* (all radio sitcoms with later TV incarnations). In a 1947 episode of *Life of Riley*, the beleaguered hero, who works as a riveter at an aircraft factory, gets his teenage son a job at the factory as an "apprentice time engineer" or assistant to the new efficiency expert, only to have his son take the job so seriously that he starts clocking poor Riley (with the very watch Riley gave him for Christmas), timing him even as he eats lunch, and repeatedly threatening to fire him for inefficiency.

That kind of irony is common in plots involving efficiency experts. In a 1952 episode of *The Great Gildersleeve*, the title character—a minor city employee with delusions of grandeur—convinces the mayor that city hall needs an efficiency expert, then convinces himself that *he* is the logical choice for that important job, and then panics when the job goes instead to a woman who doesn't like Gildersleeve. We're all in favor of a new broom, as long as it doesn't sweep *us* away.

As Gildersleeve discovers, the battle between entrenched employee and intrusive consultant can be even more poignant when opponents are also on opposite sides in the battle of the sexes. In *Desk Set*, a 1957 comedy, Katharine Hepburn is the old-fashioned, technophobic head of the research department at a big TV station, and Spencer Tracy plays a technocrat hired to computerize her department—in other words, an efficiency expert, though he says that that title is "a bit obsolete" and prefers to call himself "a methods engineer." Actually, he prefers not to name his job at all because, he says, "every time I mention what I do, people seem to go into a panic."

The Battle of the Sexes was the title of a British adaptation of one of James Thurber's greatest stories, "The Catbird Seat." In that story, a mild-mannered file clerk is so annoyed by the manner and meddling of a brassy female efficiency expert that he makes plans to murder her, but in the end contents himself with getting her fired, as she'd been planning to do to him. The movie, which appeared in 1959 and featured Peter Sellers as the hero, transplants his firm to Edinburgh but doesn't change the nationality of the villainess, who as both a woman and a Yank is twice as loathsome.

Eggheads

> *EGGHEAD WEDS HOURGLASS*
> —1955 HEADLINE IN *VARIETY* ANNOUNCING ARTHUR
> MILLER'S MARRIAGE TO MARILYN MONROE

THOUGH THE TERM in something like its current sense of "clueless intellectual" has been around since World War I (and even longer in the sense of "bald man"), it is forever associated with the venomous anti-intellectualism of the 1950s, and more specifically with the presidential campaign of 1952, when Richard Nixon used the epithet to deride the Democratic presidential candidate, Adlai Ste-

Fig. 46 Adlai Stevenson

venson. Stevenson happened to have a large cranium reminiscent of then-current images of highly evolved Martians. By singling out that feature, Nixon contemptuously ceded the Democrats the edge in pure intelligence—as Republicans have been doing ever since—but implied the same deficit of human feeling, good intentions, and common sense that we also attribute to Martians.

"During the campaign of 1952, the country seemed to be in need of some term to express that disdain for intellectuals which had by then become a self-conscious motif in American politics," wrote Richard Hofstadter in *Anti-Intellectualism in American Life*. There was already another term in the language for an intellectual with a big forehead, but as Hofstadter wrote, "The word *egghead*... acquired a much sharper tone than the traditional *highbrow*."

We can deduce that *egghead* wasn't yet a standard insult in 1933, or Frederick Henry Prince, the railroad magnate, would surely have used it in his tirade against COLLEGE PROFESSORS: "Professors are one of the chief curses of the country. They talk too much. Most professors are a bunch of COWARDS and meddlers. The sooner we get away from their influence, the better."

Can we also infer, from the wild popularity of Harold Lloyd's "glasses character" in such films as *Safety Last* (1923) and *The Freshman* (1925), that American anti-intellectualism wasn't as rabid in the 1920s as in the 1950s? Maybe so; 1920s culture, after all, was superior in almost every other way to 1950s culture. In any case, Lloyd was

Figs. 47 Egghead, Jr.

a bigger box-office draw in his heyday than Chaplin or Keaton. Not till Woody Allen would another four-eyed actor make it big in Hollywood. Offscreen, Lloyd didn't need or wear glasses, and the ones he wore onscreen beginning in 1918 had no lenses. He started wearing them because Hal Roach felt that Lloyd (like Zeppo Marx, or Chaplin without his Little Tramp getup) was too handsome to succeed as a comic actor. The glasses, then, were not a sign of intellectual hauteur, but an endearing disfigurement, one that made Lloyd easier to pity and thus easier to like. But he was, as I say, the last movie star for quite a while to win stardom with specs on his nose. By mid-century, the sentiment against eggheads—if not against all horn-rimmed types—was strong and clear, not withstanding Egghead, Jr. (**Fig. 47**), the brainy little chicken who outsmarts Foghorn Leghorn in so many mid-century Warner Bros. cartoons.

Eggheads were not only demonized in politics, but also tended to serve as villains in movies and TV shows. Think of Dr. Smith on *Lost in Space*. As a rule, if a villain is supposed to be super-intelligent, he speaks in an affected diction and makes cutting remarks to his foes and his henchmen alike about their relative stupidity. Most of the super-villains on the old *Batman* show follow that formula. The one named Egghead, whom Batman describes as the most intelligent criminal they've ever faced, may have a giant bald cranium (beneath which lurks Vincent Price), but except for a penchant for oviparous puns (*eggsquisite*, *eggstravanganza*, and so on), he sounds eggsactly like the Penguin, the Bookworm, the Riddler.

Equations

And what mean all these mysteries to me,
Whose life is full of indices and surds?

$$x^2 + 7x + 53$$
$$= 11/3$$

—LEWIS CARROLL

IN A 1963 CARTOON from *Look* magazine, three lab-coated professors stand laughing uproariously before a blackboard covered with an abstruse equation. A fourth professor says, "I thought you guys would get a kick out of it." Note the similarity to certain cartoons about MODERN ART—those that show a museum-goer moved to tears, or to lust, by an abstract painting. In either case, the joke is the emotion aroused by something of which we can make neither head nor tail.

But why does *that* amuse us? After all, if you devote your life to complicated equations, it goes without saying that they mean and matter a lot to you. So the real laugh is that some people do spend their lives thinking and caring about such things. Those people must find an extra layer of humor in cartoons involving long equations, since to them—unless the cartoonist too is a mathematician—the equations must look not abstruse but absurd. When you do get an algebraically literate humorist like Lewis Carroll—a professor of mathematics as well as a great nonsense poet and pioneering child-pornographer—the absurdity of the equation is likely to be the main joke, as with the impossible quadratic equation in the quatrain above, whose last two lines are even purer nonsense than "Jabberwocky."

Sometimes the point of the equation on the blackboard is just to show that someone is brainy. In a gag cartoon from the 1950s, a balding scientist sits in front of such a blackboard and tells the lab assistant in his lap, "My wife doesn't understand me." In a cartoon from around 1960, a rocket scientist surrounded by abstruse equations is putting the moves on a buxom assistant who exclaims, "Professor Rittenheimer! Don't you ever think about anything but sex?"

Etchings

> When a girl is invited to a man's apartment to see his etchings,
> it's usually not a standing invitation.
> —HENNY YOUNGMAN

APPARENTLY THERE WAS a moment, in the late nineteenth or early twentieth century, when sophisticated seducers lured women into their lairs by inviting them in all earnestness—the earnestness of lust—to see the man's collection of "etchings" or engrav-

Fig. 48 Etchings humor. See also OUTHOUSES.

ings. That moment, though, is now lost in the mists of time, and there is no longer much evidence of a period when the line wasn't already a joke, like "What's your sign?" (or "You have needs, I have needs") in our own day. Eric Partridge draws a blank on it in his *Dictionary of Catchphrases*, though he suspects that it started as U.S. student slang and then spread to the United Kingdom. He also associates it with Mae West's famous "Come up and see me some time," a line first uttered (in slightly different form, like so many familiar quotations) in 1933's *She Done Him Wrong*, but he isn't sure which line came first and maybe inspired the other.

In any case, "Come up and see my etchings" was enough of a cliché by the late 1930s for humorists to start ringing changes on it. In a 1939 *New Yorker* cartoon by James Thurber—a humorist obsessed with and appalled by sexually aggressive women—a man in an apartment lobby tells a woman: "You wait here and I'll bring the etchings down." A comic postcard sent in 1945 shows a well-dressed young bumpkin dragging his date toward an OUTHOUSE over the door of which he has written ART GAL-LERY. Says the blushing but not necessarily unwilling gal, "These country boys are so persistent about showin' their etchin's!"

As Partridge notes, the phrase flourished—as an effective pickup line is bound to do—on both sides of the Atlantic. In 1959's "(Have Some) Madeira, M'Dear," one of the wittiest songs of all time, an old playboy has "slyly inveigled" a sweet young thing up to his apartment "to view his collection of stamps" and not his etchings, but that's because the authors—the British duo of Flanders and Swann—needed a rhyme for "lamps" in the magnificent zeugma that followed: "And he said as he hastened to put out the cat, / The wine, his cigar, and the lamps . . ."

Etchings—like the old seducer's stamps and so many other pretexts for intimacy—allowed both parties to equivocate about their feeling and motives. For an aspiring collector, etchings were less prohibitively expensive than other forms of art, and there must have been men who collected them out of vanity or honest connoisseurship, with no view to seduction. There must have been gay men who invited women up to see their etchings with no ulterior motive, and NINCOMPOOPS who tried to impress women with their art collections but lacked the nerve or savoir faire to go any further. There were a lot of pornographic etchings in the nineteenth century, but also plenty of G-rated ones, and it would have been an easy way for a timid man to test the waters by starting with the tamest engravings and gradually working up to more suggestive ones. If he could also cloud those waters with some Madeira, so much the better.

Explainers

> *Did ya see that hawk after those hens? He scared 'em! That Rhode*
> *Island Red turned white, then blue. . . . Red, white and blue!*
> *That's a joke, son, a flag-waver! You're built too low. The fast ones*
> *go over your head. . . . Ya gotta keep your eye on the ball! Eye. Ball.*
> *Eyeball! I almost had a gag, son—a joke, that is!*
> —FOGHORN LEGHORN

> *As you know, nothing kills the laugh quicker than to*
> *explain a joke. I intend to explain all jokes, and the proper*
> *and logical outcome will be, not only that you will not laugh now,*
> *but that you will never laugh again.*
> —MAX EASTMAN, *ENJOYMENT OF LAUGHTER*

IN COMEDY, the vice of futile explanation is especially common among **BLOWHARDS**—so common I considered putting this discussion in that entry. Along with Foghorn Leghorn **(Fig. 49)**, Fibber McGee is a shining example. In almost every episode of the long-running radio comedy *Fibber McGee and Molly*, he would make a bad pun,[17] notice that his wife wasn't laughing, and try to explain why she should be, prompting her to retaliate with her catchphrase, " 'T'aint funny, McGee." The real joke is the lameness of his pun and doggedness with which he pleads on its behalf.

Note that both Foghorn and Fibber are not just explainers but *joke*-explainers. Why is it humiliating to explain a joke? We explain everything else, after all. And most of us are capable of finding a funny line funny each time we reencounter it, just as we can relive the suspense in a thriller we've seen or read before. A good joke can be perpetually surprising. But it does need to surprise, on some level; its explanation is in

---

[17] Fibber: I was a baseball pitcher in my younger days.
Molly: I never knew that. Southpaw?
Fibber: Nope, Midwest, maw.

essence a doomed effort to persuade us to feel belated or retroactive surprise for something that didn't surprise us at the time.

In the preface to his 1941 anthology, *A Subtreasury of American Humor*, E. B. White wrote what is probably the single most quoted (or, often, misquoted, and often misattributed) sentence regarding his subject: "Humor can be dissected as a frog can, but the thing dies in the process and the innards are discouraging to any but the pure scientific mind."

Since I am in the business of explaining jokes, it will come as no surprise that I find that sentence unfair. Generations of biology teachers have found dissection invaluable in helping millions of students appreciate the mystery of life, which if I remember right is almost as complex as the mystery of humor. For many people—not all of us possessors of pure scientific minds—that unit of Intro Biology was the high point of our high school science studies.

I don't know where E. B. White went to school, but in my day, everything we dissected in Biology was already dead, and so are most of the jokes I'm dissecting. That's how dissection works, except on the island of Dr. Moreau. And except for the squeamish, a dead joke is more interesting with its belly slit open and its innards on display than in a specimen jar on a shelf, pickling in the formaldehyde of cultural nostalgia.

Fig. 49
Foghorn Leghorn

F f

Fat Men

"**WHAT INDUCES US** to laugh on reading that the corpulent Gibbon was unable to rise from his knees after making a tender declaration?" So asks Herbert Spencer at the beginning of his 1860 work "The Physiology of Laughter." Being a nineteenth-century philosopher, Spencer proceeds to give his question a fifteen-page answer (something to do with the discharge of nervous energy), though most of us would call the question a no-brainer on the lines of "Why do we swear after hitting our thumb with a hammer?" In his heroic determination to complicate the issue—to analyze the irreducibly obvious and articulate the ineffably self-evident—Spencer is one of my intellectual heroes, a model for my own humble efforts in the same vein in this volume.

On *The Honeymooners*, the fat jokes are as common as—and are often responsible for—the jokes about wife-beating. "We got any lard laying around here?" asks Ralph, trying to remove a ring from his pudgy finger. "Yeah," says Alice, "about three hundred pounds." She would've had to be a saint to resist an opening like that, but even when Ralph doesn't ask for it, Alice manages time after time to turn the conversation to the subject of his weight. In the episode where Ralph and Norton want to go fishing without their wives, Ralph demands, "What do you know about fishing? When have you ever caught anything?" Alice replies: "Fifteen years ago. I caught three hundred pounds of blubber." Sometimes she says *four* hundred pounds. She also jokes about his weight behind his back. When she decides not to bake a chocolate cake for his birthday because she wants his new birthday belt to fit the day after, Trixie tells her she can always

Wish you were here to see me floating!

Fig. 50 Fat jokes: gender-agnostic

exchange the belt for a larger size. "There is no larger size," says Alice. Nor is Alice the only one to make fun of Ralph's weight. On learning that during their courtship she called him little buttercup, Norton can't help laughing; when Ralph demands to know what's so funny, Norton says "You were a little cup of butter; now you're a whole tub of lard!"

Animated cartooning, with its love of all that stretches, bounces, undulates, or jiggles as it moves, has always loved fat characters. When Chuck Jones was making "What's Opera, Doc?" and wanted to ani-mate the obese white horse as realistically as possible, he made a point of watching fat people ice-skating. Just as there are chubby chasers, there are chubby watchers. In the brilliant radio sitcom *Vic and Sade* (1932–46), the couple's odd son Russell likes nothing better than to hang out at the YMCA watching fat men play handball.

One of the first requirements of a good radio play was its ability to conjure up images in the listener's imagination. That's why fat jokes were more common on old radio comedies than on the TV sitcoms that re-placed them. On TV, a fat comic actor is a living fat joke that keeps tell-ing itself. On radio, the joke needed some help from the script, even when the voice actor was known to be as fat as his character, like Harold Peary, who created the role of Throckmorton P. Gildersleeve on *Fibber McGee and Molly* and, later, *The Great Gildersleeve*. At least once an episode, another character was sure to call attention to Gildersleeve's obesity. As for Beulah Brown, the black HOUSEKEEPER who debuted on *Fibber McGee* and eventually became the star of *The Beulah Show* (1947–54), she made constant self-deprecating jokes about her own weight. For the first two years, by the way, the title character was played by a white male. When Hattie McDaniel took over the part in 1947, the show's ratings doubled, and part of the difference must have been that actor and character not only had the same race and gender, but also the same physique.

"Nobody loves a fat man," lamented Roscoe "Fatty" Arbuckle, the great silent comedian whose career came to a noisy halt in 1921 with his indictment for rape and murder. An amazingly graceful and athletic man for his size, a master of physical comedy, and a gifted singer, too, Arbuckle rightly insisted that he was more than just another tub of lard. He refused to lend his physique to cheap sight gags like getting stuck in an armchair, and when off-duty he objected to being called "Fatty." (He probably wasn't any fonder of his other nicknames, "The Prince of Whales" and "The Balloonatic.") His indictment traumatized the whole film industry, and Arbuckle's shadow may have been the reason why, for decades afterward, there were so few morbidly fat comic actors of any importance.

Because confessional memoirs hardly ever deal with things the author is really ashamed of, we know less about the fat experience than about the criminal experience, or the experience of growing up poor, or of being addicted to drugs or alcohol or sex—circumstances that many writers take an obvious pride in. Lately fat has been seen as a feminist issue, and fat women have finally started to write about it, but for most of the twentieth century it was easier for a straight reader to get a sense of what it's like to be gay than for a thin reader to get a sense of what it's like to be fat. The only notable exception I'm aware of is *Cobb's Anatomy*, written in 1912 by the obese and then-bestselling, now-forgotten Irvin S. Cobb, and still the most candid and articulate statement I know of by a fat man about how it feels to be one.

In the chapter on "Tummies," Cobb takes issue with some doctor's published pronouncement that fat people are happier: "Did he ever have to leave the top two buttons of his vest unfastened on account of his extra chins?" Cobb goes on to list some of the other horrors of obesity:

> You pant like a lizard when you run to catch a car. You cross your legs and have to hold the crossed one on with both hands to keep your stomach from shoving it off in space. . . .
>
> You are something for people to laugh at. You are also expected to laugh. It is all right for a thin man to be grouchy. . . . But a fat man with a grouch is inexcusable in any company—there is so much of him to be grouchy. He constitutes a wave of discontent. . . .
>
> As a race fat men are fond of bright and cheerful colors; but no fat man can indulge his innocent desires in this direction without grieving his family and friends and exciting the derisive laughter of the unthinking. . . .
>
> There never was an orchestra seat in a theater that would contain all of him at the same time—he churns up and sloshes out over the sides.

Cobb also says that one of the saddest sights he knows is a fat man lying in the narrow berth of a Pullman car, "spouting like a sperm-whale and overflowing his reservation like a crock of salt-rising dough in a warm kitchen."

Fat Women

> *Fat Lady: I'm swelled with pride.*
> *Kingfish: Yeah, you is swelled with something,*
> *that's for sure. . . . Well, keep you chins up.*
> —*AMOS 'N' ANDY*, 1948

EVERYTHING IS FUNNIER when it happens to a fat lady. Even Wagner: if it were possible to sing like Brünhilde and look like Calista Flockhart, those of us who've spent our lives avoiding

OPERA wouldn't be so likely to laugh at the thought of an art form we've never experienced. Millions of us who have never sat through the Ring cycle are familiar with an allusion to its final aria that sportscasters have been making since the 1970s in an effort to keep us tuned in to obvious routs: "It ain't over till the fat lady sings."

Of course, it is seldom good news when a fat lady does appear; they're usually bad luck. Whenever the Three Stooges encounter one, she's either a snooty DOWAGER or a sexually aggressive spinster—the sort who, in animated cartoons, causes male characters to crash through walls,

Fig. 51

leaving perfect silhouettes of themselves, in their haste to get away. (Curly is no anorexic himself, of course, and his fat is part of what makes him the funniest stooge. When Moe gets tired of poking him in the eyes, he punches him in the belly instead, and the soundtrack obliges with a thump on a kettledrum.)

Groucho Marx made a lot of fat jokes at the expense of Margaret Dumont, though she really wasn't all that fat, and her bulk always seemed an expression of her social position—of the snootiness and respectability of the dowagers she played. "Twenty years of marriage make a woman look like a public building," said Oscar Wilde, in a line I've had occasion to quote elsewhere in this guide. George S. Kaufman, the main screenwriter for *A Night at the Opera*, may have been thinking of Wilde's quip when he had Groucho's character say to Dumont's, "Well, that covers a lot of ground. Say, you cover a lot of ground yourself. You better beat it—I hear they're going to tear you down and put up an office building where you're standing." In the same film, imagining Dumont's domestic life, Groucho says, "I can see you right now in the kitchen, bending over a hot stove. But I can't see the stove."

When sitcoms came along, they were more chivalrous, as if taking to heart Irvin S. Cobb's dictum: "There are women who are plump and will admit it; there are even women who are inclined to be stout. But outside of dime museums there are no fat women." The fat jokes in old sitcoms were plentiful, but most were at the expense of men, like Ralph Kramden or Sergeant Schultz. Here's an exception from *I Love Lucy*, but note how much gentler it is than all those "three hundred pounds of lard" jokes at Ralph Kramden's expense.

> Ricky: Everybody knows you can get around a lady with a little sweet talk.
>
> Fred: That's all right for Lucy, but it's a little longer trip around Ethel.

From the first, it was clear that TV's greatest value was as a way to kill time till bedtime for people trapped in one another's company all evening, every evening. For that purpose TV was even better than radio, since it gave you an excuse not even to look at your loved ones. And early on, the mostly male producers must have decided that too much joking about women's weight would tend to exacerbate the domestic tensions that TV served to allay.

No, for the real skinny on fat women, you had to go to other kinds of pop culture, such as comic strips. In the days before Johnny Hart found Jesus and started using *B.C.* to snipe at Jews and Muslims, his inner caveman amused itself (and, be it said, millions of readers) by antagonizing women's libbers with a character named Fat Broad—a fat, ugly, sadistic cavewoman who got her kicks by bashing snakes with a club. As for the big fat shapeless sexless wives of Sappo, Jiggs, Andy Capp, Snuffy Smith, Moon Mullins,[18] Major Hoople, General Halftrack, and the Wizard of

---

[18] In the Moon Mullins Game, a 1938 roll-and-move board game based on the comic strip, bumping into a fat lady causes you to move back two spaces.

Id (to name a few)—they're all versions of the same wan joke: if you let desire trick you into marrying a girl, she'll not only nag you and boss you around for the rest of your life; she'll also let herself go, having no more need to attract a mate. She'll let herself go to the point where soon you can't remember, as she wallops you with a ROLLING PIN or otherwise throws her ever-mounting weight around, why on earth you married her in the first place. What was your id *thinking*, Wizard? "Her once-dangerous curves have become extended detours," as Louis A. Safian puts it in *2000 Insults for All Occasions*.

Not surprisingly—since until recently cartooning was a man's world—the corresponding joke is seldom made at the expense of husbands, though surely Andy Capp's wife, Flo, has as much reason to regret their marriage as he does. And in reality, of course, husbands as well as wives run to fat. Sometimes they do in old comics, too—think of Walt Wallet (*Gasoline Alley*) or Major Hoople (*Our Boarding House*)—but in those cases the implicit joke is not so much that a husband no longer needs sex appeal, but that he's no longer permitted sexual conquests, what with church and state and public opinion joining forces to make him behave. His obesity is not the bait-and-switch of the safely tenured wife, but a demoralized resignation to the sexlessness of married life as depicted in family-friendly comics.

Fatness is more poignant in women, as Frances Cornford knew when she wrote:

> *O fat white woman whom nobody loves,*
> *Why do you run through the field in gloves,*
> *Missing so much and so much?*

Taking up the cudgels for fat white people everywhere, G. K. Chesterton retaliated with "The Fat White Woman Speaks":

> *Why do you rush through the field in trains,*
> *Guessing so much and so much?*
> *Why do you flash through the flowery meads,*
> *Fat-head poet that nobody reads;*

> *And why do you know such a frightful lot*
> *About people in gloves as such?*

Arthur Godfrey and his Too Fat Trio had a big hit in 1947 with the "Too Fat Polka." Everyone knows the refrain ("I don't want her, you can have her / She's too fat for me") but some of the verses are memorable, too:

> *Can she prance up a hill?*
> *No, no, no, no, no*
> *Can she dance a quadrille?*
> *No, no, no, no, no*
> *Does she fit in your coupe?*
> *By herself she's a group*
> *Could she possibly*
> *Sit upon your knee?*
> *No, no, no . . .*
>
> *She's a twosome,*
> *She's a foursome*
> *If she'd lose some*
> *I would like her more some*

The Andrews Sisters countered the same year with a transgendered cover version ("I don't want him, you can have him")—a salutary reminder of something we men are still apt to forget: that women also tend to find fat unattractive in a partner.

"Nobody loves a fat gal—but, oh how a fat gal can love!" So says a comic postcard from the 1950s, illustrating the assertion with a cartoon of a fat woman throwing herself at a man both thinner and shorter. Not all guys agree, of course, about fat gals. For that matter, not all postcards agree. Fat women have always been *the* favorite subject of comic post-cards, the favorite laughingstock, but few cards are so ungallant as to say straight out that fat gals are unlovable. On funny postcards, women tend to be fat even when fatness is not the main joke. Any woman who is meant to be neither a nubile cutie nor a desiccated OLD MAID is bound to be drawn as at least slightly obese, and often morbidly. Even some of the nubile cuties are awfully full-figured by contemporary standards. Sometimes the fatness seems an effort to compensate for the smallness and two-dimensionality of the image, as if a three-by-five postcard could never show too much female flesh, and that flesh could never bulge too much in its effort to burst into the third dimension.

Feces

Who created fake dog doo? I don't know. How far do dogs go back? When was the dog invented?
—JOSEPH (BUD) ADAMS

I just keep things moving along.
—ED NORTON, ON *THE HONEYMOONERS,* OF HIS JOB IN THE NEW YORK SEWER DEPARTMENT

Freud did not invent the
Constipated miser:
Banks have letter boxes
Built in their façade
Marked For Night Deposits,
Stocks are firm or liquid,
Currencies of nations
Either soft or hard.
—W. H. AUDEN, "THE GEOGRAPHY OF THE HOUSE"

GERSHON LEGMAN'S monumental 1954 collection of dirty limericks includes 107 under the heading of "Excrement." There are some that blur the line between scatology and pornography, like the young fellow from Twiss whose orgasms force him to piss, but in most the naughtiness is strictly pre-sexual. Here's an example from 1949:

There was an old fellow of Pittwood
Who never was able to shit good.
He'd leave small deposits
On shelves and in closets,
As a very small pup or a kit would.

The most notable thing about the limericks in the Excrement chapter, compared to the other sixteen hundred limericks in Legman's book, is their innocence. Toilet humor has always been a sort of substitute naughtiness for those who couldn't joke about sex. There seems to have been some tolerance for scatological humor even in households so strict that any allusion to sex could earn a kid a whipping. The earliest gag boxes—those joke gifts with lids designed to raise expectations that are humorously disappointed by the box's contents—were not risqué, as most of them are now, but scatological. Many, in fact, were "toilet humor" in the strictest sense, like the Original Receiving Set, made in 1924 by H. Fishlove & Company. The box cover shows a pair of radio antennae, but inside you find a miniature plastic toilet, complete with a liftable lid. An-

Fig. 52 Feces humor. See also QUADRUPEDS.

other gag box, "Dixie Pe-cans," showed pecans on its lid but contained a pair of tiny chamber pots.

In our grandparents' era, mainstream humor about feces mostly involved horseshit, which for several reasons is less offensive than manshit. (You may recall that after returning—minus his sanity—from his final voyage, Lemuel Gulliver chooses to live in his stables instead of his house because he can't stand the smell of his own wife and children, but doesn't mind the smell of horse manure.) "I'm the only guy who ever 'cleans up' at the races," says a custodian with a broom, a shovel, and a barrel labeled "Essence of Corral No. 5," on a comic postcard from the 1950s. "I swear—I'm going to move to a one-horse town," says the street sweeper on another comic postcard of roughly the same vintage, as he sweeps up horse turds that look more like eggs. Horseshit was even allowed in movies—Buster Keaton sweeps up a load in "Daydreams" (1922), during his own ill-fated stint as a big-city street cleaner (a job he misrepresents to his fiancée back home as "going around the Stock Exchange doing a bit of cleaning up"). At one point he even supplements his broom and shovel with his bare hands.

As for the fact that people defecate, you're more likely to find that acknowledged in highbrow literature than in mainstream humor. Especially if the highbrow in question is Irish: like Swift, both Joyce and Beckett joked a lot about poop.[19] What can we say about all this low humor in high places? Maybe what George Meredith said about another great comedian: "Molière's wit is like a running brook. . . . It does not run in search of obstructions, to be noisy over them; but when dead leaves and viler substances are heaped along the course, its natural song is heightened."

That brook doesn't feed into the mainstream of American humor. On the flood plains of the mainstream, though, you do find a lot of phony

---

[19] There's a fair amount of fecal matter even in Yeats, as in the lines from "Crazy Jane Talks to the Bishop" that so perfectly encapsulate the Swiftian view of the subject:

A woman may be proud and stiff
When on love intent,
But love has pitched his mansion
In the place of excrement.

dogshit. A few years ago I tried collecting phony dogshit, but soon gave up (and set my sights instead on phony VOMIT) due to a kind of snobbery. I'd imagined that there had been dozens of different models manufactured over the years, but never more than one or two at a time—all the market could bear—and that by combing estate sales and such, I could gradually amass the world's most thorough collection, and a collection made more appealing by the antiquity of most of my specimens. I imagined that fake poop had been mass-produced, in one form or another, since the dawn of the industrial revolution. But in fact the first batch wasn't made till the 1930s, and the next few decades seem to have produced only a few models.

At some point, though, our culture's sphincter opened, and nowadays you can buy every conceivable kind of bogus feces. The current *Things You Never Knew Existed* catalog offers such novelties as aerosol poop ("It's poo in a can! Very realistic & smelly!"), Oops (a phony human turd for draping on toilet seats), and Poop Soap ("Sure to cause outrageous bathroom double takes! . . . Smells great but looks like a genuine you-know-what!") available in two varieties: Plain and Corn. Obscenity laws can change overnight, but the neuroses behind them take a lot longer. What we have today is a culture where it is suddenly okay, even on after-school TV, to produce and consume the crudest toilet humor, but where the neuroses that make that stuff naughty—hence funny—are still entrenched. It's a funny overlap. And we may as well enjoy it while it lasts.

Feet

> *The rich limp with the gout, the moderately well-to-do content*
> *themselves with an active ingrown nail or so, and the poor man*
> *goes out and drops an iron casting on his toe.*
> —IRVIN S. COBB

FEET, LIKE CHEESE, are funny principally because they smell. Some even smell like cheese—or rather, some cheese smells like feet: the bacterium responsible for foot odor, *Brevibacterium linens*, is the same one that makes limburger and other stinky cheeses

smell and taste the way they do. Not even mosquitoes can tell the difference: a study in 2006
showed that the mosquitoes that transmit
malaria are equally attracted to feet and
limburger.

When Li'l Abner needs to prove
his identity in order to claim an in-
heritance, he shows the soles of his
shoes, pointing out that his "real,
genoowine Yokum feet" are
"bigger'n most people's whole
laigs." In his case and in general,

Fig. 53

the laws of cartoon logic ordain that the bigger the feet, the smaller the
brain. That's why R. Crumb's pinheaded, giant-footed characters seem
archetypal: like Abner, they are cretins with giant feet of clay.

Feet are clearly funnier than hands. Hands are seldom funny at all
except on cartoon characters, who tend to have only four fingers and to
wear white gloves, an odd but effective compromise between drawing
naked human hands and drawing paws, since either would look wrong
on anthropomorphic cartoon animals with opposable thumbs.

There is evidence to suggest that feet are even funnier than NOSES.
Newspaper cartoonists at the "cartoony" end of the realism spectrum—
guys like Mort Walker (*Beetle Bailey*), Dik Browne (*Hagar the Horrible*),
and Johnny Hart (*B.C.*), who tend to omit unnecessary details and exaggerate what's left—are sometimes referred to as "big-foot cartoonists,"
though as a rule the characters' clownish bulbous noses are at least as hypertrophied as their feet. And in fact, many cartoon characters have had
oversized feet, from Mickey Mouse and Goofy to Don Martin's humans.
Admittedly, Don Martin's characters are freaks from head to toe, but
their most distinctive feature is their big flat feet, so flimsy and thin that
when the characters walk, the front part of each foot flops over at a 90-
degree angle, as if hinged.

Like noses, feet are sometimes used as substitutes in cleaned-up dick
jokes, partly because, like noses, they vary notably in size from one man
to the next. The feet of a couple copulating in the missionary position

form such an iconic pattern that you can produce an R-rated cartoon simply by drawing the soles—a pair of large ones, close together, pointing down, flanked by a pair of small ones pointing up. In 1964, three men named Sy and Mel and Woody put out a whole book of naughty cartoons called *Sam, the Ceiling Needs Painting*—cartoons where all we see is those feet, perhaps a simple prop or bit of scenery, and a caption. One cartoon shows the four feet protruding from a big chandelier: evidently the couple is trying to spice up its love life with a change of venue. In vain: The caption reads "Y'know, I'm disappointed."

Fishing and Fishermen

*Fishing, with me, has always been an excuse
to drink in the daytime.*
—JIMMY CANNON

*Lord, give me the grace to catch a fish so big that even I, when
telling of it afterward, may never need to lie. Amen.*
—ANGLER'S PRAYER

U NLIKE MOST ANIMALS that grace the carnivore's table, fish are more fun to kill than to eat. Not even the most happy-go-lucky meat-eater really wants to think about how pigs and cows are slaughtered, much less to slaughter them himself. But people, men especially, do like fishing. Men like fishing more than they like fish; often the cleaning and eating of the catch is a sort of penance, a hangover that follows the intoxication of catching it. The first chapter of *To Hell with Fishing*, a 1945 paean to the sport by H. T. Webster and Ed Zern, is entitled "How to Dispose of Dead Fish" and suggests the following methods, among others:

1. stuffing them in a corner mailbox when nobody is looking,
2. hiding them under potted palms,

3. checking them at the Union Depot and throwing away the check,
4. hurling them from fast-moving cars on lonely roads late at night.

As a rule, the fisherman's wife disapproves of his fishing trips—because she suspects them to be pretexts for drinking and possibly womanizing (the real meaning of all the cartoons about fishermen catching mermaids?), and because, even if no other women are involved, she doesn't think it right for her husband to enjoy himself so much in her absence. On his return, it is customary for her to complain about how much he and his fish smell, and often to refuse to clean or cook his catch. Even so, he'd rather come home with something inedible than return empty-handed, since that would confirm her worst suspicions about his so-called fishing trips. So you see cartoons about homeward-bound fishermen sheepishly buying fish from chuckling grocers—fish caught by *real* fishermen.

Another tack to take with your scowling wife (or anyone else who might infer, from your paltry or nonexistent catch, that you're not a very

Fig. 54

good angler) is of course to make excuses. No other sportsmen are as legendary for making excuses. I must have seen at least a dozen crying towels (see CRYBABIES AND WHINERS) designed specifically for fishermen, and printed with traditional excuses and complaints: "They were biting yesterday"; "Too hot"; "Too much rain"; "Only thing biting today are mosquitoes"; "Water's too low."

Most of these towels also feature would-be-funny illustrations, and the central picture is invariably a fisherman with outstretched arms as he lies about the one that got away. The association between fishing and lying is so strong that not only do jokes about fishermen emphasize lying, but also jokes about liars use fishermen as exemplars. Take the Liar's License issued by Topps in 1964 as part of its Nutty Awards trading card series: it shows a braggart with his mouth wide open and his hands far apart, clearly boasting about a big fish. A 1940s postcard featured a mock ad for Fishermen's Arm Extensions—telescoping prostheses enabling the wearer to tell much bigger whoppers (up to fifteen feet across with the Deluxe model).

Fishermen, like HUNTERS, are sometimes represented as drunks for whom the sport is just a pretext to get away from the wife for a day or two, and from society's feminized, domesticated standards of good hygiene, good manners, sobriety, and so on. A black-and-white postcard from the 1940s shows nine men lounging around a fishermen's lodge, playing poker, drinking toasts, and glaring at the one guy who's holding a fishing rod. The caption reads "Every time you get a good gang of fellows together on a fishing trip . . . some guy wants to fish."

But many comic fishermen actually *did* want to fish as well as to drink, and because it's so easy to combine the activities, comic fishermen, unlike comic hunters, are often pictured doing what they said they'd be doing: catching fish, or toting fish they've caught already. There are also jokes about unsuccessful fishermen getting nary a nibble, but even they are often contrasted with a luckier buddy or child or spouse with a whole string of fish. The contrast with hunting humor (in which animals are seldom harmed, though hunters often are) reflects the strange and widespread double standard that enables some semi-vegetarians to eat fish but not flesh with a good conscience.

Flappers

B Y THE 1920S, the slapstick violence that makes early comics so funny and scary had given way to strips about PRETTY GIRLS. Everyone wanted to draw them. Even unlikely strips like *Barney Google* found pretexts for including cuties, most often in the form of *flappers*, as the mass media of the age—already showing a penchant for instant labeling of new subcultures—called the saucy, fun-loving young women whose unconventional approach to dress and sex first came to media attention during World War I. Blondie started out as a flapper (Dagwood was just one of her many beaux), and so did *Nancy*'s Aunt Fritzi. Together with their mousier, less hedonistic sisters in the working-girl strips (*Winnie Winkle, Tillie the Toiler, Somebody's Stenog*), flappers took over the funnies for more than a decade. Not themselves especially funny, they became a staple of humor because everybody liked to look at them and imagine their lives. Unlike later pop-cultural obsessions such as BEATNIKS and hippies, flappers inspired no hatred or fear (at least not among the men who controlled the humor industry), sentiments that would limit the spread of those other obsessions into the more complacent venues for humor.

The mania cut across all levels of society. Flappers were by far the favorite subject of cartoons for the first decade of *The New Yorker*'s existence. Thanks to the omnipresence of flappers, two great traditions of comic art—highbrow magazine cartoons and lowbrow newspaper strips—were closer in the late 1920s than at any time before or since. In either medium, a typical gag would involve a cute, skinny, scantily clad, and no doubt sexually licentious young woman saying something lovably airheaded to another of her ilk, and so enabling male readers to feel both

Fig. 55 *Flapper Fannie*, 1925

sexually aroused and intellectually superior. It sounds retrograde, but the flapper had a major civilizing effect on the funnies page, substituting sexiness for the rough-and-tumble violence of "mischievous kid" strips.

Flatulence

> *Confucius say, Man who fart in church*
> *must sit in his own pew.*
> —OLD JOKE

> *from every B.V.D.*
> *let freedom ring*
> —E. E. CUMMINGS

LIKE MOVIES, jokes exist at different levels of naughtiness, and till recently those levels were surprisingly distinct and well-defined—something I realized in researching this guide, as I noticed that certain funny things never appear at all in certain media. Farting is a good example: an innocuous phenomenon with no obvious reason for being tabooed (unlike masturbation, anal sex, or SUICIDE, whose suppression was more comprehensible) but one that for most of the last century was conspicuously absent from mainstream American humor.

Of course, there's always a big difference between what people joke about in private and what they do in print, on film, or on the air. This guide inevitably underrepresents the private off-the-record humor of the era it discusses. My mother, who grew up in a God-fearing midwestern middle-class household in the 1940s, recalls from her childhood the still-familiar lines:

> *Beans, beans, they're good for your heart*
> *The more you eat, the more you fart*
> *The more you fart, the happier/better you feel*
> *So let's eat beans with every meal.*

My mom also recalls such rhyming answers to the whodunit question as "He who smelt it dealt it" and "He who denied it supplied it." So a well-behaved little girl in the 1940s was exposed to fart humor. And yet there's not a whiff of it in the mainstream pop culture of the era: not on TV, not on radio, not in the movies, not in print. You have to look pretty hard to find any even in the less reputable venues of the era. Even Tijuana bibles that blithely show young Nancy performing fellatio on Sluggo, or Little Orphan Annie being sodomized by her dog Sandy, rarely challenged the taboo against farting.

It wasn't always so. In the 1890s and 1900s, a French baker named Joseph Pujol wowed the Moulin Rouge with his flatulence. His stage name was Le Petomane, and his act—which, in its heyday, would outgross Sarah Bernhardt—consisted of making all kinds of remarkable noises with his anus. As a child he'd discovered his freakish ability to suck water or air into his rectum, and long before he turned pro he was amusing fellow soldiers, during a hitch in the army, with his ability to take up water from a pan and squirt it several yards. Back in civilian life, he would amuse customers at his bakery by imitating musical instruments. At his peak, he and his amazing sphincter could play "La Marseillaise," blow out a candle from across the room, imitate all kinds of barnyard animals, and bring down the house with his deafening rendition of the great San Francisco earthquake. Everybody wanted to hear him, from Sigmund Freud to the Prince of Wales.

Fart humor, then, goes in and out of fashion. It was surprisingly common in the eighteenth century, which for all its periwigs and minuets was much less frightened by bodily functions than the nineteenth and most of the twentieth. Swift, Sterne, Smollett, and even Pope wrote memorably on the subject, though Dr. Johnson wouldn't touch it. Swift is thought to be the author of the 1722 essay "The Benefit of Farting Explain'd,"[20] under the pseudonym of Don Fartinhando Puffindorst,

---

[20] The poem on the title poem certainly sounds like Swift:

A FART, tho' wholesome, does not fail,
If barr'd of Puffage by the Tail,
To fly back to the Head again,
And by its Fumes disturb the Brain:
Thus Gunpowder confin'd, you know Sir,
Grows stronger as 'tis ramm'd the closer;
But if in open Air it fires,
In harmless Smoke its Force expires.

Professor of Bumbast in the University of Craccow. In 1787, an anonymous "Essay Upon Wind; With Curious Anecdotes of Eminent Peteurs, Humbly Dedicated to the Lord Chancellor," painstakingly distinguished five types of flatulence: the sonorous and full-toned; the double; the soft-fizzing; the wet ("easily procured" by cramming oneself with "pies, custards, whip-syllabub, prunes, &c., &c."); and the sullen, wind-bound Fart. On our side of the Atlantic, no less a paragon than Ben Franklin addressed the Royal Academy in an open letter—a Swiftian satire of the academy's pretensions and preoccupations—urging scientists to develop a drug to make farts smell better.

But then along came the Victorians and turned off the gas for about a century. In our grandparents' era, there would seem at first glance, or first sniff, to be no fart humor at all in the mainstream humor of the early or mid-twentieth century—in sitcoms, family magazines, newspaper comic strips, Broadway musicals, or Hollywood movies. (*Blazing Saddles*, which did for flatulence what *Deep Throat* did for fellatio, didn't come along till 1974.) Not even *Mad* magazine, in its early glory days, ever acknowledged the fact that *Everybody Farts* (the title of a matter-of-fact 2009 picture book presumably intended to inoculate a kinder, saner generation against fart humor).

Nowhere in the Bible, as far as I know, is farting or its discussion forbidden. And yet its discussion in mainstream culture was unthinkable till recently. *Fart* was one of George Carlin's celebrated list of Words You Can't Say on TV—not one of the original seven, admittedly, but one Carlin added when he expanded the list to ten. How on earth did a harmless joker like *fart* end up in the same cell with hardened felons like *fuck* and *cunt* and *cocksucker*? Whatever the grounds for the taboo, I've internalized it to the point that I have to override an inhibition every time I write the word—more of an inhibition than with *shit*, which has lost its charge from constant nonliteral use.

To find explicit public humor about flatulence in the mid-twentieth century, you had to go to the joke pages in men's magazines, or the walls of public restrooms. Or the Ozarks: *Pissing in the Snow: And Other Bawdy Ozark Folk Tales* includes a funny fart story that the compiler, Vance Randolph, heard in Missouri in 1954 from a Mrs. Ethel R. Strainchamps, who heard it herself in 1924. In this tale, which Randolph gives the title "Wind Instead of Water," two men and an old woman are starving to death when they find a little flour, but they have no water to wet it with, and of course you can't eat dry flour. They persuade the old lady to urinate on it, but she accidentally breaks wind instead, blowing the flour away. The notes to *Pissing in the Snow* mention another tale in which "a violinist breaks wind mightily just as he reaches the climax of an impressionistic piece about a storm. An enraptured girl interprets the section as "lightning striking a privy." Randolph's volume, though, was well outside the mainstream—so far outside that it knocked about in manuscript for twenty-two years till someone finally dared to publish it in 1976.

I'm tempted to say that, for the first two thirds of the twentieth century, flatulence—not sex, not race—was the supreme taboo in American culture. Yet further research reveals that there were some feeble drafts of fart humor wafting through the popular culture of that era, though humorists were constrained to the sort of silent-but-deadly indirection that renders the fart jokes of that era wittier (not saying much) than those of our own unembarrassed era. In *The Bank Dick*, W. C. Fields hears the name Og Oggilby and murmurs that it "sounds like a bubble in a bathtub." There's another submerged fart joke near the end of *Duck Soup*, when the lemonade vendor played by Edgar Kennedy tries to take a bath in a tub where Harpo is hiding but keeps hearing toots from Harpo's horn bubbling up from the bathwater.

Then there's the most successful fart joke of the twentieth century. The whoopee cushion **(Fig. 56)** was invented around 1930 by the JEM Rubber Company of Toronto. It encountered some initial skepticism from potential manufacturers; Soren Sorensen "Sam"

Whoopee Cushion

The Whoopee Cushion or "Poo-Poo" Cushion, as it is sometimes called, is made of rubber. It is inflated in much the same manner as an ordinary rubber balloon and then placed on a chair, couch, seat, etc. When the victim unsuspectingly sits upon the cushion, it gives forth noises that can be better imagined than described.
No. 2953. Whoopee Cushion. Price **25c**

Fig. 56 Gives forth noises better imagined than described

Adams—the great laffmeister whose S. S. Adams Company gave the world the joy buzzer, the dribble glass, the snake nut can, the squirting nickel, and all sorts of other classic laff-getters—turned down the idea, then regretted the decision for the rest of his life. He wound up selling an imitation, as did many other johnny-come-latelies. (Though *whoopee cushion* eventually prevailed as the generic term for all such noisemakers, for a while there it was one brand name among many: Poo-Poo Cushion, Whoopee Pillow, Po-Pe Ball, Razz-Z Ball, and Boop-Boop A Doop.)

Reading between the lines of old novelty catalogs, it is possible to find many precursors of the whoopee cushion. In 1924, the Heaney Magic Company offered a Joke Cigarette Holder: "When they try to smoke . . . a most peculiar noise will issue forth from the holder," says the copy, the telltale grandiloquisms "most peculiar" and "issue forth" anticipating the whoopee cushion's famous genteelism, "gives forth noises better imagined than described."[21] The illustration shows the victim looking baffled as his cigarette goes "B-R-R-T-T-U-P"—surely the transcription of a raspberry if not a fart. The same catalog uses similar wording for its Horn Cigar ("you will appear to magically control a peculiar horn or the stunt issues forth from some other source many will think"), though in the accompanying illustration, the noise produced by the jaunty young prankster in striped suit and boater is a simple "hoot."

Before it became permissible to discuss farts openly, our forebears relied on all kinds of substitutes—from DUCKS to TUBAS, from foghorns to balloons. It may be that the fully lifelike simulation of farts became

---

[21] It took a while for the copywriters at Johnson Smith to hit on this wording. In the 1935 catalog, the cushion "gives forth the most indescribable noises that can be better imagined than described." By 1944, though, the pleonasm had been fixed, so they do sometimes revise the seemingly fossilized catalog copy. Back in 1929, incidentally, the effects of the Jumping Frog, Joke Toilet Paper, and Electric Push Button were also lazily described as "better imagined than described."

possible only with later improvements in sheet rubber,[22] but in the pre-whoopee epoch it wasn't necessary or even desirable for a noisemaker to sound exactly like the real thing; it just had to sound like something sometimes used to *symbolize* the real thing. Novelty makers are always boasting about how "realistic" their products are, but in this case, realism wasn't wanted. Instead, aspiring practical jokers were offered a range of metonymies and metaphors. Even in our unembarrassed age, the whoopee cushion itself still claims to imitate a "Bronx cheer" or raspberry—not a fart but the imitation of one made by buzzing the lips in what linguists call a bilabial trill. (The reason that sound is called a "raspberry" is that it is or was cockney rhyming slang for "fart," via "raspberry tart.") The sound is the best simulation of a fart we can produce with our normal speech apparatus. In the early 1930s, when whoopee cushions took the world by storm, raspberries too were in fashion, at least on the funny pages—both Dagwood and Popeye had recourse to them now and then. A little later, Al Capp gave us Joe Btfsplk, the world's biggest jinx, easily recognized by the small black cloud—a personal fart cloud?—hanging over him at all times. When asked how to pronounce Joe's surname, Capp would respond with a raspberry, adding, "How else would you pronounce it?"

---

[22] The reason whoopee cushions counterfeit the sound so well is presumably that the real thing is produced by the same means: a small self-sealing aperture that vibrates audibly when gas forces its way through. At least, I assume, now that I stop and think, that that's what accounts for the noise when we fart. It's strange to think that I could reach the age I have without knowing for sure.

G g

Get-Rich-Quick Schemes

MOST CHARACTERS who scheme to strike it rich are doomed to fail again and again. No matter how good the scheme sounds, we know there's no way that Ralph Kramden or Lucy Ricardo or Amos and Andy are going to strike it rich, because that would be the end of the sitcom. Is it an article of faith with sitcom writers that lasting wealth can result only from honest perseverance? Clearly not: *The Beverly Hillbillies* is premised on the dumb luck of sudden unearned wealth. But sitcoms do tend to imply that social mobility is a pipe dream. It would be hard to sustain a good series that *didn't* imply that, since social and financial standing is such a big part of what defines a character. Striking it rich would be as drastic a change for an established character as going blind or going gay—changes that might work in soap operas, but not in sitcoms.

So when we laugh at Ralph Kramden's latest scheme, it isn't always because the scheme is manifestly silly in itself. Sometimes we're laughing, in effect, at Ralph's lack of insight as a sitcom character in a series that depends on him remaining a frustrated and penniless working-class slob.

Gold Diggers and Sugar Daddies

> *I never hated a man enough to give him diamonds back.*
> —ZSA ZSA GABOR

> *Always remember, honey. A good motto is: "Take all you can get and*
> *give as little as possible." . . . Don't forget, honey. Never let one man*
> *worry your mind. Find 'em, fool 'em and forget 'em!*
> —*I'M NO ANGEL*, 1933

> *There may come a time when a hard-boiled employer*
> *Thinks you're awful nice,*
> *But get that ice or else no dice. . . .*
> *Romance is divine, and I'm not one to knock it,*
> *But diamonds are a girl's best friend.*
> *Romance is divine, yes, but where can you hock it? . . .*
> *It's not compensation,*
> *It's self-preservation!*
> —LEO ROBIN,
> "DIAMONDS ARE A GIRL'S BEST FRIEND," 1953

MANY YEARS AGO, a British cartoonist named William Hewison joked that *New Yorker* cartoonists produced only four different drawings: "a sugar daddy and a dewy blonde; two hoboes sitting on a park bench in Central Park; a drunk tête-à-tête with a barman; a man and wife getting into a car after a dinner party." He was exaggerating, but anyone who has paged through old *New Yorker* cartoon albums—or spent a week perusing the mind-boggling pair of CD-ROMs including every cartoon ever to appear in the magazine— knows what Hewison meant. And of the four clichés he lists, the first— the mogul and the bimbo—was by far the most common.

That cliché was also popular in less exalted venues. *Pets—Including Women* (1956) is an odd assortment of cartoons from lowbrow humor magazines. Eighty percent of the cartoons are G-rated ones à la *Marmaduke*: for example, man with big dog asks clerk in sporting goods store

Fig. 57 Gold Digger, Sugar Daddy

for saddle. The remaining cartoons, though, are corny old sexist gags of the sort found in men's magazines of that era. It is hard to imagine the target audience for such a book—or rather, it's hard to imagine any reader, young or old, Christian or pagan, who would enjoy the whole thing, even if the cartoons were funnier. The target audience can be inferred from the cartoon on the front cover: a chuckling tycoon dangling a steak above an eager dog that begs on its hind legs, and dangling from his other hand a pearl necklace above an eager young mistress who begs for it on tiptoe.

The enduring popularity of the gold digger/sugar daddy cliché is due, I suspect, to its irresistibility as a metaphor for "normal" sexual and marital relations in our culture. To quote an old book of insults—and as someone who had never been clear on the difference between ways and means, I was thrilled to find an insult that illustrates the proper use of the two words—"She couldn't stand his ways, but she married him for his means." Some would say that simple prostitution is a better metaphor for marriage (and certainly straightforward prostitution—a simple cash transaction with no diamonds or flirtation involved—is more common than the gold digger/sugar daddy arrangement), but that metaphor is a little too brutal for most of us.

In jokes about a bimbo and a mogul, it isn't always clear just whom the joke is on—which of those stock characters we are meant to laugh at. Each is using the other, and seldom does the humor, such as it is, smack of satire, of Swiftian indignation at human misbehavior. More often, one senses schadenfreude—mirth at the expense of whichever party is getting the worst of the bargain. And that, as you'd expect, usually depends on the target audience. In magazines for servicemen and working stiffs who spend their days being ordered around by older, richer men, the joke tends to be on the mogul, who lavishes minks and diamonds on the gold digger without ever getting her into bed. Thus, a 1957 cartoon in the decidedly lowbrow *Showgirls* magazine ("Gags . . . Gals . . . and Laughs Galore") shows two balding moguls seated at a nightclub table while nearby a gorgeous stripper gyrates. Mogul 1 to Mogul 2: "Oh, I agree she's terrific. Trouble is she NO'S too much!"

In *The New Yorker*, on the other hand, at least in the 1930s and '40s, the laughingstock is usually the bimbo, whose naïveté makes her easy to seduce—as easy for the rich as taking candy from a baby. Like the ads and everything else in the magazine, the cartoons tended to flatter its well-heeled, well-educated readers, to confirm their own sense of themselves as winners in the game of life. The mogul-and-bimbo cartoons, specifically, reassured older men that, in the competition for mates, their money and power more than compensated for their age.

In any case, the relationship can be seen from several viewpoints—as a blissfully symbiotic and mutually beneficial one; as a mutually sordid one; as the exploitation of beauty by wealth; as the exploitation of wealth by beauty—and each viewpoint yields a different basic joke. And all these jokes are common in magazine cartoons but almost unheard-of in newspaper comics, making this as good a place as any to wonder why comic strips have always been so different from magazine cartoons. Even in magazines as disparate as *The New Yorker* and *Playboy* the cartoons have more in common than either has with newspaper comics. One reason, of course, is the difference between single-panel and multi-panel cartoons:

each format lends itself to a different kind of joke. But that's not the whole explanation. After all, some magazine cartoons have several panels, and there have been many wildly successful one-panel newspaper strips, from *Our Boarding House* and *Out Our Way* to *The Far Side* and *Ziggy*.

So we have to look at other factors to account for the difference. The main one is demographic: most newspapers try to reach the lowest common denominator. Those that don't address that demographic—the *New York Times*, the *Wall Street Journal*, the *Christian Science Monitor*—make a point of not running comic strips at all. Newspaper readers are less fastidious than magazine readers when it comes to slapstick violence and other broad humor, but they're more puritanical about sex. For much of the twentieth century the top newspaper cartoonists were among the richest artists in America, but they would never have stayed on top if they'd antagonized their mass audience—or incurred its resentment of moneyed privilege—with winking, "worldly" gags about rich old businessmen and young mistresses, gags that rarely register any disapproval of the sugar daddies for basically purchasing sex.

Next to the gag cartoon, the favorite venue for gold-digger jokes is probably the Broadway musical, an especially poignant venue because it was among aspiring actresses and chorus girls that sugar daddies traditionally recruited their mistresses.

> *There's an oil man known as Tex*
> *Who is keen to give me checks,*
> *And his checks, I fear, means that sex is here to stay. . . .*
> *Mister Harris, plutocrat,*
> *Wants to give my cheek a pat,*
> *If a Harris pat*
> *Means a Paris hat*
> *Bebe, Oo-la-la!*
> —COLE PORTER,
> "ALWAYS TRUE TO YOU IN MY FASHION," 1948

The Three Stooges often encounter gold diggers—though invariably after inheriting money or otherwise striking it rich, since otherwise they're three of the most ineligible bachelors in history. In "Brideless Groom" (1947), a beauty to whom Shemp has recently and unsuccessfully proposed changes her mind when she learns he stands to inherit half a million dollars. By that point, though, Shemp too has changed his mind and decided to marry another woman, so the first one traps his head in a handy book press (this is in the office of the justice of the peace) and squeezes it tighter and tighter in a scarily literal effort to make him change his mind again. "I'm gettin' a headache," Shemp cries at one point, and we think of all the future headaches this woman will inflict if they do get married.[23]

Golf

> *For me the point where any strip "jumps the shark"*
> *is when the cartoonist starts doing golf jokes. It means*
> *he is spending more time at the golf course playing*
> *with his buddies than working on his strip.*
> —GER APELDOORN, *THOSE FABULOUS FIFTIES* (BLOG)

THE LIFETIME OF RESEARCH I seem to have squandered on this book is nothing compared to the Dantean eternity of research I'm neglecting. I have never played golf, for example, and so I'm unable to say whether golf is really as unfunny as it seems to me. If there weren't so much golf humor, I would spare myself the chore of writing this entry, but that would be as unthinkable as remaining silent on the subject of DESERT ISLANDS or MOTHERS-IN-LAW. An insanely disproportionate number of the world's comic strips and gag cartoons concern golf—Gibbs Smith recently published a lavish volume entitled *Golf in the Comic Strips*—not because golf is funny, but because it has always been the favorite sport of cartoonists, a socially insecure bunch. Ever since the days of *The Yellow Kid* (there was, indeed, an episode about

---

[23] On *The Addams Family*, Uncle Fester *treats* his headaches by squeezing his head in a vise.

Fig. 58 Golfer. See also SCOTSMEN.

the Kid's wacky misadventures on the golf course), the most successful cartoonists have been rich. Like millionaire pornographers, though, they find it hard to buy their way into high society with their tainted money.

Of course, and alas, it isn't only cartoonists who care about golf. The mountain of jocular golf "collectibles" makes it clear that, whether or not they want to spend every waking minute actually golfing, a lot of people like to *think* about golf even when they're doing other things. In the middle of the twentieth century, golf humor was everywhere you looked—on cocktail napkins ("Golf is like taxes . . . You try hard to get to the GREEN . . . and end up in the HOLE"), on wall plaques, on postcards, on shot glasses ("Old golfers never die . . . they just lose their balls") and drinking glasses like the one calibrated and labeled according to how many ounces of booze are warranted by different golfing mishaps, from minor irritations ("2 oz—a flat on my golf cart"; "4 oz—slow female players") all the way up to the worst-case scenario ("15 oz—drove into the boss's foursome"). There were golf-related practical jokes, like balls designed to zigzag as they rolled. There were novelty tees shaped like the legs and buttocks of a shapely woman ("Guaranteed to keep your eye on the ball").

Above all, there were crying towels—tea towels imprinted with cartoonish images and sentiments, and meant to be presented to golfers who complain too much about their golfing misfortunes. I've seen six or seven different golf-related crying towels, and it is to them that I owe much of my knowledge of the sport. I know, for example, that golfers in denial about their own ineptitude are apt to blame their caddies, their partners, their clubs, the weather, the grass. I know that divots are good for a laugh, as are HEAD INJURIES inflicted by stray balls. I know that golfers find it hard to keep their heads down, and that hooking and slicing are to golf what wow and flutter are to hi-fi.

I knew some of that already from TV. After all, Fred Flintstone played, as did Bugs Bunny (after accidentally tunneling to Scotland), and Mickey Mouse (with Pluto as a caddy), and Donald Duck (who needs total quiet when he plays, but doesn't get it because he has unwisely brought along his nephews), and Goofy (who dutifully plays it as it lies, even when it lies on the nose of a dozing bull), and Tom and Jerry, and Woody Woodpecker, and Foghorn Leghorn (who plays an underhanded game, exploding balls and all, with his old college chum Rhode Island Red). Live-action golfers include Ward Cleaver (who breaks his driver), the Three Stooges (who destroy the golf course), Lucy Ricardo (who naturally takes up the game when Ricky gets obsessed with it), and even the Little Rascals (who play with garden tools in lieu of clubs).

To a nongolfer, the game is funniest when played by loudmouths like Ralph Kramden or bullies like Moe Howard—men accustomed to getting what they want via brute force—because force is not enough to succeed at golf. The disproportion between the size of an adult male and the size of a golf ball makes it even more galling for the former when the latter disobeys his wishes—and all the more comical that he cares about the game at all. Some guys should just stick to BOWLING.

Gossips and Busybodies

The only time people dislike gossip is when it's about them.
—WILL ROGERS

Oh, the woman on our party line's the nosiest thing;
She picks up her receiver when she knows it's my ring.
—HANK WILLIAMS, "MIND YOUR OWN BUSINESS," 1949

THE MOST MEMORABLE—AND even the witchiest—character on *Bewitched* was a mortal with no supernatural powers. Gladys Kravitz **(Fig. 59)** lived across the street from Samantha and Darrin, and she just knew that something fishy was going on over there. She was right, but that didn't make her sympathetic. Nor did her frus-

Fig. 59 Gladys Kravitz

trated efforts to convince her husband frustrate the viewer, as they might have if *Bewitched* had been directed by Kafka or Hitchcock. Instead, her plight was comical, not only because viewers identified with—and knew all about—the objects of her suspicion, but because it was clear that Gladys had *always* inflicted her prurient curiosity on NEIGHBORS, even when those neighbors had nothing to hide. Her punishment was the life of a suburban Cassandra, her hypertrophied curiosity mated to her husband's comic *in*curiosity.

Gladys was played by two different actresses, both notably less attractive than Elizabeth Montgomery, who played Samantha. That's usually the case when a busybody focuses her prurience on another woman. In *My Little Chickadee*, Mae West's nemesis is played by Margaret Hamilton, best known as the Wicked Witch of the West in *The Wizard of Oz*. Hamilton's town gossip sees Mae West's town hussy kissing a masked bandit, and not only gets West drummed out of town, but also arranges with the Ladies Guild in the town where West heads next to ostracize her there as well. From her flirtatious behavior with W. C. Fields, and her indignation when Fields proves more interested in Mae, we gather that Hamilton's nosy and meddlesome behavior is the result of envy and sexual frustration.

The comic busybody is usually a woman (for the closest male stereotype, see DO-GOODERS), but not always: after all, what else is Jimmy Stewart in *Rear Window*? Or the prurient and creepy narrator of Henry James's only full-length first-person novel, *The Sacred Fount*? Usually, though, men are given some better motive for their nosiness than idle curiosity or free-floating malice. Or maybe they're just less honest about their motives, as Phyllis McGinley—as always, an eloquent advocate for her much-maligned gender—suggests:

Women are restless, uneasy to handle,
But when they are burning both ends of the scandal,
They do not insist with a vow that is votive
How high are their minds and how noble the motive.

Gravity

> *Whenever possible, make gravity the Coyote's greatest enemy.*
> —ONE OF THE TEN RULES CHUCK JONES OBSERVED
> IN MAKING ROAD RUNNER CARTOONS

> *It seems to me that no kind of depravity*
> *Brings such speedy retribution as ignoring the law of gravity.*
> —OGDEN NASH

FOR THOSE OF US raised on the legend of the Algonquin Round Table, surprisingly few of the witticisms collected by Robert E. Drennan in *The Algonquin Wits* have retained their power to delight (perhaps because, as Antoine Rivaroli observed, "A witticism is a minor work that does not merit a second edition"). One that does is ascribed to Franklin Pierce Adams, the newspaperman who signed himself F.P.A. As Drennan tells it:

> F.P.A. once escorted George and Beatrice Kaufman to a cocktail party where Beatrice, sitting down on a cane-bottom chair, suddenly broke through the seat. . . . Adams secured her humiliation by remarking, "I've told you a hundred times, Beatrice, that's not funny!"

Part of what makes F.P.A.'s remark so good is that, of course, Mrs. Kaufman's mishap was funny—so funny that most humorists wouldn't

Fig. 60 Wile E. Coyote and his nemesis

even try to compete with the event by joking about it. Gravity has always been the funniest of the fundamental forces, and if not the funniest physical law (I vote for inertia), certainly the one most commonly referred to as a law—hence all the jokes about breaking the law of gravity, by everyone from T. S. Eliot ("McCavity, McCavity, there's no one like McCavity / He's broken every human law; He breaks the law of gravity") to Bugs Bunny.

In "High Diving Hare" (1949), Yosemite Sam wants Bugs to jump off a diving board into a tiny pool far below. When other blandishments fail, Sam traps Bugs at the end of the board and saws through it, but instead of Bugs falling, the ladder and platform and Sam fall instead. Bugs observes, "I know this defies the law of gravity, but, you see, I never studied law!" It's odd that he even mentions the law in question, since cartoon characters violate it as matter-of-factly as New Yorkers jaywalk. Think of all the cartoons where a character strolls off the edge of a cliff and continues blithely walking on midair until he notices the void beneath his feet.

Speaking of laws, gravity is so funny that it features in no fewer than four of the ten basic Laws of Cartoon Physics as codified by Mark O'Donnell:

I: Any body suspended in space will remain in space until made aware of its situation. **(See Fig. 60)**

IV: The time required for an object to fall twenty stories is greater than or equal to the time it takes for whoever knocked it off the ledge to spiral down twenty flights to attempt to capture it unbroken.

V: All principles of gravity are negated by fear.

IX: Everything falls faster than an anvil.

Though animated cartoons are uniquely suited to having fun with gravity, early live-action comedies did a lot with it, too. (The word *cliffhanger* predates motion pictures; it originally applied to melodramatic stage plays and serialized fiction.) The most famous example may be Harold Lloyd dangling from the minute hand of a big clock at the top of a skyscraper in *Safety Last* (1923), but there were plenty of precedents for that famous scene even in Lloyd's own work. Vertiginous "ledge" scenes were almost as much of a trademark with him as those big round lensless glasses.

Slapstick relied heavily on gravity-assisted gags. (What else is a PRATFALL?) In an especially cartoonish scene in "The Blacksmith" (1922), Buster Keaton needs to change a tire and uses a child's helium balloon in place of a jack. In true cartoon fashion, his makeshift jack does the trick—until the child retaliates by bursting the balloon with a pea-shooter. You can do amazing things when you fight the law of gravity in an old comedy, but in the end the law usually wins.

Grawlixes

WHEN BARNEY GOOGLE or Sgt. Snorkel loses his temper, he's liable to say "!#@!" or words to that effect. But of course they aren't exactly words. What they are is grawlixes: symbols that stand for unprintable profanities. Most of the comic-strip clichés considered in this guide are also found in animated cartoons, and some in live-action comedy, but grawlixes occur only on the funnies page. Over the decades, cartoonists have developed a standard palette of

Fig. 61 *The Five Fifteen*, 1921

such symbols, and in *The Lexicon of Comicana* (1980), Mort Walker gave them names: asterisks are *nittles*, spirals and pound signs are *jarns*, and heavenly bodies—crescent moons, ringed planets, five-pointed stars— are *quimps*. Scribbles and zigzags are *grawlixes*, which has also become an umbrella term for all symbols used in comics to represent swearing. And you need to master them all, if you want your characters to swear convincingly. "A variety of acceptable curse words are at the cartoonist's disposal," says Walker. "He may throw in a new one from time to time, but the real meat of the epithet must always contain plenty of jarns, quimps, nittles, and grawlixes."

Walker's *Lexicon* defines all kinds of other comic-strip symbols (see BRIFFITS AND DUSTUPS), but it is his names for cartoon obscenities that have proven most successful. Some, through inclusion in respected dictionaries, have attained the status of bona fide, certified words. Like most terms of art, they aren't very useful in everyday life, where nobody knows what they mean. But William Gass didn't let that stop him from including the terms in *The Tunnel*—shamelessly exhuming them from Walker's dictionary only to rebury them at once in a much thicker book, and one much less likely to be read cover to cover—in his description of a cartoonish history professor: "He does all the Popeye voices, but prefers Olive Oyl's. He has noises for the nittles, the grawlix, the quimps, the jarns. He blows each balloon up before your ears."

Though Walker gave them names, he was far from the first cartoonist to use the symbols in question. The practice of swearing in funny symbols is as old as the comics themselves, or at least as old as the kind with speech balloons. In the early days, nearly every strip involved the sort of mishap that would cause even a saint to lose his temper, and the victim's reaction to the mishap was almost always half the fun, so it wasn't long before cartoonists came up with printable ways to suggest the funny reaction of swearing a blue streak. Cartoonists didn't arrive immediately, though, at the current tool set. The development of comic-strip cussing is a fascinating case of graphic evolution.

As far as I can tell, grawlixes began as punctuation of censored speech balloons—punctuation suggesting what we're missing. On stubbing his toe, a character in an early comic strip might shout "_____! ____!?

_____!!!"ˣ24 Maybe readers were meant to imagine that the newspaper, or the syndicate, had censored the original text. (That was certainly the joke in later speech balloons that used black bars, as in soldiers' letters home, to suggest the obliteration of forbidden words.) A hundred years later, we're so accustomed to grawlixes that we no longer automatically associate them with censorship (as we still do with bleeped-out words on network TV). In the first decade of the last century, though, they were new enough that the suggestion of bowdlerization was half the joke. When that joke got old, cartoonists realized that they could leave out the blanks that stood for censored words and use the punctuation alone as a quick and funny way to indicate swearing.

Scribbles have always had a place in comic-strip cussing. They represent another variation on the censorship gag, suggesting that strong language has been used and then crossed out. The cartoonists can't show the underlying word, only a canceling scribble—hardly ever turgid enough to look like an actual obliteration—to suggest that a forbidden word lurks behind all that black ink.

Aside from scribbles and standard punctuation marks, the first grawlixes were asterisks, which printers have used for hundreds of years to indicate missing text, and five-pointed stars, which have been used by cartoonists since the late nineteenth century to signify PAIN. The world of early comics is a world of pain, and those stars are everywhere. Most of the events that drive cartoon characters to swear are not just infuriating but physically painful, so it's not surprising that stars—originally used outside speech balloons to suggest a character's sensations (on being punched in the nose, say)—found their way inside the balloons, to symbolize verbal expressions of displeasure.

The most distinctive of all the standard grawlixes, the planet Saturn with its famous ring, was one of the last adopted. As far back as 1901,

---

24 In his *Historical Dictionary of American Slang*, J. K. Lighter quotes a funny sentence from 1888 to substantiate the use of *astonisher* as journalistic slang for *exclamation point*: "What in three dashes, two hyphens, and an astonisher do you want here!" (Nye and Riley, *Railway*, 1888). Other journalistic synonyms for *exclamation point* include *screamer*, *shout*, and *bang*, whence *interrobang* for the combination question mark and exclamation point:?!

cartoonists were using planets as well as stars and crescent moons to indicate pain, but not till the late 1920s, as far as I can tell, did planets first
appear in speech balloons. And now that's the only place you find them
on the funnies page, except of course in scenes of outer space; their use in
cartoon cussing has made them unusable for other kinds of symbolism.

The last symbol to gain admission to the standard repertoire was the
pound sign or octothorpe, #, of which I've yet to find a specimen dating
from earlier than 1940. Until recently the grawlixes in speech balloons
were always handwritten, but you wonder if the top row of keys on typewriters suggested both the # and the @ to cartoonists in search of new
ways to represent swearing. In the old days, cartoonists worked in the
art rooms of their home newspapers, and though the reporters and their
typewriters were in a separate room, a newsroom, it isn't hard to imagine
a cartoonist straying into the newsroom and looking over the shoulder of
a madly typing friend, first at the dull article on the League of Nations,
then at interesting symbols on the keyboard. The ones in the top row,
especially, would have suggested themselves as grawlixes because some of
them—asterisk, exclamation point—had served that purpose all along.
Just a theory, but it would explain why Walker lumped together pound
signs and spirals (including the modified spiral that looks more like an
@) as "jarns," putting those disparate symbols in the same subclass.

Walker's book started life as an extended joke, and if we take his
terms too seriously, the joke is on us. It doesn't really matter what we
call those symbols; it's hard to think of any situation where the lack of a
clear and fully standardized nomenclature for cartoon obscenities would
drive anyone to real-life swearing. And even if we know what to call the
various symbols, we still don't know precisely what the symbols themselves stand for, which one represents which unprintable word. (Though
presumably the cartoon characters themselves know. In a sequence of *Li'l
Abner* strips from 1947, we learn that the troglodytic Scraggs family includes a juvenile delinquent named *@!!*!-Belle Scragg.)

If we did know how to translate every grawlix into a specific four-
letter word, the symbols would be as obscene as the words. As it is, they
are much more innocent than ridiculous dodges like "f__k" or "s__t." I
never find myself translating grawlixes into actual obscenities (as we do

reflexively with bleeped-out words on television), partly because the symbols seldom occur in a syntactic context. It would be different if Popeye or Jiggs said things like "Ah, go # yourself"; "Aw, you're full of *" or "You can kiss my big fat @." Syntax is everything. When a strip does incorporate the grawlixes into sentences, as a few classic strips sometimes do (*Dick Tracy*, *Wash Tubbs*, *Moon Mullins*, *Thimble Theatre*), the swearing seems much more profane.

My parade of illustrations is misleading if it gives the impression that grawlixes were ever common on the funnies page. They *should* have been everyday occurrences in early comics, given the damnable nature of everyday events in those comics. But grawlixes were never common. I think of Barney Google as especially foul-mouthed and underbred, but in fact he seldom swears in circumstances that wouldn't elicit a profanity from Mother Teresa herself. And many early comic strips—including rough-and-tumble strips like *Mutt and Jeff*, probably the most violent strip of all time—seem not to have used grawlixes at all. Maybe when you feel free to lob a brick at anybody who annoys you, you don't need the sublimation of strong language.

Guest Towels

Go, and never darken my towels again!
—RUFUS T. FIREFLY
(GROUCHO MARX) IN *DUCK SOUP*, 1933

FEW ISSUES DIVIDED the sexes as bitterly, in our grandparents' day, as the purpose of guest towels—hand towels that the inhabitants of a house, and thus the most frequent users of its bathrooms, are not supposed to use. At the beginning of *Babbitt* (1922), the hero washes his face and then discovers that the family towels are all "wet and clammy and vile"—even his own.

Then George F. Babbitt did a dismaying thing. He wiped his face on the guest-towel! It was a pansy-embroidered trifle which always hung there to indicate that the Babbitts were in the best Floral Heights society. No one had ever used it. No guest had ever dared to. Guests secretively took a corner of the nearest regular towel.

Naturally this transgression brings the expected reproach from Babbitt's wife—"Oh Georgie, you didn't go and use the guest towel, did you?"—to which the author adds, "It is not recorded that he was able to answer." At that point, barely five pages into the book, we already know that Babbitt is a blustering jackass, yet it's hard not to side with him in this case. Hard for me, anyhow. No one can really rise above the Battle of the Sexes, and most heterosexual males, however enlightened they may be in other respects, cling all their lives to a little-boy disdain of household furnishings that imitate useful objects but aren't supposed to be used: fancy candles not meant to be lit, fancy soaps that mustn't get wet, fancy chairs that no one is allowed to sit on. It could be argued that the sublimation of prosaic household objects into the poetry of uselessness is part of what makes a house a home, but so much the worse for homes. We Neanderthals would be happier in caves.

James Thurber discusses the towel question at some length in his 1929 collaboration with E. B. White, *Is Sex Necessary?* "If a husband uses a guest towel, he should be calmly reprimanded, but under no circumstances sent to his room," writes Thurber, stressing the importance of correcting the sin without traumatizing the sinner. The husband should be "told where guest towels come from," and not only told: "The wife should lead him to the drawer where she keeps the guest towels and show him wherein they differ from ordinary towels—the kind he may use." Moreover:

> The husband should also be told that the use of such towels is not pleasurable because of the hemstitching, the rough embroidery, and the like. He should be made to understand that no man ever uses a guest towel, either in his own home or as a guest somewhere else, that they are hung up for lady guests to look at and are not to be disturbed.

Note that both Thurber and Lewis insist that guests don't use guest towels, either, a claim that confines the debate to terms that men are comfortable with—those of utility versus decoration—and avoids the whole issue of hospitality. In reality, of course, no one objects to guest towels per se—at least no one who has ever washed his or her hands (especially before a meal) and then looked in vain for a way to dry them that doesn't threaten to restore the very germs that washing removed. As far as I can tell, the female view is not just that such towels beautify the bathroom, but that they figure among the minor duties of a good host or hostess; to use one in your own house and not promptly replace it is selfish and thoughtless.

Gum

> *This will never be a civilized country until we spend more money*
> *for books than we do for chewing gum.*
> —ELBERT HUBBARD

> *Presidential candidates don't chew gum.*
> —THEODORE C. SORENSEN

WHEN WOLCOTT GIBBS claimed that 90 percent of American movies were "so vulgar, witless and dull that it is preposterous to write about them in any publication not intended to be read while chewing gum," he betrayed an old-fashioned snobbery that in retrospect is more damning to him than to the object of his scorn. He may have been right about American movies, but what did he have against *gum*? Why did Ernie Bushmiller, explaining the sublime and unfaltering stupidity of his great comic strip, say that he intended *Nancy* for the "gum chewers"? Why did Emily Post, in 1922, deem it "scarcely necessary to add that no gentleman walks along the street chewing gum"?

There is far more gum sold in our time than in our grandparents', but not nearly as much gum humor. Like instant coffee, gum has lost its novelty; like the conventions of hat-wearing, the rules concerning gum-chewing have been sublimed away in the melting pot of democracy. Manners experts have to choose their battles (just like usage experts), and the brighter know a lost cause when they see one. If I called a student uncouth for chewing gum in class, he or she would find my disapproval even quainter than my adjective. Joking about the practice nowadays would seem as crotchety as joking about women's-libbers.

Fig. 62

But that wasn't always the case. Even in my own lifetime, there's been a perceptible falling-off in gum humor. When I was a kid, we used to offer one another a piece of "ABC gum," then remove a wad from our mouth and explain that "ABC" stood for "Already Been Chewed." The Johnson Smith Company used to sell *fake* ABC gum ("Stick this pile of gum anywhere and watch people get mad! Looks like a real wad of gum!"), which strikes me as one of their more pointless offerings. Why would anybody buy *fake* chewed gum? What can it do that real ABC gum can't?

"Does Your Chewing Gum Lose Its Flavor?" was a big hit for Lonnie Donegan in 1958, and is number 10 on digitaldreamdoor.com's list of the top one hundred novelty songs of all time, thanks to such questions as "If your mother says don't chew it, do you swallow it in spite?" and "Can you catch it on your tonsils, can you heave it left and right?" Donegan's version was an adaptation of a 1924 song by Billy Rose (who also wrote the Barney Google song): "Does the Spearmint Lose Its Flavor on the Bedpost Overnight?"[25]

When Donegan redid the song, he regrettably dropped some of Rose's most pertinent gum-related questions: "If you chew it in the morning, will it be too hard to bite?"; "Would you use it on your collar when your button's not in sight?"; "If you pull it out like rubber will it

[25] Like many comic-strip characters of his era, Castor Oyl—Olive Oyl's brother—was an **INVENTOR**; his inventions included a nonparkable chewing gum.

snap right back and bite?"; and my favorite (for its evocation of a simpler and more frugal era when even a wad of ABC gum might tempt a thieving sibling): "If you paste it on the left side, will you find it on the right?" The original version shows a greater familiarity with the behavior of used chewing gum. Donegan gives no evidence of ever having chewed the stuff, but it may be that by 1958 gum was so familiar that its peculiarities no longer struck people as funny.

The only good gum humor I've encountered recently was a 1994 *New Yorker* spoof by Scott Gutterman. "Gum" purports to be the shooting script for a nostalgic documentary about the early days of gum, and features a narrator who says things like "It started as an idle pursuit: a way to pass the time, to occupy the slackened jaw of street urchin and steel magnate alike. . . ." The kind of documentary Gutterman is spoofing was ripe for parody, but his spoof wouldn't be as funny if he'd picked some other lowly phenomenon like paper clips or even breath mints. Gum was an inspired choice because we all sense that its heyday was long ago, before we were born—and also because, as exhaustively as it was chewed over by the wits and wiseacres of that era, and as long as it has spent since then parked out of sight on the underside of our culture's sticky Formica-covered collective sense of humor, gum still hasn't completely lost its flavor: it still tastes funny.

H h

Ham

PART OF BEING FUNNY for a living—whether you are a cartoonist, an NPR soliloquist, a stand-up comedian, an ad-libbing actor, or a lowly comic novelist—is detecting trace amounts of humor in things that people don't usually think of as funny at all. You find laugh potential in surprising places when you make a point of spritzing every handy surface of reality with the luminol of mirth. I pride myself on my ability to say, with the calm expertise of a lifelong humor nerd, that ham is distinctly funnier than SPINACH but not quite as funny as SAUSAGE. And these days that's about as funny as life gets.

On a comic seaside postcard from around 1960, a man sits on the beach facing the water, while his fat wife lies on her belly behind him, sunbathing. Her shoulders and the backs of her legs look painfully red, but her rump—though decently clad in a floral bathing suit—is cooking even faster, to judge by the lines of heat and puffs of smoke, and by her husband's comment: "Dearie, don't I smell ham burning?"

Hams are funny because they are butt cheeks. The word itself is akin to the Icelandic word for buttock, *höm*, and in the late 1890s a *ham-rester* was an idler, a chair-warmer. "Somebody's roastin' a ham," Shemp observes in a Three Stooges episode when he sits on a hot iron. "Whoa! It's me!" Beckett's Molloy refers to his buttocks as hams—the perfect word for a character who sees his body as little more than a lump of meat in which his mind is regrettably imprisoned.

That lumpishness is implied by most of the slang senses of the word. Proceeding chronologically (with the help of Lighter's *Historical Dictionary of American Slang*): Since at least 1863, *ham* has meant "a clumsy or worth-

Fig. 63

less fellow," especially a bad prizefighter. By 1881, it had come to mean a bad actor, especially one guilty of overacting—and found such widespread application in that sense that it developed variants like *hambo*, *hambone*, and *hamola*. *Hamhead* (meaning "meathead") and *ham-handed* both date from 1918; *ham-fisted* came along a decade later. "Slamming the ham"—one of the hundreds of facetious terms for masturbation—is first attested in 1958.

Hams are clearly fun to draw, and in any cartoon depiction of a huge meal, at least one ham will be seen on the groaning board. Even if the diner is literally a pig, there will be ham. When Li'l Abner and Daisy Mae leave for New York City on their honeymoon, they lug along an enormous Dogpatch ham that inspires more affection in Abner than poor Daisy does (though not even his attentions can prevent the ham from being run over by a bus). Daisy spends her wedding night curled up with the ham in the sleeper berth of their train to New York while Abner reads comic books in the lounge car, since the berth isn't big enough for all three of them.

Hams are everywhere, in fact, in *Li'l Abner*. The Yokums own the last surviving *Hammus Alabamus* pig in existence, a sow named Salomey, and its existence is constantly threatened by scheming gourmets, since it is the main and irreplaceable ingredient in Ecstasy Sauce, a mind-boggling concentrate of all that is delectable about Hammus Alabamus: an entire pig is needed to produce a single drop.

Hangovers

The hangover became a part of the day as well allowed-for as the Spanish siesta.
—F. SCOTT FITZGERALD

The only cure for a real hangover is death.
—ROBERT BENCHLEY

THE *FUNNY BAR Book and Guide to Mixed Drinks*, published in 1955 by *True* magazine with cartoons by Virgil Partch devotes a full ten pages to "The Common Household Hangover," describ-

Fig. 64 Hungover.
See also DRUNKS AND
DRUNKENNESS.

ing eight varieties, including the Thirsty Bedouin, the Eyeball Sonata, the Mechanical Expanding Throb, and the Anchored Butterfly Phenomenon. Though jocular, this typology is the most ambitious attempt I know of to describe and distinguish variations on a single form of discomfort. The *Funny Bar Book* also provides recipes for no fewer than seventeen hangover cures, of which all but one include at least a hair of the dog, and most a whole hank of hair, along with such ingredients as clam juice, egg yolks, heavy cream, vinegar, and spirits of ammonia. Hangover cures are of course a staple of alcoholic humor, which is why so many of them have funny names: Morning Glory, the Prairie Oyster, the Harvard Equalizer.

As with so many other afflictions, medical science can't decide whether to recommend heat or cold. The hot-water bottle seems to have entered into the iconography of hangovers early on—possibly the morning after it was invented. Dagwood, who likes to sleep on his side, sometimes wears a hot-water bottle strapped to his head like a helmet. Other cartoon characters like ice, preferably in the big-block form that ICEMEN delivered back in the days of iceboxes. In the *Hogan's Alley* cartoon of December 26, 1897, set on New Year's Day, even the *children* have hangovers. The star of *Hogan's*, the Yellow Kid—who can't be more than ten or eleven—has a block of ice tied on top of his head with a strip of cloth knotted under his chin; his scalp has melted a form-fitting concavity into the underside of the block; and the caption on his famous yellow nightshirt (this was before his creator, R. F. Outcault, switched to speech balloons) reads: "Say, dat ain't as funny as it looks, see?"

After the hot-water bottle, the most common visual sign of hangover in cartoons is heavy stubble, though other just-awakened characters are seldom drawn with stubble. If you didn't know better, you could get the idea that alcohol makes whiskers grow faster. Or maybe the stubble is meant to indicate that, even though a guy is still in pajamas, it's well past his usual hour of rising and shaving. When he does get around to shaving, he might be tempted to shave his tongue as well, as a man does in a 1950s cartoon from *True* magazine.

Another funny symptom is a hypersensitivity to NOISE. "Between the earsplitting chirps of that canary and pounding tick-tocks of the wall clock, my poor head is nigh ready to crack," thinks Major Hoople, in a strip dated January 1, 1935. "No, I couldn't stand the noise," says a hungover W. C. Fields, in one of his movies, when offered a Bromo-Seltzer. "Blondie! Make Daisy stop stomping around in here!" yells Dagwood, when the poor dog pads cautiously into the master bedroom. We drink to tune out reality, and sometimes we succeed, but it always returns with a vengeance.

Hash

> *Soup is still funny, but not as funny as it was a few years back.*
> *Hash is immensely humorous.*
> —IRVIN S. COBB, 1911

> *Bring us whatever you have. Anything but hash.*
> —*SINCE YOU WENT AWAY*, 1944

> *Catherine, I'm afraid you'll have to ask the blessing. The Lord knows I'm not grateful for turkey hash and I can't fool him.*
> —*A MAN CALLED PETER*, 1955

WEBSTER'S DESCRIBES the substance succinctly: "Chopped meat mixed with potatoes and browned." In the witty slang of 1930s soda jerks—the sort who referred to prunes as "looseners," yelled "fix the pumps!" to signal the arrival of a big-breasted customer, and relayed an order for spare ribs by calling for a "first lady"—roundabout ways of calling for hash included "Clean up the kitchen" and "The gentleman will take a chance." The usual gripe against hash, though, was not that it consisted of indeterminate leftovers, nor that it was intrinsically revolting, but that it was served too often by frugal land-ladies, housewives, and soup kitchens. As with any cheap food overused when times are tough, overfamiliarity breeds contempt.

Other slang terms for hash, in its heyday, included *dog food, Irish turkey, gooey, gook* (long predating the word's racist meaning), *mystery, slumgudgeon,* and the fatalistic *yesterday today and forever.* Not that jocular types avoided the word *hash* itself—far from it. One sign that hash used to be funny is the widespread use of the word in old slang as a disparaging term for cheap food in general. A *hash house* was any cheap restaurant or boardinghouse, whether or not it specialized in hash. Ditto with *hash factory, hash foundry, hash joint, hash mill,* and *hashery.* A *hash-slinger* or *hash-burner* was a cook, a *hashhound* was a chowhound, and to *wrestle hash* or *hash up* was to eat. I assume that even the most sordid hash house boasted forks, and all but the most barbaric hashhounds used them when consuming hash, but hands were sometimes referred to as *hash hooks.*

The heyday of hash humor in America was during World War I: wartime deprivation always seems to inspire a spate of jokes about bad food, and evidently hash was for civilians what creamed chipped beef was for soldiers. Between 1914 and 1918, the film industry gave us *Love and Hash; A Hash House Fraud; Hash and Havoc; Pass the Hash, Ann; Hash and Hypnotism; Mr. Jack, the Hash Magnet; Hash and Horrors; Hash House Mashers; A Hash House Romance;* and *The Hash House Mystery.* Not all of these films had much to say about hash—a *hash house,* as I say, was just a cheap eatery—but clearly people thought the word itself was funny.

Can hash destroy a marriage? Maybe not, but it can certainly focus the sort of resentments that lead to divorce. In "All About Hash" (1940), the Little Rascals find Mickey crying one Sunday evening, and he explains that every Sunday his impoverished family is reduced to eating hash, causing Mickey's father and mother to quarrel about her inadequacies as a cook and his as a breadwinner.

We know that the Whos down in Whoville were more grateful than Rev. Marshall in *A Man Called Peter*, since Marshall considered hash a reason to sit out Thanksgiving, whereas the Whos celebrated Christmas without even that lowliest of foodstuffs. In case you've forgotten, the Grinch is so ruthless that he steals not only the Whos' gifts and decorations but also their entire larder of food: roast beast, Who-pudding, and even their last can of Who-hash.

You can still buy hash, and order it in diners, but it's no longer especially inexpensive (if anything, it tends now to be overpriced, as if subject to a nostalgia surcharge). It no longer serves as a poverty food. Nowadays, the closest thing to hash in that capacity is probably Hamburger Helper, or ramen noodles—both of which have themselves become punch lines.

Hat Takes

A SIGHT GAG THAT seems to be on its way out, now that cartoon characters no longer routinely wear HATS, is the hat take: the sudden ascent of a hat when its wearer is surprised, but not surprised enough to faint. (For comic-strip fainting, see PLOPS.) Hat takes seldom appear outside of comics and cartoons, though now and then one will crop up in an especially cartoonish live-action film, such as Buster Keaton's 1922 short "The Blacksmith": through the magic of special effects, Buster's hat leaps off his head, flips 360 degrees, and returns to its point of departure.[26]

Three decades later, the 1950 Johnson Smith catalog offered a Jumping Hat Device for fifty cents postpaid. "Your hat slowly rises and bounces up and down on top of your head," promised the ad. "Push hat back down and a little later it comes to 'life' again." If that sounds a little obscene, it was probably supposed to; sometimes a hat take is no more or less than a G-rated erection. In the days when a glimpse of a woman's

[26] "The Blacksmith" also contains the supremely cartoonish gag of a child's helium balloon used in place of a jack to hold up the front end of a car while the tire is changed.

lower leg was a serious sexual thrill (see ANKLES), an especially clever use of the erectile hat take was to show a stiff breeze lifting a woman's skirts, exposing her ankles to a lucky male passerby while also lifting the man's hat. A comic postcard from the 1930s shows a woman's dress blowing up, revealing the hem of her petticoat, and the hats of *four* male bystanders leaping in response; the caption reads "Inflation is making everything go up around here."

Hat takes are one of the most quintessentially cartoonish of all cartoon clichés, and I have the numbers to prove it, since I recently devised a pseudoscientific formula for determining the cartoonishness of any object, situation, or event: you divide its incidence in comic strips (scored on a scale of 1 to 10) by its incidence in real life. By that measure, nothing is *less* cartoonish than FLATULENCE, which occurs all the time in real life but never happens at all in old comic strips. Flatulence, then, has a Katzenjammer Index (as I'll call it, in honor of the strip that invented more cartoon clichés than any other) of 0.1, the lowest possible:

Fig. 65 *Alphonse & Gaston,* 1903

Fig. 66

> comic-strip incidence: 1
> real-life incidence: 10

At the other extreme, we have the phenomenon of sheer surprise causing somebody's hat to fly off. In old comic strips, hat takes are extremely
common—the standard way, in fact, of registering surprise. And of
course they don't occur at all in real life, so their Katzenjammer Index is
a perfect 10:

> comic-strip incidence: 10
> real-life incidence: 1[27]

---

[27] One problem with this formula is the suggestion that the less common cartoon
clichés are therefore less cartoonish. In real life, as far as I'm aware, women hardly
ever burst out of giant phony cakes; if not quite as unheard-of as a hat take, or a dollar
bill flying off on tiny wings, the stripper in the cake is surely rare enough to rate an
incidence of 1.5 at most. But it's also fairly rare in cartoons—at most a 3. So its KI
is only 2.0, which wrongly makes it sound five times less cartoonish than hat takes.

Hats, Men's

> *No matter how desperate the predicament is, I am always very*
> *much in earnest about clutching my cane, straightening my derby*
> *hat and fixing my tie, even though I have just landed on my head.*
> —CHARLIE CHAPLIN

N OW THAT MEN no longer wear hats, we find it funny that they ever did. But what was so funny about them in their heyday? It may be a stretch to say that hats per se were once considered funny. In the first half of the twentieth century, hats were standard apparel for men, so their omnipresence in silent comedies, for instance, proves nothing in itself. But when you look at how hats function in those comedies, you notice that they provided a lot more humor than, for instance, neckties, on the face of it a funnier class of garment (more phallic, less functional) or even PANTS (certainly the funnier *word*: "pants").

If it weren't for the evidence of old movies, we'd find it hard to believe that there *was* a time, little more than half a century ago, when middle-class men felt obliged to wear a hat when appearing in public—when they would have felt underdressed, even naked, without one. That's the point of a George Price cartoon that appeared in his 1942 collection, *It's Smart to Be People*. The scene is a while-you-wait shoe repair shop where customers sit in little booths that afford them privacy below the waist, since even now most city dwellers feel underdressed in public without shoes. One customer, however, sprawls on the floor of the booth so that only his legs and decently shod feet are visible—because (as a clerk explains to another customer) *he's* having his *hat* repaired.

A hat makes its wearer look taller; it also insists on the wearer's importance. There was a time when doffing your hat—on entering a church, on encountering a lady, on singing the national anthem—was universally understood as a way of showing respect by humbling yourself. Taking off your hat involves a diminution, a loss of literal and metaphoric stature, as Kafka said somewhere, and no one knew more than Kafka about catastrophic losses of stature. One reason panhandlers of yore held out their hats—as opposed to paper bags, tin cans, or Big Gulp cups—was that the hat underscored with special poignancy the social distance between beggar and prospective benefactor, and the loss of dignity involved in begging.

"In your hat" (a shortened form of "Go shit in your hat") was a popular insult in the 1920s and '30s. You might think "[Go shit] in your shoe" would be funnier, both because the words alliterate and because the recommended act would be harder to perform, and so (for me, anyhow) more tempting to picture. But SHOES are not symbolic of their wearers' dignity; shoes are already acquainted with shit.

As for humbling someone else, denting someone's dignity, one of the archetypal ways to do it was to knock off his top hat with a snowball, stick, or BRICK. Most hat humor involves the squashing or dislodging of a hat. When the prankster is an urchin and the victim a toff, the hat will be as grand as possible. Otherwise, comedy hats tend to be forlorn, misshapen things, either comically battered (like the hats of Chaplin's tramps, or Beckett's), or too small for their owners' heads, like the small TIN CAN that serves Happy Hooligan as a better-than-nothing hat substitute. Often an undersized hat calls attention to an overgrown ego: the hat stands for its wearer's actual position in the world, the head for his incongruously swollen self-conception. But not always. On hoboes, where the funny hat is as essential an accessory as the old shoes with toes protruding, the hat symbolizes the pitiable modicum of self-respect its downtrodden wearer manages to cling to. Happy Hooligan's tin can doesn't offer much protection from the elements, but proves invaluable as a shock absorber. Happy is forever getting

Fig. 67 *Pocket Cartoon Course*, 1943

conked on the head with a nightstick, and since his hat is always crushed in the process, we know that it must have absorbed part of the blow. Incidentally, fun-loving urchins should be warned, before dropping a BRICK out the window onto the head of a top-hatted passerby, that top hats sometime act like trampolines, sending the brick straight back up into the jaw of the prankster without the passerby feeling a thing.

Most of the great comedic acts of the silent-film and early-talkie eras recognized the symbolic status and comedic possibilities of hats and hat abuse. In addition to Chaplin, think of W. C. Fields and his running joke about dilapidated hats. Think of Laurel and Hardy, who were constantly knocking off each other's hats and those of third parties—as in *From Soup to Nuts*, where the two are hired as waiters at a lavish dinner party and Laurel keeps knocking off the chef's hat because Hardy has told him it's bad manners to wear a hat indoors. Sometimes their hat fights escalate into hat wars, as in *Hats Off*, where respectable businessmen and other strangers find themselves caught up in the duo's slapstick frenzy. In *Safety Last*, when Harold Lloyd scales the skyscraper, he wears not only his nerdy glasses but also a leisurely boater, the better to emphasize the incongruity of the character and the feat he's attempting. One of the most memorable scenes in *Duck Soup* is the one where Chico and Harpo Marx antagonize a lemonade vendor, at one point setting fire to his straw hat.

For a long time, hats were the strongest fashion statement permitted to males, and in the case of long-forgotten fashions, many of the statements have become inscrutable. What is the odd crownlike item that Archie's friend Jughead wears, for instance, and what if anything was it originally supposed to suggest about Jughead? What about the customized boater worn by one of the tellers in *The Bank Dick*—a straw hat with the top cut out so that the top of the teller's head shows through? That hat is still funny, but you can't help feeling you're missing part of the joke.

Hats, Women's

Her hat is a creation that will never go out of style;
it will just look ridiculous year after year.
—FRED ALLEN

LIKE ALL GARMENTS whose function is not strictly utilitarian, but symbolic or expressive, hats are asking to be laughed at—women's hats especially. Men's hats, even when they serve a comic function, are seldom funny in themselves; they can be dilapidated, or too small for the heads they crown, but mostly they function as symbols of dignity, or prosthetic enhancers of stature, like elevator shoes. Their humor potential has less to do with their appearance than with their susceptibility to disrespect or mistreatment: they sit there just begging to be knocked off, smashed, sat upon, run over, set on fire.

Women's hats, however, are not symbols of dignity but forms of self-expression—fashion statements, as we say now, and until recently the loudest such statements most women permitted themselves. These hats revealed a grandiosity, a need to feel special, that men tend to keep *under* their hats. Women's hats have always been seen by male humorists as

Invisible Tête-à-têtes, or advantages of large Leghorns.

Fig. 68

embodying everything funny about women per se—it's hard to imagine a drag queen feeling fully dressed without one—and most of the traits that men ridicule in women can be embodied by those hats. A Carmen Miranda fruit basket hat suggests that the woman is bananas. A bunch of gaudy feathers indicates the vain and feather-brained, though among actual birds it is of course the males who sport the gaudiest plumage.

If you want to characterize a woman as maddeningly indecisive, show her in a department store trying on hat after hat. (Rube Goldberg once drew a cartoon of a fat, matronly angel, freshly arrived in heaven, trying on one halo after another while a grumpy male angel gripes, "You idiot, can't you see they're all alike?") If you want to joke about what SPEND-THRIFTS women are, show one coming home with a stack of boxes—one of them always a circular hatbox—and a cute remark. If you want to show how thoughtless a woman is, let her fail to remove her large, obstructive hat when she goes to the movies. If you want to emphasize that her rosy beauty is defended by thorns, make a joke about hatpins.

Another joke about women's hats—and women's fashions generally—is that even the funkiest are mass-produced, and sooner or later the would-be-unique wearer is bound to encounter another woman wearing the exact same thing. A five-panel 1958 cartoon from the *Saturday Evening Post* shows a woman on a windy day chasing after her odd hat (it looks like a sombrero with a dove perched on its crown), only to abandon it in disgust when she sees another, identical hat blowing along beside hers. It's not a terribly funny cartoon, but real humorists have generated real humor from the irony of people trying to buy uniqueness. Think of Dr. Seuss's great parable "The Sneetches," or Flannery O'Connor's even greater parable, "Everything That Rises Must Converge," in which a smug, routinely racist southern matron in the early 1960s is proud of her garish new hat (which reminds her son of "a cushion with the stuffing out"), until she spots a black woman wearing an identical hat.

Head Injuries

*The savage who cracked his enemy over the head with a tomahawk
and shouted "Ha! Ha!" was the first humorist.*
—STEPHEN LEACOCK

I N THE 1920S AND '30S, before he decided to focus on picture
books, Dr. Seuss wrote and illustrated a series of spoofs for magazines like *Judge* and *Vanity Fair*. In a brief essay on "Monosyllabic
Ejaculations," he explains how he once attempted to pass himself off
as the Prince of Wales and how the Queen exposed the imposture by
having a pot of geraniums dropped on his head, causing him to exclaim
"OOP!" (A true Englishman, he claimed, would have reacted to that
particular head injury with a "POUF!") In an accompanying illustration,
Seuss offers a taxonomy of interjections: a gentleman exclaims "AWK"
when beaned by a load of BRICKS, "OOOF" when beaned by an alarm
clock, and "OOP" only when beaned by a Listerine bottle. It's a silly but
relatively brainy take on a mishap that appeals most to lowbrow humorists. Head injuries have always been a favorite of cartoonists and slapstick
comedians, maybe because the head is where the person really "is." And
it's certainly the locus of more than its share of annoying behavior, since
most obnoxious people are obnoxious mainly by way of their words and
facial expressions. This encyclopedia doesn't condone violence as a means
of conflict resolution, but I do consider the impulse to punch someone in
the mouth, or swat him in the head (as one swats a malfunctioning TV
set), more natural and so perhaps more forgivable than the impulse to
sock him in the stomach or stomp on his toes.

It's not even an especially sadistic impulse, since the skull, considering its contents, is surprisingly insensitive to pain. In the name of research, I just noogied myself as hard as I could, and though it hurt, it
didn't hurt as much as stubbing a toe, to say nothing of barking a shin.
(And unlike those pains, that of a noogie subsides at once. It may be
the least cruel of common school pranks.) One of the conventions of old
comics is that the head is as resilient as the rump, which is why charac-

ters who slip on banana peels are as likely to land on their heads as their tails. Characters struck by motorcars also tend to land headfirst.

Unlike a kick in the rump, a cartoon blow to the head tends to raise a funny bump. Animated cartoons will show the bump erupting, but in comic strips it tends to appear, fully formed, from one panel to the next. The provocation, the assault, the bump. Not always, though: E. C. Segar, whose Sunday strip *Sappo* tended to consist of many small panels, saw the laff potential of a gradually erupting bump. In one installment, little Sappo's huge and violent wife comes looking for him with a baseball bat at the Hardboiled Husband's Club (to which Sappo has gained entrée by lying about his home life and who wears the PANTS in his marriage). Our hero goes downstairs to face her, returns claiming to have bawled her out, and is praised by his fellow members—until they notice that, over the course of four panels, a big bump has erupted on Sappo's bald head. In another strip, the little SAP refuses to take off the new toupee his wife detests, standing firm ("You won't gain a thing by getting rough! My wig is gonna stay right where it is!") even after she clubs him on the head with her ever-ready ROLLING PIN; but the bump that erupts on his scalp over the course of the next six panels finally displaces the toupee for her.

Fig. 69 *Nize Baby,* 1926

Henpecked Husbands

Many a man that could rule
a hundred million strangers with an iron hand
is careful to take off his shoes in the front hallway
when he comes home late at night.
—MR. DOOLEY

The American woman is my theme,
and how she dominates the male,
how he tries to go away but always
comes back for more.
—JAMES THURBER

OF ALL THE THINGS that struck our grandparents—or at least our grandfathers—as funny, few have lost as much of their humor value as the henpecked husband. I've never been married, so maybe I'm missing the joke, but it's striking how seldom we encounter that joke nowadays: it used to be *everywhere*—in early silent films, on Broadway, on the funnies page, in old Warner Bros. cartoons (one of many reminders that those cartoons were originally for grownups), in the gag cartoons and light verse in magazines from *The New Yorker* down to *Playboy*, and down even further to such bottom-of-the-barrel publications as *Snappy* and *Titter*, which make *Playboy* look like *The New Yorker*.

Even the term "henpecked husband" is on its way out. We still say "pussy-whipped," but the two terms aren't synonymous. "Pussy-whipped" is the premarital equivalent, and differs from "henpecked" as much as single life differs from married. A man is pussy-whipped when sexual dependency causes him to take orders from his lover. A henpecked husband, as a rule, isn't even getting sex in exchange for his obedience (or no more sex than necessary for his wife to breed and brood): on the contrary, the joke is that he married for sex, when his

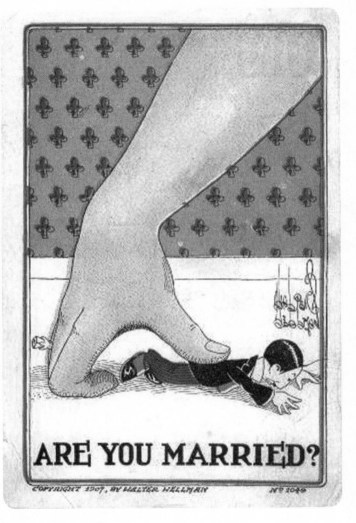

Fig. 70

wife was a spring chicken, and now he's stuck with a fat, bossy, vociferous hen.[28]

W. C. Fields, in his best comedies, plays a henpecked husband with an unbearably shrewish wife. He defers to her reflexively, no matter how vituperative she becomes, though when she's out of earshot he claims— like so many funny husbands—to be his own man. Here he is as Harold Bissonette in *It's a Gift* (1934), in the kitchen with his daughter Mildred while his wife screams at him from the living room:

> Amelia: Harold, are you listening to me?
> Harold: Oh yes, yes, dear, go on, go on . . .
> Amelia: What did I say last?
> Harold: Yes, yes, every word of it, yes.
> Mildred: I never knew such an ungrateful father.
> Harold: [to his daughter] Listen, you've all got to realize one thing: that *I* [glances tentatively toward his wife, then whispers so she won't hear] am the master of this household.
> Amelia: Harold!
> Harold: Yes, dear?

And so on. The closest Harold comes to standing up to his wife is sneaking out of the apartment during her rants, or agreeing to her commands without intending to obey them; he is never more endearing than when

---

[28] My laff-loving editor, Cal, takes issue with my contention that the harpy-wife-and-henpecked-husband cliché is, if not extinct, at least endangered. In Cal's opinion— compounded of what mixture of reflection, observation, and hard-won life experience he alone can say—the cliché still flourishes but has morphed into a different animal, "the Stupid Husband who's always getting things wrong around the house in modern TV commercials, causing the All-Knowing Wife to roll her head and smile indulgently, infantilizing her man."

Cal and I seldom disagree about our culture's basic Humor genome, but according to *my* lab notes, the eye-rolling wife and the rolling-pin-wielding wife are only second cousins in the teeming clan of marriage jokes. But the cliché Cal describes—so common nowadays in feebly humorous commercials—will surely have an entry in the updated laffopedia I hope to bring out in twenty years, if it is my happiness to live to 2032.

at his most passive-aggressive. As for Amelia and her counterparts in *The Bank Dick* and *Man on the Flying Trapeze*, they change their tune abruptly at the end, after Fields strikes it rich, as if that's all they ever wanted from him. And we Americans do tend to think that money can solve everything, but it's hard to believe that Fields himself found the domestic bliss at the end of his comedies plausible even by the logic of farce. Surely the death of his spouse (and if possible, their offspring) would do more for the happiness of Egbert Souse in *The Bank Dick* or Harold Bissonette in *It's a Gift* than any amount of sudden wealth. The happy endings of those films have a way of undercutting the satiric portrayal of carping wives, suggesting that the carping is a natural result of poverty. In retrospect, the wives look less like harpies than like the sort of tough-love coaches who berate and belittle their players in an effort to motivate them. If a football coach is justified in screaming, then why not a life coach?

Now and then you get a comedy husband whose spirit has been broken so thoroughly that it doesn't even occur to him to lie in public about who wears the PANTS. At the beginning of *Sons of the Desert* (1933), Laurel and Hardy attend a lodge meeting where members swear a sacred oath to attend the upcoming convention in Chicago. Stan starts crying and confesses to Ollie his fear that his wife won't let him go.

> Ollie: Do you have to ask your wife everything?
> Stan: Well, if I didn't ask her, I wouldn't know what she wanted me to do.

It's a funny line, but there's a limit to how much humor you can get from a ridiculous character who admits so candidly to his ridiculousness. Ollie, as it turns out, is every bit as henpecked, but won't admit it: "Why don't you pattern your life after mine? I go places and do things, and then tell my wife. Every man should be the king in his own castle." That's more like it, thinks the viewer—because hypocrisy is funnier than honesty, and self-deception funnier by far than self-knowledge. Incongruity isn't always funny, but it's almost always an essential ingredient of humor.

Hiccups

*Anyone will be glad to admit that he knows nothing about beagling,
or the Chinese stock market, or ballistics, but there is not a man or
woman alive who does not claim to know how to cure hiccoughs.*
—ROBERT BENCHLEY, "STOP THOSE HICCOUGHS!" (1934)

ANYONE WHO WORRIES about spilling tea on the hostess at a snooty tea party because of a sudden attack of the hiccups is advised to train on the Lehrenkraus Hiccough Machine, one of many mad contraptions imagined by Dr. Seuss in his early days as a cartoonist for *Judge* magazine. With its spring-loaded platform and arms to shake the trainee by the shoulders and the scruff, the machine is so good at simulating "the hiccough contortions" that after a couple of months on the machine, with a brimming teacup in hand and a tailor's dummy standing in for the snooty DOWAGER, anyone will be able to hiccup his way through an actual tea party without spilling a drop.

Hiccup, like *ketchup*, is a phonetic respelling. *Hiccough*, like *cupboard* or *breakfast*, is a philologically transparent compound whose derivation is obscured by its pronunciation. But if *hiccough* is semantically richer, *hiccup* is more onomatopoetic, and therefore—since the noise it imitates is funny—funnier.

Spell it as you will, a hiccup is a high-pitched and involuntary sound, and funniest when produced by someone with a low-pitched voice, like the booming title character of *The Great Gildersleeve*, a popular radio sitcom in the 1940s and '50s, who hiccups throughout a thirty-minute episode from the show's first season. Hiccup humor is naturally most common in media involving a soundtrack: TV, radio, movies. What makes the undignified squeak especially funny is that it's not just involuntary, like SNEEZING, but periodic, like a drip from a slow-dripping faucet, or the swipes of windshield wipers set on Intermittent, or the eruption of Old Faithful. Thanks to this combination, hiccups remind us like few other bodily events that the human body is a machine.

Another funny consequence of this intermittency, at least with hiccups recurring at long intervals, is that the afflicted have time to delude themselves again and again, as they try one cure after another, that the latest cure has finally done the trick. Gildersleeve tries every remedy conceivable (including the one I swear by: drinking a tall glass of water very slowly), but always in vain. This aspect of hiccups—the profusion of folk remedies—is naturally the one dwelt on by prose humorists on the rare occasions when they dwell on the affliction at all:

> To date, I have been advised to perform the following feats to cure hiccoughs:
> Bend the body backward until the head touches the floor, and whistle in reverse.
> Place the head in a pail of water and inhale twelve times deeply.
> Drink a glass of milk from the right hand with the right arm twisted around the neck until the milk enters the mouth from the left side.
> Hop, with the feet together, up and down a flight of steps ten times, screaming loudly at each hop.
> Roll down a long, inclined lawn, snatching a mouthful of grass up each time the face is downward.
> —ROBERT BENCHLEY, "STOP THOSE HICCOUGHS!"

Sometimes hiccups are a symptom of some other problem, and then the trick is to address their underlying cause. In *Millionaire Playboy* (1940), Joe Penner plays a man so bashful he gets hiccups any time a woman kisses him. In *That Uncertain Feeling* (1941), Merle Oberon plays an unhappily married woman who sees a PSYCHIATRIST about her frequent hiccups, and with his help realizes—as, implausibly, she'd never noticed on her own—that the attacks are always triggered by anger at her husband.

Like the smoke alarm that so often adds its voice to the pandemonium during kitchen mishaps, hiccups often serve as a complication—as one more funny thing that can go wrong. The marketing consultant J. Colossal McGenius (see CHATTERBOXES) not only charges ten thousand dollars a word for his advice; he charges the same for each of his hiccups. Lucy Ricardo gets the hiccups when she cries. And also when she drinks too much Vitameatavegamin, since of course, in comedy (though not—as far as I've observed—in real life), people hiccup when they're drunk.

High Culture

> *I've always hated*
> *That overrated*
> *Pretentious music, complicated. . . .*
> *Give me a Sousa strain*
> *Instead of a Wagner pain. . . .*
> *I want to hear a Yankee Doodle tune,*
> *The only music I can understand. . . .*
> *You may have your William Tell,*
> *And Faust and Lohengrin as well,*
> *But I'll take a Yankee Doodle tune for mine.*
> —GEORGE M. COHAN, "I WANT TO HEAR
> A YANKEE DOODLE TUNE," 1912

THOUGH HE WROTE the music as well as the words to his songs, George M. Cohan—who also gave us such bumptious classics as "Over There," "The Yankee Doodle Boy," and "You're a Grand Old Flag"—seems to have been a bona fide vulgarian where music was concerned. Or else a shameless demagogue. A man who cites the *William Tell* overture as an exemplar of snooty highbrow music, and considers Sousa's marches the high-water mark of "the popular melody craze," betrays a deafness as bewildering in a composer as Beethoven's. As a rule, though, songwriters exaggerate their philistinism. Cole Porter wouldn't have written "Red, Hot and Blue" (1936)—and his audiences couldn't have fully enjoyed it—if they hadn't known and cared more about Wagner than most of us do now:

> *Due to the tragic lowness of my brow*
> *All music that's highbrow*
> *Gets me upset*
> *Each time I hear Stravinsky's,*
> *I hurry to Minsky's*
> *And try to forget.* . . .
> *I've no desire to hear*
> *Flagstad's Brünnhilde, dear,*
> *She waves a pretty spear,*
> *But she's not*
> *Red, hot*
> *And blue.*
> —COLE PORTER, "RED, HOT AND BLUE," 1936

When educated lyricists dismiss high art and sing the praises of pop culture (something poets also do—poets as dissimilar as Philip Larkin and Frank O'Hara), it's a kind of slumming, or, more charitably, a kind of longing for a pastoral idyll, like all the songs by and for longtime New Yorkers that celebrate the simple life far from the bustle and noise of the big city.

Just as there are sacrilegious jokes that only the pious find funny, Porter's irreverence toward high culture depends for its effect partly on shock value; it assumes an audience accustomed to genuflecting at the altar of high art. There was a tiny thrill of transgression at name-checking people like Wagner at all in a Broadway musical: he stood for everything that pop culture refuses to stand for, or sit through, and his name sticks out in a show tune like a portrait of the Virgin Mary in a brothel.

Twenty years after "Red, Hot and Blue," Chuck Berry released "Roll Over Beethoven." By that time, though, our culture had dumbed itself down so completely that the existence in the distant past of a composer named Beethoven and another named Tchaikovsky was the only collective knowledge Berry could assume on the subject of classical music.

In "I'm Tickled Silly," a surprisingly modern-sounding 1921 tribute to slapstick comedy—and more generally to the virtues of an adjustable brow (now high, now low)—Ira Gershwin drops the tiresome populist pretext of being as uncultured as the most boorish of his listeners. Like most good lyricists, Gershwin was a literate and cultured person, and in the song he admits his membership in the educated class even as he chides that class for its cultural snobbery—a more appealing and convincing stance than the reverse snobbery that so many show tunes adopt.

> *All the highbrows call 'em frightful,*
> *But for my part they're delightful. . . .*
> *I'm a gent, and I'm a scholar,*
> *Yet I'd part with my last dollar*
> *Just to see a slapstick artist frolic . . .*
> *With young Lloyd or Keaton clowning*
> *(Though you know your Keats and Browning),*
> *You'll say slapstick hath a charm.*

Hillbillies

AMERICA BECAME OBSESSED with hillbillies in the early 1930s—an odd fad, you would think, for a nation in the grips of the Great Depression, but the hillbilly stereotype was in some ways an idyllic one, a pastoral of contented and voluntary poverty, and must have been consoling to the millions of Americans suddenly facing the involuntary kind.

The Ozark way of life first came to the widespread attention of city folk via broadcasts of "mountain music." Where earlier treatments of the hillbilly theme (such as *Our Hospitality*, a 1923 Buster Keaton film) focused on feuds of the Hatfield/McCoy variety, the music generated interest in the hillbilly lifestyle and worldview. By 1932, the listening audience was ready for *Lum & Abner*, a radio sitcom about two dim-witted hillbillies in Pine Ridge, Arkansas. The stereotype as we know it had already coalesced when, in 1933, Al Capp introduced a hillbilly character into *Joe Palooka*, the comic strip he was ghost-drawing for Ham Fisher. Briefly given a chance to script the strip as well, Capp invented Big Leviticus, and liked the character so much that he decided to leave Fisher

Fig. 71 Hillbilly family.
See also TRAVELING SALESMEN, SHOTGUN WEDDINGS, YOKELS AND HICKS.

and create his own strip—the one that became *Li'l Abner*—thereby touching off a feud between the two cartoonists as bitter as any between the Yokums and the Scraggs.

Although it's impossible now to imagine Al Capp's imagination thriving so luxuriantly in any other setting, the first syndicate to whom he showed his strip wanted him to lose the hillbilly angle. They recognized Capp's talent and offered him $250 a week—quite a lot of money for an unknown cartoonist in 1934—but only on condition that he keep out of Dogpatch.

Luckily for us, Capp refused, found another syndicate, and touched off a nationwide craze for hillbilly humor. In the months that intervened between the debut of Big Leviticus and the debut of *Li'l Abner*, Billy DeBeck relocated his already-long-running strip *Barney Google* to the Ozarks, and introduced a mountain man named Snuffy Smith who, together with his wife, Loweezy, promptly stole the show. Suddenly, and for many years to come, two of the funniest strips on the funnies page focused on hillbillies.

Thanks to those strips, and rip-offs like *Pokey Oakie, Possum Holler, Ozark Ike,* and *Looie Lazybones,* and animated series like *Huckleberry Hound* and *The Hillbilly Bears,* and live-action series like *Hee-Haw* and *The Beverly Hillbillies,* we know a lot about mountain folk. We know, for example, that they seldom if ever take baths, and in general are bewildered by all forms of indoor plumbing. We know that they brew their own hooch, and use their shotguns not just to feud with NEIGHBORS or escort TRAVELING SALESMEN to the altar, but to keep revenue officers away from their stills. We know they eat things most of us would rather not—things like turnips, possums, and SKUNKS.

Above all, we know that their menfolk are comically lazy. Pappy Yokum, Li'l Abner's worthless father, neither bathes himself nor clips his own toenails, leaving both those chores to his long-suffering wife. As for Li'l Abner himself, if he doesn't dread work as much as he dreads marriage, it's because no one is after him to get a job. Now and then he earns a little as a mattress tester, but otherwise he's blissfully unemployed. The same dynamic prevails in the Snuffy Smith household (which, again, evolved alongside the Yokum household): feckless daddy, hardworking mother, and simple-minded son (Jughaid, who wears a cast-iron skillet as a cap). Jethro Bodine, the idiot son on *The Beverly Hillbillies,* bucks the trend: there's no need for *him* to work, since his family has struck it rich, but his delusions of grandeur impel him again and again to pursue some glamorous vocation: brain surgeon, astronaut, "double-nought spy."

The hillbilly craze outlived the Depression because even when times are going well people like to think about bumpkins and hicks. No other figure of fun offers better support for the "superiority" theory of humor, which holds, in the words of its most articulate exponent, Thomas Hobbes, that "the passion of laughter is nothing else but sudden glory arising from some sudden conception of some eminency in ourselves, by comparison with the infirmity of others." Ever since it became unacceptable to make fun of blacks and Jews, hillbillies—or, as we say more often nowadays, rednecks or white trash—have been the easiest group to feel superior to, of all those you're still allowed to make fun of in polite society.

Hoboes

> *Chief Bloberger surveyed a party of hoboes coming down the Great
> Northern tracks. "Here they come, hog fat and crummy, short pipes
> and red noses. Won't work, ain't allowed to shoot 'em, and if you
> don't feed 'em, they'll burn your barn daown."*
> —*CAPTAIN BILLY'S WHIZ BANG*, 1922

MOST OF THE laughingstocks discussed in this encyclopedia
fall into one of two classes: things that people like, and like
to think about; and things that people hate but can't help
thinking about. The surfeit of GOLF humor is due less to anything intrinsically funny about the sport than to the fact that many humorists have
been golfers and welcomed any opportunity to think about the sport. But
there are also lots of jokes about TOOTHACHES AND DENTISTRY, because
one purpose of humor is to make light of things we hate and fear.

It's hard to say which class hoboes belonged to. They were feared, but
envied, too. Like HILLBILLIES, they embodied a pastoral alternative to

Fig. 72 Hoboes, traveling in pairs

Fig. 73 Hoboes, traveling in pairs

the rat race and inspired fantasies of dropping out. Young men hungry for adventure *chose* to be hoboes, or at least to get a taste of hobo life, like the hero of *Sullivan's Travels*, a Preston Sturges comedy from 1941 about an idealistic director who slums as a hobo (toting a **BINDLESTICK**, jumping trains, and so on) in order to "know trouble." Like Sullivan—and like young men who join the army in quest of "adventure," or any other romanticists who try to crash a subculture they've been idealizing—many hobo wannabes must have gotten a bigger helping of the lifestyle than they expected.

Like the army, incidentally, hoboes used to recruit, and their ads could be as misleading as Uncle Sam's. "The Big Rock Candy Mountain," written by Harry McClintock and recorded by him in 1928, on the eve of the Great Depression (though its peak of popularity was 1939, after that historical trauma had run its course), was not just a hobo pipe dream but an elaborate lie spun to lure a boy into the hobo life. Just *why* the older hobo wanted to lure the boy into that life is made explicit by the song's last lyric, omitted from McClintock's recorded version and subsequent recordings:

I've hiked and hiked and wandered, too,
But I ain't seen any candy.
I've hiked and hiked till my feet are sore
And I'll be damned if I hike any more
To be buggered sore like a hobo's whore
In the Big Rock Candy Mountain.

With that verse safely forgotten, what we all remember is the idyllic vision of a vagrant's paradise, where "the handouts grow on bushes" and "the boxcars all are empty / and the sun shines every day" and "all the cops have wooden legs / and the bulldogs all have rubber teeth / and the hens lay soft-boiled eggs" and "little streams of alcohol / come trickling down the rocks" and "there's a lake of stew / and of whiskey too" and "they hung the jerk / that invented work." It really is a clever song, one that vividly evokes the hardships of hobo life by telling a series of obvious lies about it.

Actual hoboes were unlikely to idealize the life, or idealize themselves. According to H. L. Mencken, hoboes in the 1930s had a merciless nomenclature for the various subtypes of their subculture: "Those who gaze longingly into restaurants or bakeshops while they gnaw at prop breadcrusts are *nibblers*. Those who dig into garbage cans are *divers*. Those who pretend to have fainted from hunger are *flickers*. Those with hard-luck stories are *weepers*."

If it were anyone but Mencken, author of a magisterial study of *The American Language*, I'd think he confused hoboes with BUMS, who in the standard distinction are vagrants who stay put instead of traveling. Bums are less exotic. No one glamorizes them or their way of life; no bored schoolboy or office boy or shoeshine boy dreams of becoming a bum. Hoboes inspired less contempt than bums and more fear, and it's not hard to see why a housewife might have been frightened by a scruffy stranger pounding on her front door in the middle of the day and asking for a handout. Hoboes lived outside of society and its laws, and some resorted to thieving—especially, in old comic strips and cartoons anyhow, thieving pies from windowsills. Homeowners in those same cartoons and strips often kept ferocious white bulldogs with names like Spike and

Towser to guard their pies from hoboes—hence the wishful line in "The Big Rock Candy Mountain" about bulldogs with rubber teeth.

Honeymoons and Newlyweds

> *Maybe the bride bed brings despair*
> *Because each an ideal image brings*
> *And finds a real image there.*
> —WILLIAM BUTLER YEATS

THE BASIS OF most wedding-night humor is the adolescent sense that the newlyweds, though now officially entitled in the eyes of church and state alike to do what they're about to do, are about to do something naughty—that, just as we are always naked underneath our clothes, sex itself is always sinful. Perhaps at least a vestige of that adolescent sense of transgression and taboo is necessary to keep sex exciting; perhaps, once the act no longer seems even a little naughty, the honeymoon is over. In any case, our culture has always done its best to ensure that newlyweds start out, at least, with an exhilarating sense of naughtiness. The SHOES thrown at the groom as he leaves the church are a form of persecution for the unspeakably filthy intentions he's nursing, the unthinkably wicked thing he's going to do that very night. The TIN CANS tied to the newlyweds' getaway car are like a leper's bell, proclaiming to the world that another pair of degenerates is embarking on a career of depravity.

For most of the era this guide is concerned with, movies weren't even allowed to show married couples sleeping in the same bed, so naturally Hollywood had some trouble representing honeymoons. In *A Smattering of Ignorance* (1940), Oscar Levant described one cinematic solution:

> [A] boat is seen pulling out of New York harbor, then there is a shot of the Savoy in London, the Champs Elysees in Paris, the pigeons at St. Peter's in Rome and finally the Statue of Liberty. In this way the Will Hays office is appeased, and the audience is given to understand that a marriage has been consummated.

Novelty postcards were almost as coy. I have one from the '50s that is divided into a triptych (Fig. 74). In the first panel, we see a couple speeding toward their honeymoon destination in a car marked "JUST MAR-RIED." In the second panel, they're shown undressing eagerly in a hotel room. In the third panel, though, they're running across a beach to the water: turns out they were only getting undressed in order to put on their bathing suits. At the top of the card, in bold black capitals, a disapproving caption: "WHAT DID YOU THINK?"

If there's less wedding-night humor in our time than fifty years ago, it's not so much because we're less neurotic about sex; it's because no one waits for marriage anymore to start doing it. There have always been couples who didn't wait till marriage, but wedding guests used to assume that the bride and groom were about to get naked in each other's presence for the very first time. Most of the old just-married gags were based on that premise— the groom's impatience, for example. "Hurry up, Honey, it's getting soft!" says a young man to his wife as he hastens up the front steps of a hotel . . . with a carton of ice cream. (This cartoon, from around 1940, appeared on an arcade card—the size of a postcard, but not intended to be mailed, and

Fig. 74 Honeymooners

thus able to be a bit racier than American postcards were permitted to be in that era. The couple aren't explicitly identified as newlyweds or even as married, but it nicely encapsulates the mixture of horniness, urgency, and anxiety that characterizes new husbands in the humor of that era.)

Another result of waiting till marriage is the wedding-night disappointment. In an early magazine cartoon by Hank Ketcham, from his apprenticeship as a freelance gag cartoonist before the birth of Dennis the Menace, a new husband sits on the hotel bed and looks sadly through the open doorway of the bathroom. We can't see his bride, but we hear her: "Don't look so sad, Freddie. Lots of girls wear them." (The moral: Never marry anyone you haven't gotten to second base with.) Sometimes it's the bride who is disappointed, though never—in the mainstream humor of the era—by the size of the groom's equipment. Since they're both supposed to be virgins, she'd have no basis of comparison for that anyhow, and it does seem that men worried less about penis size fifty or a hundred years ago, though of course we can't draw any conclusions from the absence of jokes on the subject in back issues of the *Saturday Evening Post*.

Still, it's clear that men have always worried about their performance. In the deeply dumb gags-and-gals magazines of the 1940s and '50s, you find cartoon grooms sitting sheepishly on dunce stools in dunce caps, while the sexy naked bride sits in bed and smolders. In these cartoons, as in more highbrow ones concerning honeymoons, the usual way of showing that a couple is just married is to show a suitcase labeled "JUST MARRIED." Has there ever been such a suitcase in real life? Maybe not, but it's a useful shorthand, like putting "XXX" on a bottle to show that it holds liquor.

There were of course plenty of jokes about the newlyweds' insatiability—how they lose track of the clock, and even of the calendar, in their rented love nest. There were also lots of jokes about NINCOMPOOPS—men so naïve as to have no idea what to do on the wedding night. An arcade card from the 1940s or '50s shows a sexy young bride in a hotel bed, naked except for an impossibly transparent negligee. The nerdy young groom (striped pajamas, glasses, overbite) is on the phone: "Yes father, we're at the hotel and she's in bed. Now what do I do?" It sounds implausible, but such things have happened—most famously to John Ruskin, the great nineteenth-century art critic, whose Victorian upbringing was so exemplary that it wasn't until his wedding night that he learned, to his horror, that real women, unlike statuary, have pubic hair and labia. Unable to consummate the marriage, Ruskin returned his wife to her parents. (She went on to marry a friend of his and have eight children.)

When the groom has to call his father for instructions, like a pilot calling flight control, the joke is clearly on the groom. Likewise when Li'l Abner spends his wedding night reading comic books. Sometimes, though, it's harder to say which newlywed is the butt of the joke—for instance, when the groom is more interested in FISHING than in fucking. This joke nicely balances the ones about insatiability; they flank the truth on either side at a respectful distance. The truth is that no man who likes women at all is more interested in fishing than in consummating his marriage, but few are so single-mindedly and indefatigably horny that they aren't ready for a break from sex, and from constant intimacy, after that first superheated night. Maybe it was different in the days before premarital sex became the norm: maybe, if you've been saving all your love for your lawfully wedded mate, you have more at your disposal when the time comes.

The fact remains, though, that even the most virile men eventually tire—not of sex itself, of course, but of specific partners, when they enjoy unlimited access to those partners. And this temporary exhaustion of lust, during a trip devoted to intensive sex, is ominous and poignant because it prefigures the more gradual death of passion—and all too often of simple affection—in the marriage as a whole. Some of the strangest postcards ever sent are the several series of honeymoon progress reports using the phases of the moon as a metaphor for the mutual waning of enthusiasm. My favorite series, from 1908, shows the same pair of newlyweds in a succession of tableaux, always outdoors and usually seated, with a big yellow cartoon moon low on the horizon behind them. Only in the first card, Full Moon, are the newlyweds smiling and cuddling. By the next card, On the Wane, she's sulking and facing away from him, he's scowling, and the moon, though barely nibbled, already looks unhappy and uneasy. There follow First Quarter, Half Moon, Third Quarter, and No Moon, on each of which the newlyweds turn farther away from each other; by the end of the honeymoon, they seem to be parting forever. Granting that people sent a lot of postcards in that era, I can't imagine the sense of humor that would send *those* postcards, one by one, in the proper lunar order. But some people joke compulsively about the things they fear, as if naming a possible bad outcome would somehow prevent it—a neurotic behavior having less to do with mirth than with magical thinking.

Fig. 75

And not even optimists doubt that a pair of newlyweds, no matter how idyllically enamored of each other, will eventually grow less so. In old show tunes, the newlyweds' first home is always envisioned as a cozy cottage far from the noise and nosiness of the world. Prospective couples seldom dream of spending their entire lives in such close quarters (especially not if they plan to have kids, as they usually do), but it is a measure of their initial idealism and infatuation that at first they enjoy (or think they'll enjoy—most of these songs are starry-eyed evocations of a married future by a lovesick suitor) that sort of round-the-clock involuntary intimacy. As years go by and hubby gets promoted, they move to a bigger house, which isn't just a consolation prize for the waning of red-hot passion, but a necessity for coexistence: the longer they've lived together, the farther they need to be able to get from each other. If the husband doesn't get promoted and they find themselves stuck in their newlyweds' cottage, the marriage will go sour, as even an archromantic like Keats recognized: "Love in a hut, with water and a crust / Is—Love forgive me—ashes, cinders, dust."

Even if the husband does get promoted, the honeymoon can't last forever. How long does it take for the idyll to curdle? The title of Billy Wilder's 1955 sex comedy, *The Seven Year Itch*, refers to a theory that that's how long it takes the average husband to grow restless. But there are other milestones long before that one. A 1923 ad for Dr. Eliot's Five-Foot Shelf of Books—quoted by Lois and Alan Gordon in their year-by-year history of twentieth-century America, *American Chronicle*—asked "One Year Married and All Talked Out? . . . Is there anything that would brighten their evenings? . . . How can they turn their silent, lonely hours into real human companionship?" But maybe Dr. Eliot came along too late, since the Gordons inform us that 1923 was also the year the radio craze really began, possibly in response to the very loneliness and silence the doctor diagnosed.

Housekeepers

LIKE SO MANY early sitcoms, *The Beulah Show* had both a radio incarnation (1945–54) and a TV incarnation (1950–53). Both versions concerned a black housekeeper and the white family she worked for, but in the radio version Beulah too was initially voiced by a white man. Even so, by 1940s standards, *Beulah*'s representation of blacks was fairly benign, though Beulah's boyfriend Bill was a bit of a freeloader—always hungry, liable to make himself scarce when there was work to be done, and even more marriage-shy than work-shy. Beulah herself was the most capable member of the household, the wittiest, and the most charismatic. She was clearly the model for Alice on *The Brady Bunch*, who also complained about her long-standing but marriage-averse boyfriend, and about her own appearance, though in Beulah's case, the problem wasn't homeliness but obesity.

That such a woman could serve as the model for a white housekeeper on a later sitcom shows that the point of Beulah wasn't just her

Fig. 76 Beulah . . . and Hazel

race and her flattering devotion to her white employers. That was part of her appeal to white America, but not the whole of it: there's a poignancy about a not-young woman who loves children, likes cooking, and doesn't mind housework—yet continues to cook and clean and babysit for someone else's family because she can't get a man to start one with her. It's one thing when the household help is a sexy French maid, or a young au pair with her life ahead of her, but Beulah and Alice are well along in their lives, and those lives take place in other people's houses.

So does Hazel's. Ted Key's omnicompetent domestic, whose cartoon began appearing in the *Saturday Evening Post* in 1943, is both fat and homely, but unlike Alice or Beulah she's also surly and disdainful; the couple that employs her is afraid of her. We know she's stronger than the husband: one cartoon shows her effortlessly bearing away a barbell that *he* can lift only with great effort. She also teaches his son how to pitch sinkers (and helps the boy with his math homework, since neither parent is able), talks sports with the mailman, climbs trees to retrieve kites, and makes herself at home to a degree that neither Beulah nor Alice ever dared, barging into conversations with visitors, or lounging in an easy chair reading the sports section while the head of household tries his hardest to relax in another easy chair.

In one cartoon, Hazel describes herself as a "tomboy," and that does seem to have been the mid-century stereotype of the hired housekeeper.

It's another way of explaining why a woman would devote her life to someone else's family instead of raising one of her own. In the future, when housework is no longer done by humans, even the housekeeping robots will be dykey—if the Jetsons' robot maid, Rosie, is any indication.

Hunters

FEW PEOPLE FIND the killing of animals funny, and that may explain why most hunting humor focuses on everything but. Hunters are usually portrayed as more interested in drinking and gambling. A comic postcard from around 1960 shows a man about to leave on a hunting trip. As he sticks a bottle of booze into his backpack, his wife asks sarcastically, "Taking an extra quart of bullets along?" A 1945 cartoon from the *Saturday Evening Post* shows three hunters playing poker by their tent. A moose has stuck its head into the clearing where they sit, and one of the men addresses it irritably: "Shoo! Get out of here."

When animals appear at all in hunting-themed cartoons, they're usually alive and well, and often laughing at their would-be killers. "Now be real quiet while they bag each other," says a doe to a fawn on a comic postcard from 1956, as they watch two stupid-looking hunters on opposite sides of a big tree. "There's another one we won't have to worry about," chuckles one stag to another on a 1960s postcard as they watch a drunken hunter head into the woods with a case of whiskey. Often the roles of hunter and prey are simply reversed, anticipating by decades the many such reversals in *Far Side* cartoons. The two most popular images are the hunter fleeing from the bear and the pair or trio of deer driving a car with a human carcass tied to its hood.

Unlike BLONDE jokes or PSYCHIATRIST cartoons, hunting humor is intended for the very group it ridicules. That itself is nothing special— like BOWLING, bridge, and GOLF, hunting is a pastime whose devotees like to think about it all the time; they'd rather laugh at themselves, or their fellow devotees, than change the subject. Nor is it strange that hunters are usually portrayed as bumblers: failure is always funnier than

THERE GOES ANOTHER ONE WE WON'T HAVE TO WORRY ABOUT!

BONDED
XXX

Fig. 77

success. What *is* strange, and almost unique, is that people who like to shoot animals seem not to want to be reminded, in their lighthearted moods, that that's what hunting is about. To love an activity, and love thinking about it, and yet not to be able to laugh at it—that's a strange mentality. The libertine's pursuit of women has always been compared to the hunter's pursuit of game (we even have a word, *venery*, that can refer to either hobby), but it's hard to imagine a world where the thousands of raunchy cartoons in old men's magazines never actually depicted sex, or even suggested that a couple had just done it, or was just about to, but instead joked only about impotence, overzealous chaperones, and black eyes dealt out by indignant prudes.

This huge blind spot in the humorous vision of hunting is a form of gallantry, a hard-boiled sentimentality that makes it okay to kill deer for sport, but not to disrespect them by laughing at their corpses, or joking about the actual slaughter. Significantly, in the only cliché of hunting humor that does involve a dead animal, that animal is not a deer or moose or even a duck: two lady hunters drive along proudly with a cow tied to their hood, an angry farmer in pursuit, and a caption like this below them: "Now our husbands can't say that women don't know how to hunt deer!"

Hypnotism

"WANT THE THRILL of imposing your will over someone? Of making someone do exactly what you order?" So begins an ad that ran in 1954, in magazines like *Sir* and *Wild*, for a booklet called *How to Hypnotize*. For readers of those magazines too dense to decode the copywriter's promise, a picture shows a man hypnotizing a beautiful woman while a couch waits in the background for her imminent surrender. That is the implicit promise of many such ads; in 1954, hypnotism was the closest thing to date-rape drugs available to the average fifteen-year-old boy.

It was also a favorite plot device for sitcoms, first on radio and then on television. Like AMNESIA, hypnotism has always been an easy way of shaking things up for an episode or two on shows where the same characters interact week after week. Another way, of course, is to introduce strangers—but precisely because sitcom characters become so stereotyped and predictable, a sudden personality change is usually funnier. (Sometimes AMNESIA and hypnosis work together, as on the episode of *Gilligan's Island* where a head injury causes Mary Ann to think she's Ginger. An effort to hypnotize her back to her true identity misfires, and ends up instead convincing Gilligan that he's Mary Ann.)

Even *The Dick Van Dyke Show* succumbed to the uncanny compulsion of the cliché. In an episode from 1962, "My Husband Is Not a Drunk," posthypnotic suggestion causes Rob to become "drunk" any time a bell rings, and to sober up again the next time a bell rings. Needless to say, that episode is full of bells that send Rob toggling back and forth between his sober normal self and comic drunkenness. The inspiration for the episode may have been *The Court Jester* (1956), in which a COWARD played by Danny Kaye is emboldened by hypnosis to prepare him for a duel. The sound of fingers snapping causes Kaye to toggle repeatedly between his true self and his braver alter ego.

In "The Wail of the Siren," an episode of the old live-action *Batman* series, an evil singer named the Siren hypnotizes Bruce Wayne over the phone by singing her high note. She nearly succeeds in getting him to sign over the Wayne Family Jewels before Robin comes to the rescue and forces the Siren to break Batman's spell by singing a special Antidote Note. (In another episode, another villain, the Mad Hatter, tries to hypnotize the Caped Crusader with a Super Instant Mesmerizer mounted like a miner's headlamp on the Hatter's hat, but Batman protects himself with his Antimesmerizing Bat-Reflector.)

I don't know if hypnotism by phone is really possible, but it's funny, and it accords with a sense some of us have always had about telephones as conduits through which the outer world is likely to harm us. In a 1941 *Popeye* cartoon called "Nix on Hypnotricks," the evil Professor I. Stare phones Olive Oyl and hypnotizes her into coming to his office. Ostensibly he has called her at random because he needs a subject to practice on, but given that most Popeye cartoons culminate in the attempted RAPE of Olive, and that many hypnotism fantasies are basically rape fantasies, we are right to fear the worst about Professor Stare.

Ii · Jj · Kk

Icemen

It's not always the iceman's fault when your wife treats you cool.
—*CAPTAIN BILLY'S WHIZ BANG*, 1927

THERE IS NO iceman in *The Iceman Cometh*, but there are several jokes about one. O'Neill's play debuted in 1939, when electric refrigerators were gradually replacing old-fashioned iceboxes, but it is set in 1912, when the only way for a housewife to keep her perishables cold on a hot day was to let a big beefy man into her home, several times a week, in the middle of the day while her husband was at work, to deliver a big block of ice. Like UPS drivers in our own time, these lucky guys inspired a lot of raunchy male humor. "Don't do no cheatin' wid de iceman," says a bartender to his girlfriend in O'Neill's play. Earlier, we've heard the bartender discussing a regular named Hickey, who seems positively obsessed with the sexual threat posed by the lowly deliveryman: "Remember how he woiks up dat gag about his wife, when he's cockeyed, cryin' over her picture and den springin' it on yuh all of a sudden dat he left her in de hay wid de iceman?"

Why the iceman? For one thing, they were hunks, as they had to be to lug big chunks of ice up tenement stairs all day long. (In *Ella Cinders*, a 1926 film adapted from the comic strip, Ella's boyfriend is an iceman and college football star named Waite Lifter, who in the end turns out to be rich; he's been delivering ice as part of his football conditioning.) But why not the milkman, or the guy who delivered the coal? Well, sometimes it *was* the milkman, though when you lug around bottles of milk for a living, not even the most insecure husband is likely to see you as an embodiment of unbridled male sexuality. The man who delivers the coal might be harder to dismiss, but luckily he comes but once a year, and unlike the iceman he's filthy. Neither the milkman nor the coalman, moreover, has any legitimate need to enter the home, whereas the iceman has no choice but to come in and install his dripping block of ice in the icebox personally. Look what happens in "The Dentist" (1932) when a father, played by W. C. Fields, chases away the iceman his daughter wants to marry. "Put it down there and get out," says Fields, indicating the kitchen floor; and then we get to watch Fields wrestling with the slippery block without the aid of tongs.

Another reason to fear—and thus to joke about—the iceman was his ethnicity. Unlike the milkman, as pasteurized and homogenized as his wares, the stereotypical iceman, at least in eastern cities, was a recent Italian immigrant. That's why Bavarelli, Chico Marx's character in *Horse Feathers*, is an iceman—and a highly sexed one, too, who can't keep his hands off Thelma Todd. (The film was made in 1932, at the tail end of the Prohibition, so Bavarelli also delivers bootleg liquor.)

Another highly sexed iceman appears in *The Girl Can't Help It*, as one of several RUBBERNECKING males who overreact to Jayne Mansfield's sex appeal: he spots her just as he's prepared to lift a big block of ice from his truck, and the sight of Jayne raises his temperature so dramatically that the block melts into a cloud of steam. By 1956, when the film appeared, icemen and iceboxes were on their way out, but not quite extinct. Between the introduction of household refrigerators during World War I and the final obsolescence of iceboxes around 1960, the two technologies overlapped poignantly. The Kramdens' icebox on *The Honeymooners* is one of many jokes on poor Ralph's inadequacy as a breadwinner. ("I fought for everything I own," he tells Norton in one episode. "Gee, Ralph, you must have lost most of the fights," says Norton, glancing around the Kramdens' kitchen.) Other comedy husbands of the era bought refrigerators precisely because they didn't trust their wives with the iceman.

Figs. 78

Fig. 79 Icemen. See also DISHWASHING HUSBANDS.

Indigestion Nightmares

I N 1937, THE University of Chicago Press published a slender volume called *Sleep Characteristics: How They Vary and React to Changing Conditions in the Group and the Individual.* The book (coauthored by Nathaniel Kleitman, who went on to codiscover REM sleep) reported the results of a series of experiments. The chapter on dreaming focused on the effects of food and beverages just before bedtime, found no difference in the effects of hot and cold beverages, and found that only a few of the beverage dreams were nightmares—a predictable finding, a cynic might say, given that the study was financed by the makers of Ovaltine.

On the other hand, you can hardly blame the makers of Ovaltine—a cozy bedtime drink if ever there was one—for wanting to discredit the ancient prejudice linking dairy products to nightmares. In "Ozzie's Triple Banana Surprise," a 1957 episode of *The Adventures of Ozzie and Harriet,* the title character has a night of bad dreams after consuming not one but two such concoctions that evening at the malt shop. We're not surprised that that binge had repercussions, since we've not only seen the sundaes but also heard their components listed—in reverse order, starting with the crowning cherry—by the soda jerk:

One red cherry, crème de menthe cherries, hazelnuts, walnuts, whipped cream, slice of pineapple, butterscotch syrup, marshmallow syrup, a scoop of chocolate, scoop of vanilla, scoop of pistachio nut, scoop of coffee ripple, lime sherbet, two bananas, and six macaroons.

Then night falls and hilarity ensues for Ozzie Nelson. Dairy products, as I say, are fabled for their power to cause nightmares, so we mustn't rush to the conclusion that Ozzie was lactose-intolerant. Salvador Dalí made a point of eating Camembert at bedtime in order to give himself lurid dreams he could repackage as lucrative paintings. Or so the legend goes, and there's no denying that both his art and his persona were redolent of overripe cheese.

Fig. 80 Winsor McCay's *Dream of the Rarebit Fiend*, 1909

And cheese is especially notorious for its ability to lure incubi and incubate bad dreams. In a 1967 episode of *Gomer Pyle, USMC* called "Gomer, the Welsh Rarebit Fiend," Private Pyle becomes addicted to rarebit at an eatery near Camp Henderson, though it makes him not only walk in his sleep but also quarrel and shout in his sleep, flip-flopping his sunny daytime disposition to something like its polar opposite. When Sergeant Carter tries the rarebit, *he* has a nightmare in which he and Gomer have swapped ranks and voices as well as personalities, allowing us to glimpse Sgt. Pyle bawling out Private Carter for showing up at reveille in his underwear.

The title of that episode was an homage to *Dream of the Rarebit Fiend* **(Fig. 80)**, the comic strip Winsor McCay drew from 1904 to 1914 for the *Evening Telegram*, concurrently with *Little Nemo in Slumberland*, which he drew for the *New York Herald*. Each six- or eight-panel strip depicted a nightmare caused by the rash ingestion of "that deadly agglomeration of cheese and ale," Welsh rarebit; the last panel always showed the wakened sleeper (a different one each time) vowing never again to eat melted cheese at bedtime. McCay's contract with the *Herald* forbade him to publish in other papers under his own name, so for the *Rarebit Fiend* he used a pseudonym: "Silas," the name of his garbageman, as if the cartoonist had foreseen the recent theory that the function of dreams is to sweep up the litter and leavings of the previous day. The strip was successful enough to spawn imitations, of which at least one, *Chilly Cholly's Ice Cream Dream*, would have struck a chord with Ozzie Nelson.

Little Nemo's nightmares, too, were often blamed on food—peanuts or raw onions, for instance—and McCay himself drew an earlier strip called *Dreams of the Lobster Fiend*. Both lobster *and* Welsh rarebit are implicated in an especially sinister psychological torture in *When the Clouds Roll By*, a 1919 comedy about an evil psychiatrist trying to drive one of his patients insane—feeding his victim (Douglas Fairbanks) Welsh rarebit and lobster at bedtime (along with mince pie and onions), and so inducing predictably horrible nightmares.

Each man to his poison, then. In *A Christmas Carol*, Scrooge tries to dismiss Marley's ghost as a figment of his indigestion, "more of gravy than of grave." "What a night!" exclaims Bugs Bunny at the beginning of "Hare-Way to the Stars" (1957). "I'll never mix radish juice and carrot juice again!" Pizza is the culprit in *What a Nightmare, Charlie Brown*: Snoopy pigs out, then dreams he's a maltreated sled dog in the Yukon. Indeed, these days pizza has become the most common culprit when a character in a sitcom or cartoon has a funny nightmare due to food. Sometimes the toppings are singled out for blame—anchovies especially have a bad rep—but a plain cheese pizza would probably suffice.

In *Doctor Seuss's Sleep Book* (1962), we learn that it's dangerous even to *dream* of the wrong kind of juice. A moose and a goose are shown dreaming of moose juice (orange) and goose juice (green) respectively: all well and good. But though they sleep in separate beds, they sometimes get their dreams mixed up, and "it isn't too good when a moose and a goose / Start dreaming they're drinking the other one's juice." Indeed,

> When goose gets a mouthful of juices of moose's,
> And moose gets a mouthful of juices of goose's,
> They always fall out of their beds screaming screams.
> So . . . I'm warning you, now! Never drink in your dreams.

The indigestion theory was already on its way out by the first decade of the last century, thanks in part to Freud's *The Interpretation of Dreams*, which appeared in 1899, five years before the Rarebit Fiend, and offered a more ambitious explanation. Throughout the nineteenth century, though, indigestion (or more generally the theory that dreams are caused by bodily sensations and encroaching sensory data) was the prevailing explanation—what educated laymen thought they knew about dreams before Freud came along and gave them something else to think they knew.

Infant Mortality

IN 1963, EDWARD Gorey published what remains his most popular book, *The Gashlycrumb Tinies*, an illustrated alphabet of gruesome deaths met by innocent children, from "A is for Amy who fell down the stairs" to "Z is for Zillah, who drank too much gin." Other notable Gashlycrumb deaths include those of Fanny (sucked dry by a leech), Prue (trampled flat in a brawl), and Victor (squashed under a train). A shining example of Gorey's morbid sense of humor, the book is also an homage to the vanished Edwardian world where his imagination liked to dwell—to an era that, as stolid and starched as it may seem in retrospect, laughed more readily than ours does at infant mortality.

Though the 1970s craze for Dead Baby jokes might seem like a characteristically crass product of modern times, in fact our culture has a venerable tradition of sick humor about horrible deaths befalling babies and children. The first Dead Baby joke (unless you laugh at certain grisly passages in the Old Testament, or Greek tragedy, or Shakespeare), and certainly the most elaborate, is Swift's "A Modest Proposal," which famously suggests eating the babies of the poor.

Swift, of course, wasn't writing *for* children. The comically traumatic children's story could be traced to the Brothers Grimm (though they weren't writing for children, either), or to their compatriot Heinrich Hoffmann, a psychiatrist who in 1845 wrote and illustrated a collection of nightmarish children's tales later known as *Struwwelpeter* but initially and anonymously published as *Lustige Geschichten*—funny stories—*für Kinder von 3–6 Jahren*. Among the stories Dr. Hoffmann somehow deemed appropriate for children from three to six years old was one about a girl who plays with matches and is burnt to ashes, one about a little boy who won't eat his SOUP and therefore starves to death, and one about a recalcitrant thumb-sucker whose thumbs are finally cut off by a crazy tailor with a giant pair of scissors. The book was hugely popular on both sides of the Atlantic; one of the first English translations was by Mark Twain.

Twenty years later, another German—Wilhelm Busch—wrote and illustrated *Max und Moritz*, the tale in rhyming couplets of two rotten little boys who play a series of sadistic pranks on grownups (putting beetles in their uncle's bed, putting gunpowder in their teacher's pipe, and so on), until they're caught by a farmer who takes them to a mill and has them ground to bits. *Max und Moritz* was the acknowledged inspiration for *The Katzenjammer Kids*—the first full-fledged comic strip—and so is hugely important to the history of the comics medium, and especially to its early emphasis on pranks and punishments.

The German obsession with practical jokes—from Till Eulenspiegel to itching powder—falls outside the purview of this guide, but the penchant for morbid children's tales was not limited to Germany. In 1899, a British writer named Harry Graham published a slender volume called *Ruthless Rhymes for Heartless Homes*, which featured verses like these:

> *When baby's cries grew hard to bear,*
> *I popped him in the Frigidaire.*
> *I never would have done so if*
> *I'd known that he'd be frozen stiff.*
> *My wife said, "George, I'm so unhappé!*
> *Our darling's now completely frappé!"*
> * * *
>
> *Billy, in one of his nice new sashes,*
> *Fell in the fire and was burnt to ashes;*
> *Now, although the room grows chilly,*
> *I haven't the heart to poke poor Billy.*

The ghoulish sense of humor behind such rhymes, assuming it wasn't just spontaneously generated by the Zeitgeist, derived less from the *Struwwelpeter* tradition of gruesome cautionary verses than from the unintended gruesomeness, tastelessness, bathos, and all-around badness of certain minor nineteenth-century funereal poets such as Julia Moore, the self-styled and self-published Sweet Singer of Michigan, who in 1876 gave the world a book of would-be-solemn epitaphs and dirges inspired by tragic news items:

> *While eating dinner, this dear child,*
> *Was choked on a piece of beef.*
> *Doctors came, tried their skill awhile,*
> *But none could give relief . . .* —"Little Libbie"

Mark Twain was a great fan of Moore—of her Midas touch for turning any tragedy she handled into inadvertent comedy. Moore's doggerel was the inspiration and model for Emmeline Grangerford's "Ode to Steven Dowling Botts, Dec'd" in *Huckleberry Finn*:

> . . . *Oh No! Then list with tearful eye,*
> *Whilst I his fate do tell.*
> *His soul did from this cold world fly*
> *By falling down a well.*
> *They got him out and emptied him;*
> *Alas it was too late;*
> *His spirit was gone for to sport aloft*
> *In the realms of the good and great.*

On the other side of the ocean, at the same time as Julia Moore, there flourished an even greater anti-talent, the immortal William Topaz McGonagall (1825–1902). McGonagall favored natural disasters and large-scale accidents to the domestic tragedies that fascinated Moore, but he wasn't above writing about dead children himself, as in "The Little Match Girl":

> . . . *Her body was found half-covered with snow,*
> *And as the people gazed thereon their hearts were full*
> *of woe;*
> *And many present let fall a burning tear*
> *Because she was found dead on the last night of the year.*[29]

Around the same time as Graham's *Ruthless Rhymes*, an American humorist named Charles Heber Clark wrote a whole suite of intentionally awful funereal verses in the Julia Moore vein. One of Clark's verses was entitled "Willie":

---

[29] McGonagall wrote so much about catastrophes large and small that he developed a fatalistic attitude:
But accidents will happen by land and by sea,
Therefore, to save ourselves from accidents, we needn't try to flee,
For whatsoever God has ordained will come to pass;
For instance, ye may be killed by a stone or a piece of glass.

Willie had a purple monkey climbing on a yellow stick,
And when he sucked the paint all off it made him
    deathly sick;
And in his latest hours he clasped that monkey in his hand,
And bade good-bye to earth and went into a better land.
   . . .
Oh! no more he'll shoot his sister with his little wooden gun;
And no more he'll twist the pussy's tail and make her yowl,
    for fun.
The pussy's tail now stands out straight; the gun is laid aside;
The monkey doesn't jump around since little Willie died.

At this remove, it's unclear whether Graham or Clark was to blame for the craze, on both sides of the Atlantic, in the first decade of the twentieth century, for "Little Willie" poems, thrillingly macabre precursors not only of the *Gashlycrumb Tinies* but also of Dead Baby jokes.

Willie and two other brats
Licked up all the Rough-on-rats.[30]
Father said, when Mother cried,
"Never mind—they'll die outside."

Little Willie feeling bright
Stole a stick of dynamite.
Curiosity seldom pays:
It rained Willie for seven days

Little Willie from his mirror
Licked the mercury right off,
Thinking in his childish error
It would cure the whooping cough.

At the funeral Willie's mother
Smartly said to Mrs. Brown,
"'Twas a chilly day for Willie
When the mercury went down!"

[30] A brand of rat poison.

In 1907, Hilaire Belloc published *Cautionary Tales*, probably the last great book of light verse in the language. Unlike the Little Willy poems, Belloc's tales parodied didactic verse, and in that sense harked back to *Struwwelpeter*. In "Jim," a little boy slips away from his nurse one day at the zoo and lives just long enough to regret it:

> *He hadn't gone a yard when—Bang!*
> *With open Jaws, a Lion sprang,*
> *And hungrily began to eat*
> *The Boy: beginning at his feet.*
> *Now just imagine how it feels*
> *When first your toes and then your heels,*
> *And then, by gradual degrees,*
> *Your shins and ankles, calves and knees,*
> *Are slowly eaten, bit by bit.*
> *No wonder Jim detested it!*

The meal continues, and the moral is to "always keep a-hold of nurse / For fear of finding something worse." Belloc often verges on nonsense— and given all the other stunts of which the nonsense genre is capable, it's odd how closely it was associated, in its heyday, with such parodies of di- dactic children's verse. Most of the poems in the *Alice* books parody other, once-familiar, now-forgotten poems, pious and improving poems of the sort that well-bred Victorian children were made to memorize and recite. (To the books' first audience, the recitation scenes—with their subversive garbling of humorless verses—must have seemed mildly naughty trans- gressions.) Gelett Burgess's Goops ("The Goops are gluttonous and rude / They gug and gumble with their food") don't do much more than teach good manners by negative example, like the Goofus panels in *HighLights* magazine's long-running "Goofus and Gallant" feature, and yet it is to them (and to a quatrain about a purple cow) that Burgess owes his repu- tation as a major nonsensibility. Belloc's *Cautionary Tales* are much fun- nier, and doubtless did more than the Goops to hasten the death of the genre they spoof—and so, since parody is parasitic on its model, of their own genre, too.

Years ago, as I was reading Belloc and thinking of how I'd just annoyed my brother-in-law by giving his six-year-old son a whoopee cushion for Christmas, I had an epiphany. I understood at last exactly what distinguishes nonsense from other genres of children's literature: nonsense is written not by parents but by *uncles*—by grownups who may or may not have the child's best interest at heart, but whose real object is to amuse at all costs, even if that means mocking the parents' values or subverting their efforts to raise decent, sensible, non-smart-alecky children.

It would be wrong to say that unmarried uncles and other childless men are less upset and more amused by the thought of a small child eating rat poison, but undoubtedly it's easier to laugh at things like that when you don't have kids of your own. If I ever do have kids, I'll probably stop joking about such things myself—it would feel unlucky. There's a reason why most of the great nonsense poets have been BACHELORS, and a reason why, in our own time, Dead Baby jokes appeal mainly to people too young to have kids of their own.

According to Simon Bronner in *American Children's Folklore*, one theory about the fad for Dead Baby jokes is that they represented "a response to the issue of abortion which had been thrust into the spotlight by the media." Another theory explained the jokes as a response to "the graphic coverage of the Vietnam war . . . which often featured bleeding infants." Both theories are plausible, but maybe unnecessary, given the long line of precedents for such jokes. Like another product of the era, punk rock, Dead Baby jokes expressed a perennial urge to flout certain taboos as flagrantly as possible. Once that urge is acknowledged, there's really nothing left to explain—though of course we can still ask why the urge flares up when it does, why it fixes on the taboos it does, and why those taboos exist in the first place.

Insomnia

IN 1935, ROBERT Benchley wrote and starred in a short comic film called *How to Sleep*. While nowhere near as funny or quirky as Benchley's magazine pieces, the film won an Academy Award for Best Short Subject, and still serves as a handy guide to the things our grandparents found funny about insomnia: the difficulty of finding a comfortable sleeping position; the inefficacy of counting sheep; the profusion of other folk remedies like the hot bath, or the glass of hot milk that escalates into a MIDNIGHT SNACK of Dagwoody proportions; the tendency of daytime worries to assail us with fresh vigor in the middle of the night; such consequences of "faulty bedmaking" as the sliding sheet and the "riding pajama top"; and, above all, NOISE—the flapping window blind, the dripping tap, the whining mosquito.

Insomnia humor is usually humor about NOISE, and thus often about NEIGHBORS; if there weren't so much to say about each affliction, I'd conflate them in a single entry. In *It's a Gift* (1934), W. C. Fields plays a severely HENPECKED HUSBAND who takes refuge from his wife's endless curtain lecture, one summer night around 4 A.M., by trying to sleep outside on the porch swing. There ensues the funniest and most sadistically elaborate insomnia sequence in all of cinema. As soon as Fields tries to lie down on the swing, one end of the beam from which it is suspended starts to split with an ominous creak. Fields lies down anyhow, as carefully as possible, and for the moment the beam splits no farther, but before he can fall asleep, a delivery boy approaches with a wicker basket of groceries and four loudly rattling bottles of milk. These goods are destined for the third-floor tenants of the small apartment building on whose second-floor balcony Fields is trying to sleep, so the boy rattles noisily upstairs past the hero, then, after unloading his basket, and leaving a coconut perched precariously on a kitchen windowsill, back down past him again, but not till the beam supporting the porch swings breaks, and the head of the makeshift bed crashes to the floor. Fields tries to sleep on the badly tilted swing, but as soon as the grocer's boy is out of earshot, the coconut rolls off its windowsill with a thud, and proceeds with further thuds to roll down the zigzag flights of wooden steps, now and then banging into a metal trash can, and sometimes pausing on the brink of a step—allowing Fields to hope the disturbance is over—before falling further. Next comes a pushy early-rising insurance salesman who disregards Fields's efforts to sleep and tries to sell him insurance. Then the demonic little boy on the third-floor balcony starts dropping grapes through a knothole onto Fields's head. Then there's a long shouted conversation between the child's mother on the third floor and her teenage daughter on the sidewalk, about whether they should buy syrup of squill or syrup of ipecac. Then another neighbor starts hanging wet clothes on the clothesline, causing its pulley to squeak loudly, and then an Italian vegetable peddler comes by crying his wares at the top of his lungs. The whole sequence lasts more than fifteen minutes.

Outdoors, at least, Fields isn't pestered by a dripping faucet, probably the noise most often implicated in insomnia humor, unless that honor goes to the SNORING spouse. Both noises irritate poor Joe McDoakes in "So You Think You Can't Sleep" (1953), one in a series of short, mildly funny, faintly informative films—not exactly mockumentaries, but maybe jocumentaries—made in the 1940s and '50s and starring George O'Hanlon (later the voice of George Jetson). Donald Duck was plagued by dripping faucets, too.

Over at Warner Bros., Elmer Fudd was the favorite victim of sleep-depriving noise—maybe because he was one of the few human characters in Warner cartoons, and one of the most bourgeois. In any case, he spends maddeningly sleepless nights in several cartoons like "Back-Alley Oproar," "A Pest in the House," and "Good Night, Elmer," where an early (1940) version of the character is kept awake not by noise pollution but by light pollution: the candle he uses to light himself to bed refuses to stay extinguished. By the time he finally puts it out, the sun is rising.

Why do insomniacs count *sheep*? Probably because they're so woolly, so nebulous, like the thoughts of someone on the point of losing consciousness. Just discrete enough to be countable, they are usually pictured leaping over a stile one by one; in animated cartoons they leap in slow motion. Their job is to model or embody—and thereby encourage—drowsiness. *New Yorker* cartoonists have always been fond of the cliché: a sheep counting men leaping over a stile; a ladies' man counting wolves in sheep's clothing; a mother in bed alongside a cradled baby and counting sheep for both of them—sheep-and-lamb pairs leaping over the stile two by two (that one's by Saul Steinberg). No cartoonist had more fun with the cliché than Otto Soglow, who made a specialty of the sheep gag in the late 1940s: a prisoner counting black sheep; an African counting giraffes; a tennis buff counting victorious opponents leaping the net; a sleeping cop whose sheep obey a traffic light; an insomniac scowling as the sheep in his thought balloon lie asleep in single file before the unleapt stile.

Inventors

FROM THE FIRST, the comic-strip form has had an affinity for mad inventors, maybe because mad inventions are fun to draw and fun to look at. Rube Goldberg is only the most celebrated (and only in America; England has Heath Robinson) of a long line of cartoonists who sometimes seemed better at inventing machines than inventing jokes. E. C. Segar, who created Popeye, also drew a companion or "topper" strip called *Sappo* about a henpecked little SAP, his big fat abusive wife, his inventions, and those of his friend Professor O. G. Wotasnozzle **(Fig. 81)**. Between them, Sappo and the Professor invented a mechanical dog, a two-headed matchstick, an automatic hat-hanger, a miniaturizing pill, an invisibility ray, a hair-growing ray, a rain-making machine, a Linger Liniment that makes musical notes last longer, a fish-stretcher for fishermen, a hands-free smoking machine for card-players, assorted food pills ("You can carry a complete picnic lunch for eight people in one pocket"), a joy-inducing chewing gum called Giggle Gum (with an active ingredient called Mirtholene), a scale that under-reports the weight of fat ladies and over-reports the weight of skinny ones (reminding us that, back in 1931, some women actually wanted to weigh *more*), a multi-tool the size of a cello (with all the usual attachments but also an egg beater, shaving brush, ROLLING PIN, mouth organ, and mop), and many other handy items. The strip is still funny;

Fig. 81 *Sappo*, 1935

if it's now forgotten, it's partly because Sappo himself wasn't much of an invention. His contraptions weren't an expression of his personality, since he barely had one, but of Segar's Goldbergian fondness for imagining crazy machines.

The same criticism, incidentally, applies to Goldberg's own inventor, Professor Lucifer Gorgonzola Butts, who has no personality at all, only HEAD INJURIES and similar sources of inspiration. He's not even really a character, just a forgettable framing device for Goldberg's unforgettable inventions **(Fig. 82)**. It's a pity: if the cartoonist had bothered to flesh out his mad inventor via back-formation—by imagining exactly what *kind* of lunatic would come up with such contraptions (as Flann O'Brien did so brilliantly with *his* mad inventor in *The Third Policeman*, one of the funniest novels ever written)—those contraptions would be doubly funny: in themselves and as expressions of a funny character's personality. And people might still be perusing Rube Goldberg's cartoons, rather than merely using his name to describe anything needlessly elaborate.

Two fictive inventors whose inventions do serve to express their creator's personalities are the windbag Major Hoople, from the great single-panel newspaper cartoon *Our Boarding House*, and Fibber McGee, the truth-stretching hero of one of the greatest radio sitcoms. Hoople, when

Fig. 82 Rube Goldberg's juicing machine

he isn't inventing heroic exploits or hard-luck stories (to justify his in-activity, or persuade someone to lend him money), is inventing for real: his GET-RICH-QUICK SCHEMES include matchless cigars, food pills again (a single pill is the equivalent of a steak; take five assorted pills and you have a five-course dinner), and, decades before Nair, "a solvent salve that will make the ordeal of razor shaving obsolete." McGee's brainstorms in-clude a special alarm clock for Sunday mornings (it has a foam-rubber bell so the ringing won't awaken you) and a plastic crosspiece for your radio antenna to make the neighbors think you own a TV set. Why are so many confabulating BLOWHARDS also mad inventors? Maybe because both tendencies reflect the same contempt for reality and its constraints.

Animated cartoons also love crazy inventions, especially big ones that malfunction spectacularly. Wile E. Coyote is not just a would-be preda-tor but a grandiose inventor who in episode after episode is hoisted by his own petard—one always assembled from Acme components. Other no-table cartoon inventions are found in Tex Avery's retro-futuristic "House of Tomorrow" (1949) and "Car of Tomorrow" (1951); in "The Whole Idea" (1955), which features an inventor named Calvin Q. Calculus and his portable hole; and in the Marvin the Martian cartoons, in which a runty Martian with a big head (presumably housing a more evolved brain) and an arsenal of extraterrestrial high technology is nonetheless repeatedly outwitted by Bugs Bunny's street smarts, in a series of con-frontations that make the viewer proud to be an earthling.

Irishmen

The wheelbarrow was invented to teach the Irish to walk on their hind legs.
—*CAPTAIN BILLY'S WHIZ BANG*, 1924

I GREW UP IN the heyday of Polish jokes—a heyday that arrived too late to earn that nationality an entry in this encyclopedia. One of my zanier uncles used to make what he called "Polish cannons" by taping together beer cans into a tube that used the ignited fumes of

Fig. 83 Irishman as monkey *and* policeman. See also COPS AND NIGHTSTICKS.

lighter fluid to shoot tennis balls. Either because it was a gentler era than the one in which my uncle's uncles grew up, or because ethnic slang was on the wane, or because, as much as we loved Polack jokes, no one hated the Poles, "Polish cannon" is almost the only jocular expression of its kind that I recall.

Things were very different in the heyday of anti-Irish sentiment in the late nineteenth and early twentieth century. J. E. Lighter's *Historical Dictionary of American Slang*, one of the most impressive one-man reference works of our era, lists forty-six jocular—and, as a rule, pejorative—"Irish" compounds of the "Polish cannon" variety. To name a few: *Irish ambulance* (a wheelbarrow), *Irish apple* (a potato—ditto with *Irish apricot, Irish football*, and *Irish lemon*), *Irish applesauce* (mashed potatoes), *Irish banjo* (a shovel), *Irish caviar* (meat stew), *Irish clubhouse* (a jail or police station), *Irish confetti* (stones or brickbats), *Irish hint* (a broad hint; a threat), *Irish lace* (cobwebs), *Irishman's coat-of-arms* (a bloody nose and two black eyes), *Irish necktie* (a rope), *Irish nightingale* (a bullfrog), *Irish pullman* (a railway handcar), *Irish spoon* (a shovel or spade), *Irish toothache* (an erection, a punch in the jaw, or a hangover). Most of these terms date back to the early twentieth century or before, and all of them had currency in American slang.

In the comic art of the early twentieth century, the Irish come in for more racial hatred than African Americans. Blacks were a much more *common* subject, and the blatant racism of such stereotypes as the Mammy, the Pickaninny, Rastus, and so on is evident at a glance. To find images of blacks that convey the sort of visceral loathing inspired by the Irish, though, you'd have to look at the cartoons in neo-Nazi publications. (In mainstream humor, the closest thing is the depictions of Japanese during World War II.) And anti-Irish humor at its most virulent was strikingly similar to racist humor, often representing Irishmen as simian, more ape than man, as in the quote above (from a very popular lowbrow humor magazine of the 1920s and '30s). In the era of blackface comedy, Dooley Wilson—later cast as the piano player Sam in *Casablanca*—made a name for himself with a *white*face vaudeville routine as an Irishman.

Much of the ridicule of COPS in early silent comedies and other humor of the era is less anti-authority than anti-Irish **(Fig. 83)**, and the stereotype of the Irish cop—lazy, cowardly, brutal, corrupt, hired via nepotism, fond of flirting with young women, fond of helping himself to unpurchased apples from fruit carts, fond of (and easily bribed with) a pint of beer—predates the age of movies. *Batman*'s Chief O'Hara is a relatively recent, benign, and high-ranking instance of the stereotype, but note that his superior, Commissioner Gordon, is reassuringly WASPy.

Not all the stereotypes were hostile. When Freud described the Irish as "one race of people for whom psychoanalysis is of no use whatsoever," he may have been thinking in part of their reputation for wacky illogic, a stereotype that Irish humorists from Laurence Sterne to Flann O'Brien have done little to discourage. An Irish bull is a joke, usually involving an Irishman named Pat or Mike, that depends on nonsensical reasoning:

> "Mike," said Pat to his friend who had fallen into a pit, "are you killed? Answer me! If you're killed, say so!"
> "No, Pat," replied Mike. "I'm not killed. But I can't answer you. I've been knocked speechless."

Like blacks of the same era, the Irish were sometimes portrayed as endearingly childlike and feckless (think of Fibber McGee) rather than subhuman and depraved. For eighty-seven years, beginning in 1913, the comic strip *Bringing Up Father* related the antics of a nouveau riche Irish-American couple named Jiggs and Maggie. Jiggs **(Fig. 84)** used

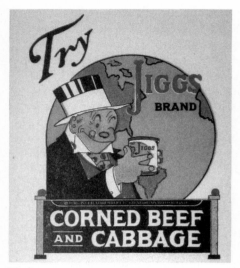

Fig. 84

to be a manual laborer (a hod carrier, like Finnegan of *Finnegans Wake*), but he struck it rich on the Irish sweepstakes, to his lasting misfortune: his socially ambitious and terrifying wife insists—to the point of hurling ROLLING PINS at him—that Jiggs behave like a millionaire.

Despite the frequent head injuries, Jiggs remains loyal to his old friends and his old idea of fun, which involves eating corned beef and cabbage and carousing till all hours. By the time its creator, George McManus, died in 1954, Americans had ceased to find the Irish screamingly funny: other ethnicities had crowded them out of the limelight and *Bringing Up Father* had become a living fossil, like most long-running comic strips. It lived on for another forty-six years because many people read the funnies not for a reflection of reality but as an escape from the real world and its real news.

Just Married

A LESS HIGH-RESOLUTION LAFFOPEDIA might have omitted this topic, which picks up where WEDDINGS leaves off, and leaves off where HONEYMOONS begins. Between emerging from the church and reaching the hotel, however, funny newlyweds do undergo enough of interest to the humorist to deserve a separate entry.

In the early part of the century, many newlyweds took a train to their honeymoon destination, and consummated their marriage en route, in a sleeper car instead of a hotel bed. Hence this quip, which Gershon Legman dates to 1938: "Niagara Falls: the bride's second big disappointment." In his *Rationale of the Dirty Joke*, Legman devotes five close-printed pages to off-color jokes about newlyweds on trains.

Other newlyweds leave the scene in the back of a limo, and many cartoons feature the bride saying something sure to alarm her new husband, as they ride off into their future together, and to aggravate any buyer's remorse he may already be feeling. "Good-bye steam baths, good-bye slenderizing treatments, good-bye low-calorie diets!" exclaims one such bride in a Chon Day cartoon, as her husband regards her uneasily. I found almost the same picture in *Let's Go to Bedlam*—a surprisingly tame 1954 collection of cartoons about courtship and marriage—except that the bride looks stern instead of triumphant, and the caption reads, "Well, I'm just reminding you. Our first anniversary is only a year away!"

By the 1950s, though, the favorite getaway vehicle was an ordinary car driven by the eager groom himself. In several cartoons of that era, the newlyweds' car—recognizable by the old SHOES and TIN CANS tied to the back bumper, and of course by the passengers' clothes—has been pulled over by an unsmiling motorcycle cop, presumably for speeding. The main joke, of course, is the groom's impatience to reach the honeymoon hotel. (In a 1905 *Mr. Buttin* strip, the title character, a compulsive DO-GOODER, chases a pair of newlyweds for eight blocks, convinced mistakenly that their car has dropped a cog. After berating him for the mistake—"That don't belong to me, you idiot!"—the groom drives off, grumbling: "That fool delayed us 27 seconds.")

After a day of being toasted and wept for and showered with rice by well-wishers, the new couple is due to be reminded that the world at large doesn't care about their happiness. That's half the joke in the Robert Day cartoon that shows a groom pleading with a traffic cop: "But, officer, this is supposed to be the happiest day of my life!"

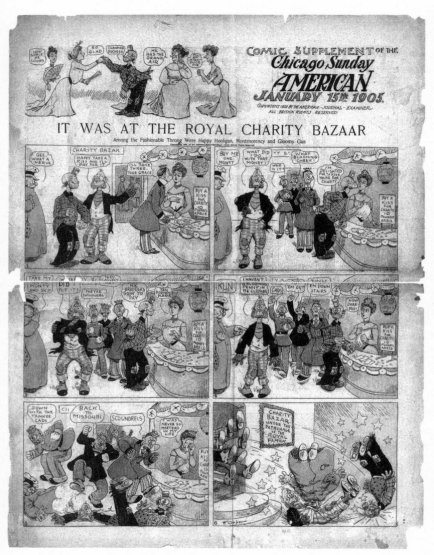

Fig. 85 The kissing booth, 1905. See also THE RICH, PRETTY GIRLS, BUM'S RUSH.

Kissing

I wasn't kissing her, I was whispering in her mouth.
—CHICO MARX

It takes a lot of experience for a girl to kiss like a beginner.
—LADIES' HOME JOURNAL

Why does a man take it for granted that a girl who flirts with him
wants him to kiss her—when, nine times out of ten,
she only wants him to want to kiss her?
—HELEN ROWLAND

CHILDREN, AND ESPECIALLY little boys, find kissing inexplicable, and only too easy to laugh at. They dimly sense that it's connected with the mysteries of sex, and that if a man and woman are kissing, the act will set in motion a mysterious chain of events involving love and marriage and culminating in a baby in a baby carriage. In times when the discussion of sex in popular culture was confined to little-boy snickers, kissing retained some of its playground naughtiness even for grownups.

As Gershon Legman points out in his magnum opus on dirty jokes, kissing was often used as a visual or verbal euphemism for sex. Among professional humorists, according to Legman, "the immediate and practical question about any sex-joke being hoked up for pop-culch presentation is: 'Can you do it with *kissing*?'" That euphemistic function, of course, was not confined to comedy. In Erich von Stroheim's *Greed* (1924), the creepy dentist McTeague leers down at the beautiful young patient (ZaSu Pitts), etherized in the chair so as not to feel his drill; after a struggle with his better instincts, he sniffs her hair and kisses her on the mouth.

Often the joke is that the woman doesn't know what the kiss means to the man, or to the audience. In *The Seven Year Itch*, Marilyn Monroe plays an actress who stars in toothpaste commercials, and Tom Ewell tricks her into kissing him by claiming to doubt her televised claims that Dazzledent eliminates bad breath; the kiss is sexier, from the male perspective, because she seems unaware of its sexual significance. Ditto with the kissing in the ridiculous film-within-a-film in *Never Give a Sucker an Even Break* (1941), in which W. C. Fields falls out of an airplane straight into a male fantasy, encountering a beautiful young woman named Ouliotta Delight Hemoglobin, who has never seen a man before and so—like an isolated aborigine with no antibodies to the pathogens of the outside world—is easy pickings. Fields promptly teaches her a kissing game he calls Squidgulum; she takes to it (and to him) at once, and there's no telling what might have happened next if Margaret Dumont hadn't shown up to spoil the party.

Once you *are* aware of the kissing/coitus equation, you become aware of the outrageous subliminal obscenity of a film like *Don Juan* (1926), in which John Barrymore set a record that still stands by engaging in 191 separate kisses. It was films like *Don Juan* and *Flaming Youth* (which appeared in 1923 and was advertised with promises of "neckers, petters, white kisses, red kisses, pleasure-mad daughters, sensation-craving mothers") that led to the draconian anti-kissing legislation of the Hays Code, which not only limited the duration of kisses, prohibiting the "red" ones altogether, but also forbade horizontal kissing, and stipulated that if two characters do kiss on a bed, at least one of them must have a foot on the floor.

Cartoons about kissing booths are seldom very funny, and certainly never as funny as the sheer existence of such booths, if they do exist, or ever did, outside cartoons. Thurber might have been thinking of kissing-booth cartoons when he said, in 1930 in *The New Yorker*, "A drawing is always dragged down to the level of its caption."[31] Cartoons about kissing booths often have captions involving the possibility of "under-the-counter" deals.

[31] He might also have been thinking—but for the anachronism—of the latter-day *New Yorker*'s Cartoon Captioning Contest.

L 1

Ladies' Clubs

. . . Ladies who pursue culture in bands,
as though it were dangerous to meet it alone.
—EDITH WHARTON

There is a woman,
There is a vulture
Who circles about
The carcass of culture.
—OGDEN NASH, 1931

IN THE FIRST decades of *The New Yorker*, one favorite butt of cartoonists, especially the great Helen Hokinson, was the plump society matron saying something philistine like (to a stockbroker) "All I want is a stock that will go up a *little* bit" or (to her assembled clubwomen) "Today Mr. Chatfield is going to show us a little—but not *too* much—of the horror in Spain." Sometimes the philistinism of such women went without saying, and it was enough to show one in a Paris bookstore asking in French for *Ulysses*—a joke that would have been inscrutable, even by *The New Yorker*'s notoriously rarefied standards of cartoon scrutability, if the customer had been a man.

Wolcott Gibbs, who briefly slummed as an art editor at *The New Yorker*, wrote that Hokinson's well-upholstered clubwomen "are forever engaged in a struggle to preserve the innocent, undaunted enthusiasms of a long-ago campus." Gibbs saw this pursuit of "the Bryn Mawr ideal"

Figs. 86 Above: *Mt. Ararat*, 1904. Below: Helen Hokinson, 1950s

"It has been moved that our recording secretary send a summary of today's discussion to Marshal Tito. Do I hear a second?"

into middle age and beyond as a touching instance of "arrested development." That may sound like sexist condescension by a male chauvinist who believes that women should forget about high culture upon graduating from college, but Gibbs comes close to summing up the spirit of the cartoons.

Since no man got more than a glimpse of the world in question, it's not surprising that the greatest chronicler of women's clubs and clubwomen was herself a woman; the surprise is that several male cartoonists covered the same beat. *The Girls*, a syndicated single-panel cartoon by Franklin Folger, ran from 1955 to 1988 and in its heyday appeared in more than a hundred newspapers. Like Hokinson's, Folger's "girls" are fat, sexless, middle-aged women in funny hats; if they are less convincing than Hokinson's—if we don't believe that Folger really knows such people—it is less a matter of gender than of class, as Folger's clubwomen have been abstracted from the social context that explains them. The humor in *The Girls* is broader and dumber: in one installment, a plump woman in a floral bathing suit stands up to her knees in the shallow end of a public swimming pool and cries "Help!" to the hunky lifeguard walking past.

Even in *The New Yorker*, of course, the joke about clubwomen is not always their pretensions to high culture; sometimes it's their ignorance of male things like automobile engines or liquor. And in any case, the *first* joke in all these cartoons, underlying the others, is that the woman is plump and no longer nubile, since everyone knows that women in cartoons are supposed to be young, slender, and sexy. Hokinson and Folger both refer to their menopausal poseurs as "the girls" to emphasize that they're anything but.

Laughter

LAUGHTER IS A big and fascinating subject, one that has inspired whole books, including this one. The present entry confines itself to cases in which laughter itself is laugh-provoking, both as a contagious emotion and as a funny phenomenon in its own right, like HICCUPS or MOTHERS-IN-LAW.

I'll start with laugh tracks, which emerged in the television era, though by the time TV took over, radio comedies had been using live audiences for decades. On the radio shows that prefigured TV sitcoms—*The Great Gildersleeve, The Bickersons, Amos 'n' Andy, Fibber McGee and Molly*—characters often laughed at one another's jokes and at their own. Sometimes compulsive laughter was an integral part of the character, as with Charles the Poet, a recurring character on *The Bob and Ray Show* who kept cracking up in mid-recital, or Senator Beauregard Claghorn on *The Fred Allen Show*, the blustering Dixiecrat who laughed at his own jokes, effectively pre-empting any other laughter, then peevishly insisted, "That's a joke, son" (he was the model for Foghorn Leghorn, the loud-mouthed cartoon rooster), and explained exactly what was funny about it.

Often, though, the actors' laughter weakened their jokes without reinforcing their characterizations. By that point, comedy as we know it had been around for more than two millennia, and comic actors must have known for at least that long that funny behavior is always funnier when those involved seem unaware of their own zaniness. In the golden age of radio, however, comic actors often found it necessary to indicate to the live studio audience—as the illuminated LAUGHTER sign would do in the TV era—that something funny had been said, modeling a response for that audience so that the audience could model one for all the people listening at home on their Philcos.

Humor theorists, who agree about so little, do agree that laughter is a social phenomenon—one of the few esthetic responses enhanced by experiencing it in a crowd. According to Robert Provine, whose *Laughter* (2001) is a notable recent book on the subject, we are thirty times less likely to laugh when alone than in company. Back in the radio era, no one seems to have thought of using a laugh track instead of a live audience, but television hit on the idea soon enough—by the evening of September 9, 1950, on a short-lived comedy called *The Hank McCune Show*, which lives on in infamy for that innovation.

But it was bound to happen sooner or later, and if Hank McCune had felt the need for ennobling precedents, he could have pointed out that one function of the chorus in Greek drama—the first form of live entertainment we know anything about—was to model and cue reactions for the audience. In the early nineteenth century, the French developed the *claque*, a group of shills paid to ensure a play's success by reacting to it in various exemplary ways. According to Robert Hendrickson in *The Literary Life & Other Curiosities*, the *claque* system was elaborate, and included *rieurs* hired to laugh at the jokes as well as *pleureurs* paid to cry at the sad parts, and *bisseurs* to cry "Bis!" ("Encore!").

Soon, anyhow, laugh tracks were standard on sitcoms, even animated ones. One reminder that cartoons weren't always for kids is the grown-up laughter on the laugh tracks for shows like *The Flintstones*, *The Jetsons*, and *The Pink Panther Show*. On the other hand, the truly puerile *Scooby-Doo* used grown-up laughter, too, so who knows what it means? Maybe it was cheaper than recording juvenile laughter, or maybe someone thought that children wouldn't *want* juvenile laugh tracks. And maybe they don't.

When Ross Bagdasarian Sr. created *The Alvin Show* in 1961, he refused to use a laugh track—he's the first producer known to have done so. Larry Gelbart wanted to do the same thing with *M*A*S*H* but usually had to settle for turning off the laughter during scenes in the operating room. (Nowadays, those watching the show on DVD have the options of watching it with or without canned laughter—which makes sense if we think of the laugh track as a layer of commentary on the shows themselves.)

But not everyone resisted the innovation. Si Rose, the executive producer for *H.R. Pufnstuf*, persuaded its creators, Sid and Marty Krofft, to use laugh tracks. Defending the decision in a recent interview, Rose made a valid point: "Night-time started using laugh tracks . . . [so] then when you see a show that's funny and there's no laugh because of no laugh track, it becomes a handicap." Like grade inflation or lying on résumés, laugh tracks became necessary because everyone else was doing it.

They aren't supposed to be funny themselves, of course, but rather to convince us that something laughable has been said or done, or even more directly to prompt the primal response of responding to laughter by echoing it, as we do with yawning. In comic strips, characters hardly ever laugh at their own wackiness, but laughter itself can be a sort of punch line, equivalent to the daily spankings or brickbats that end other strips. *Sam and His Laugh* was a 1905 comic strip about a black man who kept getting fired because he couldn't help laughing uproariously at the foibles of his various—but uniformly silly—white employers. Though Sam was drawn according to the usual blubber-lipped racist conventions of the time, he was the viewpoint character, and though his laughter and its dire consequences for him was the payoff of the strip, the whites came off looking more ridiculous.

Mocking laughter of the kind we all dread is one more funny mishap that can befall a comic villain, especially a self-important one. When a pompous character is hit with a pie or falls in a puddle and other characters laugh, they aren't just redundantly duplicating the audience's laughter; rather, they are giving us a second thing to laugh about, as if the dignitary had been hit with *two* pies, or fallen in two puddles.

Real gut-busting, knee-slapping, full-throated laughter is undignified, and therefore funny the same way as a pratfall or a tantrum when performed by someone stuffy, by a sourpuss or killjoy who normally sneers at frivolity. Laughing gas is a good way to reduce an unsmiling character to raucous guffaws.

You can deduce a humorist's own conscious or unconscious theory of humor from the situations in which he or she shows people laughing. Even if Al Capp hadn't gone on record as believing that "all comedy is based on man's delight in man's inhumanity to man," we'd know that for him laughter was inextricable from schadenfreude, not only because his strip offers so much of that guilty pleasure, but because the biggest laughers in *Li'l Abner* are the most malicious characters, and they laugh hardest when things are going worst for others.

Lightbulbs

SOME ART FORMS are born self-reflexive. Old-fashioned critics like to imply that an art begins to examine itself only when it has exhausted other subjects, and that metafiction, for example, is a sign of decadence. Often, though, the opposite is true: artists call attention to the art form because they refuse to take it for granted. They retain, and even cultivate, the power to see it afresh. It is the conventional writers, filmmakers, and so on—those who do their jobs as unobtrusively as possible, so that we never notice the art—who represent jadedness, habituation, decadence.

Like hip-hop, the comics have been "meta-" ever since their inception. By the first decade of the twentieth century, cartoonists were routinely rapping about their own rapping. In one strip from that era, Winsor McCay—the genius who gave us *Little Nemo in Slumberland*—draws himself at the drawing board, invoking aloud the muse of daily laffs: "Oh! For an idea! What is funny? What can I draw? Oh! For a joke! Let me think!" In taking as his subject his very inability to come up with a subject, McCay joins a venerable tradition whose later practitioners include Yeats ("The Circus Animals' Desertion") and Beckett.

All that, though, is by the way. My real purpose in citing McCay's strip is to point out how ill-suited the comics medium is to probing its characters' innermost thoughts. McCay's solution is a laughably stagy apostrophe; he gets away with it because laughs are what he's after, but in a "serious" strip, such an artificial exclamation would be fatal. A more recent way of representing a character's thoughts is of course the thought

Fig. 87

balloon, with its special scalloped border to indicate that the words inside are not spoken but merely thought. But the thought balloon—that brain-fart linked to its source by a chain of diminishing bubbles—is as silly a convention as McCay's apostrophe; it too works best as a joke, like the theatrical aside, another mind-reading convention that is all but extinct now in serious drama.

One problem with all these conventions—thought balloon, apostrophe, aside—is that they represent thought as much more *verbal* than it really is. Nabokov made the same point about Joyce's celebrated stream-of-consciousness technique: as wonderful as that technique could be in Joyce's hands, it's no more "realistic"—and no less conventional—than any other bookish means of representing thought. Whether or not our thoughts are as predominantly *visual*, as Nabokov insisted, there's no question that the comic strip is mainly a visual medium. Long before the verbal thought balloon became the norm, cartoonists were drawing iconographic thought balloons: a hungry character enters a restaurant picturing the steak he's going to order; then, on receiving the check, he pictures his money winging away. A jealous character pictures his sweetheart in another man's embrace. An errant husband returning late from a poker game pictures his wife awaiting him with a ROLLING PIN. And when someone has a bright idea, a lightbulb appears above his or her head—generally in a thought balloon, though we're no more supposed to think the character is thinking about lightbulbs than we are to deduce from a black cloud over an unhappy character's head that the guy is picturing clouds.

Although many comic strip clichés date back to the pre-history of the medium, the bright-idea bulb doesn't. The first patent for a lightbulb was issued in 1841 to Frederick de Moleyns, an English inventor whose design featured platinum wires in an evacuated glass bulb. (Then as now, the purpose of the bulb itself was mainly to protect the filament from oxidation by isolating it in a vacuum.) "Illumination" has been used as a metaphor for inspiration ever since the Middle Ages—longer than it has been used (in English) in the purely optical sense. But it wasn't until the 1930s that lightbulbs became the standard way of indicating cartoon inspiration. When McCay, in the early strip I mentioned, finally gets his idea, it comes not in the form of a lightbulb but a living creature—a bird, presumably, since it has a beak and two webbed feet, and flies away the instant another cartoonist diverts McCay's attention (**Fig. 87**). It looks less like a bird, though, than a flying porcupine; it looks, in fact, uncannily like the Thing I pictured the first time I read Emily Dickinson's line "Hope is the thing with feathers." We know it's a funny idea, as McCay wished for, because it's funny-looking. And we know it's an idea because it's labeled "IDEA." That sort of labeling is now confined mainly to editorial cartoons but was common in the early days of comics.

People have been speaking of ideas "dawning on" them since the mid-nineteenth century, and there are old comic strips that use a sunrise to represent a sudden inspiration. Cartoonists finally opted for lightbulbs rather than dawns, probably because lightbulbs are easier to draw. And most funny-page epiphanies are in fact pretty dim, better symbolized by a ten-watt bulb than a rising sun. A 1940 strip shows Barney Google's bright idea as a candle, reflecting both the dimness (and precariousness) of his epiphany and his humble hillbilly origins; he must have grown up thinking that electric lighting, like UNDERWEAR or indoor plumbing, was a newfangled invention strictly for city slickers.

The first cartoon lightbulbs, like the first real lightbulbs, were teardrop shaped, tapering to a point at the top to suggest a stylized flame, as chandelier bulbs still do. When real lightbulbs got more bulbous, so did cartoon bulbs, though not immediately. Sometimes iconographic inertia (to borrow a phrase from Nicholson Baker) creates quite a lag between changes in the real world and their reflection in the mirror of art (or, for that matter, the mirror of language; some people *still* say "icebox" rather than "refrigerator"). Will tomorrow's energy-conscious cartoonists retrofit their idea balloons with compact fluorescents or LEDS? It remains to be seen.

Limburger

IN ITS 1929 catalog, the Johnson Smith Company describes the Anarchist Stink Bomb as "more fun than a Limburger cheese." How fun would that have been? Fun enough: as the smelliest cheese most Americans were likely to have encountered, limburger was the funny cheese par excellence in the early twentieth century. In our time limburger humor is almost extinct, but back then, when German immigrants were legion, it was an irresistible target.

Rube Goldberg liked to joke about smelly cheese, as you'd guess from the name of the mad scientist to whom he attributed his mad inventions: Lucifer Gorgonzola Butts. In Butts's machine for keeping a hat from blowing off on a windy day, a piece of cheese falls into an old shoe, and "strength of cheese causes shoe to walk away" (thereby pulling a shoelace which opens the lid of an upside-down box and releases a ten-pound biscuit, and so on). We can't say for sure that the cheese in question was limburger, but Goldberg is more specific in describing another invention, the painless tooth extractor, where a sequence of events involving peanuts and a squirrel leads a piston to work a bellows so that it "blow fumes of limbourger cheese in patient's face, knocking him cold." As usual when cartoonists draw cheese—even when the cheese's stinkiness is the whole point, even when it's identified as limburger—Goldberg drew a wedge of Swiss, because that's the only cheese that says "cheese" at comic-strip resolution.

Limburger was a favorite laughingstock in early comic films—films like "Oh! That Limburger: The Story of a Piece of Cheese" (1906), "Love and Limburger" (1913), "The Adventures of Limburger and Schweitzer"

(1914), "Limburger's Victory" (1915), "A Case of Limburger" (1915), "A Limburger Cyclone" (1917), and "Where the Limburger Grows" (1917), the last an animated short featuring the Katzenjammer Kids. People deprived of one sense compensate by developing their other senses to an abnormal degree, and that may be why silent comedies were filled with jokes about stinks, though of course viewers could no more smell the cheese than they could hear the gunshots. In *Shoulder Arms* (1918), Charlie Chaplin plays an American soldier in the trenches of World War I France. One day he receives a food package from home and it includes a limburger—one made right there in Europe, perhaps, and returning to its native continent after a pointless trip to America. In any case, the cheese is so ripe that Charlie must put on his gas mask in order to unwrap it; instead of eating it, he lobs it into the German trench, causing a panic there.

Though the region of Limburg is partly in Belgium and partly in the Netherlands, it is the Germans who make and eat most of the cheese, and limburger humor in the United States peaked at the same time as German humor, in the first two decades of the twentieth century. Germans were so funny, in that era, to everyone else in the melting pot, and limburger—like lederhosen—was such a tempting pretext for ridiculing Germans, that we probably needn't look any further to explain the vogue for limburger humor.

The reason such humor has just about vanished in our era is that limburger itself is an endangered species in America, as it already was in my childhood. Though I grew up in Ohio, not far from the dairy states (and from the only American cheesemaker still making limburger), I was in my thirties before I first encountered the cheese, and only because I'd sought it out, confronted it, as a writer must face anything he's been reading about all his life without ever laying eyes on, or getting wind of. Back in 1979, when the B-52s released "Dance This Mess Around" with its immortal cri de coeur, "Why don't you dance with me? / I'm not no limburger," I knew that limburger was a famously smelly cheese, but at that point I'd never actually smelled one, and I suspect that the B-52s hadn't, either.

So let's hear from someone who has. In *Eating in Two or Three Languages* (1918), Irvin S. Cobb sings the praises of a cheese he never names but that clearly belongs to the same cheese family as limburger, the washed-rind family, whose members are repeatedly moistened with beer during aging to foster the growth of the bacteria that flavor them—the same bacteria we have to thank for foot odor:

> It comes in a flat cake, which invariably is all caved in and squashed out, as though the cheese-maker had sat upon it. . . . When its temperature goes up, it becomes more of a liquid than a solid; and it has an aroma by virtue of which it secures the attention and commands the respect of the most casual passer-by. . . . It is to other and lesser cheeses as civet cats are to canary birds. . . . Among strangers, eating it—or, when it is in an especially fluid state, drinking it—comes under the head of outdoor sports.

Ripe limburger is as soft and spreadable as brie; indeed, it was once sold in jars, as we know from episodes of both *Our Gang* and *The Three Stooges* where a character (Chubby; Curly) mistakes it for salve and applies it topically. In "Bear Shooters" (1930), Chubby brings along a jar of limburger cheese spread on the Gang's hunting trip. He likes to smear it on BANANAS and even to eat it straight from the jar. When Mary asks him to "grease Weezer"—to rub salve on her ailing little brother when he coughs—Chubby uses the limburger instead, and of course Weezer becomes a pariah: at his approach, a duck buries its head under its wing, Pete the dog covers his snout with his forepaws, a mule shakes its head, and Farina exclaims, "Boy, you sure don't smell like no violet!" Even a skunk flees at Weezer's approach.

In 1933, Harry Langdon upped the ante by setting the limburger/ointment mix-up on an airplane. The movie is *The Hitchhiker*, a two-reeler that resonates with modern anxieties about flying. Sporting a nasty chest cold that accounts for most of the sounds he makes in the movie, and most of the annoyance he causes, the baby-faced Langdon sneaks onto a passenger plane and spends the next fifteen minutes coughing and sneezing all over his fellow passengers. What finally gets him ejected midflight, though, is limburger cheese: what with his cold, Langdon can't smell anything, so when he confuses a jar of limburger spread with a like-shaped jar of ointment and smears the cheese on his chest and face, he's the last one on the plane to notice. He keeps dabbing the stuff on even after everyone else aboard is gagging and craning and asking, "What's that horrible smell?"

Since the Pepé Le Pew cartoons are about stinkiness the way the Mr. Magoo cartoons are about blindness, it was probably inevitable that some of them would laugh at limburger as well as skunks and Frenchmen. In "Odor-able Kitty," a cat uses white paint and ripe cheese to look and smell like a skunk in order to scare away dogs, but thereby earns Pepé's unwelcome attentions. In "Really Scent," Pepé falls for Fabrette, a cat with an unfortunate white streak on her back, but despite Pepé's endearments ("Come back, my leetle melon baby collie!"), Fabrette can't stand his smell. But she's more desperate for a mate than most of Pepé's quarries, and in a touching gesture of love, dips herself in a vat of limburger ("150 proof") in order to smell as bad as Pepé. He, however, has gotten the same idea, diving into a vat of chlorophyll ("For her, I weel make myself dain-TEE") in an O. Henry twist. The next time he sees Fabrette, now enveloped by a foliage-wilting cloud of stink, Pepé flees *her*.

Little Audrey

Little Audrey came home holding a dollar bill.
When her mother asked her where she got it, she said
that the neighbor boys paid her a dollar to climb a tree. "Don't ever
do that again, Little Audrey," said her mother. "Those boys just
want to see your underwear." Little Audrey laughed and laughed,
because she knew she wasn't wearing any underwear.
—1930S JOKE

LITTLE AUDREY IS a stupid little girl who laughs and laughs at what she takes to be other people's misconceptions. According to folklorist B. A. Botkin, there were thousands of jokes about her, clean and dirty, in the 1930s. Partridge's *Dictionary of Catch Phrases* dates the expression "little Audrey laughed and laughed" to the late 1920s, and presumably some of the jokes go back at least that far. The much-spanked

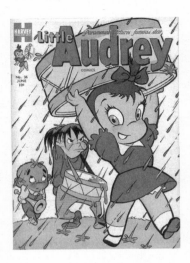

Fig. 88

Harvey Comics character (modeled on Little Lulu) didn't come along till 1948 and so is a rare example of pop culture working as it should: as a recycling of folklore, not just a substitute for it.

Like her comic book avatar **(Fig. 88)**, Little Audrey was ostensibly a child, and some of the jokes about her are reminiscent of the vintage Dead Baby jokes discussed in the entry on INFANT MORTALITY (unless I rename it KINDERTOTEN-LIEDER, since those sick old jokes remain our culture's embarrassing answer to Mahler's haunting songs on the death of children):

> People came from far and near to see Little Audrey parachute-jump. She went way up high in the airplane and got ready to jump. . . . On her way down she just laughed and laughed, because she knew she was going to fool those people: she didn't have on her parachute.

For such a sweet and innocent little girl, such a ray of sunshine, many of the jokes were alarmingly raunchy. They have less in common with G-rated comic books (already kinky enough—see SPANKING) than with the crudely illustrated pornographic fan fictions known as Tijuana bibles. Legman, whose flabbergasting typology of dirty jokes classifies Little Audrey jokes as "female-fool" jokes (and says they were especially popular in college humor magazines), quotes a literate specimen from 1940: "When her boyfriend said that it was so dark he couldn't see his hand in front of her face, Little Audrey laughed and laughed, because she knew his hand wasn't in front of his face."

So some of the jokes, like certain comic books, were clearly for adults. But others were just as clearly by and for kids, like the parachute joke. I sometimes wonder, from my debauched and degraded adult perspective, how children can take as much pleasure as they do in squeaky-clean jokes, considering that many grownups laugh only at dirty ones, and others have ceased to get any pleasure at all from humor, and resent having to fake the orgasm of mirth every time a joke is told by anyone they fear or pity. Most children, even little ones, are smarter than Little Audrey. Some are as smart as most grownups. And most grownups—even pious grownups who would never buy a book of dirty jokes—know to avoid books of *clean* ones. And websites devoted to clean ones. I'd be surprised if many of my readers spend much time chuckling at the thousands of clean ones found so easily online at websites run, I like to think, by sinister soccer moms taking a break from the PTA and the Neighborhood Patrol to splash around with me in heavy-duty waders in the open sewer of American humor, though unlike me the moms are looking not for funny but for sterile sewage. If jokes were breakfast cereals, then the clean ones scavenged, disinfected, and reposted on the Clean Joke pages would make Cream of Wheat taste positively spicy. If jokes were movies, the Clean Ones would demand an MPAA rating even tamer and more namby-pamby than G. And yet most children subsist (or did in the days before the Internet) on a diet of mostly clean jokes.

One way the sense of humor changes at adolescence is that at that point we discover the most embarrassing thing in life, and it turns out to be the instinct and process by which human life perpetuates itself. Once you learn about sex,[32] you find it hard to believe that you were ever embarrassed by anything else, or ever laughed at anything else. But you

---

[32] Some children, of course, get obsessed with sex before adolescence, and though I wasn't one of them, I've noticed that such prodigies often go on to be the funniest grownups. Maybe that's because only children with a hyperactive sense of humor would choose to think about sex a minute sooner than their glands compel them to. Or maybe the prodigious sense of humor comes from the years of observing and inferring and interpreting grown-up behavior with the cold eye of childhood. I know I was more attuned to the sheer funniness of BOSOMS AND BREASTS back before I learned to like them again.

were and you did, after all. Long before children learn to be embarrassed by their bodies, they are embarrassed by their minds.

Children "are intensely preoccupied with the issue of smartness and dumbness," writes Martha Wolfenstein in *Children's Humor,* explaining why, "from the age of six to about eleven, children tend to identify jokes with riddles." (I'd add that riddles are easier to recall and recount than anecdotal jokes, and that a lot of grown-up jokes are riddles too, including nearly all the jokes that spring up in response to certain news items, like the Michael Jackson scandals.) Wolfenstein argues that children tend to use the two terms interchangeably, and that the confusion is related to children's concern with smartness, with knowing the answer.

And of course all jokes depend for their effect on the teller knowing something the listener doesn't. And children know and tell more jokes than all but the most buffoonish grownups. In the same way that some intelligent adults who never went to college will compensate for real or perceived defects in their knowledge by teaching themselves about some esoteric subject like computers or science fiction, enabling them to feel smarter for a change, the huge body of children's folklore, of which few grownups have retained more than scraps, serves children as a rival expertise, an esoteric or countercultural knowledge, to set against the official grown-up knowledge in which they are daily made to feel inadequate.

The lore of schoolchildren also embraces urban legends, counting-out rhymes, playground games, and so on, but when it comes to making children feel smart, nothing beats the lowly joke. After all, many thinkers from Plato onward have argued that the essence of humor is superiority, and that a laugh is really a roar of exultation on beholding someone less intelligent, attractive, successful, or lucky than oneself. Even if you find the superiority theory insanely reductive (as I do), you must admit that a lot of laughter expresses scorn. At the mention of superior or scornful laughter we may think of haughty aristocrats like Nabokov or Wilde, but in fact such laughter is at least as common among the lowest of the low. Indeed, according to Descartes, "the least perfect are usually most given to mockery . . . desiring to see all others held in as low an estimation as themselves."

Even when children's jokes don't take the form of riddles, they often deal with stupidity, and Little Audrey jokes derived their humor precisely from the penchant of the very stupid to indulge in superior laughter:

Little Audrey was playing with matches and burned the house down. Audrey and her mother were looking at the ruins. Audrey's mother said, "Little Audrey, your daddy is going to kill you when he gets home." Little Audrey laughed and laughed and laughed because she knew her daddy was asleep on the couch.

Little Audrey is notably stupid even by juvenile standards, and the jokes about her belong to the same family as MORON jokes and Polack jokes: jokes about stupidity. The special ingredient in Little Audrey jokes is Audrey's mistaken conviction of being smarter—knowing better—than other people, and her way of positively reveling in that delusion, laughing and laughing. Her delusions of cleverness are endearing in the same way as Curly's in Three Stooges shorts: his trademark "nyuck-nyuck-nyuck" is his way of laughing and laughing at whatever moronic solution he's just hit on and mistaken for clever.

Curly is, indeed, a Little Audrey of a larger growth—and that, I'd argue, is one reason he is not just the funniest but the most lovable of the Three Stooges. He's a FAT MAN with a bald head, a high voice, and a funny Brooklyn accent, and he's the stupidest of the Stooges, but what makes him so endearing is his amazing emotional transparency. The only kind of thinking he can handle is thinking aloud, and as befits the all-but-subhuman dimness of his thoughts, half the sounds that accompany them are not words, but squeaks of surprise and growls of annoyance and woo-woos-woos of fear or agitation and—most famously—chuckles of pure unearned self-satisfaction.

Marriage

Marriage—a book of which the first chapter is written in poetry
and the remaining chapters in prose.—
BEVERLY NICHOLS

Good morning, sir. I'm the census taker. Are you married or happy?
—MOE HOWARD, "NO CENSUS, NO FEELING," 1940

IN *THE AMERICAN Language*, H. L. Mencken quotes another commentator's observation that *The American Thesaurus of Slang* (1942) lists fifty-two synonyms for *wife* but "not an affectionate reference in the lot." Mencken cites this as an instance of the mean-spiritedness of slang, but it could also serve as an instance of the ingratitude of humor, since most slang partakes of humor, and what Henri de Montherlant said about happiness—that it "writes in white ink on a white page"—is also true of gratitude, especially among humorists. If your wife is a constant joy, you count your blessings in private. You won't win many laughs by singing the praises of her cooking or drawing cartoons that show how sweet and forgiving she is when you come home drunk.

So the humor of marriage mostly takes the form of bellyaching. In "I Do, I Will, I Have," Ogden Nash defines the institution as "a legal and religious alliance entered into by a man who can't sleep with the window shut and a woman who can't with the window open." Nash allows that he may not know the difference between flotsam and jetsam, but he does know that "marriage is the alliance of two people one of whom never remembers birthdays and the other never forgetsam." He concludes, though, that "a little incompatibility is the spice of life, particularly if he has income and she is pattable."

When two people live together day after day and year after year, they develop a morbid sensitivity to each other's eccentricities, and unless both are saints, they will now and then get comically annoyed at what strike outsiders as comically minor offenses. In *That Uncertain Feeling* (1941), a comedy directed by Ernst Lubitsch, a woman is so irritated by her husband's harmless habit of poking her in the belly with a finger and saying "Keeks!" that she develops a case of psychosomatic HICCUPS and has to see a PSYCHIATRIST about it. In such instances, the prognosis for the marriage depends on the humorist. A gentle humorist will wind up concluding, and getting the couple to conclude, that for all its aggravations, marriage is worth it. A more savage humorist will joke about SPOUSE-KILLING or the joys of single life.

The other big joke about marriage treats it as a sort of punitive "sin tax" on sex. Why buy the cow when you can get the milk for free? A lot of marriage humor concerns men's efforts to get the milk for free, and the efforts of society—in the form of chaperones, shotgun-toting HILLBIL-LIES, virtuous maidens, and so on—to prevent such thefts and reform such thieves. A comic postcard from the 1950s pictures two men leering at a passing blonde. Says one guy to the other: "She can be had for a song . . . the wedding march!"

For some reason, this unromantic view of marriage was once seen as positively racy. On the cover of *The Gag Writer's Private Joke Book*, a 1956 Ace paperback by "leading jokesmith" Eddie Davis, featuring "the special howlers that top comics tell each other . . . the real belly-laughs they couldn't use over the air," an indignant mother scolds the young man seated on her COUCH and making out with her daughter: "If you're not buying, please don't handle the merchandise." The girl is scantily clad and absurdly big-breasted, but there is nothing especially daring—even by staid 1950s standards—in the implication that marriage is a commercial proposition; Jane Austen was making the same point two hundred years ago.

Marriage Counselors

A S ONE WHO has never been married *or* counseled, I find it all too easy to laugh at marriage counselors, and I've been wondering why cartoons about them tend to be so lame. Gag cartoons in general are seldom very funny, but no cartoon cliché, not even the BUMS on the park bench, has a lower Laff Quotient than this one. There have been savagely funny cartoons about marital discord (see, for instance, SPOUSE-KILLING), and funny cartoons about therapy and therapists (see PSYCHIATRISTS), but most marriage-counselor cartoons are as coy as Norman Rockwell's 1963 illustration—painted for the *Saturday Evening Post* but never used—of a young couple seated side by side in a counselor's office, he with a black eye and a sorrowful expression, she giving him a cute sidelong scowl. The picture tells a story, but not much of one because Rockwell had to give so wide a berth—though evidently not wide enough for the *Saturday Evening Post*—to the sort of problems that actually send couples to counselors. We can't even be sure that the wife gave her husband that shiner; in the humor of the era, men usually get black eyes not from their wives but from other women, after the men get too fresh.

The real problem is that marriage counseling as we know it didn't come along until the 1950s. (Until then, the term meant "birth control" and was associated with the eugenics movement.) By that point our culture had become very coy about sexual matters. One could argue that marriage counseling was one symptom of that coyness. In any case, humorists joke about marriage the most when they're forbidden to joke about sex. And marriage-counselor humor is notable for its avoidance of sex.

Take, for instance, a 1965 cartoon from *Parade* magazine. A middle-aged couple sits in a counselor's waiting room; she looks shell-shocked and he sits blithely nearby, holding (wearing?) a sousaphone. That's a joke about TUBAS, not about marriage or counseling. In a cartoon from 1960, another couple sits in another waiting room, he frowning and she smiling; through the open door we see the counselor on the phone to his own wife: " . . . Yes, dear . . . of course, dear . . . I'll do that, dear . . . yes, dear." As usual, Charles Addams managed to be funnier than average: a cartoon from *Black Maria* (1960) shows a prince and princess in the office of a medieval marriage counselor. The prince explains why they're there: "We're not living happily ever after."

Married Sex

Sex in marriage is like medicine. Three times a day for the first week. Then once a day for another week. Then once every three or four days until the condition clears up.
—PETER DE VRIES

The gods gave man fire, and he invented fire engines. They gave him love, and he invented marriage.
—HENNY YOUNGMAN

Personally I know nothing about sex because I've always been married.
—ZSA ZSA GABOR

Marriage is the miracle that transforms a kiss from a pleasure into a duty.
—HELEN ROWLAND

Fig. 89 Married sex (or lack thereof), part I. See also RUMPS.

Marriage isn't a process of prolonging the life of love,
but of mummifying the corpse.
—P. G. WODEHOUSE

Marriage is like a bank account.
You put it in, you take it out, you lose interest.
—IRWIN COREY

Lucy [to Ethel]: Ever since we said "I do,"
there are so many things we don't.
—I LOVE LUCY

Do you know what it means to come home at night
to a woman who'll give you a little love, a little affection,
a little tenderness? It means you're in the wrong house,
that's what it means.
—HENNY YOUNGMAN

Fig. 90 Married sex (or lack thereof), part 2. See also NINCOMPOOPS.

Meat

How beautiful is the universe when something digestible
meets with an eager digestion.
—DON MARQUIS

IN ITS EARLY years, the *Popeye* comic strip was even more violent than the animated cartoons it inspired. There is one especially gruesome Sunday strip from 1933 that must have changed the way some readers thought about hamburgers. Wimpy has just inherited a cow from his cousin, and tries to trade it to Popeye for a burger, since burgers are the only thing that Wimpy cares about. When Popeye refuses, Wimpy converts the cow into burgers himself with the aid of some knives and a meat grinder. We aren't shown the butchering, but the aftermath is bad enough: Wimpy sits by the side of the road, next to a heap of ground beef as tall as he. Nearby lie the cow's severed head (still tied to a stake by a rope around its neck) and hooves (one of them still standing upright, with leg bone attached). The only other cow part to remain intact, the tail, protrudes from the hopper of the meat grinder.

Though we tend to think of high art as more truthful than low art, it isn't always. The fact that eating meat means eating animals has always been acknowledged most candidly in cartoons and comic strips. *Li'l Abner*, for example, constantly insisted on the regrettable connection between animals and meat. The Yokums, Abner's family, eat more than their share of pork, though they are turnip farmers and their prize hog Salomey is a beloved pet, not a future source of food. In a Sunday strip from 1947, Abner takes Salomey for "a nice in-viggy-ratin' ride" in the country, past all sorts of lurid billboards for pig's feet, pork sausages, roast suckling pig, and the like. On returning, he can't understand why Salomey looks sick instead of inviggyrated, till Mammy asks how he'd feel after such a ride with "a fambly o' kine-hearted pigs," in a world where the roles of eater and eaten were reversed. Abner—and Al Capp—proceed to envision just that, and we see billboards for boys' feet, human sausage ("Made From the Finest Boys!" says the ad, which pictures a naked Li'l Abner as well as a string of sausages), roast suckling lout (showing Abner's straw-hatted head on a platter, with an apple in the mouth), and so on.

Though not a vegetarian himself, Capp was strangely obsessed by meat and by the idea that meat is murder. He even imagined a state of affairs where meat *wouldn't* be murder: in 1948, Abner discovers a creature called the Shmoo, which stands about three feet high, looks like a walking scrotum with a penis for a head, reproduces asexually and unstoppably, and loves to be eaten. Shmoos are so fond of being eaten that they die of sheer happiness when anyone looks at them hungrily. And they're delicious: when fried they taste like chicken; when broiled, like steak.

The quintessential funny cut of meat is probably the pork chop. In a *Li'l Abner* strip from 1939, Pappy Yokum contemplates Salomey and a pork chop side by side: "How dreamy ah feels . . . What a lovely sight . . . a li'l pig an a li'l po'k chop . . . The pig rep-re-sents th' po'k chop befo' . . . an the' po'k chop rep-re-sents th' pig aftuh!!" Pork is funnier than beef because it's more fatty and more flavorful. But steak is funny too, especially the kind with an eye that a comic character holds over his own eye after getting the worst of a fistfight. I can imagine a vegetarian nodding grimly at the juxtaposition of two forms of barbarism, brawling and meat-eating, especially since the steak in question is always raw, straight from the cow. Or almost always: in *Top Hat*, a bumbling servant brings a cooked one straight from the grill and applies *that* to his master's shiner.

Steak, by the way, was not always classy fare. When T. S. Eliot wrote "The winter evening settles in / With smell of steaks in passageways," he was evoking a squalid tenement, not a fancy restaurant. And when in 1921 Edward E. Paramore Jr. wrote, "Oh, tough as a steak was Yukon Jake / Hard-boiled as a picnic egg," the comparisons not only evoked the qualities under discussion, but also suited Jake's all-round character and the mood of the poem. (And nowhere in poetry are connotations more important than in the choice of metaphor: it would be fatal to all but the most farcical poem to speak of a beauty "with skin as white as lard" or "a delicious pudding the color of pus.") Even today, a big chuck steak is often the cheapest thing in the meat department.

Meat has been used as slang for a sex object since the early sixteenth century, and as slang for the penis since Shakespeare's time. In the 1890s, to *brown your meat* was to have sex—standard missionary sex, not anal sex—while to *flash your meat* was to expose yourself. By the end of World War I, to *hang your meat* was to urinate, though *beat your meat* has referred to masturbation only since the 1930s. These idioms are interesting because meat is something less than living flesh; to call your penis your meat—like calling it your tool—is to treat it as a possession, an accessory, rather than a part of your body with an embarrassing mind of its own.

Mental Undressing

Take Mother Eve in her cute dress;
Think of that and picture less.
—BUDDY DESYLVA, "MAGNOLIA," 1927

TO JUDGE BY my own decades of coveting women, the feat of imagination portrayed in cartoons of mental undressing is not a very accurate portrayal of what actually happens when a man looks at a woman with lust in his heart. Certainly we try to deduce the size and shape of the parts that interest us. But I doubt that many men undress PRETTY GIRLS from head to toe in their imaginations. Who but foot fetishists, for instance, would go to the trouble of picturing a woman's FEET minus their footwear?

But mental undressing is a funny sight gag, partly for its acknowledgment of the open secret that, at any given moment, that respectable businessman on the commuter train is probably thinking X-rated thoughts. It's also a pretext for the cartoonist to draw naked women—a favorite subject of single-panel gag cartoonists, in the 1940s and '50s, not only in lowbrow publications like *Snappy* and *Joker*, but at *The New Yorker*. It was *The New Yorker*, after all, that gave us Sam Cobean, one of the most outrageous one-trick ponies in the history of cartooning.

To be fair, not *all* of Cobean's cartoons involved mental undressing. He was actually a three- or four-trick pony, with several other running gags, like the drunk being thrown out of the bar (see BUM'S RUSH), or the flood washing whole houses downstream while survivors cower on the rooftops. And his nudes were never as lovingly—or lustfully—drawn as, say, Peter Arno's. You can imagine a porn-deprived adolescent in the 1940s getting aroused by Arno's cartoons, but hardly by Cobean's. He wasn't the only cartoonist who played with the premise: A 1948 cartoon by Eric Ericson (not the psychoanalyst, though I wish it were) shows a rooster ogling a chicken and picturing her without feathers; an R. Taylor cartoon from the same era shows a male doctor staring at a sexy nurse and envisioning her skeleton.

But Cobean made the gag his own. He wasn't a lecher, just a cartoonist who developed a fatal fascination with the possibilities of a particular joke. And he was in good company: George Herriman was fascinated with all the ways you could show a mouse beaning a cat with a brick. Rudolph Dirks was fascinated with all the ways that a pair of mischievous little boys could earn themselves a spanking. And Sam Cobean was fascinated with all the ways he could vary the basic guy-sees-pretty-woman-and-pictures-her-naked gag. To list only a few of his variations:

2/5/49: Man at nightclub ogles scantily clad dancer and pictures her completely nude; she, however, pictures herself in mink coat.

4/23/49: Man in bar looks at blonde on next barstool and blurrily imagines her naked; then puts on eyeglasses, looks at her again, and mental picture is much sharper.

8/6/49: Arab man sees woman in full burqa and imagines her without her veil but otherwise fully clad.

1/21/1950: Man in department store sees woman trying on hat in front of triptych mirror and pictures group of four identical naked women.

3/18/1950: Man sees young woman walking along between two middle-aged women; mentally undresses her but not them.

4/8/1950: Man at circus sideshow stares at half-man, half-woman Zelda and, exercising superhuman control of imagination, pictures only female half.

4/29/1950: (1) Male pedestrian mentally undresses female pedestrian. (2) He pauses to greet her, tips hat, briefly stops envisioning her in the nude. (3) As they continue on their separate ways, he looks back over shoulder and picture woman naked again, but now from behind.

7/8/1950: Man at beach sees suntanned woman in bikini and pictures her naked with tan lines.

6/23/51: Male umpire for woman's baseball game watches starting pitcher disconsolately walking off field, pictures her in shower.

6/21/51: Woman spends ten panels meticulously getting dressed for date, then heads downstairs, where waiting boyfriend instantly undresses her in imagination.

9/20/52: Little boy sees voluptuous woman and pictures her as naked stick figure.[33]

So if it's cartoons of naked people you want, the highbrow *New Yorker*, mid-century edition, is one place to look. The lowbrow men's magazines are, of course, another. You won't find much nudity, however, in the middlebrow, middle-class periodicals of the era. The *Saturday Evening Post* might run a funny poem about Lady Godiva by someone like Richard Armour; *Reader's Digest* might venture a tame, unillustrated joke about nudist colonies. But images—even hazy low-res photos or artless vandalistic scrawls—have a primal power that censors fear and writers can only envy.

---

[33] By my calculation, that little boy must have reached manhood right around the time that Twiggy replaced Marilyn Monroe as a sex symbol.

Middle Initials

AMIDDLE INITIAL IS a riddle awaiting a solution, and sometimes the solution is funny. On *The Honeymooners*, Edward L. Norton's middle initial stands for "Lilywhite." The "L." in "Larry L. Lawrence"—the crime reporter played by Bob Hope in *The Ghost Breakers* (1940)—stands for "Lawrence." In *North by Northwest*, Cary Grant plays a character named "Roger O. Thornhill"; when asked what the "O." stands for, he says "Nothing." Maynard G. Krebs, the beatnik sidekick of Dobie Gillis, claims absurdly that the "G." is silent and stands for "Walter." Old sitcoms could get a whole episode of mirth out of an embarrassing middle name, as with the *Dick Van Dyke* episode "What's in a Middle Name?," where we learn that Ritchie's middle name is Rosebud—or, actually, R.O.S.E.B.U.D., an acronym for the names of his father, grandfathers, and great-grandfathers: "Robert Oscar Samuel Edward Benjamin Ulysses David."

Groucho Marx favored middle initials for his characters: "Otis B. Driftwood," "Hugo Z. Hackenbush," "Rufus T. Firefly." Those examples illustrate two laws of the funny middle initial:

1. It is usually one of the nine letters in our alphabet that ends in an "ee" sound. For some reason, comic writers who favor middle initials favor that sound—if not quite nine times out of ten, certainly more than nine out of twenty-six.
2. It will invariably contribute to a name that is already sufficiently distinctive without it. The singer Mark E. Smith can be excused for using an initial to distinguish himself from all the other Mark Smiths, and likewise with Samuel L. Jackson, but how many Otis Driftwoods are there?

A middle initial tends to connote wealth and distinction, and outside of Marx Brothers movies, the most common function of the comedic middle initial is as part of a comically misleading misnomer for a character utterly lacking in wealth and distinction—a character like Alfred

E. Neuman or his Brand-X counterpart at *Cracked*, Sylvester P. Smythe.

In addition to their other roles in funny NAMES, middle initials are indispensable to contrivers of *joke* names—ones that don't just sound funny, and may not sound funny at all, but function as puns—I. P. Freely, I. M. Horny, and the like. The annals of forgotten comic strip characters include B. O. Plenty, H. E. Butzin, O. U. Chump, and Kinney B. Alive. The huckster played by W. C. Fields in *You Can't Cheat an Honest Man* is named Larson E. Whipsnade. It should come as no surprise that an American who chose to use his first two initials instead of his forename, when those initials were "W.C.," was fond not only of funny names in general, but of funny initials in particular. And while we're on the subject of the great film comedians: when Fatty Arbuckle returned to Hollywood as a director years after the RAPE-and-murder scandal that virtually ended his acting career, he worked under the pseudonym of "William Goodrich." According to legend, Arbuckle's old friend Buster Keaton had suggested "Will B. Goode," but they decided that that was too transparently an alias.

Surprisingly rare—since it's funnier than the middle initial—is the *first* initial with the middle name spelled out, à la J. Pierpont Morgan or E. Power Biggs. I forget who said, "Never trust a man who parts his name on the left," but it's good advice in Funnyland, where the practice betokens a stuffed shirt or blowhard, or sometimes just a rich guy like the one in *Thimble Theatre*, I. Canniford Lotts, or the ruthless Pork King in *Li'l Abner*, J. Roaringham Fatback. Abbreviating the first name instead of the middle does more than tell us that a character prefers his middle name to his first. It also implies a desire for specialness, even if the middle name itself is nothing special, as with G. Gordon Liddy. But usually the middle name *is* special; often it's a family name insisting on its owner's illustrious ancestry. In a way, there's something *humble* about calling yourself E. Power Biggs instead or Edward Biggs—an admission that you yourself, and perhaps your organ-playing, are less important than the Power lineage from which you have the privilege of descending.

In pop culture as in real life, parting one's name on the left is an almost exclusively male affectation. Sometimes, as with initials in general, the joke is in the contrast between the mighty-sounding name and its mousy bearer, as with E. Pluribus Dingbat, hapless head of household and star of *The Dingbat Family*—the early George Herriman strip best remembered for spinning off *Krazy Kat*. In other, lesser strips like *O. Heeza Boob* (1912–13), the name was parted on the left simply for the sake of a lame pun.

Midnight Snacks

> *McGee: I et something last night that didn't agree with me.*
> *Doc Gamble: What?*
> *McGee: Oh, just a little sandwich I fixed up about midnight. Fried egg, bologna, Bermuda onion, cream cheese and mustard pickles.*
> —*FIBBER MCGEE AND MOLLY*, 1946

ALTHOUGH ONE PURPOSE of a good humorist is to detect and amplify trace amounts of humor in things nobody ordinarily thinks of as funny—COUCHES, for instance—sometimes it isn't clear whether the funniness in question has been discovered or rather imparted by the humorist. Just as the coolest kid in junior high could single-handedly make pocket protectors or high-water pants fashionable by wearing them often enough, comic geniuses like Charlie Chaplin or Al Capp or Samuel Beckett (or, in our own time, Roz Chast) can impart a radioactive charge of humor to any unpromising subject or object simply by exposing it often enough to their high-voltage sense of humor.

It was Chic Young, I'm convinced, who made midnight snacking funny (or "taught us to laugh at" it) in his comic strip *Blondie*, through the agency of a once-minor character who married the title character and crowded her out of the limelight. Dagwood's insistence on marrying Blondie caused his rich and snooty parents to disinherit him, or else he'd never have had to go to work for Mr. Dithers. The marriage had still graver consequences: Blondie settled down and became a happy housewife and a model mother, in the process losing much of her sex appeal. As for Dagwood, he lost his libido and gave free rein to another appetite.

Dagwood's trademark vice is perfect for the strip's G-rated humor. In comic strips about nice couples—*Hi and Lois, Toots and Casper, Blondie*—

the husband isn't allowed to get drunk (except perhaps on New Year's Eve) or chase after showgirls. Maybe he gets to play cards now and then, but the middle-class, middle-American audiences of the mid-twentieth century weren't comfortable with anything racier, so cartoonists replaced the manly sins of old with suburban peccadilloes like chore-shirking, oversleeping, noonday napping on the sofa, and, especially, midnight snacking. That vice reaches its apotheosis in Dagwood's magnificent Pisan (or Jengan?) sandwiches **(Fig. 91)**.

In our era, a sandwich like that is a sure sign that its architect has given up on sex and settled for the consolation prize of food. We like to think that in the past, people weren't as fat-obsessed or body-conscious, and maybe they weren't, but fat as a form of despair—and a cause for despair in the fat person's spouse—is an old joke. Dagwood, though, is blessed with a metabolism that enables him to snack all he wants without putting on a pound. Like Blondie, he still has his youthful figure, and if he were ever to pursue some young receptionist, it would hardly be more of a long shot than his original pursuit of Blondie herself (who was always out of his league); but she must be reassured by the fact that when his id wakes him in the middle of the night and prompts him to sneak from their sexless bedroom, the desire he seeks to gratify is for sandwiches, not sex.

In his discussion of jokes about men "substituting food satisfaction for sex," Gershon Legman—who has done more than anyone else to re-

Fig. 91 *Blondie*, 1944

interpret our culture's humor on Freudian lines—christens the behavior "Dagwoodism" or "the Dagwood complex." Such explanations of midnight snacking were common enough by 1959 that a cartoon from the *Saturday Evening Post* showed a pajamaed husband, caught red-handed in front of an open refrigerator with a bottle of milk in one hand, a HAM and a big slice of pie in the other, telling his wife: "I'm NOT insecure—I'm HUNGRY!"

One of the best midnight-snacking sequences I've seen is in *How to Sleep*, a 1935 MGM mockumentary written by and starring Robert Benchley. Benchley enters the kitchen for a glass of hot milk, but while returning the bottle to the fridge discovers a plate of cold lobster, and then a dish of coleslaw, and samples both with his bare hands. "Funny these things never tasted like this at dinner," the voice-over observes. Next comes some chicken, at which point, as his appetite continues to snowball, he reasons, "Oh well, might as well be comfortable about it," and in a jump cut transfers his center of operations to the kitchen table, where he has set half a dozen different leftovers and a bottle of beer. No wonder the narrator concludes that, "in using the hot milk method, it is better to have the milk brought to you by someone else."

Milquetoasts

> *Pity the meek, for they shall inherit the earth.*
> —DON MARQUIS

> *It's going to be fun to watch and see how long the meek can keep the earth once they inherit it.*
> —KIN HUBBARD

I OWE THE TITLE of this entry to H. T. Webster, whose panel cartoon *The Timid Soul* introduced Caspar Milquetoast in 1924, and had made him a household word by the time of Webster's death in 1954. Caspar is so meek, he deserves to inherit the earth single-handedly. In one cartoon we see him standing on a street corner in the rain, and saying to himself, "Well, I'll wait one more hour for him, and if he doesn't come then he can go borrow that money from someone else." In another, he stands on a sidewalk staring at his hat, which has blown off his head and lies ten feet away on a lawn with a KEEP OFF THE GRASS sign. "Oh, well," he tells himself, "I had to buy a new hat anyway." In another we see him standing at his front door glancing sideways at his wife and wondering how to answer the census taker, who has just asked him, "Are you the head of the family?" But it's regrettable that Webster felt the need, every few panels, to illustrate his antihero's meekness with examples from his marriage, because the last thing the comics need—or needed back in 1924—is another strip about a HENPECKED HUSBAND. And Caspar, at least potentially, was something much more interesting: a Kafka character whose free-floating sense of doom leads him to imagine horrendous punishments for the smallest infractions.

What did people call men like Caspar before H. T. Webster came along? There have been many good synonyms for *coward*, such as *poltroon*, *dastard*, *shy-cock*, and *lily-liver*. But a milquetoast isn't the same as a COWARD, any more than a chickenshit is the same as a wimp. Mr. Smith on *Lost in Space*, and Shaggy on *Scooby-Doo*, and Bob Hope in the Road movies, and Falstaff, and Lou Costello, and Barney Fife, and the Black Adder: *those* are cowards. But not meek ones. On the contrary, cowards in comedy tend to be BLOWHARDS, fleeing ingloriously from any real danger but spending the rest of the time thumping their chests and acting bold. A milquetoast is someone who never acts bold because for him *every* situation seems fraught with unspeakable danger. Milquetoasts rank lower on the totem pole of comic types than cowards of the blustering Falstaffian variety. Up to a point, our culture prizes bluster and bravado more than it minds hypocrisy; and after all, someone who's constantly fearful is more crippled psychologically than someone who fears only danger.

No, the best term for a milquetoast before 1924 was probably *milksop*, which not only has the same literal meaning as "milk toast"—bread soaked in milk—but has been used in the same figurative sense, the H. T. Webster sense, since the fourteenth century. Nowadays neither is used much—we say "wimp" instead, or "wuss."

Fig. 92 Caspar Milquetoast, 1929

Wimp, by the way, has been around since at least the 1920s, though it didn't make it big till the '60s, and no one knows where it came from. One suggested derivation is *whimper*, and it can't have hurt that *gimp* and *simp* were both current slang when *wimp* first appeared. J. Wellington Wimpy, Popeye's hamburger-maddened acquaintance, has also been suggested as the origin of *wimp*, and anything is possible, but for the record Wimpy *wasn't* wimpy in our sense of the word. True, he wasn't as macho as Popeye or Bluto, but his cardinal trait was gluttony, not meekness, and in the pursuit of burgers he was so audacious that his ruses often got him clobbered. On the other hand, Mr. Wimple, a character developed by radio actor Bill Thompson in the mid-1930s and made famous in the 1940s on *Fibber McGee and Molly*, really was a classic wimp: mild, mousy, mush-mouthed, and henpecked. (So was Wimple's counterpart on *The Great Gildersleeve*, Mr. Peavey, with his famous catchphrase "Well, now, I wouldn't say that.") The bird-watching, wife-fearing Wimple was so popular that he inspired a cartoon character, Tex Avery's Droopy Dog, also voiced by Thompson.

Missiles

THIS ENTRY CONCERNS a cartooning cliché, not the missiles that warring countries aim at one other. (*Those* are seldom drawn except by the most consistently unfunny class of cartoonists, the editorial.) Comic strips focus on much smaller battles, and the missiles they favor are the heavy objects that cartoon civilians throw at one another (or at ALLEY CATS). The most common of these, in descending order of frequency, are BRICKS, SHOES, bottles, flatirons, frying pans, ROLLING PINS, vases, TIN CANS, plates, and bootjacks.

Some cartoonists are especially fond of missiles. In *Mutt and Jeff*, the title characters are constantly dodging (especially Jeff) and throwing (especially Mutt) not only the usual objects but also horseshoes, house cats, lead pipes, eggs, books, inkwells, baseball bats, spittoons, bowls of soup, glasses of wine, and now and then a dog or two, a piglet, a turkey, a roast duck.

Most cartoonists, though, tend to arm their characters with the same few throwable objects, maybe because those objects are so easy to recognize. Or maybe the *reason* the objects are easy to recognize, no matter how crudely depicted, is that we're looking for them. Old shoes are so strongly associated with alley cats, for instance, that once we've determined that things are being thrown at a cat, we need only the slimmest resemblance in order to recognize an airborne blob as a shoe, though in another context it might be unrecognizable.

Thrown objects are especially funny when thrown through windows or down flights of stairs. Cartoonists understood early on that if they've shown X doing something that will infuriate Y, it's at least as funny for the next panel to show X fleeing a hail of objects as to show Y looking furious. Drawn by a good cartoonist, an airborne shoe can be as expressive as an angry face.

Fig. 93

Modern Art

If that's art, I'm a Hottentot.
—HARRY S TRUMAN

Abstract art is a product of the untalented,
sold by the unprincipled to the utterly bewildered.
—AL CAPP

OF ALL THE universal middle-class ordeals, few are as funny as that of going to an art museum and being confronted with works of Important Art you can't make head or tail of, forcing you either to sneer in disgust and feel like a philistine, or to suspend disbelief and fight back the mounting sense of being duped, like a rube too meek to call a spade a spade.

In magazine cartoons, the most common gag about modern art is the viewer reacting to its abstractions the same way we do to old-fashioned representational art. Museumgoers are often shown blushing or leering at a heap of twisted metal labeled "Nude Woman" or "Figure of Woman." An H. T. Webster cartoon from 1940 shows the famously timid Caspar Milquetoast averting his gaze from an amorphous blob labeled "Venus"; the caption helpfully explains that "Mr. Milquetoast never likes to be seen looking at undraped statuary."

Lust is not the only unlikely reaction provoked by abstract art in old cartoons. In a J. W. Taylor cartoon from around 1950, a middle-aged, middle-class woman in an art museum has been moved to tears by a modern painting consisting of nothing but a white square and a black circle—a moment recalling the one in Samuel Beckett's novel *Watt* where the servant is moved to tears by contemplating a painting of a circle and a dot. I don't know what year the Taylor cartoon was published, but it would have been not long before or after *Watt* appeared in England in 1953. It's fun to imagine one inspiring the other. But hard to imagine a 1950s *New Yorker* cartoonist making it that far into *Watt*. Easier to imagine Beckett paging through Peggy Guggenheim's copy of *The New Yorker* one afternoon in Paris while she tidied up on the bidet, and no-

Fig. 94 "His spatter is masterful, but his dribble lacks conviction." Peter Arno, 1961

ticing a cartoon that appealed to his absurdist, almost-dadaesque attitude toward the arts.

In cartoons from the 1950s and '60s, artists themselves are sometimes shown relating to their avant-garde artworks in ways more appropriate to old-fashioned art. William Steig drew a cartoon of a sort of cubist Pygmalion, raptly embracing a nude that looks like it was carved from a big block of Swiss cheese. In a *Playboy* cartoon from the 1950s, a brainy-looking painter stands at his easel working on a Mondrianesque grid of rectangles and perpendicular lines; beyond the easel is a nude model, and the painter is saying, "Miss Gaylord! You've moved again!"

Difficulty in modern art is itself a difficult question, and the scorn with which its high priests dismiss its detractors is no more satisfactory a response than the reflexive and defensive ridicule that the laity expresses for painting and sculptures it doesn't understand. To be sure, a sullen fear of being hoodwinked is more likely to make you look like a YOKEL than like a connoisseur, but it's also true that American culture—at its high end no less than its low—has always placed a premium on skepticism. From Twain to Mencken to Vonnegut, American satirists have prided themselves on seeing and saying that the emperor has no clothes.

Note that it's mainly the visual arts that are chastised for their difficulty by mainstream humorists. Modern music is every bit as difficult, but how often do you see it ridiculed in a *Nancy* strip, or a politician's quip, or a *Beverly Hillbillies* rerun? There was a lot of nervous humor about rock and roll in the 1950s and '60s, but not much about Stockhausen or Cage. Likewise with modern poetry, though poets themselves have always struck the rest of us as laughingstocks. The people who'd be likely to make cheap jokes about the inaccessibility of T. S. Eliot or Ezra Pound have never encountered their work in the first place. There's no readerly counterpart to the compulsion that sends philistines to art museums and then forces them, once there, to mortify themselves by leaving the Edenic prettiness of the Impressionist wing for the postlapsarian bafflements of the Modern and the end-times provocations of the Contemporary.

Once there, such museumgoers are likely to say what Norman Rockwell said on seeing Picasso's *Still Life with a Bull's Head*: "My little granddaughter of six could do as well."[34] A favorite target of such sneers was and still is Jackson Pollock (nicknamed—by *Time*, I believe—Jack the Dripper), even for humorists as smart as Phyllis McGinley:

> *Jackson Pollock had a quaint*
> *Way of saying to his sibyl,*
> *"Shall I dribble?*
> *Shall I paint?"*
> *And with never a instant's quibble,*
> *Sibyl always answered,*
> *"Dribble."*

A famous 1961 cartoon by Peter Arno also deals with Pollock or someone who paints just like him, though the real target is the pompous discourse inspired by such painters. The cartoon shows two connoisseurs regarding a spatterdash canvas. Says one expert to the other, "His spatter is masterful, but his dribble lacks conviction" **(Fig. 94)**.

Then, as now, the obfuscations of art *criticism* were ripe for parody. In the 1950s, Peter De Vries published a piece in the *Saturday Review* about his supposed career as a primitivist art critic. Showing up in blue jeans and a mackinaw at all the fancier openings, and giving his name as Moe Juste, this no-bullshit critic starts off with such homely comments as—in connection with a gouache still-life of a trout—"Gimme sardines

[34] In 1973, the Tate Gallery published a collection of cartoons about modern art entitled *A Child of Six Could Do It!*

in oil." Soon, though, he learns the lingo of the trade, but without relinquishing his homespun manner: an abstractionist is "mighty evocative of latter-day internal stresses"; a certain surrealist is "a heap more delirious than most," though the movement itself is "flatter'n a flapjack"; and as for pointillism, Moe pronounces it "dead as a stewed chicken."

Moochers

> *Let the others make statues of Apollo and Mercury and Hercules.*
> *You're the man I want to chisel.*
> —GRACIE ALLEN

LIKE THE GREAT satirists, practical jokers sometimes disguise their schadenfreude as righteous indignation. Among the wide range of mail-order laff-getters (joy buzzers, itching powder, garlic gum, and so on) available in the first half of the twentieth century, cigarette-related gags were especially bought—or sold, at any rate—for purposes of retribution. Most such gags worked by booby-trapping a cigarette so that after a few puffs, it would do something surprising and unpleasant. And the vice they thereby proposed to punish was, invariably, mooching. "Fool the Moocher," proclaimed the display card for Exploding Cigarette Loads, tiny land mines or depth charges sold in tiny red tins. ("Just place one in a cigarette or cigar. When the 'moocher' smokes down to the load . . . it goes 'BANG!'")[35]

"Cure the Moocher," urged a similar product called Shooting Plugs. (In the parlance of old novelty catalogs, a "shooting" gag was one that detonated a cap, not one that fired a projectile.) Blue Devils—tiny smoke

---

[35] The war on moochers must have been one reason for exploding cigars, though another was the phallic shape of the cigar, and thus the dirty joke whenever one "went off." Both motives are suggested by the package copy for the Shooting Cigar made by R. Appel in the 1940s: "When your ever-borrowing friend lifts this cigar off the table, it explodes in his hand!"

bombs—sold themselves as a "Sure Cure for Cadgers." Stink Loads ("When it starts to burn, tastes awful and smells even worse") were "sure to stop moochers."

The S. S. Adams novelty company used to sell a special variety pack of "Smokers Jokers": Stinko Stinkers, Bitter Cigarette Powder, and Snow Storm Tablets. The last, when properly embedded in a burning cigarette, were supposed to "emit clouds of snowlike fuzz," and seem to have been intended more as a magic trick than as an anti-mooch technology; but some smokers must have used them on especially hateful moochers without mentioning the safety information: "Do not inhale smoke while tablet is burning. May be dangerous. Contains methaldehyde."

"There are different ways of discouraging the persistent cigarette borrower, and this is one of the best," says the 1929 Johnson Smith catalog of its Snapping Cigarette Case, which seems to have worked on the same lines of the more familiar snapping gum pack—thus on the same lines as a mousetrap, with a spring-loaded device snapping shut when the bait is taken.

For much of the twentieth century, then, the persistent cigarette borrower was the most detested variety of moocher, perhaps the only one to merit its own stereotype. On a vinegar valentine that looks to date from the 1930s, an attractive blonde stubs out a cigarette in a teeming ashtray and helps herself to yet another from a scowling man's cigarette case. The cartoon, captioned "Cigarette Chiseler," is accompanied by a venomous quatrain:

> *You don't carry your own, you always BUTT IN,*
> *You ask for a cig—and leave my stock thin.*
> *So here is a valentine that fits to a T,*
> *You never can carry your own with me!*

One suspects that the blonde in the picture would be offended to be called a "chiseler," and not just because that term—like *blowhard*, EGG-HEAD, and so many other vintage put-downs that might seem equally applicable to either sex—is generally reserved for men, like *asshole* in our own day. She might not mind an epithet like *gold digger*, but *chiseler* sounds so penny-ante!

The title character of Cab Calloway's "Minnie the Moocher" (1931) is not really much of a moocher, any more than the hero of "Willie the Weeper"—the 1927 song that inspired Calloway's—is a CRYBABY. At least, neither song wastes any time demonstrating the justice of those epithets; both are too busy telling a story. Minnie is a prostitute, and her dream about the king of Sweden does suggest some gold-digging tendencies:

> *He gave her a home built of gold and steel,*
> *A diamond car with a platinum wheel.*

We're also told, though, that she had a heart as big as a whale, and that she posted bail for a lover who promptly skipped town: Minnie is more mooched from than mooching.

Names can be misleading. The biggest mooch in the annals of comics is not Baron Mooch (an early George Herriman protagonist) but Popeye's tormentor Wimpy, one of the most inspired comic-strip characters of all time. Though he was always broke and never looked for gainful employment, he expended superhuman energy in his quest for a free lunch ("I'll gladly pay you Tuesday for a hamburger today") or dinner (he frequently invited friends to his house for a DUCK dinner, but always added, "You bring the ducks.")

Baron Mooch is a less memorable character, a penniless aristocrat whose very ancestry dooms him to poverty, since of course a job would be out of the question, though somehow the Baron's dubious noblesse doesn't prevent him from seeking out free lunches. One of many early characters auditioned by Herriman before he discovered Krazy Kat, Mooch is notable solely as a reminder that most great comic-strip creators hit on their immortal creations only after years of inglorious trial and error.

Morons

Dulness, insensible to the Comic, has the privilege of arousing it.
—GEORGE MEREDITH

No one had ever done a show about an idiot before.
I decided to be the first.
—MEL BROOKS, ON *GET SMART*

MANY OF OUR most emphatic slang terms for mental disability were official euphemisms in their day. In the early twentieth century, *moron*, *imbecile*, and *idiot* were scientific terms for the mildly, the moderately, and the profoundly retarded, respectively. The title of this entry, then, is a dated synonym for "the mildly retarded." It is probably best that we reserve *that* label (and other well-intended Latinisms—"intellectually challenged," "developmentally disabled") for noncomic discussions, but there's no denying that if it were possible to infer the IQ of a fictional character from his or her words and actions, an alarming number of the best-loved characters in American comedy would have IQs in the borderline-retarded range.

Since humor takes all of human folly as its province, it shouldn't surprise us to reflect that many of our favorite comic characters are foolish to the point of disability. In the same way that a Road Runner cartoon can make us laugh at injuries that wouldn't be funny at all in real life, so a sitcom or comic strip can make us laugh at mental disabilities we'd be ashamed to laugh at in a real life. And make no mistake: when we laugh at lummoxes like Gomer Pyle **(Fig. 97)** or simpletons like Harpo Marx, we are in essence laughing at the mildly retarded. Ditto with goofballs like Goofy, clodhoppers like Jethro Bodine, cretins like Krazy Kat, mooncalves like Barney Fife, chuckleheads like Private Zero in *Beetle Bailey*. Some are more than mildly afflicted, such as Alfred E. Neuman **(Fig. 95)**. Or Curly: in a Three Stooges short called "A Bird in the Head" (1946), a mad scientist wants a human brain to put in a gorilla's skull, and naturally picks Curly's as the only brain that's small enough.

Curly, incidentally, is a good example of the confusion between mental

"What~~me worry?"
(I read MAD!)

Fig. 95 Alfred E. Neuman

Fig. 96 Mortimer Snerd

illness and mental retardation so common in old humor. His hallmark, of course, is stupidity, but in many shorts he also suffers from a cartoony kind of insanity. In "Punch Drunks" (1934), Curly goes crazy whenever he hears "Pop Goes the Weasel." In "Horses' Collars" (1935), he goes crazy whenever he sees a mouse. In "Grips, Grunts and Groans" (1937), he goes crazy when he smells a certain perfume, Wild Hyacinth. In "Tassels in the Air" (1938), he goes crazy any time he sees tassels.

As for the others named above, none of them is notably smarter than Forrest Gump, who makes no secret of *his* disability. You don't think Jethro Bodine belongs on the short bus? What about the episode where he gets a job feeding the fish at Marine Land and fondly believes he's enlisted in the Marines? Granted, he can throw a baseball with big-league force and accuracy, provided it's smeared with possum fat. But that only makes him an idiot savant, like Harpo, or the golden-throated Gomer Pyle.

If it's jarring to think of all those people as retarded, that's partly because their stupidity is stylized out of all recognition; they suffer from a special set of mental defects found only in old sitcoms, movies, comics, and jokes. When I was a child, my mother scolded my brothers and me for telling Polack jokes, and insisted that we substitute *moron* for *Polack*. You could say that she was replacing one oppressed group with another, but the morons in moron jokes—sillies who took a ruler to bed to see how long they slept—existed only in jokes; it never occurred to me to associate them with the retarded girl down the street.

One of our own era's dubious achievements was to laugh at cruelly recognizable portraits of real retardation—and especially of Down syndrome—like the ones on *South Park*. (Something to keep in mind whenever we're tempted to scold our grandparents for not sharing some of our own taboos.) The change is recent enough that you can see it by comparing two movies by the Farrelly brothers—the stylized stupidity of the two main idiots in *Dumb and Dumber* (1994) versus the much more realistic retardation of Mary's brother in 1998's *There's Something About Mary*.

Fig. 97 **Gomer Pyle**

In our culture, "That's not funny" really means "It's wrong to laugh at that," which is why we sometimes say it even while laughing. "That's not funny" is only secondarily a report on the speaker's true reactions, though it can be an effort to *train* those reactions. If you strongly disapprove of something and therefore insist it isn't funny, that isn't quite as dishonest as insisting that O. J. Simpson was never a great running back because you hate the psychopathic asshole he later became. No, it's more like refusing to find an actress beautiful because you hate her personality. Given the determination, you really can suppress your sense of humor, like your sense of beauty. But if you say, "There's nothing funny about mental retardation, and for the life of me I've never understood why anybody thinks there is," you must be either a hypocrite or a saint. Either way, you've clearly forgotten the jokes of your childhood, and how many of them concerned extreme stupidity:

Q: Why did the moron throw the clock out the window?
A: Because he wanted to see time fly.

As it also was in my day, that was the best-known moron joke in 1952, when Martha Wolfenstein published *Children's Humor*. Moron jokes were so big in that era, among the younger set, that Wolfenstein devotes a sixty-four-page chapter to the genre, including interviews with children (most of whom envision the moron as a grownup, often an old man) and paying special attention to the clock-out-the-window joke:

"Having heard this from one child after another, I was at first baffled at what they could find so interesting in it," confesses Wolfenstein before embarking on a five-page psychoanalytic explanation of the joke. She begins by arguing that throwing things out windows can be an expression of sibling rivalry: "The child thus intends in a magical way to get rid of the unwelcome baby." She also emphasizes that "flying is a symbol for intercourse," and concludes from the expression "wanted to see" that the moron wanted to see his parents copulating; being prevented, he reacted with "a raging effort to prevent it." Throwing something out the window can also symbolize defecation, and we all know that "children may try to interrupt the nocturnal activities of the parents by wetting and soiling."

As for the clock, it is "a symbol of imposed routines, which in the major early instance are those of toilet training." Throwing a clock out the window "may thus represent a rebellion against the rules of cleanliness." Moreover:

As the ticking of the clock may symbolize genital pulsations, throwing the clock out may further express the wish to get rid of frightening sexual excitement. . . . The child, envious of the parents, wishes that time would fly so that he could be quickly grown-up and able to do what they do. In this connection throwing something out the window may mean giving birth. . . . The child wishes that he too could have a baby.

And so on. Unlike the joke itself, Wolfenstein's interpretation is still funny—but funny inadvertently. It suggests not just an abject loyalty to Freud, but a fundamental mirthlessness: no one capable of empathizing with the state of mind that laughs at moron jokes would indulge in all that unconvincing ingenuity on their behalf. There *are* jokes (see SQUIRT-ING) to which only a psychoanalytic approach can do justice. But in general that approach just obfuscates. Humor tells us more about psychology than psychology can tell us about humor.

Mothers-in-Law

> *Secretary: It must be hard to lose your mother-in-law.*
> *W.C. Fields: Yes it is, very hard. It's almost impossible.*
> —*NEVER GIVE A SUCKER AN EVEN BREAK*, 1941

> *They had never heard the other side of the story.*
> *It was always the* man's *mother-in-law.*
> —PHYLLIS DILLER

HENPECKED HUSBANDS ARE often bullied more by their mothers-in-law than by their wives—especially in old silent films, where it isn't always spelled out whether the old battle-ax is living with the couple or just visiting. (Mothers-in-law were as proverbial for their protracted stays as for their nagging; that's the point of Mencken's remark that "conscience is a mother-in-law whose visit never ends.") In either case, she sits at the breakfast table with them, scowling at her son-in-law as if it were she whom he'd disgusted or disappointed during the night. She's like a ghost or emanation of her daughter, an embodiment of the kind of person the daughter may one day become, and a personification of the daughter's most unpleasant moods and traits. In other words, the mother-in-law represents not only the mundane threat of an unevictable houseguest, but also a reification of fears that all husbands must feel, even those who marry orphans.

Endora, poor Darrin's hostile, meddling mother-in-law on *Bewitched*, is such a fixture that when Samantha threatens to leave her husband and

Fig. 98 Mothers-in-law, before . . .

Fig. 99 . . . and after

says, "I'm going home to mother," he replies, "What do you mean 'going home to mother'? Your mother's always here." Endora is an exemplary mother-in-law because she's *literally* a witch; that witchery not only explains her hostility to Darrin (the mere mortal her daughter Samantha has married), but also gives her all sorts of supernatural means to harass him.

When a mother-in-law finally departs after an extended visit, it is customary for the husband to exalt—sometimes so openly that his wife trounces him for disrespect, though comic mothers-in-law are only too able to fend for themselves. On a postcard from 1906, an especially formidable specimen—stocky, sturdy-looking, standing with arms crossed belligerently—is pictured thinking: "So, my daughter's husband says he'll put me out of the house, does he? Well, we shall see. Here I am, and here I shall remain, to protect my poor dear girl."

In *The Rationale of the Dirty Joke*, Gershon Legman argues that the reason fathers-in-law are so much rarer in humor than mothers-in-law is that once a woman marries, her father becomes irrelevant. His duty was to guard her virginity—and thus, as it were, her bride-price—but once he marries her off, his wife takes over. There are lots of jokes about farmers, daughters, and TRAVELING SALESMEN, but once a salesman marries a farmer's daughter, the farmer ceases to be funny and his wife takes his place as comically menacing protector.

Radio comedies and early TV sitcoms had a lot of visiting mothers-in-law, though as a rule the husbands' complaints about them behind their backs were funnier than the sparks that flew when the old lady was present. Here's the Kingfish on the phone with the beauty parlor in a 1951 episode of *Amos 'n' Andy* in which he tries to find a husband for his wife's mother in order to get her out of his life:

> That's right, Madam Olga, I'm bringin' my mother-in-law in to your beauty parlor here this afternoon for a complete overhaul job. . . . Well, Madam Olga, I'm gonna give ya the problem with my mother-in-law. Have you ever been down to the beach and seen a grapefruit washed up on the sand, one that's been in the water for three or four weeks and then washed up and left to dry in the sun for a few days?

And here's Ed Norton to Ralph on *The Honeymooners*:

> My mother-in-law coming! Boy, compared to her coming, the invasion of locusts was a boon to mankind! . . . I can't even afford to feed her. Boy, can she eat! When she comes to dinner, she clears that table like a hurdler. Gee, and is she fat. From the front, she looks like you from the back!

Both men insist so strenuously on the mother-in-law's UGLINESS as almost to give credence to Freud's claim that the real reason men disparage their wives' mothers is to repress a sexual attraction toward them. We can imagine what Nabokov—a famously outspoken anti-Freudian—would say about *that*, and yet in *Pale Fire* (1962) he forces Gradus the assassin to illustrate Freud's theory: "After his wife . . . had left him (with a gypsy lover), he had lived in sin with his mother-in-law until she was removed, blind and dropsical, to an asylum for decayed widows."

In old humor, "mother-in-law" almost always meant the *wife's* mother, the husband's in-law. In reality, of course, a mother is at least as likely to quarrel with her daughters-in-law as with her sons-in-law, and it's hard to believe that that was ever different, but most of the humorists retaliating against their in-laws were men. Jokes about the wife's mother-in-law are surprisingly rare.

Murphy Beds

IN 1900, WILLIAM Lawrence Murphy formed the Murphy Wall Bed Company to mass-produce an ingenious space-saving bed he'd designed for his own tiny San Francisco apartment, a bed that folded up into the wall when not in use, like a jackknife blade into its handle. Immediately comic artists started drawing—and comic actors getting trapped in—what at that point weren't yet known as Murphy beds. In "The Burglar-Proof Bed," a short film released in July 1900 by the American Mutoscope & Biograph Company, a bachelor is sleeping peacefully in his newfangled bed when a burglar enters the room and

Fig. 100 "One A.M.," 1916

demands his money at gunpoint. The bachelor hits a switch that returns his bed to its full upright position, and we see that the bed is a special model customized with a crenellated top and guns projecting from the underside as from the slots of a citadel. The guns belch lead and smoke, the burglar flees, and the proud homeowner hoists a little American flag from inside his turn-of-the-century panic room. Three years later, an Edison film called "Subub Surprises the Burglar" ripped off the plot of "The Burglar-Proof Bed" down to the last detail—the American flag— with the difference that this time around the burglar is blown away.

In "One A.M.," a Chaplin short from 1916 **(Fig. 100)**, Charlie comes home drunk one night and spends a good six minutes wrestling with his Murphy bed, in a long series of sight gags: first he can't find the bed and looks out the window and under the rug for it; then he remembers the switch that causes a section of his wall to pivot like a secret panel in a haunted-house movie, but because he's standing too close to the wall in question, he pivots with it about a dozen times; then, when he finally gets the bed side facing into the bedroom, the bed flops down on top of him, incidentally pinning his bowler hat under one of the legs of the bed; and so on. Finally he decides to sleep on the floor.

Murphy beds still exist, and so does the Murphy Bed Company, despite the setback of a 1989 court ruling that the thitherto-proprietary term "Murphy bed" may also be used by competitors, as it has long been used by the public, for any bed that folds into a wall. (The former owners of that name can console themselves with the thought that the same fate had already befallen elevators, trampolines, and whoopee cushions.) For the most part, though, the public no longer needs a name at all for Murphy beds because it no longer refers to them much, and neither do the forms of popular entertainment by which we can gauge the public's sense of humor. But that public used to find those beds hilarious: last time I did a keyword search for "murphy bed" on the Internet Movie Database, forty-two of the fifty-eight hits were comedies.

More than half of those fifty-eight films appeared between 1928 and 1948. Then came the Levittown era, when the relative affordability of housing put a crimp in the sales of Murphy beds, and so in the humor about them. Between 1954's *Phffft* (tagline: "Don't Say It! See It!") and 1965's *Dr. Goldfoot and the Bikini Machine*, only 1960's *The Savage Eye*—not a comedy—deployed a Murphy bed.

When inanimate objects strike us as funny, it's often because they strike us as defective or outlandish variations on familiar objects. Henri Bergson argued that only humans are funny—humans and things that remind us of humans. When we laugh at pets, we are laughing at a real or imagined resemblance to human behavior or appearance. In the case of a funny contraption, what really makes us laugh is the thought of the person who invented it, or the sight of the people who buy it or use it. Segways, for example, are funny only while in use, and if used more widely, would soon cease to strike us as especially funny—though, paradoxically, they would appear more often in gag cartoons, sitcoms, Hollywood comedies, and the like, simply by virtue of being more central to our lives. That's what happened to bicycles, which initially struck a lot of observers as ludicrous, but now retain only the faintest charge of funniness.

N n

Names

ROGER EBERT'S FIRST Law of Funny Names decrees: "No names are funny unless used by W. C. Fields or Groucho Marx. Funny names, in general, are a sign of desperation at the screenplay level. See 'Dr. Hfuhruhurr' in *The Man with Two Brains*." But is a Groucho name like "Rufus T. Firefly" really any funnier than "Dr. Hfuhruhurr"? As for W. C. Fields, he was a great comedian, but the strange names in his films are evidence less of a talent than a penchant. His best movie, *The Bank Dick*, is an encyclopedia of nomenclatorial hijinks, but few are laugh-provoking. Written and directed by Fields under the pen name "Mahatma Kane Jeeves," the film features a son-in-law named Og Oggilby, a bank robber named Filthy McNasty, a bank examiner named J. Pinkerton Snoopington, a swindler named A. Pismo Clam, and all sorts of minor characters with names like Miss Plupp and Mr. Cheek. Fields himself plays a souse named Egbert Sousé.

So maybe we should strengthen Ebert's Law and say that names meant to be funny never are. That may be an overstatement, but there's no denying that nowadays we find joke names so painfully *un*funny that they make it hard for us to see what still is funny in the works of writers who used them. If anything: there's no surer sign that a piece of would-be-comic writing won't be comic than a name like Murgatroyd or Percy. (I should know, but don't, how these Officially Funny Names attained their status. Why is "Percy" so much funnier than "Larry"? Because "Percival" is funnier than "Lawrence"? Is it, though?)

One of James Thurber's rules of thumb for funny stories is to avoid such names as Ann S. Thetic, Maud Lynn, Sally Forth, and Bertha

Twins, because "the reader's attention . . . never recovers from such names." He's right: nothing dates old humor more disastrously. If Pynchon often seems stuck in the 1960s and its wacky mind-set, his weakness for joke names is one big reason. *The Crying of Lot 49* is a brilliant novella, but Pynchon made it easy to dismiss by giving his characters painfully unfunny names like Oedipa, "Mucho" Maas, Stanley Kotex, and Dr. Hilarious. The difference between such names and the great Dickens names—Pecksniff, Jarndyce, Murdstone, Micawber, and the rest—is one of subtlety. Dickens as a rule chose surnames that might have belonged to real people, and that evoked his characters by connotation and clang association. Naming a character "Jarndyce" is very different from naming him "Jaundice."

The presence on Thurber's list of "Sally Forth"—not yet a comic strip when Thurber wrote his rules—reminds us that funny names have always flourished in the funny pages. They are less annoying there; sometimes they're outright amusing, maybe because we expect, or accept, higher levels of silliness and stylization from the comics than at the movies. George Herriman, best known for Krazy Kat, also gave us Baron Bean and his wife, Lucinda Bean (at the time, *bean* was common slang for "head"), and—more wittily—a dog named Mr. Wough Wuph Wuff. Milt Gross had characters named Izzy Human, Babbling Brooks, and Kinney B. Alive. Rube Goldberg's characters include not only Professor Lucifer Gorgonzola Butts (the deranged inventor to whom Goldberg attributed so many of his famous contraptions), but also countless minor figures with bizarre and rhythmic names like Rococo Mandamus McStark and Macy Toledo McFigg. Jimmy Hatlo also had a penchant for unlikely names—Iodine, Sediment, Linseed, Lushwell, Angora, Squatwell, Medulla, Mr. Tremblechin, Mrs. Pandoodle—and used them every time in *They'll Do It Every Time.*

Most of the characters in the *Archie* comics have joke names, though the jokes are obscured by nicknames and familiarity. Their full names include Archibald Andrews, Reginald Mantle III, Forsythe Pendleton Jones III (better known as Jughead), Ethel Muggs ("Big Ethel"), Marmaduke Mason ("Moose"), his girlfriend Midge Klump, and Dilton Donald Doyle. Notable exceptions to the pattern are Betty Cooper and

Veronica Lodge, whose more realistic names may be seen as the ono-
mastic counterpart of the graphic double standard whereby cartoonists
used to draw the PRETTY GIRLS more realistically than the other characters. As for Archibald, Reginald, and the others, their names offer a
good cross section of the names Americans found funny in the 1940s,
and more specifically the sort of names that lowbrow humor favored for
upper-class twits, though except for Reggie and Veronica the characters
aren't supposed to be rich kids.

The cartoonist with the greatest knack for funny names was incon-
testably Al Capp, who over the decades peopled *Li'l Abner* with such
characters as Lucifer Ornamental Yokum (Abner's pappy), Moonbeam
McSwine, Joe Btfsplk, Tobacco Rhoda, Romeo McHaystack, Skeleton
McCloset, Hamfat Gooch, Concertino Constipato, Jinx Rasputinburg,
Global McBlimp, Slobberlips McJab, Dumpington Van Lump, Swami
Riva, Sir Orble Gasse-Payne, and Henry Cabbage Cod.[36]

The passing of the fashion is no cause for regret, though it may be due
in part to a decline in literacy, and specifically an unfamiliarity with Restoration drama, which gave us characters like Mrs. Malaprop and Mr.
Witwould, as well as the first character in English literature with a name
like a modern superhero, Sheridan's Captain Absolute. Much that was
good about the popular literature of our grandfathers came from their
greater knowledge of and zeal for the classics. Much that was bad came
from an inability to see which aspects of the classics were and weren't
worth emulating. So you had humorists whose otherwise sound instincts
couldn't quite prevent them, when it came to naming characters, from
emulating Restoration drama. (As for why Restoration playwrights used
them, can one reason be that they followed a twenty-year ban on theater
in England during the Commonwealth era, and that a whole generation
had lost touch with the stock characters of comic drama?)

---

[36] You might think that *no* name is too stupid for the comics, but I draw the line at
the villains in *Dick Tracy*, of whom far too many had unlikely, uninspired, and consistently unfunny surnames consisting simply and moronically of a salient trait spelled
backward—the murderous Frankie Redrum, the bloodthirsty Junky Doolb, the cos-
mopolitan Mr. Kroywen, the lawless Professor Emirc, and so on.

Or maybe the change in taste has more to do with the rise of television. Funny names flourished on radio sitcoms like *Vic and Sade* (1932–46), which gave us such characters as Miss Appelrot, Oyster Crecker, Ike Kneesuffer, Dottie Brainfeeble, Orville Wheeney, Dwight Twentysixler, B.B. Baugh, J. J. J. J. Stunbolt, and Rishigan Fishigan (from Sishigan, Michigan). But a TV sitcom doesn't *need* a funny name to let us know at a glance not just that a character is ridiculous, but in what way he or she is ridiculous. It would have been a disaster if Norman Lear had named his archetypal bigot Archie Bigot. "Archie Bunker" is funny and fitting enough without taxing our credulity. The same goes for "Ralph Kramden," "Barney Fife," "Gladys Kravitz," and most of the other great sitcom characters. Their names are less deafeningly meaningful than the names I've been discussing, but that initial lack of semantic saturation was precisely what allowed a name like "Gladys Kravitz" to become imbued with its owner's personality (to the point where it's hard to imagine her being called anything else), rather than the other way around, with characters reduced to two-dimensional clichés every time their names ("Ann S. Thetic," "Mr. Tremblechin") are uttered.

Another problem with meaningful surnames is the implication—almost never intended—that the trait in question is hereditary, and that the character descends from a long line of Fogbounds, Witwoulds, Milquetoasts, or what-have-yous. It is fitting that the name Snopes has become a synonym for "shiftless white trash," because what makes Faulkner's Snopeses hateful runs in the family, and is handed down from generation to generation along with the surname. We are not meant, though, to assume, that Egbert Sousé is a souse because his forebears were. Another unintended absurdity is likely to result when the allegorical name belongs to a married woman, except in the minority of cases where she is supposed to share the trait with her husband. Congreve's randy Lady Wishfort wouldn't be so desperate if Lord Wishfort wished for it too.

Neighbors

YOUR NEIGHBORS' ABILITY to annoy you depends on their
location. Next-door neighbors—Thursty and Irma Thurston
in *Hi and Lois*, Herb and Tootsie Woodley in *Blondie*, Barney
and Betty Rubble on *The Flintstones*—tend to have large deciduous
trees overhanging the property line. They tend to borrow power tools.
In old slapstick comedies and comic strips, they may even throw TIN
CANS over the fence and into your yard. The Hatfields and McCoys
were next-door neighbors. Nonetheless, the couple next door are often
your best friends, which means that when they fight, one or the other is
likely to seek refuge in your house, and of course to prove an exasperat-
ing houseguest.

In old sitcoms, the folks across the street may be a factor, as Gladys
Kravitz is on *Bewitched*. The street between you keeps them from annoying you as much as a next-door neighbor can, but they're well placed to
spy on you—or for you to spy on them, as Jimmy Stewart spies on the
SPOUSE-KILLER across the courtyard in *Rear Window*.

In urban comedies about apartment dwellers, the neighbors who
matter tend to live upstairs or downstairs rather than next door or across
the hall, although of course in real life it's easier to visit neighbors on
your own floor, to know them as people and not just as nuisances, and
so to coexist peacefully. On *The Honeymooners*, the Nortons live upstairs
from the Kramdens; on *I Love Lucy*, Fred and Ethel live downstairs from
Lucy and Ricky. In *The Seven Year Itch*, Marilyn Monroe lives above the
temporarily single man who finds her so tempting. In *It's a Gift*, W. C.
Fields's most annoying neighbors live in the apartment above. The people

Fig. 101 George Herriman's *Dingbat Family* confronts the neighbors upstairs.

above or below your apartment are more likely to annoy you with their noises and their leaks, or to complain about your own. It's simply a funnier relationship than the next-door one. An apartment building is supposed to afford as much apartness as is possible for dwellers in a densely populated city, but as long as someone lives in the apartment overhead, you are never allowed to forget that your life is insanely adjacent to some random stranger's.

In 1925, the great cartoonist Milt Gross published a book consisting entirely of dialogue—voices of inhabitants of a four-story tenement on the Lower East Side. Dedicated to "the guy that invented dumb-waiters and thin walls," the book, *Nize Baby*, switches among four households, one on each floor, with an occasional street cry from an ICE MAN or greengrocer. Though there may be no one vantage point from which a listener would really be able to audit all the different arguments, gossip, scoldings, take-a-bite stories, and so on that Gross transcribes, the impression you get while reading is that from *any* point inside this immigrant Tower of Babel, all those voices are constantly audible, like a radio playing four or five different stations at once, so that only by consciously tuning your attention to one or another is it possible to extract any sense from the cacophony.

Not that the different broadcasts are always mutually oblivious. Much of the book is devoted to (presumably) shouted conversations between the yentas on the first and second floors:

> Second Floor: Did we hev excitement lest night in de houze, Mrs. Feitelbaum. Was almost by us a calumnity!
> First Floor: What was?
> Second Floor: Hm! What was, she esks!! I tut what we'll gonna hev to call a nembulence!
> First Floor: Iy-yi—yi—yi—yi—yi—yi—yi!! WHAT WUSS???
> Second Floor: What was? Mine woister enemies shouldn't hev it. De baby ate opp all de pills!

Though it's a joke we associate with low-to-middlebrow humor—

with the Kramdens and the Nortons, the Bumsteads and the Woodleys,
Mr. Wilson and Dennis the Menace—the annoying neighbor has occupied
the minds of highbrows, too. And after all, they're as aware as anyone else
that, in Sartre's words, Hell is other people. No one who has read Nabokov's American novels is surprised to learn that after losing his ancestral
estate to the Russian Revolution, the novelist chose to spend the rest of his
life in rented houses and hotels, where he could always pull up stakes and
move again if his neighbors proved too horrible. *Pale Fire* is narrated by a
horrible neighbor, a demented COLLEGE PROFESSOR named Kinbote whose
many delusions include the belief that the famous writer in the house next
door considers Kinbote a close friend and not a pitiable nuisance. Kinbote
is so obsessed with his famous "friend" that he spies on him nightly, sometimes tiptoeing next door to peer through the man's windows.

Newspapers at Breakfast

> *Before marriage, a man declares that he would*
> *lay down his life to serve you; after marriage,*
> *he won't even lay down his newspaper to talk to you.*
> —HELEN ROWLAND

> *My recipe for marital happiness is,*
> *Whenever you can, read at meals.*
> —CYRIL CONNOLLY

WHEN IS A HONEYMOON really over? When the newlyweds
get back from Niagara Falls? No, some couples are already
en route to divorce court by that point, while some are still as
enamored of each other as on their wedding night. A less arbitrary way to
mark the reassertion of grim reality might be to say that the honeymoon
ends the first morning the husband reads the newspaper at breakfast instead of looking at and talking with his wife. I myself have never been
married, but to judge by old magazine cartoons, sitcoms, and movies,
that morning arrives sooner or later for even the happiest couple.

In *Citizen Kane*, Orson Welles used a sort of time-lapse montage of breakfast-table scenes to show the decline of Kane's first marriage over the course of nine years. In each successive phase, husband and wife are seated farther apart, their conversation is more acrimonious, and the background music more dissonant. In the final scene, they sit at far ends of a long table, not talking at all but reading different newspapers—he his own, she the competition's. Why did Welles chart the marriage by way of breakfasts, rather than dinners or Christmases? Perhaps a sense that it is in the morning, before we've booted up our elaborate daytime personas, that we show ourselves as we really are. *Lunch* is a funnier word, but breakfast is the funnier meal because no one is hungry, no one is quite awake, and no one wants to be awake at all, or even alive. Or at least that's the joke.

How long have men been reading at breakfast? In one Charles Addams cartoon, we see an archaeologist and his wife eating breakfast outdoors, in what must Egypt, by the site of a dig; he's sipping coffee and reading a big stone fragment covered with hieroglyphics. Given Addams's penchant for jokes about SPOUSE-KILLING, we probably shouldn't read too much significance into the cartoon, circa 1950, where a housewife prepares to electrocute her husband, as he sits reading the paper at a breakfast table cluttered with newfangled electric appliances (coffeemaker, waffle iron, toaster) with an electric wire coiled around one leg of his chair—but what should we make of the fact that in 1958 *The Saturday Evening Post* ran a cartoon by one Al Kaufman that exactly reprises the Addams gag, down to the three appliances on the table (though the waffle iron has been replaced with an electric chafing dish)?

Well, it may be that people routinely fantasize about killing spouses who ignore them at meals, just as, according to a French proverb, people count up the faults of those who keep them waiting. (In one episode of *I Love Lucy*, Lucy gets so annoyed with Ricky for ignoring her at the breakfast table that she turns the toaster sideways and fires two pieces of toast at him; he catches the toast without interrupting his reading.) In any case, I've come across more than a dozen cartoons about husbands ignoring their wives by reading the paper. All were drawn by male cartoonists, suggesting that husbands know exactly how much their newspaper habit exasperates their wives, but persist with it anyhow, or for that very reason. No wonder some of those wives resort to murder. In a cartoon that appeared in *Playboy* around 1960, we see a plump woman in a floral housedress being grilled by the police. "Then I buried his head in the sports page," she tells them. "He would have liked that."

Such a cartoon would be unthinkable in a newspaper. I don't think I've encountered the newspaper-at-breakfast cliché even once in a newspaper comic strip, presumably because it's considered an anti-newspaper gag. It may also be that a single image says it all so well about a failing marriage that a sequence of images on the subject would be superfluous. But it's equally hard to imagine a newspaper printing a multi-panel gag like the one that appeared in 1957 in *The Saturday Evening Post* in which the wife takes out her hostility on the paper instead of on its reader. We see the poor woman gloomily watching her husband and his precious newspaper, then jumping up and gleefully snatching it, shredding it, and stomping on the shreds, then sitting down again and asking pleasantly, "What's new?"

The Newspaper at Breakfast works so well as a sight gag that comic novelists and poets have mostly ceded the joke to cartoonists and screenwriters, but there are bright exceptions. In "Daniel at Breakfast," Phyllis McGinley observes her title character with the intensity of a loving but exasperated wife, though for all we know for most of the poem, Daniel may well be a bachelor:

> *His paper propped against the electric toaster*
> *(Nicely adjusted to his morning use)*
> *Daniel at breakfast studies world disaster,*
> *And sips his orange juice.*
> *The words dismay him. Headlines shrilly chatter*
> *Of famine, storm, death, pestilence, dismay.*
> *Daniel is gloomy, reaching for the butter. . . .*

Not until the last couplet of the twenty-two-line poem do we learn that Daniel has a wife, and that she's presumably been there in the kitchen with him all along, though till now the poem ignored her just as Daniel does. Finally, though, he sets down his newspaper, finishes his coffee, "And, kissing his wife abruptly at the door / Stamps fiercely off to catch the 8:04."

Nincompoops

NINCOMPOOP, POSSIBLY DERIVED from *non compos mentis*, is usually encountered as a comic synonym for MORON. That's how Mo uses the word in Three Stooges shorts. Here, though, I'm using it in the specialized sense assigned it by Gershon Legman in his monumental *Rationale of the Dirty Joke*: "the child who has grown up without learning the meaning of sex." Legman himself claims to be restoring the word's original sense, and quotes two earlier definitions that, in their different degrees of explicitness, nicely reflect the difference between eighteenth-century lustiness and nineteenth-century pudibundity: "one who never saw his wife's ____" (1785), and "a term of derision, applied by a young lass to her lover, who presses not his suit with enough vigour" (1823). Nabokov uses the word in this sexual sense in *Lolita* when he has Humbert Humbert describe the young males in his daughter's orbit: "from the perspiring nincompoop whom 'holding hands' thrills to the self-sufficient rapist with pustules and a souped-up car."

James Thurber and E. B. White have a whole chapter on nincompoops in their 1929 spoof of a sex manual, *Is Sex Necessary?* The chapter is entitled "Frigidity in Men" and focuses on two manifestations: Declination of the Kiss (and dislike of KISSING generally) and the Recessive Knee, a shrinking away from physical contact coyly initiated by the woman: "A frigid male . . . will move his knee away at the first suggestion of contact, denying himself the electric stimulus of love's first stirring."[37] The author of this pseudoscientific discussion (who emphasizes that "my laboratory has been the laboratory of life itself," and admits to suffering from Recessive Knee) was probably Thurber, who made no secret of his horror of sexually aggressive women.

In the first half of the twentieth century, slang terms for sexually unassertive men included *flat heel*, *flickering flame*, and *pussyfoot*. The adjec-

---

[37] Such behavior, we are told, is likely to provoke Fuller's Retort, named for its originator, a Miss Lillian Fuller of Paterson, New Jersey: "Say, what is the matter with you, anyhow?"

Fig. 102

tive *bashful* also tended to imply not just any shyness but male shyness vis-à-vis women, as in movie titles like *Are Blond Men Bashful?* (1924) and *Bashful Romeo* (1949). Hollywood has always found bashful males both ridiculous and lovable, and if the humor at their expense is seldom very funny, it is nonetheless a refreshing change of pace from the usual joke about men and sex, namely that it's all men think about—the thing that makes us tick. In *Girl Shy* (1924), Harold Lloyd plays Harold Meadows, a stuttering young bachelor working in a tailor shop[38] and writing a self-help book for other shy young men. In *Millionaire Playboy* (1940) Joe Penner plays a rich young nincompoop who gets bad HICCUPS any time a woman kisses him—the only women who *don't* frighten him are old ladies. His father's hirelings cure Joe by taking him to a resort and convincing him that all the young women are really old ladies with facelifts.

---

[38] In those days the profession had connotations of fussiness and even effeminacy: real men don't measure inseams.

Noise

Nowadays most men lead lives of noisy desperation.
—JAMES THURBER

IN THE ENTRY on INSOMNIA, I discuss the brilliant sequence in *It's a Gift* where a tenement dweller played by W. C. Fields tries to sleep on his balcony and is constantly disturbed by urban noises. He probably thinks that moving to the suburbs would solve his problems, but what happens in the suburbs is that your ears grow more acute, so that you can be tormented by noises you'd never even notice in the city. Besides, suburbia can be noisy too, as George Babbitt knows. Sinclair Lewis's *Babbitt* (1922) begins with George waking prematurely, on the sleeping porch of his house in Floral Heights, on the outskirts of Zenith:

> Rumble and bang of the milk truck. . . . The furnaceman slammed the basement door. A dog barked in the next yard. As Babbitt sank blissfully into a dim warm tide, the paper-carrier went by whistling, and the rolled-up *Advocate* thumped the front door. Babbitt roused, his stomach constricted with alarm. As he relaxed, he was pierced by the familiar and irritating rattle of someone cranking a Ford: snap-ah-ah, snap-ah-ah, snap-ah-ah.

Humorists like to enumerate noises like that. Here's Ogden Nash on an annoying caddy:

> *He had chronic hiccups.*
> *He had hay fever too.*
> *Also, he was learning to whistle through his teeth.*
> *Oh yes, and his shoes squeaked.*

A classic comic situation is the character who needs at all costs to avoid making noise, and who can't help making one noise after another. In *Duck Soup*, Chico and Harpo sneak into Margaret Dumont's house one night to steal Freedonia's war plans for their foreign paymaster. They've been cautioned not to make a sound, but Harpo resets the grandfather clock to midnight (to match the alarm clock he carries in his pocket) and it starts chiming; then he picks up a DUCK-shaped music box, which starts playing loudly; then he joins in by plucking the strings of a handy grand piano as if it were a harp. Chico yanks him away, causing the sounding board to crash down. A little later, Harpo gets hold of the combination to the safe where the plans are kept, but mistakes a big boxy radio for a safe, and when he twists its knob back and forth according to instructions, the radio starts blaring a raucous Sousa march at full volume. Harpo tries to turn the music off, but the knob comes off in his hand instead. In his panicked and futile attempts to silence the infernal radio, he tries to cover it first with a cushion and then with a curtain, then he spritzes it with seltzer (in old comic films there's usually a seltzer bottle handy), then shuts it in the bathroom, then takes it back out and dashes it to the floor, then hacks at it with the steel pedestal of a standing ashtray. Finally he throws the radio out the window.

Noise annoys, as the Buzzcocks sang, and during the era covered by this guide, the world got a lot noisier. When nickel jukeboxes started to appear in restaurants and bars around 1940, it was possible to buy silence as well as music: a nickel bought three minutes of surcease. But even when no one is comically annoyed by them, noises tend to be funny. Funny noises are a big part, for example, of the humor in Three Stooges comedies: their antics wouldn't be half as amusing without the cartoonish sounds that accompany all those eyeball pokes (made by plucking a ukulele string), stomach punches (kettledrum), ear twists (ratchet), hair ripping (torn fabric), and so on.

Comedy is noisier than tragedy, and farce is noisiest of all, partly because stupid people yell a lot. Even the objects are noisier in farce, as if they too wanted to speak, whether or not they have anything intelligent to say. (Usually not: as grade school teachers have insisted for generations, empty BARRELS make the most noise.) Naturally such noises are everywhere in animated cartoons, which so often express an animistic worldview, and tend to caricature sounds as well as shapes, and to amplify inaudible or outright nonexistent ones to the point where we can hear the blinking of an eye or the sparkling of a diamond.

There are also live-action cartoons, like the 1960s *Batman* show, with its notorious preference for printed sound effects—all those BIFF!'s and POW!'s—rather than audible ones; on the soundtrack, each blow was accompanied by a sforzando, a brief brassy blare in the high-excitement music, rather than by some simulation of a fist hitting a jaw, or a foot a solar plexus. Someone on the Internet claims to have enumerated these sounds for every episode; according to the list, the most frequently occurring sound is *kapow*, occurring in no fewer than 50 episodes of *Batman*. Other popular sounds are *pow* (49), *boff* (43), *zap* (42), *sock* (41), *biff* (34), *ooooff* (33), *splatt* (32), *bam* (31), *crash* (31), *whamm* (30), *whap* (24), *whack* (22), and *zowie* (22). Some of the less common sounds are still a lot more common than they have any right to be, like *zlopp* (11), *klonk* (10), *vronk* (9), and *zlonk* (9). *Glipp*, on the other hand, occurs only once.

Batman, of course, aimed for maximum silliness, and the actual onomatopoeias were pretty uninspired, but that shouldn't blind us to the fact that the best place to look for funny sound effects is in fact in print, and especially in comics. The February 1955 issue of *Mad* features a spoof of hard-boiled detective comics with no words at all except for onomatopoeias (the typewriter goes "KLAKETTY KLAK"; the femme fatale descends the stairway with a "BOING GONG GONG GONG VA VA VOOM KPOW") and pseudo-onomatopoeias (when the cops batter their way though a door, it goes "SPLINTER!"). The characters are also allowed some inarticulate grunts like "GNNG!" (stabbed in back) and "ROWF!" (laying eyes on sultry redhead), as well as one pseudo-inarticulate grunt: victims of the killer die exclaiming "AARRGH," which we discover in the final panel to be the killer's name: Joe Aarrgh.

Like most of the content in the early issues of *Mad*, that spoof was written by the great Harvey Kurtzman. It was two later *Mad* artists, however, Basil Wolverton and Don Martin, who raised the comic-book onomatopoeia to a high art. Wolverton even wrote an article claiming to have researched each of his sound effects: to ascertain what it sounds like when a horse steps on a man's head, for instance, he rented a horse and got it to step on his BROTHER-IN-LAW's head. One can only wish that all writers were so dedicated to checking their own facts—though even if

they were, written sound effects would remain egregiously nonstandard-
ized, since no two earwitnesses to a given sound will hear or transcribe it
the same way.

QUIZ: Identify the following sounds by matching each with its
source. For extra credit, guess which sounds are Don Martin's and which
are Basil Wolverton's. (Answers appear at the end of this entry.)

1. FAMP	a. BB hitting cow's udder
2. FLIP BLAP BLAP	b. Cigarette extinguished on eyeball
3. GA-SHPLUCT	c. Fat person falling backward into vat
4. GLINK	of peanut butter
5. KRANG	d. Farmer stepping in cowshit
6. PADAP PADAP	e. Garter snapping on varicose vein
PADAP, KADOONK	f. Glass eye falling into pitcher of thick
7. PWIP	syrup
8. PLOFF	g. Guard dribbling meat loaf like a
9. SCHWIPP	basketball, then "dunking" it into
10. SIZAFITZ	inmate's mouth
	h. Stray toenail clipping landing in
	beer can
	i. Surgeon tossing gallstones into
	empty garbage can
	j. Wallpaper coming unglued and un-
	rolling from wall

Answers: 1c, 2j, 3d, 4h, 5i, 6g, 7a, 8f, 9e, 10b. Sounds # 2, 3, 4, 6, and 10
are by Don Martin, the other five by Wolverton.

Noses

When it comes to noses, you're a retailer. I'm a wholesaler!
—JIMMY DURANTE TO BOB HOPE

*All through my life, even when I was making a fortune on account
of the big beak, and while I'm out there on the stage laughin' and
kiddin' about the nose, at no time was I ever happy about it.*
—JIMMY DURANTE

O N *TV LAND to Go*'s list of the "TV's Ten Best Moments," Marcia Brady's getting hit in the nose with a football ranks #5—not as high as Neil Armstrong's first steps on the moon or the Beatles on *The Ed Sullivan Show* (#1 and #2 respectively), but the highest-ranking comic moment. And that makes sense, because the nose is the funniest part of the body, or the funniest one that can be exposed on network TV. And an injured nose is funnier than an injured eye or ear. As all fans of the Three Stooges know, the Nose Tweak was one of Moe's favorite means of self-expression. ("Nose tweak" is also a gossip-column synonym for *rhinoplasty*, but never mind that.)

"The first thing any clown or comedian thinks of in the dressing room is to put on some more nose," says Max Eastman in *Enjoyment of Humor*, adding, "It takes only a little more of the human nose to be too much." For that reason, a big nose can be enough to doom an actress to a career in comedy. Think of Barbra Streisand or, more recently, Catherine Keener and Sarah Jessica Parker. Many male comedians—Jimmy Durante, W. C. Fields, Bob Hope—have also had notable noses, but here as so often, men have always enjoyed a double standard, as witness the careers of leading men like Dustin Hoffman and Sean Penn. Is it because we associate noses with PENISES, and big ones with big ones? Here's a limerick that Legman dates to 1942:

> *A man in the battle of Aix*
> *Had one nut and his cock shot away,*
> *But he found in this pickle*

Beautiful Noses and Disguises
- LOTS OF FUN -
Even Your Best Girl Won't Know You
One of these prominent features will quite change your style of beauty

No. 4331, 25c   No. 4332, 25c   No. 4333, 15c   No. 4334, 20c   No. 4335, 50c
(Assorted Shapes)

No. 4337, $1.00   No. 4336, $1.00   No. 4338, $1.00   No. 4339, $1.00

No. 4340, 75c   No. 4341, $1.00   No. 4342, 75c

No. 4343, 75c   No. 4344, 75c   No. 4345, 75c   No. 4346, 75c

N. B. Disguises Nos. 4344 and 4345 come in assorted animals, etc., such as Cows, Cats, Dogs, Horses, Mules, Chickens, Alligators, Parrots, Elephants etc.

Fig. 103 From the Johnson-Smith catalog, 1929

His nose could still tickle,
Though he might get the snuffles some day.

In Japanese comics and anime, a nosebleed is a graphic euphemism for sexual arousal, specifically for an erection. Gogol's great story "The Nose," in which a man awakes one morning to find that his is missing, has been read as an extended dick joke, and for once the Freudian interpretation is convincing. Someone in Russia has published a version substituting a blank for every instance of "nose" and trusting the reader's dirty mind to do the rest.

The main reason we associate noses with penises is presumably that the nose is "the extreme outpost of the face," as Ambrose Bierce put it, and the penis the extreme outpost of the male abdomen. Another reason is that both outcroppings are affected by syphilis. There was a lot of cruel humor in the seventeenth and eighteenth centuries—in Voltaire, in Swift, in Pope—about noses rotting off because of venereal disease. In *Hudibras* (1663), in the course of a long comic simile whose other half needn't concern us, Samuel Butler alludes to prosthetic noses carved out of buttocks and retaining a magical affinity with their source:

> *So learned TALIACOTIUS from*
> *The brawny part of porter's bum*
> *Cut supplemental noses, which*
> *Wou'd last as long as parent breech;*
> *But when the date of nock was out*
> *Off drop'd the sympathetic snout.*

And, as Michael Jackson's nasal misadventures reminded us all, few things are more grotesquely funny than prosthetic noses. In *Cat Ballou* (1965), Lee Marvin plays a villain nicknamed Silvernose because the schnozz he was born with was bitten off in a fight, and now he wears a silver one held on by a rubber band. In Lucille Ball's own favorite episode of *I Love Lucy*, "L.A. at Last" (1955), Lucy disguises herself before a visit from William Holden with horn-rimmed glasses and a putty nose that grows gradually longer during his visit because she keeps nervously pinching it. When Holden tries to light Lucy's cigarette, the tip of her nose catches fire; she puts it out by dipping it into a teacup, like one of those drinking birds.

There is, of course, a long tradition of comic-strip characters with big noses. The artists sometimes referred to as "big-foot cartoonists"—Mort Walker, Dik Browne, and their ilk—could just as well be called "big-nose." So could E. C. Segar, though his most famous character, Popeye the Sailor, is more notable for a missing eye, a speech impediment, and grotesquely hypertrophied forearms. But several other Segar characters, like O. G. Watasnozzle, have ridiculously long and phallic snouts. Describing the genesis of his great comic strip, Segar recalled: "Olive Oyl was the first character to be born to *Thimble Theatre*. Ham Gravy came along about a minute later. I was eating a banana at the time and he was born with, or rather marked with, a nose not unlike that fruit." Since both bananas and noses remind us of penises, it makes sense that some noses remind us of BANANAS. "Banana-nose" has been a slang expression since at least the 1920s. Lighter cites an example from 1936: "Schnozzle, is that your nose or are you eating a banana?"

Segar not only drew funny noses on some of his characters, but also joked explicitly about their deformities. In one early Thimble Theatre strip, Ham Gravy gets his nose stuck in an antique vase. In another, when Olive refuses to marry him because of the length of his nose, he paints the tip black and proposes to her at night, claiming to have had a nose job. In a third, he's lifting weights and tells Olive that the exercises will make all his muscles twice as big, a boast to which Olive replies: "Gosh—it's lucky your nose ain't a muscle."

Another strip with explicit schnozzle humor was Bill Holman's *Smokey Stover*, a famously wacky (though seldom very funny) screwball strip that ran from 1935 to 1973. The title character secured his fire helmet (which had a tendency to fly off his head, and fly to pieces, whenever Smoky was surprised) with a string whose other end was tied around his nose, a feat possible only for those with the SAUSAGE-shaped nose so common in the comics.

Most cartoonists, though, were content to let the funny noses contribute to a strip's overall humor without ever striking the characters within the strip as humorous. It's probably the wiser choice, and not only for cartoonists. One measure of Jimmy Durante's inferiority to W. C. Fields is that Durante made so many nose jokes, while Fields hardly ever joked about his own unfortunate nose. Now and then another character does, as in *The Bank Dick* when a bratty child says, "Mommy, doesn't that man have a funny nose?" and his mother scolds him: "You mustn't make fun of the gentleman, Clifford. You'd like to have a nose like that full of nickels, wouldn't you?" But such put-downs at the expense of Fields's most salient feature are rare.

O o

Old Maids

OFTEN WITH THE humor of the past, the puzzle isn't how anyone found it funny, but who on earth could have found it *so* funny. Most of us have enough free-floating schadenfreude at our disposal to laugh in passing at a cruel portrayal in a movie or a novel of a ridiculous old maid. Who, though, would have wanted porcelain salt-and-pepper shakers shaped like a nightcapped old maid kneeling in prayer (salt) and a bed with a burglar's feet protruding from one end (pepper)? Who would have wanted to chuckle, day after day, every morning at breakfast, over some old lady's lifetime of loneliness and sexual frustration? Who, for that matter, would have wanted to send any of at least a dozen early comic postcards depicting that very scene, or similar scenes— the old maid gleefully discovering the burglar; the ugly old lady wistfully watching a happy young couple and saying, "Gee, I wish I had a beau"; the old maid alone with her black cat on any of several cards captioned "The Old Maid's Honeymoon"; the old maid pursuing a man with a rifle on Leap Year Day, or asking a father for the hand of his son? No doubt some of those cards were sent by old maids themselves, pre-empting ridicule by laughing at their own plight—but part of their plight was precisely that they lived in a world where unmarried women were heartlessly mocked.

Most of the cruelest postcards date from before World War I; the fad for Leap Year jokes was largely confined to 1908. To trace the iconography of spinsterhood after that, we must put away the postcards and get out the playing cards. Old Maid dates back to the nineteenth century and can be played with an ordinary deck (using a joker as the title card) since it's basically just a matching game like rummy. But there's more pathos in the game when all the cards are face cards: at the end, everybody has paired off except for the odd woman out, the ugly old maid. And some of the customized decks, especially those dating from the days before the game was relegated to the nursery, are a lot of fun, less for their depiction of the old gal herself than for their array of other human types. My favorite is a Jazz Age deck by Whitman with a cast of characters of which the humor would have been wasted on all but the most precocious five-year-olds of the era: Agonizing Sue, Azz I. Said (a BLOWHARD, and possibly an Arab), Bugs Boggs, Caspar Hotstuff, Cop Emoff, Ebeneezer Picket (a YOKEL), Eric Faintheart, Hazel Hazzit (a shopaholic), I. M. Cranky, Iva Lipstick, Jazzbo Jackson (a Cab Calloway look-alike), Jennie Twinkletoes, Lemmie Think (an EGGHEAD), Mandy Struts, Mr. I. Never (a killjoy), Oswald Shy, Sallie Splash (a bather), Slim Pickens, Tuffy Yegg, Weary Stoops (a HOBO), and Yotta Fall (a vamp). As for the Old Maid in that deck, she isn't as ugly as some, despite crossed eyes and a large red nose.

Fig. 104 Old maid, 1905

The long bony nose (Fig. 104), often red, is as much a hallmark of old maids in comic art as the black cat. In a Parker Brothers deck from the 1930s, the Old Maid has an even bigger nose than Flatfoot Floogy, the W.C. Fields look-alike. What does it mean? Like crossed eyes or BUCK TEETH, a big nose is an easy way for a less-than-masterly artist to suggest that a woman is unmarriageably ugly. It may also indicate horniness, or unladylike sexual aggression, given that NOSES are often equated with PENISES. As for the redness, is that meant to hint that the old lady has sought the consolation of drink? (*Nose paint* was 1920s slang for alcohol.) Maybe so, but it's seldom supplemented with any other hints.

Jokes about old maids are hardly ever funny,[39] and almost always cruel, though some are crueler than others. Sometimes the old maid's unmarried status is blamed on her personality, on her refusal to charm, as in an insulting greeting card from around 1910:

> *Your crabbed actions are enough to vex*
> *The most ardent admirer of your sex,*
> *And you care for nothing we can see*
> *Except your cat and your cup of tea.*

At least as often, though, the old maid is doomed to spinsterdom by homeliness, as in a vinegar valentine from the 1940s that shows a comically ugly woman, with cup-handle ears and warts on her nose, and a poem beginning:

> *You simper and smirk and primp with care*
> *In hope that you'll find a mate somewhere.*
> *No doubt you peek 'neath the bed at night*
> *Praying there will be a man in sight.*

Part of the lore about old maids was their fear of strange men—often imagined lurking under the bed—and the prurient desires concealed by the fear. W. H. Auden nicely captured that sexual ambivalence in "Miss Gee," a poem about a prim and proper spinster whose only male acquaintance is the vicar. One night she dreams that she is out biking and "a bull with the face of the vicar" is chasing her:

> *She could feel his hot breath upon her,*
> *He was going to overtake,*

---

[39] The only funny old-maid joke I know of—the slang use of *old maids* to mean unpopped kernels of popcorn—dates back to the 1940s.

And the bicycle went slower and slower
Because of that back-pedal brake.

Interestingly, old maids are seldom portrayed as fat. Usually they are beanpole thin. Is the skinniness a metaphor for sexual frustration?

With some exceptions (such as the too-hot-to-handle ethnic slurs), I've opted, in giving titles to the entries in this guide, for terms that reflect the outdated and sometimes appalling attitudes I'm discussing. We no longer speak of "old maids," but of course they still exist. What should we call them? *Spinster* is even worse—it's hard to see how it could ever have been anything but insulting, whereas *old maid* must once have been a euphemism, in an era that valued chastity and condemned all nonmarital sex, since what the term literally means is a woman who has remained a maiden—a virgin—longer than most. Forty years ago, some people spoke of "bachelor-ettes," especially on the original *Dating Game* (1965–73), but the same cultural revolution that has made the single life more acceptable has made *-ette* less so, if not as a diminutive then at least as a transgendering suffix.

Opera

NEAR THE BEGINNING of *A Night at the Opera*, Groucho arrives at the opera house in a horse-drawn cab. When he learns that the show is still in progress, he scolds the cabman: "Hey, you, I told you to slow that nag down. On account of you I nearly heard the opera." Groucho speaks for most of us: no other art form inspires such contempt—not just indifference but active contempt—from so many people who have never actually experienced it. But despite Groucho's quip, and the title of the film, surprisingly few of the many laughs in *A Night at the Opera* come at the expense of opera itself. Yes, there is Lassparri, the self-important, temperamental tenor; but Allan Jones and Kitty Carlisle—the young attractive pair in the (regrettable, contractual, unfunny, sentimental) subplot—are also cast as opera singers, so the film is forced to glamorize the art.

The pomposity and artificiality of opera would have been a perfect target for the Marx Brothers, but some people must have known there wouldn't be much mockery of opera in the movie as soon as they learned that the operas sampled were *Pagliacci* and *Il Trovatore*. When pop culture makes fun of opera, the opera is almost always Wagnerian, because the humorlessness of Wagner's weltanschauung makes him so laughable to those of us who are more adept at laughter than at solemnity. Also because of the kind of lungs needed to belt out his arias. It isn't the howling or even the horns on the helmet, though they don't help: what makes it hard for most of us to think of opera without smiling is the image of a three-hundred-pound diva howling to embody feminine allure.

In "The Lady Is a Tramp" (1937), Rodgers and Hart not only sing the pleasures of the simple life, but also claim to take a simple pleasure in sophisticated entertainments: "I like the theater, but never come late. . . . I go to opera and stay wide awake. . . ." That's not an opera joke, since it implies that there are better reasons for attending the opera than simple snobbery. But it also implies that most people at the opera don't know why they are there, and see it as at best something to be endured, not enjoyed.

Men, especially, are apt to be depicted as suffering at the opera, to which they've been dragged along by their wives. In a Peter Arno cartoon, two frowning businessmen sit in an opera box behind their plump, bejeweled wives, whose eyes are shut in rapt attention, or esthetic transport, or sleep, or sheer hauteur. One man consults his pocket watch and mutters to the other, "Well, we're over the hump." In another Arno cartoon, a man sits serenely in his box while the soprano wails onstage and his wife upbraids him: "You have SO got it turned off!"

As codified by Emily Post, operagoing in 1922 was as elaborate and pompous a charade as opera itself—one reason that so many people who've never attended an opera have any opinion about it at all, and have the opinion they do. "There is no occasion where greater dignity of manner is required of ladies and gentlemen both, than in occupying a box at the opera," according to Ms. Post, who adds, "For a gentleman especially no other etiquette is so exacting." He must always be in full dress, for example, in white tie and white gloves, and he must never sit in the front row of the box even if he has that box to himself. No wonder men hate to go to the opera.

Outhouses

IN 1941, SOMEONE published an elaborate spoof called the *Rears and Robust Catalogue*. I own a copy. Roughly the size of a Sears catalog, it consists mostly of blank sheets of tissue, and comes complete with a hook and a loop of twine for hanging it "in your Castle of the Half Moon." There are also pages printed with joke ads for fake products. Many of the jokes are tamely scatological: portable fireplugs for dogs to pee on, non-FLATULENCE-inducing canned BEANS, a combination high chair and potty, a bicycle built for two *buttocks* (with just one set of handlebars and pedals but two seats side by side: the illustration shows a FAT WOMAN resting one ham on each).

More exciting, for a writer who loves formal innovations and gimmicks generally, is an assortment of inserts and tip-ins that make *Rears and Roebuck* as fun to page through as a pop-up book. Among other things, the volume features a sheet of carbon paper (still capable, after seventy years, of faint duplication) "for those who like to make an impression . . . ditto"; a sheet of sandpaper "for the tired businessman" to "loosen up an otherwise tight situation"; a hotel-style DO NOT DISTURB sign; and a little envelope labeled "How to make your own MOON-SHINE" and containing yet another piece of toilet paper.

The love and ingenuity that clearly went into this "catalogue," and the costliness of its special effects (could even Jonathan Franzen get a publisher to include a sheet of sandpaper in *his* next catalog-sized volume?), testify to an interesting fact: for much of the twentieth century, in much of America—roughly in the red states and the rural parts of blue ones—most slightly naughty humor featured defecation rather than sex.

On the comic postcards of the mid-twentieth century, the second most common image (admittedly a distant second to the FAT WOMAN

WHEN YOU SAID COME OVER AN' SEE MY NEW TWO SEATER I THOUGHT YOU MEANT A BICYCLE!

Fig. 105

seen from behind) was probably a ramshackle outhouse. Usually we see only the exterior, though sometimes we get a glimpse inside at the untenanted seat (just a round or oval hole cut out of a plank) and the mail-order catalog hanging from a hook. Sometimes there are two holes, side by side without any partition, suggesting that the HILLBILLIES or hicks who own the outhouse are in the habit of defecating in tandem with their spouses, siblings, parents, or children. One comic postcard shows a lovesick carpenter's assistant being upbraided by his boss for cutting heart-shaped holes in a two-seater. Another shows three children of different ages and heights being measured by a carpenter for a custom-made three-seater. There are many outhouse postcards that pun on the word *hole*, like the one depicting an outhouse at night, with a smiling crescent moon above, and lines radiating from the walls like the ones drawn around a cartoon character's face to indicate shock or chagrin, and the message "Just a Line to Say—On the WhOle Everything's Okay."

Seldom do we see a bare-assed defecator seated on that hole, though we often see people—tourists or hicks—queuing for or sprinting for the outhouse. Cartoon HILLBILLIES are so accustomed to outdoor plumbing as to be unaware that any other kind is possible; if they accidentally order a toilet from the catalog that serves as toilet paper, they are apt to use the seat as a picture frame, the lid as a bread board, and the bowl as a hog trough. Hillbillies are also unaware of such a thing as single-purpose toilet paper; such a product would strike them as just another sissified luxury for city folks.

Like other toilets, outhouses are associated with masturbation as well as defecation. One 1940s postcard shows a pair of outhouses in a romantic lakeside setting. The signs on their crescent-vented doors read TOMMY and TABBY, and there's a tidy little quatrain in the postcard's lower right-hand corner: "You go here and I'll go there / We'll both be out of view / And while I sit in silent bliss / I'll think sweet thoughts of you." Outhouse humor is not only scatological but often sexual as well, because outhouses are places of nudity, privacy, shame, and, often, sexual segregation. In a 1952 postcard, two cartoon dogs sit contemplating two outhouses marked HIS and HERS, and one dog says to the other, "Well—I guess one must be for Setters and one's for Pointers."

Fig. 106

Pain

THERE IS, AS far as I know, not one scene in all of Henry James where a character of either sex sits on a THUMBTACK. I haven't read everything by Henry James, but I've read enough to know what the rest must be like, and nowhere do I see a thumbtack penetrating an unsuspecting buttock. Stubbed toes are also few and far between, if they occur at all. And unlike all those hapless dads on *America's Funniest Home Videos*, the males in James's arcadia never get hit in the balls.

What does Henry James have to do with mainstream American humor? Not a lot. But he was alive (though mostly overseas) during the rough-and-tumble heyday of early comic strips and slapstick comedy. He could have followed *Mutt and Jeff*. He could have seen the first films of Fatty Arbuckle and Charlie Chaplin. As far as I know, he never did. It's safe to say that if he had, he would have been appalled by the brickbats and PRATFALLS. James reminds us of the correlation of low- and high-brow humor with physical and mental pain respectively.

Among the forms of bodily harm most likely to befall characters in silent movies and old comic strips were being kicked in the RUMP, punched in the gut, socked in the NOSE, clubbed by a COP, hit by a car (after which it was customary for pedestrians to flip and land on their heads), launched over a fence by the hind legs of a mule, tossed by a bull, bucked by horse, treed or bitten by a dog, beaned with a ROLLING PIN or flatiron or skillet hurled by an angry wife, crushed by a falling SAFE or grand PIANO (ANVILS came later), whacked on the head with a cane or umbrella, spanked by an angry parent (usually with a hairbrush or SHOE instead of a bare hand), squirted by a hose or seltzer bottle, beaned by brickbat hurled by an urchin (extremely common, even before *Krazy Kat*), slipping and falling hard on the rump or head (since one of the conventions of old comics and silent comedies was that the head is as resilient as the rump), and falling from a ladder, window, tree, or rooftop.

No one knows why we find this stuff so funny—not even Max Eastman, who said so memorably in *The Sense of Humor* (not as good a book, alas, as the quotation makes it sound) that "humor is the instinct for taking pain playfully." If the definition makes humor sound like schadenfreude, that's because the two have a lot in common. There are crepe-hangers like Hobbes who insist that *all* humor partakes of schadenfreude. Not true. But both are ingenious inventions for extracting pleasure from pain. Schadenfreude is a bad invention, humor a good one. The humorist doesn't shake the Tree of Pain, or pluck the fruit, but windfalls are fair game.

When Eastman speaks of "taking pain playfully," he of course means mental pain as well as physical. For most people—those not being tortured by other people or by bodily afflictions—pain is mostly mental. Even for children, physical pain is usually only the tip of the iceberg. It's the kind of pain that children laugh at because it's the kind they find intelligible. Children aren't convinced yet that other minds are as real as their own, but no one doubts the reality, and vulnerability, of other *bodies*.

The better you're able to empathize with other people and imagine their feelings in a given situation, the more gratuitous and uninteresting any vivid depiction of their physical pain will seem. It's hard to picture Isabel Archer dropping a brick on her foot, because James is so exquisitely attuned to her psychic distress.

Fig. 107 Pain from head . . .

Conversely, the scary thing about so many early comic strips and silent movies, and so many Warner Bros. cartoons, is what they imply about the audience and its sociopathic inability to believe in, or even to imagine, any sort of mental activity in other people except when that activity is accompanied and illustrated by flamboyant physical symptoms. The reason there are so many SUICIDE attempts in old comic strips and movies is not that people used to find suicide funnier, but that it was the only way for adult characters to exhibit unbearable mental pain.

You could almost say that the difference between juvenile and adult narrative (in novels, movies, comics, and so on) is precisely that the latter, instead of confining the characters' feelings to the most basic and easily depicted passions and sensations, sometimes concerns feelings that *can't* be shown but must be imagined instead.

Sometimes, especially in comedies, a story switches back and forth between adult and juvenile representations of pain. When the heroine of *The Palm Beach Story* (1942) writes a "Dear John" letter to her sleeping husband and tries to pin it to his blanket before stealing out of his life, she accidentally pokes him with the pin instead. Henry James would have deplored that pinprick. James was a great American writer, maybe the smartest ever,

THE SORE TOE JOKE

A MOST EFFECTIVE DECEPTION

Makes One Shudder!

IT LOOKS SO PAINFUL

FITS OVER THE TOE OF YOUR SHOE

Price 15 Cents Mailed Anywhere

It is strongly molded in papier mache and it slips easily on to the toe of your shoe. A badly bruised and inflamed big toe projects through the end, that has been cut to relieve the pressure. A slight limp will elicit many sympathising enquiries. It can also be used as the finishing touch to a tramp's make-up.

No. 2190.   THE SORE TOE.   Price Postpaid.................................**15c**

Or Three for 40 cents, or One Dozen for $1.35 by Mail Postpaid.

Fig. 108 . . . to toe

and one of the wittiest, too. But he tactfully ignored the 95 percent of life he didn't like to think about. He was unsurpassed at describing the other 5 percent, but he was no more able to address the tragicomedy of physical pain than the Three Stooges were able to write like Henry James.

Pants

> *Your eyes, your eyes, they shine like the pants of a blue serge suit.*
> *That's not a reflection on you—it's on the pants.*
> —GROUCHO MARX, *THE COCOANUTS*, 1929

> *Is there any word more expressive than . . . pants?*
> —*REARS AND ROBUST CATALOGUE*, 1941

WHEN YOU ASK people to list the funniest words they can think of, *pants* often makes the list alongside more obvious candidates like *lollygag*, *platypus*, *kumquat*, and *gubernatorial*. The question of exactly what makes a word funny falls outside the scope of this encyclopedia, but usually the humor is semantic and not just phonological. To be sure, a disproportionate number of funny words feature *p* or *k*; and *oo* (as in *poot* or *bazooka*) shows up more often than it should, but seldom do funny letters alone add up to laughter. Now and then, as with *Kalamazoo*, we need look no further than the phonics for the funny; but *hooters* is funny because BOSOMS AND BREASTS are funny, *Kickapoo* because FECES is funny, *Titicaca* because both are.

As those last two examples suggest, it isn't necessary for a funny word to designate a funny thing, as long as it reminds us of one. It is goobers and not governors that do the trick with *gubernatorial*. With *pants*, part of the humor is the happenstance that the noun sounds like an unrelated third-person verb for heavy breathing (as well as a noun for heavy breaths): "He pants when she takes off her pants." But that barely begins to explain why *pants* is so much funnier than *pints* or *rants*. To explain that, we need to look beyond our grandfathers to our great- or great-great-grandfathers, and one of their most endearing neuroses.

Slang and Euphemism, a 1981 dictionary compiled by Richard A. Spears, focuses specifically on sexual and scatological terms, making it both funnier and more depressing than any other compilation of slang I've seen. I own the abridged edition, but it still features ninety-two synonyms for *pants*, evidence in itself that people have been laughing at pants for a long time now. No other garment comes close, and though that's partly because of the book's focus on the vulgar and obscene, it's notable that Spears could find only twenty-six synonyms for *underwear*.

The dictionary focuses on low subjects, but Spears doesn't confine his research to lowlifes and their ways of discussing those subjects. He lists genteelisms alongside vulgarisms. As a result, the entry on pants is an interesting mix of euphemisms, dysphemisms, jocularities, and clinicalities. At the low end of the sociolinguistic spectrum, there are such terms as *arse-rug*, *bum-curtains*, *farting-crackers*, *ham-cases*, and *sin-hiders*. Moving to a slightly better verbal neighborhood, we encounter *leg-covers*, *limb-shrouders*, and *sit-down-upons*. Note that all these terms, lower-class and lower-middle alike, reflect not just a sense of humor about the lower half of the body but also a neurotic inability to think of pants without also thinking of the body parts they conceal.

If those parts are naughty, so are the pants that cover them. Back when standards of modesty were much stricter, legs (and even ANKLES) were eroticized to the point where a glimpse of a woman's bare calf could affect a horny man the way a bare breast does nowadays. And though back then it was only men who wore pants, their legs too—and the legs of the pants that encased them—were suspect because they converged at the crotch. Thus the spate of crazy euphemisms designating pants—not underpants but outer pants—at the height of the Victorian era: *don't-name-'ems, mustn't-mention-'ems, never-mention-'ems, indescribables, indispensables, inexplicables, inexpressibles, innominables, unhintables, unspeakables, unutterables, unwhisperables.* Most of these terms were used on both sides of the Atlantic, and a few of them survived into (or were revived during) the twentieth century as synonyms for women's underpants—garments so unmentionable in Queen Victoria's time that they couldn't be referred to even as "unmentionables."

Paperhanging

LIKE PLUMBING, HANGING wallpaper is something you can either do yourself or pay a pro to do. If your goal is to fail amusingly, by all means do it yourself. "Why should I, an able-bodied man, pay a paperhanger for a simple job?" asks Baby Snooks's father, shortly before he steps on his glasses, drips paste on his daughter's face, and finds himself trapped in the room when he papers over the door and windows so thoroughly that he can't tell which way is out.

In "So You Want to Be a Paper Hanger" (1951), one in a long series of short comic how-to films from the 1940s and '50s, the protagonist also papers over the doorway and windows, as well as an annoying DOOR-TO-DOOR SALESMAN. Laurel and Hardy made a paperhanging film, as did Abbott and Costello. There's a zany paperhanging sequence in *A Day at the Races* (1937) **(Fig. 109)**. Donald Duck tries to hang a floral pattern in 1948's "Inferior Decorator" and ends up doing battle with a bee who mistakes the flowers for real ones. In "You Nazty Spy" (1940), the Three

Fig. 109 *A Day at the Races*, 1937

Stooges, who seldom reach the end of a two-reeler with the same vocation they pursued at the beginning, start out as paperhangers but before
they have a chance to screw up that job are promoted to dictators of
Moronica—a career change that makes better use of Moe's uncanny resemblance to Hitler, but also makes the film an unaccountable exception
to the rule that whenever someone tries to hang wallpaper in a comedy,
sticky mayhem will ensue.

According to Don Martin, the sound of wallpaper coming unglued
and unrolling from a wall is FLIP BLAP BLAP.

Parking and Petting

Girls who balk
Always walk.
—*CAPTAIN BILLY'S WHIZ BANG*, 1933

There's none so classy
As this fair lassie
Oh! Oh! Holy Moses, what a chassis
We went riding, she didn't balk,
Back from Yonkers
I'm the one that had to walk.
—"IF YOU KNEW SUSIE," BUDDY DESYLVA, 1925

BETWEEN THE TWO world wars, there was a major change in the mating rituals of American youth. Traditionally, the young man had paid court to the young woman on her living-room sofa, with her parents watching the clock and otherwise serving as superegos to keep young libidos in check. With the widespread availability of cars, though, horny couples discovered that they could get more privacy by driving off—ostensibly for some other wholesome and chaperoned location—and then stopping en route on a lonely stretch of road, or scenic overlook, or Lovers' Lane.

Though (as always) gag cartoonists took a while to register the change—well into the 1950s you still found plenty of cartoons about old-fashioned courtship on COUCHES—the locus of jokes about oversexed teenagers and undergrads eventually shifted from the sofa to the backseat, possibly a setting with less comic potential, what with the girl's nosy dad and bratty little brother out of the way, but one that lent itself more readily to risqué humor, as in the cartoon from a 1954 issue of *Sexations* showing a stretch limo pulled up in front of a hotel: the doorman has opened the car door to reveal a sugar daddy tucked into a bed, wearing pajamas and reading a newspaper. "Tell Miss Lulu her date is waiting," he commands the doorman.

More often, though, the struggle buggy (1920s slang for a car as a place to pet) lent itself to humor about the things that can happen when, as so often happens, only one of the youngsters is in the mood. That one is usually the male, but not always. "Can't you think of anything else to do when we run out of gas?" says the sexy redhead in the passenger seat to the NINCOMPOOP pushing their car uphill, on a comic postcard from the 1950s. The caption alludes to the male fantasy of running out of gas with a date on a deserted road, and/or the male ploy of pretending to have done so, though I've never been clear about how that eventuality was supposed to make the girl feel romantic. Like DESERT ISLAND cartoons, jokes about motoring couples stranded after dark in the middle of nowhere were sometimes jokes about RAPE.

Often they were jokes about sexual pressure and sexual rejection. The cover of a 1952 issue of *College Laughs* shows a young college man picking up his date in his yellow roadster; the young man is scowling because his date—although she's wearing stiletto heels and a skintight, tissue-thin dress—is also prudently carrying a gas can. Not many young women brought their own gas, but many did bring cab fare to get home ("mad money") in case a young man got too fresh. There were all sorts of variations on the theme. In a routinely racist comic postcard from the 1940s, a little black girl in a bathing suit brings along a life preserver as she joins her beau in his canoe for an evening boat ride lit by a winking moon: "I'm prepared in case you get fresh . . . and I have'ta get out and walk!" If you accept a ride on someone's magic carpet, what you need if he gets fresh is not cab fare so much as a parachute, like the one used by the indignant girl in a 1959 cartoon from *Man's Magazine*, who has just leapt from an airborne Lothario's carpet with a cry of "Fresh!"

William Fawcett, editor of a racy Jazz Age rag called *Captain Billy's Whiz Bang*, was obsessed with parking, and joked about it constantly: "The best of friends must park" (1924). "Her hair was bleached, her eyebrows penciled, her lips painted, her cheeks rouged, her eyes belladonnaed, her nose powdered, and when she entered the car with him, even her mind was made up" (1924). "Some girls walk home from an auto ride because they want to, some because they don't" (1930). "Chains won't keep one from slipping in a parked car" (1930). "Flapper Lily: 'Did you girls come in Pete's car?' Flapper Hulda: 'No I came in Shortie's and Babe came in Teddie's'" (c. 1930). Then there's the cartoon in a 1930 edition of *Smokehouse Monthly* (another early Fawcett publication; *smokehouse* was a jokey euphemism for OUTHOUSE[40]), one of the minority showing the woman as sexual aggressor: a sultry flapper and her date sit in a Model T that still looks less old-fashioned than the two-speaker caption:

> He: Something's gone wrong in this car.
> She: Well, get out your jack.

Henny Youngman was another humorist who couldn't stop joking about parking, at least in his 1967 collection, *400 Traveling Salesmen's Jokes*: "To most couples, curbing their emotions means parking." "If, as the scientists say, sex is such a driving force, why is so much of it nowadays found parked?" "A used-car dealer tells us that the usual standard sales pitch for a car that was owned by the little old lady who only used it on Sunday has been replaced by a nymphomaniac who only used the back seat."

In cartoons about parking and petting, the car is almost always a convertible, the better for us to see what all is going on inside. Even SAPS and MILQUETOASTS—unsporty guys who have nothing to show at the end of a date but a black eye—are given sporty convertibles.

Copping a feel in a parked car is a quintessentially youthful form of sexual activity, so it's automatically funny when practiced by anyone over the age of thirty—for instance, by the pompous and avuncular Throckmorton P. Gildersleeve, who in one episode of *The Great Gildersleeve* makes a fool of himself by trying the old out-of-gas subterfuge. Gildersleeve is a BACHELOR; a married man would hardly try to hoodwink his wife into "parking," though he might of course run out of gas for real. A

---

[40] *Outhouse*, too, is of course a euphemism. In everyday speech, there are no *non*-euphemistic terms for the places set aside for shitting and pissing. We are so accustomed to speaking in circumlocutions about these bodily functions that most of us routinely speak of "going to the bathroom"—as I do—without reflecting that the expression is a euphemism every bit as coy as "powdering my nose." Would life be better if we spoke with perfect frankness ("I'll be over in a minute—I just need to defecate") about such things? I doubt it.

postcard from the same era shows a glum middle-aged man standing by a car in which his scowling wife still sits, on a lonesome country road by a sign reading BILL'S GAS STATION—5 MI; and the caption reads, "What was a lucky break in courting days . . . is now just another pain in the neck!"

Pay Toilets

THOUGH I CAN'T pretend to emulate their erudition or their scholarly dedication, my role models as I write this guide are folklorists—scholars of modern low culture like Gershon Legman (*The Limerick* and *The Rationale of the Dirty Joke*), Vance Randolph (*Pissing in the Snow and Other Ozark Folktales*), Iona and Peter Opie (*The Lore and Language of Schoolchildren*), and Reinhold Aman (editor of *Maledicta*). Not least among my heroes is Alan Dundes, whose many publications include a 1966 monograph entitled "Here I Sit—A Study of American Latrinalia," in which Dundes proposed that Latinate word for what till then had been called "shithouse graffiti."[41] The change in nomenclature gave the subject an instant academic legitimacy, and the tree of knowledge sprouted a new limb. Subsequent studies of latrinalia have tended to focus on gender differences in graffiti, since no other form of folklore comes so handily pre-filtered by gender. A 1980 study by E. M. Bruner and J. P. Kelso concluded that

> women's graffiti are more interactive and interpersonal; one woman will raise a question and others will provide a string of responses and serious replies. . . . Men write about sexual conquests, sexual prowess and frequency of performance. . . . Women's graffiti are more conversational and deal with relationships; men's are more individualistic and deal with isolated sex acts and organs.

---

[41] A more recent article by Dundes is entitled "Six Inches from the Presidency: The Gary Hart Jokes as Public Opinion."

It's fun to think of other ways to crunch the data. Does the ration of sexist to racist graffiti increase or decrease between junior and senior high? How does the graffiti in toilet stalls at nursing homes and senior centers differ from the norm, and how is it depressingly or cheeringly the same? What about left-handed graffiti (since it doesn't take a Sherlock Holmes to deduce that certain inscriptions were made by left-handers): do those inscriptions differ from common latrinalia in ways that bear out the things we south-paws like to tell ourselves about our greater creativity? And what about the wit and wisdom scribbled in *pay* toilets? Does pay-toilet humor tend to be more literate than normal toilet humor, since those who can afford a decent education are presumably more likely to spring for the price of admission? Or is it just more meta-, since nothing is more likely to make one reflect on the mixed blessing of indoor plumbing than a tariff on its use?

The title of Dundes's seminal article alludes, of course, to the most famous of all shithouse poems, a poem existing in at least two versions:

1: Here I sit, / Broken-hearted: / Tried to shit / But only farted.
2: Here I sit, / Broken-hearted: / Paid a dime / But only farted.

Which of those is funnier? I ask because I much prefer the second. If you don't, read them aloud. Unless you're young enough that the word *shit* is enough in itself to make you laugh, I think you'll agree that *sit/shit* is not a terribly funny rhyme. A New Critic could argue that it's a *clever* rhyme, emphasizing both the kinship and the crucial difference between the two activities: shitting is sitting with something extra, something added; and for one who hoped to shit, mere sitting is heartbreakingly inadequate. With lines this short, though, the rhymes in the first version come at such close intervals as to drown out everything else, including humor. The ABCB rhyme scheme of the second version, with lines one and three un-rhymed, is more workable. More important, the "heartbreak" that is the real joke, in either version, is funnier when it's due not just to constipation but also to miserliness—and as Freud convinced the world in his discussion of the "anal-retentive personality," the two afflictions are linked.

Besides, pay toilets are intrinsically funny. Like liposuction, Christian rock, or nasophilia, they are funnier than anything we can say about them, which must be why they're underrepresented in the huge and steaming heap of mid-twentieth-century toilet humor. There are only a few basic gags—all lame—about them. There are gags about tightwads, usually SCOTSMEN in kilts, crawling under the door to the stall. ("Hoot, Mon! When comfort costs a fee / I grunt and strain to get in free!") There are jokes about means of payment—credit cards, go-now-pay-later plans, and so on. There are jokes about parking meters and dogs, as on a 1940s postcard where a frugal Scottie warns a companion, "Hoot mon! Not there—that's a pay station!" (A 1958 postcard more notable for its BEATNIK lingo than its humor shows a parking meter and a dog beside it saying, "Dig this crazy pay toilet!") And, again, there's the anguish of the constipated user whose dime unlocked the door but not his bowels.

Penises

> *Mrs. Hardy: You know, Charley, I haven't seen you*
> *since you sang in the choir.*
> *Charley Chase: And you used to pump the organ, remember?*
> *You little organ pumper you!*
> —*SONS OF THE DESERT,* 1933

> *Osgood: Which of these instruments do you play?*
> *Daphne: Bow fiddle.*
> *Osgood: Oh, fascinating! Do you use a bow or do you just pluck it?*
> *Daphne: Most of the time, I slap it!*
> —*SOME LIKE IT HOT,* 1959

IN 1929, THE Johnson Smith Company's mail order catalog offered a self-inflating balloon called the Hot Dog:

There is a small rubber tube . . . less than two inches long. It contains a very curious chemical that acts in a most remarkable way. You have merely to grasp it tightly in the hand and it suddenly becomes inflated with air just as if you had blown into it.

. . . Put it in someone's pocket, and then watch his astonishment when, after friction has developed, he finds the enormous thing in his pocket. . . . Each Hot Dog is packed in a small tube-shaped box, and is ready for business any time.

That's how our grandfathers used to joke about penises, and the "very curious" behavior of penises, back in the days when explicit dick jokes were banned from mainstream culture. A few decades later, someone manufactured a gag gift consisting of a little box with this teasing sentence fragment on the lid: "9 out of 10 WOMEN AGREE THE BEST PART OF A MAN IS . . ." Gag gifts are easy to spot, though, and no one who has already encountered even one specimen of the genre is likely to be tricked into getting his or her hopes up by the lid of such a box, or to be surprised on finding a plastic billfold and some phony bills. In the middle of the last century, there was a whole inane subgenre of gift boxes that raised X-rated expectations only to deflate them with G-rated contents; the joke, such as it was, was on the dirty minds of those who read obscene meaning into an innocent text.

A more prosperous relative of the gag box is the jumping snake gag, of which the most familiar now is probably the can that claims to hold mixed nuts but actually contains a spring-operated snake that surges out when the can is opened. Like box gags, snake gags are packages that appear to contain one thing but turn out to hold another; unlike box gags, they can make actually make even sober people laugh, because they make people jump. And they used to be suspiciously popular. The 1938

Squirt Rubber Snake

This snake resembles the real thing, and if you hold it concealed in your hand and suddenly let it go, it will jump quite a distance and startle everybody. It can be filled with perfume or water and with a gentle pressure will emit a fine jet in a very snake-like manner. It is made of rubber, effectively colored, and as large as life.

No. 2178. **Squirt Rubber Snake**... **50c**
3 for $1.25, or $5.00 per doz.

Fig. 110 Resembles the real thing

Johnson Smith catalog offered snake matches, a snake flashlight, a snake chocolate box, a snake whiskey bottle, a snake cigar lighter, a snake tulip and a snake rose (like a squirting flower, except that squeezing the rubber bulb caused a rubber snake to burst out of the blossom instead of a jet of water), a snake purse, a snake fountain pen, a snake salt shaker, a snake radio, a snake phonograph, a snake jam jar, and a snake cold-cream jar.

You don't have to be a Freudian to see that snakes and penises are frequently equated in jokes,[42] in slang ("one-eyed trouser snake"), and elsewhere. Johnny Hart, whose strip *B.C.* regularly featured a circle of unhappy clams in group psychotherapy, surely had the snake = penis equation in mind when he gave the proto-feminist Fat Broad a penchant for clobbering snakes with her club.

Some jokes, some metaphors, are harder to be sure about. When a popular kid-oriented comic strip from the early 1900s is entitled *Foxy Grandpa*; when G-rated books and songs and movies from the 1920s and '30s routinely speak of "making love"; when, for that matter, a beloved folk song includes such lyrics as "She'll be wearing pink pajamas when she comes"—such relics remind us that our grandparents spoke a different language. In some cases, of course, it isn't clear if semantic change has made a once-innocent phrase seem dirty to our dirty minds, or if the double entendre was intended all along. In those cases, the *Oxford English Dictionary* is helpful, and often decisive: with humorous writings, it's safe to assume that if a word or phrase had already acquired an off-color sense when the author used it, the author intended a double entendre, even if one pitched to only the sharpest ears. All humorists deserving of the name—however clean their acts—have dirty minds.

Sometimes not even the *OED* can settle the question. When, in a Three Stooges short from 1946, Moe says, "You'all done ejaculated a mouthful," it is just possible that neither he nor the writer was aware of the double entendre. *Ejaculate* had been used in connection with semen since the early fifteenth century, but by the nineteenth that sense seems

---

[42] Here's one from my boyhood: "Harry Houdini had a forty-foot weenie. / He showed it to the lady next door. / She thought it was a snake / And she hit it with a rake, / And now it's only four foot four."

to have gone into remission; until it was revived in Kinsey's *Sexual Behavior in the Human Male* (1948), the word was mainly used, outside medical circles, as an innocently hifalutin synonym for *shouted* or *blurted*.

It's harder, though, to shrug off a line from another Stooges short, "Ants in the Pantry" (1936). At the end of that film, Larry, Moe, and Curly intone in unison, "If at first you don't succeed, keep on suckin' till ya do suck seed!" It's hard to believe that either the Stooges or their audience could have failed to hear that as a fellatio joke. Seed, after all, has been a synonym for semen or sperm for hundreds of years. (In the 1611 King James version of the only passage in the Bible that might be construed as forbidding masturbation, poor Onan is smitten for spilling his "seed" on the ground.)

Can there be a witty and civilized dick joke? Yes, if the joker is someone like James Merrill. After all, sophisticates have penises too, and spend as much time thinking about them as the rest of us do. On his return from a trip to China, Merrill told some friends about his experience with opium. When a woman archly mentioned that opium is said to cause impotence, Merrill instantly retorted "Poppycock"—a pun so good (assuming it was unrehearsed) that even those of us who pride ourselves on our own puns can only shake our heads in wonder at the miracle of the human mind at its most nimble.

Phooey

> *Baloney mahoney malarkey, you big kabloona.*
> —SURLY WAITRESS TO W. C. FIELDS IN *NEVER GIVE A SUCKER AN EVEN BREAK*, 1941

> *Oh, fiddle-faddle.*
> —AUNT BEE, *THE ANDY GRIFFITH SHOW*

SLANG IS FAMOUSLY ephemeral, and its unplanned obsolescence is due to the constant replacement of new terms by even newer ones. If the speakers of a language stop coining slang for a thing, it's usually because the thing no longer plays a part in everyday life.

But not always. No one would deny that there's at least as much bullshit spoken, written, sung, or broadcast nowadays as there has ever been, yet we really have only that one word for all these manifestations of obnoxious nonsense; the other words for it sound as quaint and geriatric as "Blast!" or "Rats!" in place of "Fuck!" or "Shit!"

It wasn't always like that. The 1920s (and, to a lesser extent, the '30s) was a golden age of anti-bullshit slang: *applesauce, baloney, balloon juice, banana oil, bibble-babble, bilge, birdseed, bosh, buckwheat, bugle oil, bumf* (short for *bum fodder*—toilet paper), *bunk, bushwah, claptrap, Durham, eyewash, flipflop,*[43] *gobbledygook, grapefruit, hokum, hooey, hornswoggle, horse apples, horsefeathers, hogwash, malarkey, meadow dressing, mumbo-jumbo, piffle, poppycock, tommyrot . . .* There were also all sorts of interjections like *in your hat, it's the bunk, nerts, nuts, phooey, says you, ish kabibble,* and *woof, woof,* though it's no accident that most of the nouns on the list above also served as interjections. When someone is spouting bullshit, an interjection is exactly what you want to squelch it—something closer to a belch or a Bronx cheer than a full-fledged word, because bullshit doesn't deserve the honor of an articulate response. But interjections can wear out, like other parts of speech. That must be one reason Jazz Age slang was so fond of anti-bullshit words: as the bullshitters kept finding new ways to lie and obfuscate, bullshit detectors kept developing new ways to fight it, like new antibiotics.

Bullshit detection has been a favorite occupation of American humorists, from the cynicism of Twain's darker pages through the compulsive debunking of Bierce and Mencken to the fake ads in *Mad*. By the way, just as *Mad* touched off a craze in the 1950s for naming humor magazines with synonyms for "insane"—*Cracked, Crazy, Sick, Unsane,* and so on—there was a fad around 1930 for naming the zaniest humor magazines with synonyms for "nonsense" or "hoopla": *Ballyhoo, Hooey, Hullaballoo.* (After leaving *Mad* in 1956, its founder, Harvey Kurtzman, started another humor magazine with a retro title: *Humbug.*) It's an in-

[43] From *Babbitt* (1922): "The first thing you got to understand is that all this uplift and flipflop and settlement-work and recreation is nothing in God's world but the entering wedge for socialism."

Fig. 111

teresting shift. Where misfits in the Eisenhower '50s tended to think of squares as boringly sane and irremediably incapable of saying anything odd, their counterparts in the 1920s and '30s found nothing more ridiculous than the nonsense spouted daily with a straight face by so many of the officially sane.

Whole comic strips were devoted to making that point. In a 1924 feature by Sals Bostwick called "The Bunk Artist's Degree," one character spouts bullshit, the listener says "Grapefruit!" and a tiny professor appears to confer the diploma in question. The best such strip, though, was *Banana Oil* by Milt Gross. In each installment of the 1920s strip, a character says something flagrantly untrue and another character—or sometimes a whole chorus—responds "Banana oil!" In one typical strip, a heartless mogul refuses to give money to a beggar, claiming that he only gives to "recognized charitable institutions." When he encounters a woman collecting for just such an institution, though, the mogul changes his tune: "I don't believe in these organized charity things. When I see a worthy case, I contribute privately." Whereupon an ALLEY CAT who has witnessed both encounters exclaims, "Banana oil!"

Nowadays we seldom say anything but "bullshit." Did that word prevail the same way the gun prevailed over spear and slingshot, simply by being so much more lethal than any of its rivals as to make them all seem feeble? Or is it that we're so inundated with nonsense these days that we've lost our sensitivity to it, our ability to discriminate fine shades? Maybe our grandparents would have said "bullshit" too, if they'd been allowed, and only the taboo on using that word in public forced them to keep finding substitutes, trying out one after another because none was strong enough. (In *private*, off the record, Americans have been saying and writing "bullshit" since World War I.)

Or could it be that bullshit, like bacteria, has grown more resistant and more virulent, and is now too obnoxious to be adequately named by any of the words our grandfathers used in mixed company fifty years ago? Or is it that, just as euphemisms grow less and less euphemistic with use, until they have to be replaced (as *handicapped* gave way to *disabled*, and that to *challenged*), dysphemisms grow less damning with time? So Grandpa compensated for his inability to use the strongest synonym for *nonsense* by always using the freshest, while it still had the impact of novelty.

Not that the culture as a whole seems to have kept abreast of the latest fashions in "nonsense" synonyms; otherwise, we'd be able to pinpoint the heyday of each, as attested by its appearances in print, to a specific year. One reason we can't is that people back then were still able to laugh about nonsense, insincerity, and obfuscation, and so were inclined to speak of it more gently and indulgently than we do, and often to favor funny names for it instead of damning ones. These days, people who haven't lost their sensitivity to bullshit are often too oppressed by it to want to joke about it—just as those of us with a life-threatening allergy to NOISE find it hard to joke about car alarms and barking dogs.

Physical Infirmities

THE EXPRESSION "FUNNY as a crutch," meaning *not funny at all*, first appeared in 1916, a year before America entered World War I. Three years later, the war was over, two hundred thousand American soldiers had been wounded, and the expression had developed a second and opposite sense: *really funny*. Granted that people laugh more readily when their country isn't at war, the scary thing about this mutation is that it seems to have been due to an honest misunderstanding: people heard the phrase "funny as a crutch" and assumed it meant funny indeed—funny as an old lady slipping on an icy sidewalk, say.

There are other signs that during and after World War I, American civilians reacted with sick humor to the shocking sight of maimed veterans returning from the bloodiest war the world had yet seen—and a war whose veterans weren't warehoused as discreetly and efficiently as badly maimed soldiers nowadays. The term *halfy*, meaning "a beggar with both legs off at the hips," first appeared in 1918. That era saw many cartoons involving beggars faking disabilities—most often blindness, though sometimes a grifter would pretend to be an amputee by standing against a board fence and sticking one leg out of sight behind him through a hole. Many humorists seem to have reacted with shocked incredulity to the horrors suddenly confronting them on city streets. There is *some* validity to the charge often leveled against humor by the humorless: it can be a way of refusing to acknowledge the reality of other people's suffering.

Speaking of beggars and legs: in 1921, when flappers were shocking the world by wearing dresses with hemlines so shamelessly high as to reveal not only their ANKLES but their calves,[44] the October issue of *Captain Billy's Whiz Bang* featured a funny cover illustration of an os-

---

[44] Like the sudden influx of cripples and crutches, if not as directly, the rise of flappers has been attributed to World War I.

Fig. 112 The blind beggar fraud, spotted in the wild. See also ANKLES.

tensibly blind beggar raising his dark glasses to get a better look at a pair of shapely gams. Two months later, the very same gag appeared on the cover of another magazine, *Snappy Stories*. Well, there's no honor among thieves, and most gag cartoonists are kleptomaniacs.

Our culture's sense of humor has changed enough since World War I that some jokes from that era are not only no longer funny, but no longer even intelligible. A bizarre cartoon from 1915 showed a beggar sporting an army uniform, two peg legs, a sign around his neck reading BLIND AS A BAT, and a pair of dark glasses he's raising to examine a dollar bill: ha ha, he isn't blind after all, though apparently he *is* a bona fide cripple.

Pianos

PIANOS ARE RIGHT up there with ANVILS and SAFES as the heavy objects most likely to fall from great heights in cartoons and land on cartoon characters. When the point of an object is simply to be bulky and heavy—as in cartoons about movers—pianos are bulkier, heavier, and funnier than steamer trunks or even Frigidaires.

Posher, too. Like fancy dinner parties, grand pianos are symbols of wealth and targets of class resentment; that's one reason the Three Stooges are almost as likely to smash up a piano as a gala. In "Ants in the Pantry" (1936), they play exterminators who disrupt a ritzy dinner party and destroy a mouse- and cat-infested piano. In "Brideless Groom" (1947), Shemp's wedding ring gets lost in the works of a baby grand, and in his efforts to retrieve it he becomes hopelessly entangled in piano wire—and, needless to say, is cracked on the head several times by the sounding board.

Pickles

ALONG WITH ICE cream, pickles are the stereotypical thing for pregnant women to crave. In one of the first episodes of *The Honeymooners*, Alice develops a sudden appetite for them, leading Ralph to deduce that she's pregnant. (Turns out she isn't: her doctor was just testing for a pickle allergy.) Notably sour and salty, pickles make sense as a craving—at least insofar as salt-and-vinegar potato chips make sense. But it's a funnier craving than most. If cucumbers are phallic, pickles are shrunken, warty, blighted phalluses (in 1942's "Matri-Phony," the Three Stooges encounter a squirting pickle at a banquet table), and there's a symbolic appropriateness to their association with the often less-than-joyous results of sex. When a cartoon pauper is reduced to wearing a BARREL to hide his nakedness, it's often labeled as a pickle barrel.

So pickles are funnier than most other preserved foods—and preservation itself makes food funnier. (That's why canned vegetables are more amusing than fresh ones, and why cheese grows steadily droller as it ages.) Pickles Sorrell—Buddy's wife—is a fondly remembered ditz from *The Dick Van Dyke Show*, though she appeared in just three episodes. I like to think of her name as a verb and not a noun.

In "The Pickle Story," a second-season episode of *The Andy Griffith Show*, Aunt Bee makes a batch of pickles so inedible that Barney and Andy call them her "kerosene cucumbers." Rather than eat them, they replace them with store-bought pickles while Bee is out. Barney gets rid of the originals by handing them out to drivers as Safe Driving awards.

Pie Fights

My heart's aglow
When they find things are slow
And they start slinging pastry and dough.
—IRA GERSHWIN, "I'M TICKLED SILLY"
(AKA "SLAPSTICK"), 1921

MORE THAN ANY sight gag except perhaps the PRATFALL, the pie in the face is emblematic of old silent comedy, especially the rough-and-tumble kind perfected by Mack Sennett and his stable of brilliant buffoons. In retrospect, it's surprising that it took so long for someone to think of the gag. The movie industry had been

Fig. 113 *The Great Race,* 1965

cranking out sight gags for almost fifteen years by 1909, when Ben Turpin made cinematic history by provoking a waitress in a diner into smashing a pie in his face. The film was called "Mr. Flip," and in those days a *flip* was "a saucy, impertinent, or forward person." Turpin played a funny-looking little man who can't keep his hands off barmaids, shop clerks, hairdressers, phone operators, and the like, and persists in chucking their chins, touching their napes, and even stealing kisses, till they retaliate. In the course of the short film, Mr. Flip is doused with seltzer bottles, wheeled off on a hand truck, jabbed in the RUMP with a pair of sewing scissors, and nearly electrocuted in a phone booth, but the final retribution—the climax—is the pie. It would be four more years, though, before someone (Mabel Normand) *threw* a pie at someone (Fatty Arbuckle), in a Mack Sennett short with the flatulent title "A Noise from the Deep."

Ever since, pie humor has been popular—so popular that someone recently compiled a list of the 100 Best Pie Scenes of All Time. Not all the scenes involve somebody getting hit in the face, but many do. In *The Battle of the Century*, a Laurel and Hardy short from 1927, a deliveryman from the L.A. Pie Company (whose truck is parked at the time with its back doors wide open) slips on a BANANA PEEL discarded by Ollie and retaliates by throwing a pie—the first shot in an enormous fight that is said to have involved four thousand pies in all. Pies 2 and 3 hit a FLAPPER, one in the rump and one in the face. As she calmly walks over to the truck and gets another pie, the other characters stand by and wait for her to take her turn—even Ollie, whom she clearly plans to hit. Maybe he knows that in a cinematic pie fight, the intended target is no more likely to get hit than an innocent bystander; and sure enough, the pie misses him by a mile and hits a man at a nearby shoeshine booth. At that point a pompous mayoral type tries to intervene and stop the nonsense, is predictably clobbered, and as predictably renounces his pacifism. A battle royale ensues, with pie-spattered pedestrians milling around the truck and stray pies flying into nearby shops and offices—one hits a man sitting in a dentist chair with mouth agape, one hits a customer in a barbershop as he's admiring his new haircut, one flies down an open manhole and hits a sewer worker, one hits a DOWAGER in an open car as she peers through a lorgnette at the ill-bred kerfuffle.

An even bigger pie fight—supposedly the biggest in cinematic history—occurs in *The Great Race* (1965), when Tony Curtis, Jack Lemmon, Natalie Wood, and other contestants in a transcontinental road race find themselves in a bakery **(Fig. 113)**. The fight is not as funny as the one in *The Battle of the Century*—1960s zaniness hasn't aged as gracefully as 1920s zaniness—but visually it is more ravishing because it's shot in color, and the characters get pasted with red and purple fruit pies as well as plain white cream pies. Like most extended pie fights, it gets less funny as it goes on: when an already-pie-spattered character is hit again, it's never as thrilling as it was the first time. That's why the director, Blake Edwards, waits till the end of the scene before the charmed, immaculate, white-suited Tony Curtis is finally pied.

The immortal pie fight in the Three Stooges short "In the Sweet Pie and Pie" (1941) begins when a butler trips and hits Moe in the face with a cake. Moe retaliates in kind and things escalate as they can only at a dinner party where the buffet features no fewer than twenty-nine pies. The sequence is a veritable anthology of pie-related gags: accidental pieing (as when the intended target ducks), people pied while laughing at other pieings, pompous voice-of-reason types joining the fray after being hit, Curly repeatedly pied while preparing to throw a pie (one he finally hits himself with), involuntary auto-pieing when someone jogs the thrower's arm; non sequitur attacks where A pies B so B pies C; pies thrown backward so that they hit the person *behind* the thrower—a trick reminiscent of the old Statue of Liberty play. (Was this scene the inspiration for the "aversion therapy" scene in the early *Simpsons* episode "There's No Disgrace Like Home," where the family therapist wires the Simpsons so that each can shock any of the others at the touch of a button?)

Insofar as the morality of a movie or a sitcom can be gauged by its allotment of punishment, the morality of pie fights is unusual; it's not the Old Testament pie-for-a-pie you might expect. Screenwriters discovered early on that, where pies are concerned, almost anything is funnier than simple retaliation. To be sure, anyone who throws a pie will probably be pied at some point, but it's even riskier to laugh at a pieing. Riskiest of all is to make a humorless grown-up plea to stop the shenanigans.

Because pies are hard to throw accurately, successful real-life pieings are usually executed at point-blank range; they're more akin to stabbings than to shootings. When they're not point-blank, movie pieings usually involve a cut from a shot of the thrower to a shot of the victim. Only in cartoons do we get to watch a pie leave the thrower's hand, travel across a room, and hit its victim in the face.

Pink Elephants

THE FIRST KNOWN reference to pink elephants in print is by Jack London. In 1913, in his memoir *John Barleycorn*, London sets himself apart from other, more stereotypical alcoholics, such as

> the man whom we all know, stupid, unimaginative, whose brain is bitten numbly by numb maggots; who walks generously with wide-spread, tentative legs, falls frequently in the gutter, and who sees, in the extremity of his ecstasy, blue mice and pink elephants. He is the type that gives rise to the jokes in the funny papers.

That passage suggests that, by 1913, pink elephants were already a cliché; as more and more old books and periodicals are scanned and put online, older references are bound to show up. I have a comic postcard from 1906 that shows a drunk leaning against a lamppost and hallucinating a tiny winged *green* elephant, so evidently the animal was associated with funny DTs before it assumed its definitive color.

The important thing, in any case, is not that the elephant be pink, but that it look like something you'd see only in hallucinations. When Felix the Cat gets drunk on moonshine in "Felix Finds Out" (1924), he too promptly starts hallucinating, and though he can't very well see pink in a black-and-white cartoon, his main hallucination is a winged elephant whose coloration alternates between throbbing polka dots and flashing stripes.

By the early 1930s, the cliché was well established. In "Pink Elephants," a 1932 novelty song, the singer swears off booze forever one morning after seeing pink elephants on the table, on the chair, on the ceiling, everywhere. A decade later, a whole generation of young moviegoers was traumatized by the "Pink Elephants on Parade" sequence in Disney's classic *Dumbo*. After his first taste of alcohol, the title character hallucinates a whole marching band of hot-pink elephants strutting around on their hind legs, dancing, belly dancing, figure skating, merging, multiplying, changing colors, shifting shapes, mutating into motorcars and camels, hurling lightning bolts, and otherwise behaving so outlandishly as to scare even Dumbo— himself an elephant, himself outlandish. As for the human children who shared his delirium, the movie must have frightened some away from alcohol for life.

Fig. 114 So drunk his pink elephant is green, 1906.

It didn't scare away everyone, though, and several vintage drinking games featured pink elephants. In Pass Out (1962), players roll a die and move around a board, taking a drink whenever a square instructs them to. Each time you pass "start" you must take a "Pink Elephant" card with a tongue twister printed on it. If you can say the tongue twister correctly three times in a row, you get to keep the card; the first player with ten cards is the winner. The game must often have ended unfinished, especially when the players were drinking anything stronger than beer. As with most packaged drinking games, the printed instructions include a ridiculous disclaimer: "Not intended for use with Alcoholic Beverages."

The decade most associated with pink elephants is neither the 1940s nor the 1960s but the 1950s, when suburbanites throughout America seem to have turned to alcohol as an escape from the appalling blandness of their lives, but needed to sweeten their drinks with all kinds of corny humor. The popularity of pink-elephant kitsch in our own time (when, among other things, "Pink Elephant" is the name of a liquor store in Hollywood, a nightclub in Manhattan, and a song by the Cherry Poppin' Daddies—as well as a term for gay Republicans) is due to nostalgia for corny 1950s stereotypes about drunkenness: as befits an animal famed for its memory, elephants are now a retro fad.

Plewds

WHAT ARE PLEWDS? You may not know the word, but you know the thing: those little drops of sweat that fly off a cartoon character when he or she is alarmed or dismayed. Because their purpose is to indicate an emotion, they always emanate from the head, though we do most of our sweating below the neck.

Plewd doesn't sound much like a real word, and some lexicographers would say it's not. For the longest time, there were no words at all, not even made-up ones, for many phenomena common in comics but otherwise rare or nonexistent. Then along came Mort Walker and his facetious *Lexicon of Comicana*, which reveals a wittier mind than you'd suspect from the stale recent decades of *Beetle Bailey* and *Hi and Lois*. Like Adam in Eden, Walker invented names for everything, and though his lexicon started as a joke, some of its names have caught on, for lack of better words. A few have even found their way into the dictionary, though most are known only to cartoonists and comic-strip buffs. Here are a few of Walker's other coinages, with my definitions (I'd use Walker's, but for the most part he illustrates rather than defines):

Agitrons are short curved lines, like nested parentheses, around a trembling or vibrating object.

Blurgits are the comic-strip equivalent of time-lapse photography, suggesting motion by indicating the many positions a moving body occupies in rapid succession. Like other conventions that might mistakenly be seen as compensating for the static nature of the comic-strip panel, blurgits are also common in animated cartoons, especially when a character tries to accelerate so quickly from a standstill that he or she runs in place for a moment before getting out of the starting blocks. (The Road Runner is so fast that, except when at rest, his feet are *always* a blur.) In comics as well, the best blurgits tend to involve circular motion, but linear blurgits are possible too; as Walker points out, that's the technique of Duchamp's *Nude Descending a Staircase*.

A *lucaflect* is a way of suggesting the roundness and shininess of an

Fig. 115 A man and his plewds; thermometer reacts sympathetically.

object (a bubble, a bald head, a billiard ball) by showing the tiny curved reflection of a four-paned window. The only place this really makes sense is indoors, where a window might be the brightest source of light in a room, but great cartoonists are not afraid of nonsense, and have no qualms about lucaflecting outdoors too. Lucaflects must never be confused with *neoflects*, the bristly little parallel lines that create an aura of newness (or sometimes just cleanliness) around an object.

A *spurl* is a spiral—what Yeats called a "widening gyre"—drawn above a character's head to indicate intoxication, grogginess, unconsciousness (usually due to head injury), or nausea.

Plewds and spurls are examples of what Walker calls "*emanata . . .* the things cartoonists have emanating from their characters . . . to show what's going on inside them." The oldest and most common emanata are the stars used to indicate pain or grogginess, especially the kind resulting from head injuries, and those stars are so common in old comics because head injuries are so common. (Classic comic-strip characters should be forgiven if they act a little punch-drunk: many of them—Barney Google, Krazy Kat, Dagwood, Happy Hooligan, Beetle Bailey, Mutt and Jeff, Popeye, Jiggs—have sustained more blows to the head than an aging boxer.)

Walker named all sorts of other comic-strip symbols—*solrads, crottles, indotherms, waftaroms, oculamas, sphericasias, boozexes, swalloops,* and *squeans,* to name a few. But if you want to know about those too, you ought to buy his book.

Plops

THOUGH THEORISTS SOMETIMES speak of the comic strip as an equal partnership of words and images, in truth the medium is mainly visual. No matter how clever a joke is, if it's strictly verbal—something funny someone says to someone else—we feel gypped. We need a visual payoff. And that payoff almost always takes the form of what's known in Hollywood as a reaction shot. If the characters don't visibly react to a verbal joke, not only do we feel cheated; we may even fail to notice that something funny has been said. It's essential that the audience know when to laugh. That's one reason sitcoms use laugh tracks and nightclub comedians use rimshots.

How should the "straight man" in a comic strip react when someone says something outrageous? Chuckling won't do; that's the kind of laughter that pre-empts the reader's. Even the stupidest sitcom knows enough to keep the laugh track offscreen, to have the characters themselves unaware of how zany they are. Laughter itself can be funny, of course, but the funniest reactions are surprise, dismay, and anger; that's why, in the little illustrated ads for mail-order pranks, the victim always exhibits one of those emotions, and in exaggerated form.

Cartooning is exaggeration. If Henry James had been a cartoonist, *his* straight men might have reacted by raising an eyebrow or coloring slightly, but most of the classic cartoonists worked at the other end of the subtlety spectrum, and were more likely to indicate comic dismay by having a character fall over backward:

Fig. 116

Cartoonists call that a "plop" or "plop take," and it implies that a blast of absurdity has knocked the character on his ass, or caused him to lose consciousness altogether. Ideally the character plops right out of the panel, so that only his or her feet are visible; in this context, feet are more expressive than faces:

Fig. 117

Sometimes, to emphasize the violence of a plop, the cartoonist endows the plopper's accessories with extra inertia, so that they remain hanging in midair, in the space just vacated:

Fig. 118

We sometimes warn people to sit down before we divulge a surprise, but comic-strip characters have a way of fainting catastrophically even from a seated position:

Fig. 119

It is also possible to plop *forward*:

Fig. 120

Ingenious artists like *Mutt and Jeff*'s Bud Fisher liked to find zany variants on the the basic sight gag, including some that are easier to show than to describe:

Fig. 121

If ever a cliché seemed native to the cartoonist's art, it's this one, which is hard even to picture in any other medium. We can trace its origins back to the birth and even back to the fetal stages of the comic strip, at least if we understand the plop as an exaggeration or reductio ad absurdum (and in comics such reductios are inevitable) of the flinch or startle, in which the straight man reels from the zaniness but nonetheless keeps his feet. On the first page of the first book to resemble even remotely our modern conception of comics, Rodolphe Töpffer's *Histoire de M. Vieux Bois* (1827), M. Vieux Bois' ghostly ancestors respond to his effrontery with an embryonic plop:

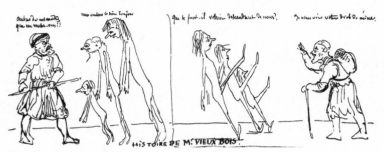

Fig. 122

So the plop has been there from the start—from the very second panel of comic-strip history, when the zygote had divided only once.

Some endangered or extinct clichés of American cartooning are still found in foreign comics, like defective pharmaceuticals dumped on the Third World after being banned in developed countries. Japanese cartoonists, in addition to giving the world a new set of sight gags (nosebleeds to signify sexual arousal; sneezes to indicate that someone is discussing a character behind her back), have revived a number of outmoded Western cartooning conventions. Remember the giant wooden mallets Bugs Bunny used to whisk from behind his back to clobber Elmer Fudd or Yosemite Sam? Those mallets are now in the hands of deceptively sweet Japanese schoolgirls, who use them to wallop perverts.

Similarly, the plop is hardly ever seen anymore in American comics (not counting self-consciously retro work by nostalgics like Crumb and

Seth), but lives on in South America's most popular comic strip, *Condorito*. In this crowd-pleaser by the Chilean cartoonist "Pepo" (as in certain American screwball strips of the 1920s and '30s—*Smokey Stover*, *Salesman Sam*, the first, pre-Popeye years of *Thimble Theatre*) almost every strip ends with a plop, though now and then the straight man manages instead to keep his feet and demand an explanation for the zaniness: "¡Exijo una explicación!" Like rimshots or laugh tracks, plops can be habit-forming: if you use them day after day to punctuate a joke, how can you stop using them without implying that you've suddenly ceased to be funny?

Plumbers

> *He must come at crack of dawn, with all his instruments*
> *and blow-torches, like a fiend from hell. The water must be shut off,*
> *pipes must be hammered and banged, and, above all,*
> *strangers will be poking their heads in and out of doors where you*
> *are accustomed to seeing only familiar faces.*
> —ROBERT BENCHLEY

IT'S INTERESTING TO compare the plumber with another beefy proletarian stock character, the ICEMAN. Both have entrée to suburban homes and middle-class apartments, sometimes when only the woman of the house is home, but while the iceman figures in all sorts of fantasies about horny housewives, you seldom see jokes about housewives seducing plumbers. The plumber's trade is rife with potential sight gags and double entendres, but somehow, because his locus of household operations (at least as imagined by humorists) is the bathroom rather than the kitchen, and because we associate him with human sewage rather than with perishable foodstuffs, he doesn't impress anyone—not even the raunchy men we have to thank for risqué postcards and *Playboy* party jokes—as a Casanova. When he does get cast in a dirty joke or gag cartoon, the plumber seldom gets to do more than barge in, accidentally or not, on a lady in a bathtub.

HANDYMAN

IS THAT GADGET ON THE BLINK?
YOU CAN FIX IT-SO YOU THINK.
NEXT TIME YOU FEEL LIKE HELPING OUT
DO SOMETHING THAT YOU KNOW ABOUT.

Fig. 123

Really, it's a pity. If plumbers could just find a way to farm out toilets to some other, lowlier profession—as dentists have done with the degrading work of cleaning teeth by giving the chore to hygienists—we'd see them differently. Toilets are only part of a plumber's job, but that part contaminates our image of the job as surely as a few drops of sewage suffice to contaminate a gallon of fresh drinking water. All the plumber's other image problems—the surliness, the tendency to overcharge (how can you justify charging as much as an electrician, say, when you deal not with alternating current but with feces?), and even the recent lowbrow jokes about the plumber's butt-crack as revealed by low-riding pants—can be traced back to that one.

Most plumbing jokes, though, don't concern certified plumbers, but do-it-yourselfers whose delusions of grandeur lead them to think they can save money by fixing their own leaks—leaks that always start small and get bigger or more numerous with each misguided effort to stop them. In most comic representations of amateur plumbers, the result is disaster. If the plumber's union had a monopoly on plumbing humor, it could hardly paint a grimmer picture of the dangers of doing it yourself.

Few of us, though, could fail as disastrously at plumbing as the Three Stooges, who in "A Plumbing We Will Go" (1940) impersonate plumbers to evade a cop, and wreak all kinds of havoc on the fancy house where chance has brought them. My favorite scene is when Curly tries to contain the water gushing from a pipe by screwing on additional sections of pipe, one after another, each time enjoying a brief "nyuck-nyuck-nyuck" of short-sighted self-satisfaction before noticing that the water is still gushing, just farther downstream. By the end of the scene, he has imprisoned himself in a cage of plumbing without impeding the leak at all. The other great sequence is when the house's plumbing gets crossed absurdly with its wiring, causing water to gush from light fixtures, kitchen appliances, and—in a sight gag that will never cease to be hilarious—from a television set (still, in 1940, a new and magical device) during a live broadcast from Niagara Falls.

Pratfalls

> *A kitten is better than a dog. A baby is better than a kitten. A kiss is*
> *better than a baby. A pratfall is better than anything.*
> —PRESTON STURGES (ON WHAT MAKES
> FOR A SUCCESSFUL COMEDY)

> *It is not funny that anything else should fall down,*
> *only that a man should. . . . Why do we laugh?*
> *Because it is a gravely religious matter: it is the Fall of Man.*
> *Only man can be absurd: for only man can be dignified.*
> —G. K. CHESTERTON, "SPIRITUALISM"

> *The drowsy stillness of the summer's afternoon was shattered*
> *by what sounded to his strained senses like*
> *Mr. G. K. Chesterton falling on a sheet of tin.*
> —P. G. WODEHOUSE

WHAT CAN I add on the subject of pratfalls, after G. K. Chesterton has already—and as usual—said more than can safely be said? Maybe I'll start not by adding but subtracting. It is, of course, untrue that humans alone are funny when they fall. As anyone who owns a fat, ungainly cat will tell you, it's distinctly *funnier* when a cat falls off a couch in mid-stretch than when a man slips on an icy sidewalk and lands on his rump; *that's* really only funny in Buster Keaton

Figs. 124 From *Blondie*, 1936

films, not in real life. Granted, our grandparents seem to have gotten a bigger laugh from pratfalls than we do, and perhaps enjoyed the real-life variety as well as—if not indeed as much as—the slapstick, but only Chesterton would claim that only human falls are funny.

He is even wronger about the pratfall as an emblem of the Fall of Man: few comic victims seem more *innocent*, less deserving of their misfortunes, than the ones who slip on icy sidewalks, BANANA PEELS, or roller skates, and land on their asses. Chesterton should have asked himself why—if pratfalls really stand for something so momentous—they almost always serve in comedies as isolated sight gags, not as plot points. With very few exceptions (*The Man Who Came to Dinner*), pratfalls serve a strictly ornamental function in old comedy, from *Steamboat Bill, Jr.* to *Singin' in the Rain* to *The Dick Van Dyke Show*.

Now and then a pratfall does befall and deflate some puffed-up dignitary, but more often it singles out the lowly—not Mr. Dithers but Dagwood, not Margaret Dumont but Groucho, not Franklin Pangborn but W. C. Fields. In the movies, this was partly due to the fact that actors with a flair for physical comedy were seldom cast in roles with much gravitas. It might have been funnier to see the STUFFED SHIRTS take the pratfalls, but those parts were seldom played by masterful gymnasts like Keaton, Chaplin, Fields, Lucille Ball, Red Skelton, or Carol Burnett.

The first two actors in particular tended to play characters so harmless and hapless that they were the last people in the world we longed to see suffering the comeuppance of a pratfall. Their only crime was to defy the law of GRAVITY, to the extent that we all do from the day we learn to crawl. Like other laws, that one is selectively enforced, and it is the meek who are most often forcibly returned ass-first to the earth they will one day inherit.

Predictability

*She pigeon-holed her fellow mortals with a hand as free
as that of a compositor scattering type.*
—HENRY JAMES

*The fact is that all of us have only one personality,
and we wring it out like a dishtowel. You are what you are.*
—S. J. PERELMAN

RUBE GOLDBERG'S CARTOON machines are still funny, but not because they do things the hard way. Unlike the children's game inspired by them—Mousetrap, which involves the linkage of assorted inanimate parts, mostly plastic, to "catch" a toy mouse—Goldberg's inventions never relied solely on Newtonian mechanics. His contraptions owed their humor not just to the needless complexity that made them famous, but also to Goldberg's knack for incorporating sentient beings expected to behave with the mindless predictability of levers or pulleys. Thus, his Simple Fly Swatter requires a "butler dog" to mistake the fly's buzz for a door buzzer. The Self-Rolling Rug requires a housemaid to fall back in fright when a HOBO steals a pie from the windowsill, and a dwarf circus elephant to roll over when he hears a song called "Oceana Roll." The Self-Watering Palm Tree requires a hound to turn three somersaults when squirted with seltzer.

Predictability is really or mainly a meta-topic, since it occurs less often as a joke in itself than as a condition for many of the other kinds of funniness considered in this guide. To call a character a TIGHTWAD, for example, is not to say that in a given situation he seems excessively frugal, but that he'll *always* be excessively frugal, in any circumstances where the question of thrift arises at all, so that if the character recurs—in a sitcom, say—we don't expect new insights into his psychology, but at most a new expression of his ruling passion.

But it's worth wondering why we find *that* so amusing, week after week. Any excessive behavior is potentially funny—too stingy or too prodigal, too bold or too timid, too tidy or too slovenly—but shouldn't it be funnier when it takes us by surprise, showing up in people from whom we'd never expect it? Sometimes, but not as often as you'd think, if you subscribe to what is now the leading theory of humor, which explains it as a perception of incongruity. Excess itself, by definition, is incongruous, but comedy has always favored predictable excess. We can't blame the stupidity of sitcoms on their use of stock characters: comedy has always relied on stock characters. **BLOWHARDS** like Ralph Kramden and Major Hoople trace their lineage all the way back to the *miles gloriosus*— the braggart soldier—of ancient Roman comedy.

Even if we confine ourselves to the twentieth century, it's unfair to single out sitcoms. The medium in which predictability has flourished most profusely is the comic strip. If you imagine what *Peanuts* would have been like if Schulz had called it *Placekicker Charlie* and every strip had featured Charlie Brown's attempts to kick that football and Lucy's yanking it away, you've just imagined hundreds of early comic strips.

"What is character but the determination of incident?" demanded Henry James. "What is incident but the illustration of character?" Those thumbnail definitions don't do justice to the complex characters and artful plots of his own fiction, but they fit the funny pages, which are peopled largely by what E. M. Forster called "flat characters," ones "constructed around a single idea or quality." If a comic strip stars the same character day after day, and if the character is defined by a single passion, quirk, neurosis, or vice, the result will be a one-note strip. You can see the appeal of such characters to cartoonists obliged to crank out a new installment every day: all they needed was to place the one-trick pony in a new situation, and they'd know just what form of hilarity should ensue. The joke rewrites itself.

Prior to *Peanuts* (a title Schulz himself disliked; he wanted to call his strip *L'il Folks* but was overruled by his syndicate), nearly all comic strips were named for their protagonists, like nineteenth-century novels, and the very titles indicate the one-dimensionality of many: *Absentminded Abner, Absentminded Augie, Acrobatic Archie, Ambitious Ambrose, Archie the Amateur & Boggs the Optimist* ("Well, it might have been worse," says Boggs at end of every strip, after the daily disaster), *Babbling Brooks* (who can't keep his mouth shut), *Balmy Benny, Baron Mooch, Barry the*

Boob, Bashful Bob, Billy Bragg (who debuted in 1906, almost eighty years before his namesake cut his first album), *Bobby Bright and Sammy Slow, Bonehead Barry, Boob McNutt, Book-Taught Bilkins, Brainy Bowers, Charlie Harduppe, Charley the Chump, Cicero Sapp, Cissie Changeful* (who can't make up her mind), *Citizen Fixit, Clumsy Claude, Crazy Charlie, Curious Charlie, Cynical Susie, Daffy Dan, Doubting Thomas, Dreamy Dave, Dreamy Mary, Dud Dudley, Dudley Dudd, Dumb Dora, Economical Bertie, Efficiency Ed* (a bumbling EFFICIENCY EXPERT), *Faithful Jeems, Fathead Fritz, Flirting Flora, Flora Flirt, Foolish Fred, Foxy Grandpa* (who always turns the tables on his prankster grandsons—this was back when *foxy* meant "wily" and not "sexy"), *Generous George, Genial Gene, Good Deed Dotty, Hard Hearted Hickey, Hard Luck Bill, Hazel the Heartbreaker, Heavy Hannah, H. E. Butzin* (a busybody not to be confused with *Mr. E. Z. Mark*, that all-day sucker, or *O. Heeza Boob*, a bumbler), *Helpful Henry, Highbrow McAllister, High-Pressure Pete* (a salesman), *Hungry Hal, Hungry Henrietta, Hungry Tommy, Ingenious Ruggles, Innocent Ike* (a fancy-talking mama's boy the rough kids love to play practical jokes on), *Inquisitive Clarence, Jingling Johnson* (a compulsive musician, like *Joe of the Musical Habit*), *Joe Jinx, Know-It-All Jake, Lady Bountiful* (whose philanthropies always misfire), *Lazy Larry, Lazy Lew, Little Mary Mixup, Little Sammy Sneeze* (who has no personality whatever, only allergies), *Meddlesome Millie, Miss Ann Teek—She's Willin'* (one of several mean-spirited strips about desperate OLD MAIDS—another was *Miss Lonely*), *Mister Makepeace, Modish Mitzi, Mr. Always Wright, Mr. Fallguy, Mr. Grouch, Mr. Hypo* (a hypochondriac), *Mr. Nutt, Mr. O. U. Absentmind, Mr. Show-Me, Mr. Smarty, Mrs. Fret-Not, Mrs. Rummage the Bargain Fiend, Mrs. Simpleton, Mrs. Sourgrapes, Mrs. Timekiller, Mrs. Trubbell, M. T. Dome, Musical Maurice, Naughty Ned, Naughty Pete, Nervy Nat, Noah Numbskull, Noodlehead Noonan, Obliging Otto, Oliver Meddle, Optimistic Oswald, O. U. Chump, Peevish Polly, Percy Vere* (who tries and tries again), *Peter Putoff, Phil Ossifer, Pretending Percy, Roaming Rowley, Romantic Rosalind, Scary William* ("scary" in the sense of "fearful"), *Si Swapper, Sime the Simp, Simon Simple, Simple Sylvia, Simp Simpson, Singing Sammy, Sinned-Against Samuel, Sleepy Sid, Sleepy Willie, Slumbering Slocum's Somnambulistic Sleeps, Stumble-Toe Joe, Superstitious Muggs, Superstitious Sam,*

Swapping Silas, Time-Table Watkins, Tumble Tom, Unlucky Looie, Weary Willis, Ysobel the Suffragette, and so on.

This guide features entries on dozens of human types, and is itself a testament to the Laff Potential of predictability: what makes it possible for me to generalize about BLOWHARDS, DO-GOODERS, TIGHTWADS, and so on, just as a naturalist generalizes about different animals, is that humorists have always approached the human comedy as a battle royale among distinct subspecies. This guide, indeed, has barely scratched the surface of that biodiversity. Riffling through my collection of early-twentieth-century vinegar valentines—insulting anti-greeting cards for familiar types of pest—I see that I've overlooked the following types: Tough Guy, Fresh Guy, Flat Tire, Coffee Hound, Auto Fiend (aka Autoist, Road Hog, or Speedster), Sourpuss, Big Shot, Night Owl, Know-It-All, Lounge Lizard, Shirk, Free-Lunch Grabber, Teacher's Pet, Mama's Angel, Social Snob, Borrower, Muscle Moll, Fake Invalid, Always Late, Factory Belle, Scrappy Sweetie, Heartbreaker, Bargain Hunter, Camera Bug (aka Camera Nut or Camera Fiend), Radio Bug, Car-Seat Hog, Office Wife, Masher, and Flirt. To name only a few.

Pretty Girls

AROUND 1920, PERHAPS as an oblique result of World War I, newspaper cartoonists got sick of drawing naughty little boys and took to drawing pretty young women instead. Not that the look of the comics section changed all that much. There were fewer brickbats and more beauties, and the need to make those beauties sexually attractive—not just to other characters, as Olive Oyl is so inexplicably to Popeye, but to readers in the real world—dictated that they be drawn more realistically than cartoon characters usually are. You'd think it would follow that the rest of the strip would likewise have to be drawn more realistically, but for a while there cartoonists managed to have things both ways, offering readers both the titillation of pretty girls lovingly depicted and the more innocent pleasure of funny pictures: of the exaggeration, simplification, and stylization that make the comics fun to

Fig. 125 From *Bringing Up Father*

look at even when they don't engage your id. Cartoonists combined these incongruous pleasures not just within the confines of a single strip, but frequently within a single panel.

As a rule, the background was drawn at roughly the same level of stylization as the nonsexy characters, making the pretty girl seem even more out of place. Often she seemed to have strayed in from another comic strip. It could be a problem. In general, cartoonists are better than novelists, say, at reining in their virtuosity and subordinating their technical skills to the laws of their imaginary worlds, but in the 1920s, few could resist the temptation of drawing young women as pretty as possible, whether or not that suited the look and mood of the strip. You often get the sense that the cartoonist has put the main business of his strip on hold in order to show off—to show how good he is at drawing pretty girls.

It's not quite as jarring as a black-and-white character would be in a Technicolor movie, or a funny thinking animal like Garfield in *Mary Worth*, but it often does suggest confused intentions on the part of the artist. Cartooning is all about simplification, stripping down and leaving out, knowing what doesn't belong. Think how damaging it would have been to the *Peanuts* ecosystem if Charles Schulz had ever let a grownup wander into the strip.

Of course, those otherworldly beauties in the midst of cartoon uglies must have looked less out of place when everyone was drawing them. Good cartoonists, too, had sense enough to exploit the incongruity for humorous effect. Often the men are not just less attractive and less well drawn—less evolved graphically—than the women, but also much *shorter*. They look like shapeless, sexless little boys with shapely sexy mothers, a sight gag emphasizing the imbalance of emotional intelligence and sexual dependency that such cartoon couples embody. The man may be a ruthless tycoon and the woman a ditzy wage slave, but as soon as he acknowledges her physical attraction, the whip changes hands. One can find a feminist affirmation in the "working girl" strips of the 1920s and '30s, but it's a muffled affirmation, since it's only as sex objects that those typists and stenographers manage to wrest any power from the patriarchy. As long as Miss Blips, General Halftrack's plain-Jane secretary in *Beetle Bailey*, fails to command as much respect as the luscious Miss Buxley, it remains a stretch to speak of Miss Buxley's power as a blow for women's rights.

Besides, the same graphic double standard applies to comics about women and *children*. When Ernie Bushmiller's homely little cartoon kid stole the spotlight from her gorgeous Aunt Fritzi in the late 1930s (marking a symbolic end to the "pretty girl" era of newspaper comics), the cartoonist not only changed the name of the strip from *Fritzi Ritz* to *Nancy*, but changed the overall look from one reminiscent of the *ligne claire* of the Tintin books to the all-but-rubber-stamped simplicity for which Bushmiller is famous. Aunt Fritzi, however, continued to appear in the strip from time to time, almost unchanged, a sort of living fossil of an older graphic style.

In Fritzi's case, as in the case of pretty cartoon wives like the one in *Dennis the Menace*, the special treatment may be due in part to gallantry, since Fritzi was modeled on Bushmiller's fiancée—and, later, wife—Abby, just as Phil Fumble, Fritzi's boyfriend, was modeled on Ernie himself. Phil is drawn much more cartoonishly than Fritzi; they seem not to belong in the same universe.

The tradition of drawing the pretty women more realistically than other characters is not quite extinct, though the incongruity tends to be more subtle—so subtle that sometimes I'm not sure I haven't just imagined it. Am I right that Daisy Mae, despite the almost pornographic exaggeration of her secondary sexual characteristics, is more realistically drawn than most of the other characters in *Li'l Abner*? That the barmaids in *Andy Capp* are not just prettier but more realistic than long-suffering Flo? That one reason the Lockhorns lock horns daily is that Loretta must vie for Leroy's interest with a bevy of sex kittens who are not only better-looking but better—more lovingly—drawn?

Psychiatrists and Psychoanalysts

"You say you don't like it. Psychology says you do."
—CAPTION FROM A 1933 *NEW YORKER* CARTOON

A psychiatrist asks a lot of expensive questions
your wife asks for nothing.
—JOEY ADAMS

Let the credulous and the vulgar continue to believe
that all mental woes can be cured by a daily application
of old Greek myths to their private parts.
—VLADIMIR NABOKOV

LUCY VAN PELT'S five-cent-psychiatry booth first opened for business on March 27, 1959, though it wasn't till 1961 that it assumed its definitive form with the adjustable sign: THE DOCTOR IS IN. It's a mark of how original and edgy *Peanuts* was in its early years that Schulz had a running joke about a little girl selling psychiatric advice to other children. Lucy's most frequent patient was the most neurotic of the *Peanuts* crew, Charlie Brown. He was also her first patient; in their first session, when he complained of feeling depressed, she said, "Snap out of it"—advice we've all given ourselves and our gloomier acquaintances, though unlike all-business Lucy, we don't follow the advice by demanding: "Five cents, please."

Psychiatry, of course, has come a long way since 1951. In a later strip, when Charlie Brown complains of depression again ("Everything seems hopeless"), Lucy has a more elaborate prescription: "Go home. And eat a jelly-bread sandwich folded over. Five cents, please." More often, though, she favors a tough-love approach. Charlie Brown complains of feeling scared, and Lucy tells him, "You're no different from anyone else. Five cents, please." When Sally complains that all the other girls hate her because they envy her naturally curly hair, Lucy is even blunter: "Don't kid yourself, sister! Five cents, please!" The mercenary refrain serves as a rimshot, and also underscores the secondary joke that Lucy is charging a nickel simply for saying the first bitchy thing that pops into her head— and back in those days, a nickel was a substantial sum to a second grader, the price of a bottle of pop or a full-sized candy bar.

If children since the early 1950s have formed their first impression of psychotherapy from *Peanuts*, grownups have been looking to *The New Yorker* for even longer for their first grown-up notion of the profession. By 1930 the iconography of the gag was pretty much set. The analyst is bald or balding, bearded, and bespectacled. If we get his name, it's usually foreign, often Teutonic. His office may or may not have a diploma on the wall, and usually contains a bookcase. Why are psychiatrists— and psychoanalysts even more so—represented as especially bookish? Is the idea that their heads are full of bookish notions—Greek myths and untranslatable puns—rather than hard scientific facts? Maybe so. In the heyday of the talk cure, psychoanalysts really did have more in common with literary critics than with, say, urologists.

One component of the current stereotype is surprisingly recent. Psychoanalysts have been using COUCHES since the birth of the discipline, but not till the 1940s did cartoonists install couches in the offices of their head-candlers and dome doctors, possibly because the healers in older cartoons were not psychoanalysts but psychiatrists—a distinction I choose to blur in this entry, as our culture does in its humor.

In a 1936 cartoon by Charles Addams, the balding, business-suited psychiatrist sits in a spindleback chair and says to the middle-aged female patient in an easy chair: "Now in this dream you're always having of being chased by a plumed alligator and Ronald Colman, which one is usually in the lead?" In another cartoon from 1936, doctor and patient sit knee to knee as he exhorts her. "Get out and mingle with the other schizophrenes." In a Thurber cartoon from 1937, a middle-aged woman in an easy chair and a giant rabbit in a swivel chair face each other across his desk; she looks anxious and he looks blasé as he speaks: "You said a moment ago that everybody you look at seems to be a rabbit. Now just what do you mean by that, Mrs. Sprague?" In a Whitney Darrow cartoon from 1939, the analyst, looking distinctly less sane than his patient, leans intently toward the latter, across the intervening desk, and asks: "These dreams of yours wherein you find great tubs of money, Mr. Croy—can you describe the spot a little more exactly?"

When a cartoon situation becomes a cliché—the shipwrecked couple on a DESERT ISLAND, the horny boss chasing the sexy SECRETARY around a desk—it's because the situation itself is funny, above and beyond its uses in particular cartoons. One reason cartoon clichés get a bad reputation is that cartoonists lazily allow the humor of the basic situation to do all the work. Psychotherapy cartoons go through the motions of joking, but most of the jokes are equally clichéd. There are the ones about the patient boring the analyst, as in an old *New Yorker* cartoon by Whitney Darrow in which the doctor glumly stares off into space while the cheerful matron on the couch divulges a recipe: " . . . and then I add the flour and shortening, and a tiny pinch of salt, of course . . ." There are the ones that emphasize the analyst's greed, as in a Cobean cartoon from 1952 where, as another matron babbles on obliviously, the analyst glances at his wristwatch and imagines its dial marked not with hours but with increments of money: $5, $10, $15 . . . There are the ones—found mostly in men's magazines—that comment on the danger of leaving a mixed-up young woman alone in a room with a couch and a middle-aged man in a position of authority. (Freud himself became aware of that danger early on, and even coined a fancy term for it, *counter-transference*, implying that although it's only natural for the patient to fall in with her analyst, it is counterintuitive, or anyhow counterproductive, for the analyst to love his patient.) And of course there are the ones about the analyst's own mental instability, which as a rule takes the form of what we now call obsessive-compulsive disorder. In a 1963 *Saturday Evening Post* cartoon, the analyst scolds a patient for stepping on a black square of his office's black-and-white checkerboard floor; he himself, we notice, is standing on two white squares. Maybe he thinks he's a bishop. The same year, a multi-panel cartoon in *Parade* showed a gabbing male patient noticing that the diploma on the wall above the couch is hanging crooked; the patient straightens the diploma, but as soon as he leaves, the analyst carefully tilts the picture again.

Another theme that goes way back is the shrink who urges patients to blame it all on mom. In a ten-panel *New Yorker* cartoon from 1929 by Otto Soglow (one of Nabokov's favorite cartoonists), a music-hall performer sings "Mammy" in blackface, à la Al Jolson, then walks dejectedly to his dressing room, broods, removes his makeup, pays a visit to Dr. Loop, Psychoanalyst, and then a visit to his white-haired mother, pulling a gun and blowing her off her rocker.

Is it by resisting obvious jokes like those that humorists find funny ones, or is it that only a rare originality enables lucky humorists the luxury of spurning the obvious jokes? In any case, here are two psychiatrist cartoons that do strike me as funny.

1. In a 1963 *Parade* cartoon, the psychiatrist sits in his chair as usual, taking notes, but his patient, a middle-aged housewife, stands with her elbows propped on a little section of board fence erected in the middle of the office, and free-associates for him as if gossiping with a next-door neighbor.

2. In a 1952 cartoon by Sam Cobean, a respectable matron lies on the couch nattering away. A secretary has just stepped into the room to put a file in his in-tray; the analyst, meeting her

eye, points at his temple with a circling forefinger to indicate that the patient is cuckoo. Uniquely among the psychiatrist cartoons I've seen, this one puts the eyeglasses on the patient rather than the analyst, who bears a prophetic resemblance to Bob Newhart.

I don't know why I find that last cartoon so funny, and I don't know if a prose description can convey its funniness. (The real humor of a cartoon inheres in the artwork, which is why we rightly celebrate a cartoonist like George Price—who never came up with his own gags—more than the lowly gag writers whose ideas he brought to life by illustrating.) I could imagine an editor rejecting it as not even a joke, or not enough of one. But it seems to me to make a point about the limitations of theory, and to make that point more gracefully than I can do here.

Qq  Rr

Quadrupeds

IT MAY BE one of the less noticed consequences of political correctness that humorists as a class have discontinued a wide repertoire of xenophobic humor at the expense of other species, those strange fellow earthlings. Animal humor used to be especially common in light verse, in part because the genre overlaps with children's verse. Most of the poems in *Alice in Wonderland* involve animals, real or fantastic, and so do most of Edward Lear's poems. In the first half of the twentieth century, even poets better known for wry poems about taxes, bills, suburban dinner parties, or grumpy bosses found time to poke fun at the animal kingdom. Even the panther, though it notably fails the Rilke Test of Funniness,[45] was funny enough for Nash to rhyme out six lines on the subject. And if you want to read a funny poem about a hippopotamus, you can take your pick of Oliver Herford ("'Oh say, what is this fearful, wild / Incorrigible cuss?' / 'This creature . . . fierce is styled / The Hippopotamus'"), Hilaire Belloc ("I shoot the hippopotamus with bullets made of platinum / Because if I use leaden ones, his hide is sure to flatten 'em"), Don Marquis ("oh do not always take a chance / upon an open countenance / the hippopotamus's smile / conceals a nature full of guile"), Ogden Nash ("Behold the hippopotamus! / We laugh at how he looks to us, / And yet in moments dank and grim / I wonder how we look to him"), or T. S. Eliot

---

[45] Rainier Maria Rilke was arguably the most humorless of all major modern poets. His instincts unerringly steered him away from any topic with comic potential. (Not the case with many lesser would-be-solemn poets, whose humorlessness makes them prone to bathos and other forms of accidental humor, and who find out the hard way that, as Chesterton said, "It is unwise in a poet to goad the sleeping lion of laughter.")

Fig. 126 Quadruped. See also FAT WOMEN.

("The broad-backed hippopotamus / Rests on his belly in the mud; / Although he seems so firm to us / He is merely flesh and blood. . . .").

There are would-be-funny poems about everything from the whale to the microbe, though as a rule the smallest creatures have a way of crawling below the humor radar. Insects are seldom funny (Don Marquis's cockroach poet Archy is an exception), though the annoyance they cause can be funny when you're not the one they're annoying. Bees are seldom funny, though a human fleeing from a swarm of bees and diving in a swimming hole is comedy gold. Small *humans*—children, short men— are a timeless source of humor, but when we consider the smallest animals, we are impressed by their proportionate strength. In the words of Georg Christoph Lichtenberg, the shortest and the wittiest of all great aphorists, "Strength without bigness is never laughable," though, he adds, the opposite—bigness without strength—often is. The fact is, we're in awe of the whole insect class, and it's hard to laugh convincingly at the things that awe you. Both Ogden Nash and Richard Armour have poems called "The Ant," but neither manages to score many points against the species.

As they move higher up the food chain, though, our humorists relax. Frogs are also small and strong, but no one hesitates to laugh at them. When humorists turn their attention to frogs, they seem to think they're picking on someone their own size. From Mark Twain's tale of the celebrated jumping frog to one of the all-time greatest animated cartoons ("One Froggy Evening"), from the classic arcade video game Frogger to the *National Lampoon* drawing of the double-amputee frog leaving a French restaurant, it's clear that amphibians and their misfortunes are fair game. Frogs, in fact, came within an afterthought of having their own entry in this guide, as did bulldogs, cows, geese, goats, hippos, mules, and turkeys.

As discussed elsewhere, the funniest animals are DUCKS. Compared to quadrupeds, birds are both more alien and—as fellow bipeds—more akin to us. And that somehow makes the funny ones especially funny. Even the swan—another creature so unfunny Rilke wrote a poem about it—is a funnier thing to be chased by than most quadrupeds. I find flightless birds distinctly laughable, and I always liked the Apteryx in *B.C.*, who introduced himself with his dictionary definition: "I am an apteryx, a flightless bird with hairy wings." Aside from him, though, and some tired gags involving ostriches, there hasn't been much mirth at the expense of such birds.

As for animals that walk on all fours, all but the biggest stand with their heads much lower than ours, and they're perfectly built for butting or biting fleeing humans in the RUMP. In the infancy of newspaper comics, when many readers still lived in the country, characters were constantly butted by goats, bucked by horses, tossed by bulls, treed by dogs, launched over fences by the hind legs of mules, and otherwise harassed by other species.

If you try to picture a funny sponge or sea anemone, you see the importance of a face to any organism hoping to pursue a career in comedy. Quadrupeds—especially our fellow mammals—have faces capable of registering some of the funnier moods and emotions: anger, boredom, fear, confusion, greed. We can relate to them because they are in fact our relatives. We relate to them so thoroughly, in fact, that it sometimes comes as a shock to be reminded that they play by different rules. They're notably indifferent to human notions of cleanliness, for instance, and are apt to void their bowels without warning. I suspect that every time an animal appears onstage, be it in a grand OPERA or a grade school Christmas pageant, the entire audience is waiting for the animal to defecate. Some wait anxiously. Most wait eagerly. It doesn't take much to amuse us.

Rape

Yes, if every other form of persuasion fails.
—W. C. FIELDS, WHEN ASKED IF HE
APPROVED OF CLUBS FOR WOMEN

When I was a child I was of an affectionate disposition,
but not enough to get arrested.
—ROBERT BENCHLEY

QUICK, WHICH DID our grandfathers laugh at more openly, flatulence or rape? The answer is rape, and the contest wasn't even close. In my entry on FLATULENCE, I point out that before our own malodorous era—the era of *South Park* and the Farrelly Brothers—the phenomenon was virtually unacknowledged by popular culture. Rape, on the other hand, was an admitted and culture-wide obsession; if never graphically portrayed, it was constantly alluded to, and chuckled at. In "Brush Up Your Shakespeare," one of Cole Porter's most celebrated songs from one of the most successful musicals of its era, *Kiss Me, Kate* (1948), the singer is ostensibly advising amorous young men to impress women with quotes from the Bard, but the real message is, Don't take no for an answer:

If she says she won't buy it or tike it,
Make her tike it, what's more, "As You Like It." . . .
If because of your heat she gets huffy,
Simply play on, and "Lay on, Macduffy!" . . .
Better mention The Merchant of Venice
When her sweet pound o' flesh you would menace.

If her virtue, at first, she defends—well,
Just remind her that All's Well That Ends Well!
And if still she won't give you a bonus,
You know what Venus got from Adonis!

But there's no use blaming Cole: the joke was everywhere. We're so used to the rape humor in old movies and cartoons that we tend to forget it's there—tend to forget, for example, that virtually every classic *Popeye* cartoon culminates in an attempted rape. (So do most of the early *Betty Boop* cartoons, before the Hays Code forced her to clean up her act.) Most of us were children when we first saw those cartoons, and we're used to seeing them with the eyes of children. Even if we watch with the eyes of adults (and as with most early cartoons, they were originally meant for adults), some of that era's coyness overcomes us when we view or discuss them; that's why it sounds jarring if I say that Bluto is essentially a rapist. But after all, what else is he planning to do with Olive Oyl when he snatches her away from Popeye and bears her off against her will? Will he just make her wash his sailor suits and cook his dinners?

It is possible to argue, with old cartoons and silent comedies, that the real function of the attempted rapes is not humor but suspense. The great Fleischer cartoons tended to be interested in everything but plot (the early Betty Boop cartoons, especially, weren't narratives so much as music videos for songs by people like Cab Calloway); and the abduction and rescue of the heroine was an easy way to throw in a little old-fashioned "story" at the end. But the silliness of the cartoon world tended

Fig. 127 Gag gift, c. 1950

to spread to the abduction scenes, too. Poor Olive is never more ludicrous than when she is borne off kicking and screaming.

Two popular early comic strips, *Hairbreadth Harry* and *Desperate Desmond*, replayed for laughs, day after day and year after year, the old melodramatic formula of the top-hatted villain abducting the maiden who refuses to marry him. There were other forms of rape humor on the funny pages; *Li'l Abner*'s Daisy Mae, for one, was forever warding off advances from gruesome inbred creeps who wouldn't take no for an answer. Indeed, rape jokes were as common as corncob pipes in *Li'l Abner* (whose creator himself faced charges of sexual improprieties toward the end of his life). When, in a 1964 strip, one of the more troglodytic denizens of Dogpatch says he likes girls, Abner's brother Tiny replies, "Ah'll say! Yo' likes 'em so much they hafta put yo' in jail three or four times a month!"

The Marx Brothers made their funniest comedies before the Hays Code spayed and neutered all of Hollywood, and we shouldn't let their zaniness distract us from the fact that theirs was the most highly sexed of all the great comic acts. Groucho, whose specialty was not physical but verbal comedy, let words do most of his wooing and harassing, but the speechless Harpo knew no other way to express his interest in PRETTY GIRLS than by literally chasing them. Each of the pre-code films features at least one scene of Harpo spotting a pretty young woman, of her sizing him up in an instant and fleeing in panic, and of Harpo in hot pursuit. And unlike the abductions in *Betty Boop* and *Popeye*, Harpo's quasi-rapist antics are played not for suspense but strictly for humor. Part of the humor, of course, is that the chases take place in polite and populous surroundings—a luxury cruise ship, a DOWAGER's mansion—where the rules of civilization can be trusted sooner or later to come to the woman's rescue. But what are we meant to imagine he'd do if he ever caught one in a lonely place? And yet no one thinks of Harpo as primarily—or even secondarily—a would-be rapist. No one holds it against him at all. Most women hate the Three Stooges, but few if any hate Harpo, who perfectly embodies the mystery of old-time rape humor.

The Rich

THERE ARE AT least two time-honored ways of ridiculing people who pride themselves on their wealth and ancestry:

1: Expose them as parvenus and imposters, would-be aristocrats descended from stable hands or prostitutes.
2: If they really do come from nobility, point out how little they themselves have accomplished in comparison with their illustrious forebears.

The first approach was the standard for centuries, and the faux-aristocrat still appears, here and there, in twentieth-century humor. Li'l Abner's dirt-poor, corncob-smoking mammy has a sister Bessie who married a duke; she's so ashamed of her lowly origins that when she revisits Dogpatch with her husband, she makes the Yokums pretend not to know her. Such examples notwithstanding, the would-be aristocrat is an endangered species in American humor, which is so populist, so dedicated (in theory) to democracy, and opposed (in theory) to hereditary privilege as to find the social anxieties of someone like Bessie née Yokum all but incomprehensible. American humorists are more likely to insist on the actual *inferiority* of all those superior people, whatever their origins. Especially in lowbrow media like animated cartoons, Three Stooges shorts, and newspaper comic strips, the rich are portrayed as twits, sissies, starched shirts, or mama's boys, when they aren't ruthless moguls or pathological misers.

Since Americans also believe in Opportunity, the nouveau riche seldom inspire the same hostility in mass culture as the old rich. But no one denies that sudden wealth can be funny in itself, like the growth spurt at adolescence or any other drastic change that happens fast enough to leave the changed person looking ludicrously miscast. Like a teen-age boy's new muscles, or a feral child's new clothes, new money takes a while to get the hang of. The Beverly Hillbillies never did get the hang of it—of behaving as if they'd always had it, which is the ideal to which

Fig. 128 The rich, distaff edition. See also OUTHOUSES.

the new rich are supposed to aspire. Neither did Jiggs, the Sweepstakes-winning husband in *Bringing Up Father*, who doesn't mind wearing a tux or living in a mansion, but would rather hang out at Dinty Moore's eating corned beef and cabbage with his cronies from the old days.

Portrayals of the new rich in the comics, incidentally, are especially interesting because in the early decades of the last century, successful cartoonists themselves embodied some of the most celebrated rags-to-riches sagas of the era. Bud Fisher (*Mutt and Jeff*) was the first cartoonist to become a millionaire through his cartooning, and it was big news when he did, as it later was for Sidney Smith (*The Gumps*), Al Capp, and Charles Schulz. With such examples to aspire to, it's no wonder that other cartoonists like Harold Gray (*Little Orphan Annie*) and George McManus (*Bringing Up Father*) celebrated the all-American self-made millionaire (as opposed to the snooty Europhilic hereditary millionaire) even before their strips had made them rich, too.

Poets are less likely than cartoonists to glamorize the rich, probably because they know that they have no chance of ever being rich themselves. Even songwriters, who do stand a chance, often take a sour-grapes approach to fabulous wealth. Think of "The Lady Is a Tramp," or "Who Wants to Be a Millionaire?":

> *Who wants a fancy foreign car? I don't.*
> *Who wants to tire of caviar? I don't.*
> —COLE PORTER, 1956

But if you can laugh at the life of the rich, you can also laugh at those who claim not to envy it:

> *The rich man has his motor-car,*
> *His country and his town estate.*
> *He smokes a fifty-cent cigar*
> *And jeers at Fate.*
> *. . . Yet though my lamp burns low and dim,*
> *Though I must slave for livelihood—*
> *Think you that I would change with him?*
> *You bet I would!*
> —FRANKLIN P. ADAMS, 1912

Rolling Pins

THOUGH THE SUCCESS of *Andy Capp* has shown the perennial comic appeal of wife-beating, as a rule it is the husbands in comic strips who get the worst of domestic spats. For one thing, their spouses tend to outweigh and outpunch them: think of Snuffy Smith and Loweezy. In addition, their kitchens are veritable arsenals of comic-strip MISSILES like cast-iron skillets, crockery, milk bottles, saucepans, and rolling pins.

Especially rolling pins. Whether hurled like a brickbat or swung like a bludgeon, the rolling pin is the weapon of choice for disgruntled hausfraus in the battle of the sexes as conducted in old comic strips. It's the distaff counterpart of the policeman's nightstick, that most common weapon of all in early comic strips.

Fig. 129 *Winnie Winkle,* 1927.
See also HENPECKED HUSBANDS.

The rolling pin's fame is probably due to its frequent deployment in *Bringing Up Father.* In that immensely popular and long-lived strip (1913–2000), Maggie threw rolling pins at Jiggs so often that as early as 1919, Jiggs reflected that "the man who invented rolling pins must've been a bachelor." When he happens to pass a factory labeled DENT CO. MANUFACTURERS OF ROLLING PINS, he buys the factory in order to shut it down.

Comic harridans were throwing rolling pins before the advent of Maggie and Jiggs, though, and no doubt before the advent of comic strips per se. The Bellicose Rolling Pin probably originated in rambunctious stage comedies. It would not be out of place, in fact, in *Ralph Roister Doister* or *Gammer Gurton's Needle,* the first comedies in the English language.

In any case, the gag was well established by the outbreak of World War I. In a 1914 strip, Frank King (later inventor of *Gasoline Alley*) pictured women as soldiers: "Unmarried ladies will be eligible to join the formidable Hatpin Brigade," whereas "the Rolling pin Brigade will be made up of married ones." The picture shows a formation of scowling middle-aged women on horseback, with rolling pins erect. Rolling pins are effective against all bad men, not just drunken husbands. And since they take almost as much abuse as drunken husbands in early rough-and-tumble comic strips, it's helpful that rolling pins are sturdy enough to use repeatedly.

A surprisingly disproportionate number of comic-strip housewives (to judge by my admittedly unscientific sample) hold the pin in their left hand. Even *Bringing Up Father*'s Maggie, though otherwise a rightie, is ambidextrous when it comes to brandishing her rolling pin. Was left-handedness itself once considered funny? Did left-handed women have a reputation for irascibility?

Rubber

RUBBER IS FUNNY because bounciness is funny. BOSOMS, PENISES, RUMPS—nearly all the naughty parts are bouncy. Plastic can be funny too, but the humor of Plastic Man, Jack Cole's tongue-in-cheek superhero, was the humor of rubber, not plastic. As you may recall, he acquired his famous stretchiness after getting some acid in an open wound during a robbery of the Crawford Chemical Works. "Great guns!! I'm stretchin' like a RUBBER BAND!!" he exclaims. "The acid! That's it! Must've gotten into my bloodstream and caused a PHYSICAL CHANGE!!" With a moral pliability almost as astounding as the physical, he vows to renounce his life of crime and use his new superpower for good instead of evil. The result is an amusing but necessarily minor superhero, since there's no way to accommodate Plastic Man's deformations to the

Fig. 130 Rubber goods, from the Johnson-Smith catalog, 1929

Rubber Doughnuts

These delicious-looking doughnuts are made of sponge rubber, and sugar coated. When placed upon a plate or dish with real doughtnuts they absolutely defy detection. Have a few on hand and we guarantee your next party will be a riot. Each doughnut comes packed in an individual glassine envelope. No. 2944. Rubber Doughnuts. Each 15c 3 for 40c, or $1.35 per dozen postpaid.

Rubber Hot Dog

It looks so real you are almost tempted to eat one. It is made of sponge rubber and resembles a Wiener in every respect. Try a few on your unsuspecting guests and watch the fun. No. 2949. Rubber Hot Dog........ 15c 3 for 40 cents, or $1.35 per doz. postpaid.

Rubber Bananas

Made of pure para rubber, and colored to resemble a real banana. Placed on a dish with real bananas no one will detect the difference, but the one who gets the rubber one will get a very great surprise. It is a great novelty and a big fun maker. No. 2946. Rubber Bananas. Each...15c 3 for 40c, or $1.35 per dozen postpaid.

Fig. 131 Rubbernecking, 1910. See also ANKLES.

body fascism, the eugenicist cult, of standard straight-faced superhero comics.

Bad checks are called rubber checks because they too "bounce," but maybe also because rubber is ideally suited to counterfeits of all kinds, and so the word is used as a synonym for *phony*. Rubber bullets are non-lethal; rubber biscuits are inedible; a rubber ducky is a toy. On the Big Rock Candy Mountain, the bulldogs all have rubber teeth. Rubber was once the preferred substance for a popular class of mail-order laff-getters: simulacra of everyday items sold as practical jokes. The 1939 Johnson Smith catalog offered rubber pretzels, rubber bananas, rubber doughnuts, rubber wieners, rubber eggs, rubber cigars and cigarettes, rubber choco-lates, rubber ice cream, rubber nuts, rubber gum, rubber dollars, rubber-pointed pencils, rubber hunting knives. When rubber is used to simulate a more rigid substance, and what reveals the imposture is precisely its lack of rigidity—rubber pencils, rubber coat hooks, rubber knives—the joke is (among other things) a dick joke.

Rubbernecking

IN LESSON #5 of the Girl Watcher's Guide, a series of educational full-page magazine ads sponsored by Pall Mall in the early 1960s, readers are warned of "the importance of head control." The ad's image is a cartoon of a businessman rubbernecking so abruptly that his eyeglasses remain hanging in midair, facing forward, as his head whips around and his eyes bulge; the caption tells us that the aspiring rubber-necker "must learn to restrict his movements to the eyeballs. The girl watcher never moves his head. Undue head-turning, particularly if it is accompanied by shouts or whistles, is the sign of the amateur."

It's a lesson many men never learn. In *The American Language*, H. L. Mencken quotes another philologist's opinion that *rubberneck* is "one of the best words ever coined," and seconds the opinion.[46] "It may be

---

[46] Other slang terms of which Mencken thought highly were *stooge*, *yes man*, *phony*, *debunk*, *highbrow*, and *tightwad*.

homely, but it is nevertheless superb," writes Mencken, adding that *rubberneck* is "almost a complete treatise on American psychology" and that "whoever invented it, if he could be discovered," merits "thirty days as the husband of Miss America." Even during that month of bliss, the term's inventor would probably continue to rubberneck, since the urge to do so seems to be hardwired into even the most happily married male.

One staple of gag cartoons is the middle-aged, middle-class man (often identified as a husband) leering at a cute girl and conspicuously failing to keep his mind on whatever he's supposed to be doing. In a 1950s cartoon by Ted Key, a family man is seen mowing his driveway while ogling a cute sunbather in the next yard. In a Jerry Marcus cartoon from the same era that appeared in *True* magazine, a new husband trips as he prepares to carry his bride over the threshold, distracted—already!—by a passing **BLONDE**. The cover of *Another Jimmy Hatlo Book*, a 1958 mass-market paperback collection of Hatlo's "They'll Do It Every Time" cartoons, shows a mousy husband with a pair of hedge clippers absentmindedly cutting a big gap in his hedge as he watches the sexy young woman next door, daintily sprinkling her flowers with a watering can; his fat wife leans out the window, preparing to dump a big washtub of water on his head.

The ogler is always pictured as grinning dopily—cartoonists use the grin to distinguish the stare from one of resentment or alarm. And that dopey grin does have a symbolic truth: no matter how intelligent and cultured you may be, when you gaze at a stranger with lust, your inner Village Idiot takes over.

Rubbernecking is often combined with a double take, and it's funny partly for the same reason as double takes (and other exaggerated reactions—spit takes, **HAT TAKES, PLOPS**): it's a comically unsubtle way of reacting to a spectacle. Like the wild takes in Tex Avery cartoons, rubbernecking is also a comically exaggerated way of paying attention to something that catches your eye. It's an open secret that men think about sex all the time, and that even the gravest among them will sometimes find their attention diverted by someone sexy. We are expected, though—and for the most part manage fairly well—to dissimulate our interest, to let our thoughts and even eyes be turned, but not our heads.

In old cartoons and comedies, rubbernecking is almost exclusively a male trait—perhaps another indication that all boys go insane at puberty. But rubbernecking isn't always sexual: men will crane their heads to covet their neighbor's Porsche as surely as their neighbor's wife. An early, wordless Hank Ketcham cartoon consists of five images of the same driver: smiling, grinning, laughing, laughing uproariously, and then suddenly mangled and hurting, with the steering wheel wrapped around his head. If not for the caption—"Burma Shave"—we'd have no idea what to make of the cartoon.

Rumps

> Did you hear about Mimsie Star?
> Got pinched in the As-tor bar.
> —COLE PORTER, "WELL, DID YOU EVAH?" (1939)

> Lee Chan: [after his father kicks his rump]
> Oh, gee, Pop, how'd you know it was me?
> Charlie Chan: Frequent spankings when young
> make rear view very familiar.
> —CHARLIE CHAN AT THE RACE TRACK, 1936

ACCORDING TO *AMERICAN Chronicle*, a year-by-year account of the twentieth century by Lois and Allan Gordon, the fad for "mooning" peaked in 1955. That year also saw Glenn Gould's debut recording; the publication of *Lolita* and *Notes of a Native Son*; the premieres of *Guys and Dolls*, *The Night of the Hunter*, and *The Blackboard Jungle*; the final episode of *The Honeymooners* (and Jackie Gleason's effort to patent the catchphrase "And away we go"); the advent of roll-on deodorant; the craze for Davy Crockett hats; the introduction of Crest toothpaste, Gorton's fish sticks, Special K, and Kentucky Fried Chicken; the opening of Disneyland; and—to complete this sentence's descent from the sublime to the ridiculous, and so bring us back around to fat buttocks and tight rectums—the first issue of the *National Review*.

Speaking of *Lolita*: Until I started collecting old postcards I never understood what Humbert Humbert meant when, enumerating the

Fig. 132

highlights of lowly roadside eateries, he mentioned "'humorous' picture post cards of the posterior 'Kurort' type." Alfred Appel Jr.'s note in *The Annotated Lolita* got me only so far by glossing *Kurort* as "spa." What Nabokov knew that neither I nor (evidently) Appel did was that, on American comic postcards in the first half of the twentieth century, by *far* the most common image was a rear view of a FAT WOMAN in a bathing suit. The seaside has always been a favorite holiday destination, so the beach imagery is understandable. And for many people in 1920, say, the most memorable impressions from a beach vacation were probably of bodies in swimsuits. But why those belonging to fat ladies?

For me, the most striking thing about fat people—and the most lamentable aspect of my own middle-aged weight problem—is the big belly. Big bottoms, though, are more often used as synecdoches for obesity, maybe because sitting on your bottom (though of course also stuffing your belly) is what makes you fat. In a comic postcard from the 1930s **(Fig. 89)**, the loss of romance in a marriage is explicitly equated with the fattening of the wife's behind. The card is divided in half diagonally. In the first panel, captioned "It's the same old moon," we see a rear view of an attractive young couple in swimsuits cuddling on a beach at night and watching the moon rise over the water. In the second panel, captioned s" . . . but oh! How it has changed!," we see the same couple in their bedroom. *He* looks about the same, though he's wearing pajamas that speak of sexless domesticity as he sits at the bed and scowls disgustedly at his now fat and fat-assed spouse, who stands with her back to him at her dresser mirror powdering her nose.

Considering the genre's obsession with rumps, it's notable that American comic postcards virtually never allude to the anus.[47] The few exceptions feature animals rather than humans. A card postmarked 1950 shows one dog saying to another, at the approach of a third, "Look, Emma! Let's sit down—here comes that dog with the cold nose." A card from the same decade shows a barfly pointing at something we can't see and saying to the bartender: "Sho you think I'm DRUNK eh? Well I can see that one-eyed cat coming through that door." "Now I know you're drunk," replies the bartender, "that cat's going *out* the door!"

I've also seen a cartoon of a firefighter sliding blithely down a fire pole while, directly beneath him, another fireman sweeps the floor, bending over and holding the upright broomstick by its neck as he sweeps dirt into a dustpan; neither man has seen the other, and in a few milliseconds, the first fireman will impale himself on the other man's broomstick. That, though, was on the cover a 1960 pamphlet of raunchy jokes and cartoons called *Gags a Go-Go*, the sort of item that would never be put out by a reputable publisher or sold in a respectable bookstore. Like the bawdy limericks collected from bus-station restrooms by fieldworkers like Gershon Legman, or the crude pornographic comic books known as "Tijuana bibles," *Gags a Go-Go* and its sodomy humor belong not to the collective consciousness of mid-twentieth-century America, but rather to its unconscious. (For the sanitized sodomy gags that even the *Saturday Evening Post* was okay with, see THUMBTACKS.)

---

[47] Neither did any other genre of mainstream humor in the era we're considering, except for a sly reference in "Brush Up Your Shakespeare," a naughty Cole Porter song from 1948: "If she says your behavior is heinous / Kick her right in the 'Coriolanus'!" A song about Shakespeare—who in *Hamlet* punned on the "cunt" in *country*—is the perfect place for such a joke.

Buttocks are, among other things, cushions, and their relative insensibility to pain makes them ideal for kicking. Al Capp—whose opinion of mankind started low and just kept getting lower—more than once implied that kicking other people in the rump is a universal urge, if not in fact a universal need. In a 1949 sequence of *Li'l Abner*, the Yokums inherit fifty million kigmies—hairy little animals specially bred for kickability. Unlike shmoos, which love to be eaten, kigmies live—and love—to be kicked in the caboose, to use an old slang term for "rump." (When a bawdy song from World War I informs us that the Mademoiselle from Armentieres "waggled her headlights and caboose," it means she shook her tits and ass.) Kigmies are little more than walking rumps that salivate at the sight of big FEET, position themselves obligingly whenever somebody is angry and looking for a way to let off steam, and exclaim with pleasure when a kick sends them sailing. They're so good at absorbing human aggression that they put a lot of people out of work: generals, lawyers, liniment makers. But every reform has its victims, and despite the jobs eliminated by the kigmy revolution, it may be that what the world needs most is more rumps.

Rye

RYE IS A cereal grass. Its seeds are used for flour and chicken feed, and (roasted) as a coffee substitute. Rye whiskey is just whiskey made from rye instead of corn mash. It used to be common—if not in real life, at least in pop culture, and especially in cartoon images of booze. This was due less to any specific lore about the drink, as far as I can tell, than to the fact that its name was short enough to fit on the label of a cartoon bottle. When a cartoonist wanted to indicate that a bottle contained whiskey, the options were to label it either "rye" or "xxx" (a less satisfactory solution since real liquor bottles don't say "xxx"). Why not "gin" or "rum"? Maybe cartoonists shared my opinion that, especially for those guzzling straight from the bottle, as cartoon drinkers tend to do, a bottle of rye is a better friend than a bottle of gin or rum.

Rye also lent itself to puns, as in Frank King's cartoon of a drunkard making "a rye face," or the Three Stooges episode entitled "Three Hams on

Fig. 133 Rye humor, 1905. See also THE RICH.

Rye." I own six different postcards issued between 1905 and 1910 that pun on "Comin' through the rye." Four of them show happy tipplers walking between two rows of bottles or barrels (Fig. 134); a fifth (which substitutes "going" for "comin'") shows an even happier tippler lying among the barrels; and the sixth shows a mouse emerging from a loaf of rye bread.

The other place you'll find rye whiskey (and more easily than at your local liquor store, unless you live in Canada) is in light verse about booze and boozers, maybe because no other hard liquor—again with the exception of gin, which also turns up in light verse—has a name that rhymes with so many words. Here's Ogden Nash (born, incidentally, in Rye, New York):

> *There is something about an old-fashioned*
> *When the dusk has enveloped the sky,*
> *And it may be the ice,*
> *Or the pineapple slice,*
> *But I strongly suspect it's the rye.*
> —"A DRINK WITH SOMETHING IN IT," 1935

S s

Safes, Falling

TO JUDGE BY old comics, safes became a standard feature of modern office buildings before elevators did, and so a common urban sight was a massive, heavy safe being hoisted to its roost by a pulley or crane. This was back in the age of recklessness, before seat belts, bicycle helmets, or flame-retardant pajamas, and sometimes the rope holding the safe would snap or slip. Old comics give the sense that that was an everyday occurrence, but it would need only to have happened once, on a busy Manhattan sidewalk, for cartoonists everywhere to register it as one more cartoonishly funny mishap they could inflict on their characters. And unlike the falling **ANVILS** in old Warner Bros. cartoons, the safes had a sensible reason to be way up there, suspended in midair, hundreds of feet overhead, and so offered a magnificent slapstick payoff without the suspension of disbelief required by Road Runner cartoons.

According to Don Martin, the sound of Superman failing to catch a falling safe filled with Kryptonite is "McPWAF!" As for the sound of an ordinary safe falling on ordinary mortals, that's "FOOMP!" Basil Wolverton hears it differently: "Few people realize that the noise of a safe fall-

Fig. 134 From _Mutt & Jeff,_ 1910

ing on a man is invariably '*JWORCH!*'" With so many safes dropping from the skies of Cartoonland, it's lucky that in cartoons a direct hit by a falling safe is seldom fatal. It can even prove an inspiration: "A safe falls on the head of Professor Butts, and knocks out an idea," says Rube Goldberg, in the era when he not only attributed his mad inventions to a mad inventor, but also specified the mind-clouding circumstances of each brainstorm. In this case—one of the few where the circumstances and the content of the brainstorm have any discernible connection—the idea is an elaborate fly-swatting machine.

Saps, etc.

> *I don't have to look up my family tree,*
> *because I know that I'm the sap.*
> —FRED ALLEN

> *There are nineteen words in Yiddish that convey gradations of*
> *disparagement, from a mild, fluttery helplessness to a state of*
> *downright, irreconcilable brutishness. All of them can be usefully*
> *employed to pinpoint the kind of individuals I write about.*
> —S. J. PERELMAN, IN AN INTERVIEW
> FOR *THE PARIS REVIEW*

THE PROCESS OF writing this guide has gotten me thinking hard about taxonomies of human folly. Humorists have always been drawn to such taxonomies, with stage comedy in particular relying heavily on stock characters like the *senex*, *meretrix*, and *parasitus* of Roman comedy; the Harlequin, Pantaloon, and Pulcinella of commedia dell'arte; or the fops, rakes, and wits of Restoration comedy. And of course this reliance on comedic stereotypes continues up to our time in Hollywood, though now that we're all such wised-up postmodern sophisticates, those stereotypes are sometimes openly subverted or lampooned, as in *Not Another Teen Comedy* (2001), whose characters are identified by their clichéd roles: the Token Black Guy, the Best Friend, the Pretty Ugly Girl.

Fig. 135 Saps = drips. See also PRETTY GIRLS.

Since I want this book to be in some sense comprehensive without being dauntingly long, I've thought a lot about the stock characters of American humor. Just how many are there? How many different types must I describe in order to do justice to the human comedy as it appeared to our grandfathers? Which are dispensable? Clearly there must be BLOWHARDS, TIGHTWADS, GOLD DIGGERS, MOTHERS-IN-LAW—but must we also have separate entries for Dips, Clucks, Drips, and Saps? Can the obsolescence of those terms be taken as proof that they were redundant all along—that they never represented distinctive patterns of human behavior meriting names of their own?

Linguists assure us that words drop out of the language only when no longer needed, but that isn't always true. There's no one-word synonym for *yonder*, and we have as much need as ever to say what it says so tidily ("way over there"), but the word is vanishing, as are *hither* and *thither*. So we shouldn't assume, from that fact that people no longer refer to one another as "saps," that saps are extinct. Saps are as plentiful as ever, in this observer's opinion, but old insults are dying off: the kudzu-like spread of a few invasive species, like *asshole* and *loser*, has crowded out many more-delicate epithets, leading to a catastrophic loss of logodiversity.

What or who exactly is or was a sap? Of the few surviving terms, *loser* probably comes closest, but not close enough. All it takes to qualify as a loser is bad luck, but to be a sap you need a bad attitude, too. (Job in the Old Testament was a loser, not a sap.) A sap is a loser who loses through stupidity, so maybe *chump* or *sucker* are closer to the mark, except that both reflect a heartless and almost eugenic contempt for the bad luck of a low IQ, just as *loser* reflects a heartless contempt for bad luck *tout court*. A sap is a loser who loses due to wrongheadedness; his behavior (and the term was pretty much confined to men) represents a sort of elective stupidity, rather than expressing a genetic limitation.

Whatever they were, saps were everywhere in the Jazz Age. They were as common as FLAPPERS in that era, to judge by the movies the era produced: *The Fighting Sap* (1924), *Two Gun Sap* (1925), *The Sap* (1926), *The Perfect Sap* (1927), *The Sap* (1929), *Singing Sap* (1930), *The Sap from Syracuse* (1930). Of course, no flapper worthy of the name would give a sap the time of day.

Sausage and Hot Dogs

I've knuckles of pigs
And tails of oxen,
And if the prospect should leave you glum,
Cheer up, for the Wurst
Is yet to come.
—PHYLLIS MCGINLEY,
"CHANT OF THE OPTIMISTIC BUTCHER," 1945

IN "DOG FACTORY" (1904), a short film by Thomas Edison, we glimpse an invention that Edison never perfected: a Dog Transformator. This amazing machine, basically a box with a hopper on top and a door in the side, can almost instantaneously turn a live dog into links of sausage. Draped on pegs on the wall behind the machine are coils of sausage labeled by breed—Poodle, Spaniel, Pointer, Setter, and so on. But this factory is more than just a butcher shop; it's a pet store, too, because the transformator also works in reverse. If you want a dachshund, you point to the corresponding sausage, which the clerk drops into the machine, and out scampers a living wiener dog. If the customer changes her mind, as lady shoppers proverbially will, back into the hopper goes the dachshund, returning to its low-maintenance sausage state. Apparently I'm not the first pet owner to daydream about putting my beloved pets in suspended animation whenever I need a vacation from them.

Except perhaps for wiener dogs, the similarity between true dogs and hot dogs is slight at best. But the fact that we refer to one unaccountably popular sausage as a "hot dog" has given rise to a lot of verbal and visual punning. A recurring sight gag in *Felix the Cat* cartoons involved hot dogs behaving like normal dogs. When Felix wants to go to Alaska, he harnesses six hot dogs to a sled.

But dogs are not what hot dogs are most often compared to. Freud saw phallic symbols in places where most of us see nothing of the sort, but sometimes they're hard not to see. Unless you're so pure-minded that you could browse in a dildo emporium without seeing a phallic symbol, you'll agree that the resemblance of hot dogs and sausages to PENISES exists not just in the dirty minds of Freudians, but in the dirty mind of popular culture. There are borderline cases—we may never know how much of a smirk we're entitled to during the *Patty Duke* theme song ("But Patty goes for rock and roll, / A hot dog makes her lose control")—but sometimes it takes an act of willful piety to miss it. Foot-long wienies are funny because men are obsessed about the length of their own wienies. As for the endless hot dog invented by Pansy Yokum in a 1955 episode of *Li'l Abner* ("As the customer chomps one end o' th' endless hot dog," reads a hand-lettered sign in Pansy's hotdog stand, "the machine is manufacturin' t'other end—and since this machine don't never stop, the hot dog is endless—as any fool kin plainly see!!")—I don't know where to begin.

When Irvin S. Cobb made his pronouncements on the relative funniness of various foods, he asserted that "a sausage is positively uproarious." A good example of an uproarious sausage occurs in *Some Like It Hot*, when thirteen young women join "Daphne" (a cross-dressing Jack Lemmon) in his sleeper berth for drinks and innocent horseplay. Many of the guests bring refreshments of one kind or another—cheese and crackers, Southern Comfort, peanut butter—but the salami brandished by one of the lady musicians is indisputably a dick joke. After all, what makes the scene so memorable is that one of the fourteen girls is actually a boy. The salami is a metaphor (though so crudely obvious it barely counts as one) for the secret subtext of the scene—a secret that Jack Lemmon had been preparing to expose (so to speak) to Marilyn Monroe when a dozen party crashers ruined his tête-à-tête, and a secret all too likely to expose itself when a sexually excited man is crammed into a tiny sleeper berth with thirteen grabby gals. That's the real reason Jack pulls the emergency brake.

Some Like It Hot was notoriously racy for its time, its country, and its medium—but that's not saying much. Off camera, offstage, off the air, and off the record, ordinary Americans were telling rawer jokes than Hollywood could stomach. My favorite dirty sausage joke is one that Gershon Legman heard in New York City in 1936 and classified, in his flabbergasting typology of dirty jokes, as one about "Traces of the Other Man":

> The day before marrying for money, a girl has one last fling with the man she really loves. He has no condom and they use the scooped-out skin of a bologna, which slips in during intercourse and cannot be retrieved. On her wedding night it comes out on her husband's penis. When he asks what it is, she says it is her maidenhead. "Well that's the first one I ever saw with a government stamp on it!"

When they aren't reminding us of penises, sausages may remind us of turds, a resemblance *Mad* magazine's Al Jaffee exploited so effectively in a 1975 feature called "Mad Solutions to Big-City Doggie-Do Problems." Jaffee's own doggie-do problem as a cartoonist was how to illustrate his fanciful solutions—such as coating each dog turd with quick-drying acrylic—without picturing actual turds. (Even Don Martin shrank from drawing recognizable turds, though he did give us some good turd humor, usually involving the telltale sound effect "GLITCH!"). Jaffee drew chubby little links of sausage instead.

The sausage/stool resemblance may explain why a string of sausages is the single most common form of meat for a dog to steal in old cartoons, though there are all sorts of other funny and delicious things in butcher stops, like HAMS. The angry butcher shaking his fist at the mutt reminds us that dogs are thieves who eat what isn't theirs. The string of little sausage links reminds us that the other end of the implacable canine digestive tract is equally lawless.

Or maybe it's just that anything is funnier when you involve a sausage. Steve Allen, in a stunt prefiguring by several decades those of David Letterman, once rushed out of his TV studio dressed as a policeman and holding a big salami. He put the salami in the back of a cab and told the driver: "Get this to Grand Central Station as quick as you can!" The driver obeyed.

Scotsmen

No McTavish / Was ever lavish.
—OGDEN NASH, "GENEALOGICAL REFLECTION"

IN 1935, THE Exhibit Supply Company of Chicago published a series of humorous photographic postcards called "Your Future Husband and Children." Strictly speaking, these were arcade cards—the size of postcards, but printed on heavier card stock, with blank backs (because they weren't intended to be sent, and some of the racier series would have been unsendable), and sold from vending machines in penny arcades. The "Future Husband" series, like several similar series of arcade cards from that era, was a precursor of *Mystery Date*, that 1960s board game in which little girls were taught a typology of possible beaux, some more desirable than others. Because the arcade cards were sold to bigger girls, they acknowledged more of the variety and complexity of prospective mates. You could end up with a dashing aviator, or a rich but tyrannical geezer, or a dumpy but good-natured gas station attendant, or a fast-talking, skirt-chasing salesman, or any of a dozen or so other destinies.

One of the least desirable husbands was the Scotsman, pictured in a tam-o'-shanter and full lowlands regalia, and smiling drunkenly above this caption:

> YOUR FUTURE HUSBAND will be a tight Scotchman, in fact he will be tight most of the time. Every time he opens his pocketbook, the moths fly out. He will be so cheap that he will squeak, and he will pinch the pennies until the Indians howl. He will love his grog and his eight little Scotties [the future children, also pictured], who will show you a good time by all playing bag-pipes at the same time.

Aside from the howling Indians—clearly an old joke by 1935, since Indian-head pennies were discontinued in 1909—the only witty thing about that clumsy caption, with its awkward repetitions of "time" (was the writer a clock-watcher paid by the hour?), is the punning use of "tight." IRISHMEN are also proverbially drinky, and Jews proverbially stingy, but only Scotsmen unite these two traits, which otherwise are as immiscible as oil and water.

In the popular imagination, Scotsmen even are stingier than they are drinky. "Genealogical Reflection" is the second poem of Nash's first collection, and shows that in 1931, it was still okay to imply that the Scottish have an innate predisposition to miserliness. You won't find a chapter of Darky Jokes in Louis Untermeyer's *Treasury of Laughter*[48] (1943), but you'll find a chapter of jokes about Scotsmen and their stinginess. In one

---

[48] You won't find a chapter of Jewish jokes, either, though one of the Scottish jokes concerns "a Scotchman, an Irishman, and a Jew" who have dinner together. The Scotchman offers to get the check, and the next day the newspaper reports "Death of a Jewish Ventriloquist." Untermeyer, incidentally, was best known for his poetry anthologies. A poet in his own right, he was presumably the subject of this quatrain by e. e. cummings:

mr. u will not be missed
who as an anthologist
sold the many on the few
not excluding mr. u.

joke, MacDonald reminds his wife to make their son take off his glasses whenever the lad isn't looking through them. In another, MacPherson buys a single spur, reasoning that if one side of his horse goes, the other will too. In a third, Sandy grieves that his wife has died before she had time to finish the pills the doctor made her buy.

Because of their proverbial frugality, Scotsmen were a natural choice for toy banks. One made in Germany in the 1930s was designed with a protruding tongue that withdrew when a coin was placed on it: the Scotsman swallowed the coin. Another old tin bank portrayed the Scotsman as drunk as well as miserly, with a head that bobbed when coins were inserted.

"The Irish gave the bagpipes to the Scots as a joke," wrote Oliver Herford about a century ago, "but the Scots haven't got the joke yet." The Scottish are supposed to be humorless, too, as are TIGHTWADS in general. No doubt this is unfair to Scots, but is it fair to tightwads? Is pathological solemnity itself a form of stinginess? That would make humor a form of generosity and not, as Freud contended, a form of parsimony: "The pleasure in the comic [arises] from an economy in expenditure of ideation . . . and the pleasure of humor from an economy of expenditure of feeling." In other words, we laugh as a way of expending *less* thought and feeling on events that otherwise would be prohibitively thought-provoking and upsetting. So it makes perfect sense that a tightwad like Jack Benny would also be—where humor is concerned—a spendthrift. It makes less sense, if you swear by Freud, that certain nationalities (the Dutch are another) should be proverbial for both lack of humor and lack of generosity. But economic metaphors are only metaphors.

Secret Societies

THOUGH MANY MISTAKE him for nothing but a lowly bus driver, Ralph Kramden is also the treasurer of the International Order of Loyal Raccoons, the lodge to which his buddy Norton also belongs (just as, on that shameless *Honeymooners* rip-off *The Flintstones*, Fred and Barney belong to the Loyal Order of Water Buffalo).

All the hubbub on the show about lodge activities was one of its more inspired features, perfectly summing up Ralph's pitiable need to feel important.

The producers of *The Honeymooners* weren't the first humorists to find such lodges funny, or to see the poignancy of their appeal to losers in nowhere jobs and nowhere lives—and indeed to any man whose sense of self-importance far outstrips his importance in the eyes of his spouse, employer, and neighbors. One such figure was BLOWHARD par excellence Major Hoople from *Our Boarding House*, the great one-panel newspaper cartoon from the 1920s and '30s. In a 1927 installment, Hoople explains the appeal of the lodge: "Hmf! To a nettlehead, this costume *would* provoke coarse guffaws and rude gibes, but in my lodge, it is the symbol of dignity and power. I . . . am the Exalted Prince of the Mystic Ruby." ("What do they call th' guy with th' next reddest nose?" asks one of the wisecracking boarders who function as a sort of pitiless Greek chorus puncturing the major's hubris.)

Laurel and Hardy's best movie, *Sons of the Desert* (1933), is the locus classicus for all subsequent humor about lodges. It involves a plot that became de rigueur in any radio or television sitcom with lodge-related episodes: husbands want to go to big lodge convention in big wicked city (usually Chicago); wives forbid them, rightly or wrongly suspecting that convention is pretext for all kinds of male misbehavior; husbands use deceit to go anyhow; wives get wind of deceit. Both Stan and Ollie play severely HENPECKED HUSBANDS whose wives routinely throw crockery to enforce decrees (at one point, Ollie wears a pot on his head as a helmet). Comedy husbands who belong to secret societies are almost always henpecked, because that's the obvious way to deflate the adolescent male fantasy of power and importance that lodges cater to.

It was a fantasy that appealed to many men, and to many scriptwriters who made light of male grandiosity at its most endearingly silly. It goes without saying that self-aggrandizing buffoons like Fibber McGee and Chester A. Riley (star of *The Life of Riley*) belonged to lodges, but who'd have guessed that Andy Griffith would, or Gomez Addams? On *Amos 'n' Andy*, both the title characters belonged to the Mystic Knights of the Sea. On the immensely popular radio show *Vic and Sade* (1932–46),

Victor Gook was by day a mild-mannered accountant for the Consolidated Kitchenware Company, but when the sun went down Vic had a secret life as Exalted Big Dipper of the Drowsy Venus Chapter of the Sacred Stars of the Milky Way—and whole episodes were devoted to his lodge regalia ("boots, sword, tunic, plume hat, robe"), lodge outings, lodge speeches, and lodge library.

Secretaries, Stenographers, and Typists

> *This Month's Drawing Account: The Boss drew the cork, the stenog drew the curtains and the office boy drew his conclusions!*
> —*CAPTAIN BILLY'S WHIZ BANG*, c. 1930

> *When the struggling stenographer quits struggling, she discovers she doesn't have to be a stenographer.*
> —HENNY YOUNGMAN

THE TYPEWRITER AS we know it, or knew it, was developed in the 1860s—Mark Twain, an early adopter, used one for *Life on the Mississippi*—and almost at once a new stock character joined the Central Casting department of our culture's collective consciousness: the Typewriter, named for the machine she operated. In the early days, in fact, *typewriter* was more likely to mean the operator than the machine, but its very ambiguity was exploited by humorists. In a cartoon dating from around 1910, a young male job applicant stands before an elderly boss and his cute young typist. "I see you can write shorthand," says the boss, "but are you familiar with the typewriter?" "No," replies the applicant, staring at the typist, "but I can soon manage that."

As the cartoon implies, typing wasn't thought of as strictly women's work. When Henry James bought a typewriting machine in 1897, his first typist was male. In 1901, James replaced the man with a woman, for reasons that suggest why the corporate world was soon to kick the men out of the typing pool: "I can get a highly competent little woman for half. It's simply that I don't want to put so much more money into dictating than I *need*."

There was of course another reason: unlike Henry James, most of the men employing stenographers and typists were attracted to the opposite sex, and even happily married bosses preferred to share their corner offices with pretty young women rather than surly young men. As the phrase implies, "taking dictation" demands submissiveness, a trait that our culture encouraged in women in a way it never did in men.

By the 1930s, *typist* had become the standard term for the operator, though as recently as 1953, *typewriter* could still mean the person and not the machine, to judge by a risqué joke published that year: "Confucius say, 'Typewriter not permanent until screwed on desk.'" By then, of course, typists were usually female, as stenographers had been for several decades—had been, indeed, ever since that term emerged. (The word derives from *stenos*, Greek for "narrow" or "close"—stenogamous insects are ones requiring no nuptial flight to mate—and means a writer of shorthand.)

And it's easy to pinpoint the nation's fascination with stenographers so designated. The Internet Movie Database lists fourteen films with *stenographer* in the title, and twelve of them date from between 1910 and 1916: *The Stenographer's Friend, Mutt and Jeff and the Lady Stenographer, Oh! You Stenographer, The New Stenographer, Stenographer Wanted, The Ranch Stenographer, Dad's Stenographer, The Substitute Stenographer, The Stenographer, The New Stenographer* (again), *Mr. Jack Hires a Stenographer*, and *The Good Stenographer*. Though the Mutt and Jeff title might suggest otherwise, stenographers were almost always women, at least in popular culture; that was of course the secret of their fascination. Not that there's anything especially female about the work; until the twentieth century, in fact, scribes were usually male, like Bartleby the Scrivener, the unwilling office drudge in Melville's 1853 novella.

The word and the job were still around in the 1920s, but so taken for granted that the title was often abbreviated, as in *His New Steno*, a film from 1928. *Somebody's Stenog*, an A. E. Hayward comic strip that debuted

Figs. 136–139

in 1924, starred a ditzy blonde named Cam O'Flage, and ran until 1940, when its increasingly archaic title may have contributed to its demise. (*Public Stenographer*, the only other movie title turned up by my IMDB search, came out in 1934.)

In the American workplace, *secretary* began as a pretentious synonym for *typist* or *stenographer* (itself originally a pretentious euphemism), and was subjected to the sort of ridicule later heaped on other occupational grandiloquisms like *mortician*, *custodian*, and *sanitary engineer*. Whatever you call her, the stereotype of the inept, airheaded office worker who owes her job to sex appeal has been around for more than a century now. An insult postcard dating from 1907 showed a pretty BLONDE typing above this caption:

> *THE TYPEWRITER*
> *We're on to you, you're very bum;*
> *You cannot strike a key straight;*
> *You sit there just to play goo-goo*
> *With poor old Mister Staylate.*

It was a common joke in lowbrow humor magazines like *Captain Billy's Whiz Bang*, which in the 1920s and '30s entertained those who found *The New Yorker*'s sense of humor too uppity. "The faster a stenographer is, the more likely she is to stay in one place," observed Captain Billy in 1927. Six years later, lamenting the high unemployment, he complained that "jobs have been scarcer than a stenographer on the Virgin Islands." Decades later—long after anyone still described herself as a stenographer—Diana Vreeland wrote of Coco Chanel, "Her first customers were princesses and duchesses and she dressed them like secretaries and stenographers." With so many slurs against the profession, it's no wonder stenographers decided to stop calling themselves that.

Shoes

You want to fall in love with a shoe, go ahead.
A shoe can't love you back, but, on the other hand,
a shoe can't hurt you too deeply either.
And there are so many nice-looking shoes.

—ALLAN SHERMAN

LESSON #6 IN the *Pocket Cartooning Course* (1943) was devoted to Shoes, either because cartoonists as a class are shoe fetishists, or because shoes are funny. Shoes *are* funny. Maxwell Smart's shoe phone appears in the very first scene of the pilot episode of *Get Smart* (1965), ringing in Symphony Hall during a stuffy Beethoven concert—as real-world cell phones wouldn't do for several decades. Shoes are a key ingredient in Kickapoo Joy Juice, the almost lethally intoxicating beverage brewed by two denizens of *Li'l Abner*'s Dogpatch.

And clearly shoes are also fun to draw. In Rube Goldberg's elaborate machines, the single most common component, not counting standard machine parts like pulleys and gears, is a heavy-looking shoe or boot, usually used either to kick or to step on the next item in the unlikely chain of causation. In Goldberg's orange-juicing machine, a diving boot stomps on the head of an octopus who then mistakes the orange for the diver's own head and squeezes it in anger. Goldberg's portable fan, on the other hand, involves six shoes mounted on a sort of paddle wheel in such a way that when the wheel turns, the shoes kick a little bear in the rump repeatedly, though several more steps intervene between the maltreated bear and the waving fan.

Old shoes as well as TIN CANS were sometimes tied to the back bumper of the newlyweds' getaway car. Tin cans and old shoes: a very common pairing in old comics. Goats eat shoes when no cans are available. Hapless cartoon fishermen tend to snag one or the other; indeed, the old shoe (or boot) is the single most common non-piscine object for a cartoon fisherman to catch, and the tin can the second-most common. Dr. Seuss included two cans and a boot in his cutaway view of McElligot's Pool ("'Young man,' laughed the farmer / 'You're sort of a fool! / You'll *never* catch fish / In McElligot's Pool!'"), along with a teakettle, a milk bottle, a whiskey bottle, and a busted alarm clock. Since fishermen keep their worms in a can (was it once possible to *buy* canned earthworms?), it figures that some of those cans would end up in the water, but boots are just a funny form of litter. A trash-strewn cartoon alley is sure to feature both, not just because both are thrown at ALLEY CATS and songful DRUNKS, but because back in the good old

Fig. 140 From *Li'l Abner*, 1949

days, when civilization was only beginning to be poisoned by its own excretions, these mass-produced and inconveniently durable objects must have been just troubling enough to laugh about.

Shoes were also thrown at newlyweds by the groom's fun-loving friends, if the groom's friends were drunken assholes. Dagwood Bumstead is beaned by a flung shoe on his wedding day as he leaves the church with Blondie. The custom was so common—if not in real life, at least in comedy—that Ira Gershwin wrote a song about it:

> *You may throw all the rice you desire,*
> *But please, friends, throw no shoes.*
> *For 'twill surely arouse my ire,*
> *If you cause my wife one bruise.*
> —"YOU MAY THROW ALL THE RICE YOU DESIRE," 1917

There is something expressive, almost touching, about a discarded shoe— maybe because we know it did a dirty job for years and now is tossed aside ungratefully. Not everyone, of course, could afford to throw away old shoes. Because many victims of the Great Depression blamed their poverty on Herbert Hoover, shoes with holes in them were referred to in the 1930s as "Hoover shoes" (just as newspapers used for warmth were

"Hoover blankets," wild rabbits used for food were "Hoover hogs," and pockets turned inside out to emphasize their emptiness were "Hoover flags"). No other article of clothing is so often used to indicate the poverty of its wearer, be he a HOBO with his toes protruding, or a HILLBILLY with holes in the soles of his clodhoppers. But better old shoes than no shoes at all.

Shotgun Weddings

> *Everything is funny as long as it is happening to someone else.*
> —WILL ROGERS

I T IS USUALLY portrayed as a HILLBILLY custom: some outsider—generally a city slicker, often a TRAVELING SALESMAN—has dallied with Paw's nubile daughter and either been caught in the act or made the mistake of returning to the same hills a year later, when the evidence of his transgression is unignorably present in the shape a swaddled infant. And now Paw and his shotgun are going to make the young man do the honorable thing. Not that the young man needs to impregnate the hillbilly gal to seal his fate; in some parts, the Code of the Hills dictates that even a kiss has the binding force of a formal marriage proposal.

Sometimes the gag is varied by making the father something other than a hillbilly, and his persuader something other than a shotgun. A 1963 cartoon showed the young man, his sweetheart, and her angry father all dressed in swimsuits, goggles, and flippers, and still dripping from the ocean; the couple stands before a justice of the peace, and the father holds a harpoon gun at the groom's back. A 1947 cartoon by William Standing, a Native American artist, sets the scene on a reservation. The priest and the middle-aged groom are white; the bride is a Native American, and her father makes do with a bow and arrow. A Charles Addams cartoon showed a pith-helmeted explorer being wed at blowgunpoint to a bare-breasted pigmy.

A related joke of the same vintage is the breach-of-promise lawsuit—the shotgun wedding's hifalutin city cousin, so civilized that it furnishes

WE WERE KINDA WISHIN' YOU'D SHOW UP AROUND HERE!

Fig. 141 Invitation to a wedding. See also HILLBILLIES, YOKELS AND HICKS.

the premise of a Henry James story ("The Bench of Desolation"), as well as a musical (*We're in the Money*), a Mae West comedy (*I'm No Angel*), and an episode of *Amos 'n' Andy* where Andy avoids the suit by faking SUICIDE. Robert Benchley was thinking of such lawsuits when he wrote, in 1930, "Sand is also a good place on which to write, 'I love you,' as it would be difficult to get into court after several years have passed."

Skunks

> *Three more years and our encyclopedia will be finished.*
> *Let's not bog down in the middle of the letter S.*
> —GARY COOPER, *BALL OF FIRE*, 1941

"THE FOX KNOWS many things, the hedgehog one big thing," wrote Archilochus, invoking two animals insufficiently funny to merit entries in this guide (though a truly

Fig. 142

unabridged encyclopedia of humor would have to say a word or two about the hedgehog). The skunk, too, knows one big thing, and it's so different from what most animals know as to muddle our notions of physical courage. A 1940s issue of *World's Finest Comics* shows Superman, Batman, and Robin fleeing in panic from a skunk. We can debate whether it's brave or merely foolhardy to stand your ground when faced with a hostile rattlesnake or rottweiler or redneck, but when the hostile critter is a skunk, there's no argument. Reckless courage flourishes in shame cultures where the prospect of losing face is more daunting than that of death or grievous bodily harm. If skunk spray were lethal, manly men would be more likely to risk the creature's wrath. As it is, there's no glory in killing a skunk, and if it beats you to the draw, you end up stinking for a week.

Since skunks are proverbially smelly, one way to insult someone is to suggest that he is even smellier than a skunk. In "Tokio Jokio," a virulently anti-Japanese cartoon made by Looney Tunes in 1943, we see a panicky Japanese general running through a forest in search of somewhere to hide during an air raid. He finally dives into a hollow log that proves already to harbor a skunk; with a look of horror, the skunk hastens to put on a gas mask.

The most famous cartoon skunk is Pepé Le Pew, and what makes him funny is comic obliviousness: not only does he persist is misconstruing unambiguous sexual rejection as mere coyness, but he repeatedly mistakes cats for skunks. Depending on which of these misunderstandings we focus on, the Pepé cartoons can be viewed either as devastating satires on male sexual aggressiveness or as sinister anti-miscegenation fables. Or of course as neither. However you interpret them, you must admire their creator, Chuck Jones, for his ingenuity in devising one way after another for a cat to wind up looking like a skunk. Only once, in "Really Scent," is the unlucky feline simply born with a white stripe. More often she acquires it by accident in the course of the cartoon (as in "A Scent of the Matterhorn," where she happens into the path of a street-painting machine), or on purpose (as in "Heaven Scent," where a cat paints a stripe down her back to ward off dogs), or as part of someone else's scheme (as in "Two Scents Worth," where a bank robber paints a stripe on a black cat in order to clear out a bank).

In "Private Ralph Skunk," the third episode of *Gomer Pyle, U.S.M.C.*, Gomer finds and adopts a skunk, predictably annoying Sergeant Carter, and names the critter fondly after his uncle Ralph. Only someone as stupid as Gomer, you'd think, would name a skunk in tribute to someone, and yet Walt Kelly modeled Mam'selle Hepzibah—the sexy French skunk in *Pogo*—on his French mistress, who became his second wife. In her case, the choice of comic-strip avatar may have been determined by the comic French accent and difficulty with English that the second Mrs. Kelly evidently shared with Pepé Le Pew (who predated her), as Mam'selle Hepzibah certainly does. "Never dark on my door again!" she exclaims at one point to a fickle boyfriend.

And in fact, it makes sense to draw your adorably cute mistress as a skunk, since cartoonists usually do portray skunks as adorably cute. But also as pitiable: Caspar the Friendly Ghost was constantly befriending them. With the exception of Le Pew, cartoon skunks are usually juvenile and, like paintings of big-eyed waifs, designed to tug at heartstrings. Their stink is a metaphor for a baby's dirty diaper as well as for social stigmas of every kind.

Smoke Signals

THIS JOKE IS seldom encountered except in single-panel magazine cartoons. In one from 1950 by a not-yet-famous Mort Walker, two Indians regard a distant mushroom cloud; one says to the other, "Whoever it is, he sure uses big words." Most of the cartoons, though, involve the transposition of some aspect of telephony into a low-tech, pre-electric, Native American key; an "original" smoke signal cartoon is one that adapts a feature of phone communication that we haven't seen adapted in previous cartoons. In a 1959 cartoon from *Boy's Life*, for example, an Indian couple stands at the edge of a bluff above a huge heap of flaming timber. As the woman uses a blanket to send smoke signals, her husband says, "I hope you realize what these long distance messages cost!" Even at their best, such cartoons are ingenious rather than funny; if we laugh, it is a laugh of admiration—at Peter Arno's ingenuity, for instance, in imagining a cliff-dwelling Indian couple responding to distant puffs of smoke. The husband has built a little signal fire in front of their dwelling, but his squaw calls down to him from a higher ledge where she too has a fire: "Never mind. I'll take it up here."

Sometimes an analogy is made with letters rather than phone calls. In a wartime Charles Addams cartoon, one Indian produces dark puffs of smoke and another Indian perched on a higher cliff uses a stick to disperse certain puffs. Looking on, one squaw remarks to another: "They're censoring everything now."

Since an inveterate bore can bore you by semaphore, hand signing, or even body language, it's not surprising that smoke signals too can be boring. In a 1966 cartoon by Charles Rodrigues, two Indians stand by a small campfire, one holding a blanket of the sort used to send signals, and both watching an enormous cluster of separate smoke puffs from another, distant campfire. Says one Indian to another, "You never should have asked him about his operation."

Sneezing

I am pretty sure that, if you will be quite honest,
you will admit that a good rousing sneeze, one that tears open
your collar and throws your hair into your eyes,
is really one of life's sensational pleasures.
—ROBERT BENCHLEY

THE FIRST MOTION picture copyrighted in the United States, "Edison Kinetoscopic Record of a Sneeze" (1894), was a five-second film of a man taking a pinch of snuff and sneezing. The man, Fred Ott, was an employee of Thomas Edison known for his sense of humor and the violence of his sneezes. Since the birth of cinema, then, sneezes have been associated with humor, though seldom as closely as in Robert Benchley's pseudoscientific 1937 essay "Why We Laugh—Or Do We?," which asserts that "all laughter is merely a compensatory reflex to take the place of sneezing." After all, Benchley points out, when we say that something is "nothing to sneeze at," we mean it is nothing to *laugh* at. "What we really want to do is sneeze, but as that is not always possible, we laugh instead. Sometimes we underestimate our powers and laugh and sneeze at the same time."

The most common cause of sneezing in American cartoons is ground pepper. Like onion tears, pepper sneezes are especially funny because of the impressive reaction to a purely mechanical trigger. But all sneezes are funny. As mentioned elsewhere in this guide, NOSES often stand for PENISES, and no other physiological phenomenon is as similar to an orgasm as a sneeze: the gradual excitation, the point of no return, the violent release, and even the ejaculate.

Sloppy serial orgasms of uncontrollable sneezing were the main symptom of sitcom allergies, back in the golden age before we came to associate allergies with anaphylactic shock. As a rule, the allergy was— or seemed at first to be—to another character, the funniest one for the sufferer to be allergic to. So of course it's Dennis who makes Mr. Wilson sneeze in a 1963 installment of the *Dennis the Menace* show. Skipper develops an allergy to Gilligan, and then, just in case that's not funny

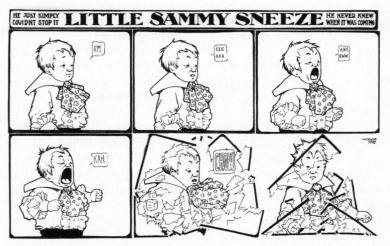

Fig. 143 One of Winsor McCay's many one-joke strips: *Little Sammy Sneeze*, 1904

enough, so do all the other castaways. Meanwhile, on *The Patty Duke Show*, Patty seems to be allergic to her identical cousin, Cathy, while over on *The Dick Van Dyke Show*, Rob fears that he's allergic to his wife, Laura. On *Petticoat Junction*, Steve Elliott is banned from his own house because his baby seems to be allergic to him. Luckily things almost always work out in the end, when it turns out the allergy isn't to the person per se, but to some nonessential aspect of the person, like the papaya oil in Gilligan's new hair tonic.

Another funny thing about sneezes is that they also occur among nonverbal beings like cats and dogs and mutes. Harpo never says a word in any of the Marx Brothers movies, but he sneezes audibly in *At the Circus*. Scooby Doo's sneezes are a running gag, especially likely to occur when he and Shaggy are hiding and need to keep silent, and though no funnier than the rest of the show, they usually elicit a laugh from the laugh track. (And it *is* funny when animals sneeze. YouTube has many videos of sneezing animals, always with human laughter in the background.)

Like joy buzzers, sneezing powder was a favorite weapon of bad guys on the old *Batman* show. In one episode, when the dynamic duo raid an apothecary shop, one of the villains incapacitates them with a handful of sneezing powder, evidently something apothecaries keep in stock. Batman should have taken precautions, as he did in another episode from earlier in the same year (1966), when the Joker tried the same form of chemical warfare. "No use, Joker," says Batman impassively. "I knew you'd employ your sneezing powder, so I took an Anti-Allergy Pill! Instead of a sneeze, I've caught you cold!"

There are also jokes about the *art* of sneezing. "Contrary to the prevalent fallacy, sneezing into the gas mask is to be avoided rather than practised," advised Wally Walgren, a cartoonist and Marine, in the caption to a cartoon that appeared in *Stars and Stripes* during World War I. The drawing shows a doughboy blowing off his gas mask, and incidentally his helmet, with a thunderous "KAH-CHOW." "If a sneeze is absolutely unavoidable, let it be through the ears . . . as the ears are not covered and afford a free air passage." And about fifteen years later, Dr. Seuss—or rather a Seuss character, Dr. Farquarharson Fohsnip—declared that "not one child in a hundred can sneeze with grace." Dr. Fohsnip conducts sneezing tutorials, where children listen to phonograph recordings of world-class sneezers like Sinclair Lewis, Mussolini, and Lydia Pinkham.

Snoring

> *Baby! Please!*
> *Please don't snore so loud!*
> *You're just a little bit o' woman but you*
> *Sound like a great big crowd.*
> —LANGSTON HUGHES, "THE MORNING AFTER"

THE MOST ANNOYING snore in all of twentieth-century humor probably belongs to John Bickerson, the harried husband played by Don Ameche on the radio comedy *The Bickersons*. For its time (1946–51), the program was striking, even scandalous, in its portrayal of a marriage gone sour—a portrayal that foreshadowed the vision of marriage offered by *The Honeymooners* and, much later, *Married with*

Children. In an era of model couples like Ward and June or Ozzie and Harriett, *The Bickersons* voiced a dissenting opinion of America's most sacred institution. When they're both awake, John's shrewish and carping wife, Blanche, is more annoying by far, but when he manages to falls asleep, John gets his own back with a deafening, mucusy snore punctuated by high-pitched giggles (convincing Blanche that John is dreaming about their sexy next-door neighbor, Gloria Gooseby). Most of their fights are provoked by Blanche waking John in the middle of the night—and insisting on talking—in retaliation for his snoring.

Like MIDNIGHT SNACKING, snoring was a handy metaphor for sexual incompatibility, in an era that couldn't talk about sex as directly as ours does. "Ma—he snores!" says the bride to her mother in an emergency wedding-night phone call (on the front cover of a racy 1956 Ace paperback collection entitled *Love and Hisses*), as her new husband sleeps in the bed behind her and a suitcase labeled JUST MARRIED stands by for clarification.

In comic strips, the standard way to indicate snoring is with a handsaw cutting a log in two. Usually the saw and log are tidily enclosed within an ordinary speech balloon, though sometimes the cartoonist will make the balloon more nebulous, to acknowledge the fact that the "speaker" is sleeping and the contents of the balloon is not a word or even an onomatopoeia, but an image. Given how common the "sawing logs" convention was in early comics—Barney Google alone must have snored his way through a cord of firewood per annum—it's odd that cartoonists almost always felt the need to accompany the image with at least one "zzz" or "bzz," a redundancy suggesting a mistrust of strictly visual storytelling. One of the quaintest things about early comics is the cartoonists' obvious uncertainty as to how much could be told through pictures alone.

Why a saw? Why a log? The cliché dates back to an era when woodstoves were more than just a cozy and nostalgic way for suburbanites to pollute, and when handsaws were not just for handymen and carpenters. The sawing of wood was an everyday sound, and a handy approximation of an everynight one. But a poor approximation, one that understates how funny, loud, and irritating real snoring can be. (Arguably, it's not approximation at all, but rather the substitution of a funny image for a

Fig. 144 *Nancy*, 1960

funny noise—a sight gag for a sound gag, as befits a medium whose real glory has always been visual, not verbal.)

No cartoonist was fonder of sight gags than Ernie Bushmiller, the mastermind we have to thank for *Nancy*, and no cartoon child snored more than its title character. In one strip, Nancy saws right through the log and wakes up when its end drops off. In another, she falls asleep sitting up and her snore is symbolized by a saw cutting lengthwise through an upright log **(Fig. 144)**. In a third, she goes to sleep with a clothespin on her nose to muffle her snores, and the saw in the log is replaced by a pocketknife cutting through a pencil.

You seldom see comic-strip characters sawing through logs nowadays, though we continue to find logs per se funny—certainly funnier than boards or trees or sawdust. (Think of the Log Lady on *Twin Peaks*, or of Ren and Stimpy's singing commercials for Log.) As for animated cartoons, the saw-in-the-log gag was never as common there. With a soundtrack there's no need for symbols to indicate snoring, and animators have found other sight gags, better suited to the medium, to accompany the sound: the sleeper's belly rising and falling massively, as Fred Flintstone's does when he naps in his hammock, or the blanket over a supine snorer's chest furling and unfurling with each breath.

Recalling the thunderous snorts and long descending whistles that comprise Fred's snores, I'm reminded of exactly how inadequate "zzz" is as a written notation for snoring. Suppose you wanted to convey the sound more accurately in print. How would you transcribe it? On a comic postcard dating from 1911, a wife is shown sitting up in bed scowling at her sleeping husband, whose snores are spelled out "Z-Z-Z-Z-R-R-

Soap Chocolates

A fancy box containing seven or eight what appear to be delicious looking chocolates. They look so nice and so real that few persons will refuse one, though we promise you they will never 'bite' at a second one.

No. 2704. Soap Chocolates.
Price per box **50c**

SOAP BISCUIT

A splendid imitation of genuine crackers made out of soap. A few of these mixed in with a dish of regular crackers ought to liven up any party. **15c**

No. 2701. Soap Biscuit...........

SOAP BISCUIT
(ROUND)

They are similar to soap biscuit described above, but are of the round variety, instead of square. Get some of each to make up an assortment. **15c**

No. 2702. Soap Biscuit (round)...

SOAP GUM DROP

A large gum drop that is made of delicately scented transparent soap. It fools them all. Mix one or two with other candy and see who gets the "surprise" piece.

No. 2703. Soap Gum Drop.........**15c**

Soap Surprise Egg

It is made of soap, though could easily be mistaken for a hard boiled egg cut in half. It is same size as an ordinary egg though not quite as appetizing.

No. 2699. Soap Surprise Egg.....**15c**

SOAP CHEESE

The most natural looking piece of Swiss cheese you ever saw. It might fool even the mice if it were not made of soap.
No. 2703. Soap Cheese 15c

SOAP PICKLE

A real imitation of a genuine pickle, which is made of green scented soap. It makes a great table joke.

No. 2700. Soap Pickle...........**15c**

SURPRISE SOAP

This "Soap" contains a chemical that acts with surprising results as soon as you commence to use it.

No. 2198.
Surprise Soap
15c

Everlasting Soap

An exact duplicate of a piece of soap, but it is impossible to wash with it. Contains no dye or chemical.

No. 2696. Everlasting Soap.......
15c

SOAP CIGAR

It looks like a real cigar, but it is made of soap! Place a few of these with a box of genuine cigars and watch the fun begin.

No. 2697. Soap Cigar ....
15c

SOAP CIGAR BUTT

Another good practical joker. Has size, shape and appearance of a real cigar half consumed, but it is made of soap.

No. 2698. Soap Cigar Butt ....
10c

Fig. 145 No soap radio?

R-R-Z-Z-Z-Z-R-R-R-R"—a transcription that at least acknowledges that snoring is a two-part sound like sneezing in its rhythmic alternation of inhales and exhales. Don Martin, whose ear was prodigious as his eye, came as close as anyone to the quiddity of snoring—especially the hiccupy or apneac variety—with onomatopoeias like "ONNNNNGHK FWEEEEEEEEE" and "ZZZZ ZZT-ZNIK SNUFFLE SNORK." Don Martin is dead, though, and no one has stepped forward to fill his giant floppy SHOES.

Soap

ALL PERSONAL-HYGIENE ITEMS are funny—mouthwash, toothpaste, toilet paper, and so on—but soap may be the funniest. Cartoon HOBOES exhibit a phobic reaction to the substance, and all-American boys aren't too fond of it either, especially when having their mouths washed out[49] or being told to wash behind their ears. In a 1941 episode of *Nancy*, the title character uses a bar of soap to scare the HICCUPS out of Grimy Gregory (her strip's forgettable answer to Pig-Pen). The soap in the bathtub is probably the second-leading cause of indoor comic PRATFALLS, after the roller skate on the stairs.

Over the decades, the Johnson Smith Company has offered a product variously labeled as Dirty Soap, Sucker Soap, and Forget-Me-Not Trick Soap, which looks and feels like ordinary soap (and claims to smell like it, too: "gardenia scented") but contains a water-activated dye that will blacken the face and hands of anyone who uses it. "Exceptionally good for BOARDING HOUSES," claims one 1940s ad; and one reason I'm glad I don't live in a boardinghouse is that they're just the kind of place where you'd encounter practical jokers who shop from the Johnson Smith catalog.

[49] In a brief illustrated essay, c. 1930, entitled "Punish Your Offspring Scientifically," Dr. Seuss improved on the time-honored practice by recommending a different brand of soap for every different swear word. The picture shows a mother standing by what looks like a vending machine, with bars of soap labeled HECK, DAMN, HELL, DRAT, GOLLY, and so on.

Soup

In taking any liquid either from a spoon or drinking vessel,
no noise must ever be made.
—EMILY POST, *ETIQUETTE*, 1922

"SOUP IS STILL funny, but not as funny as it was a few years back," pronounced Irwin S. Cobb, author of *Eating in Two or Three Languages* (1919). It's safe to say that many people have agreed with Cobb about the basic funniness of soup, including the several cartoonists for whom a favorite last-panel sight gag is a bowl of soup upended on somebody's head. What bricks are to *Krazy Kat*, and pies to the Three Stooges, soup is to *Mutt and Jeff*; Jeff often works as a waiter, and more often than not, when someone orders soup, someone will be wearing it before the meal is over.

Why is soup funny? Because it's messy? Because it's neither meat nor drink? Because it often serves (or did in my house when I was a kid) as a punitive or penitential surrogate for more substantial food? Because, like SAUSAGE, it's a way to use up leftovers and parts that no one would otherwise eat?

One reason is that it's noisy. "The soup sounds good," observes the Great McGonigle in *The Old-Fashioned Way* (1934), on hearing a meal in a BOARDINGHOUSE. In a pre-Popeye episode of *Thimble Theatre*, Olive Oyl makes soup for herself and her boyfriend, Ham Gravy, but he makes so much NOISE eating it—not slurping but slupping, to judge by the "slup slup slup" sound he makes—that she flounces off in disgust, abandoning her bowl to a roaming hog that makes the same slupping noise. Soup is an ambiguous food, neither solid nor liquid, too thick to be sipped from a cup but too thin to be forked into the mouth. Especially when it's piping hot, it almost demands to slupped, *pace* Olive Oyl and Emily Post. And here—I announce it beforehand for the sake of readers who prefer to skip such things—is a scatological limerick:

There was an old fellow from Roop
Who'd lost all control of his poop.

One evening at supper
His wife said, "Now Tupper,
Stop making that noise with your soup!"

Its noisiness was so proverbial a hundred years ago that Guy Wetmore
Carryl, in his retelling of "Little Boy Blue," compares the sound of rogue
cows tramping around in mud to the sound of schoolboys eating soup,
instead of the other way around. In a 1934 *New Yorker* cartoon by William Steig, a sort of field guide to different types of eaters (the Slow
Careful Masticator; the Jackal who raids the icebox in his pajamas; the
Pseudo-Correct, who extends the pinky on her crumpet hand as well as
the one on her teacup hand), the Beast is a fat man slurping his soup.
"You can get all the noise you want out of a tramp and a bowl of soup,"
reads the caption to one of Rube Goldberg's simpler cartoon inventions,
a New Year's Eve noisemaker consisting of a chair tied to a reveler's back
with what looks like a piece of ordinary kite string; a tramp sits in the
chair noisily spooning up a big bowl of soup with a ladle, and a sort of
giant hearing trumpet mounted on the chair collects the ensuing noise
and broadcasts it to the world at large.

And what exactly *is* the noise of a man eating soup? Slup slup slup?
No, "GURGLE GURGLE GURGLE," according to Goldberg. Don
Martin hears it differently: "SLURK GLURKLE GLUP SLOOPLE
GLIK SPLORP SHPLIPLE DROOT GLORT." The soup dripping
back into the bowl from the spoon gets its own sound effect: "DRIPPLE
BLIT." (According to Martin's precursor as *Mad*'s Maddest Artist, Basil
Wolverton, the sound of a glass eye falling into a bowl of tomato soup is
"PLOOP!" while that of a glass eye falling into heavy syrup is "PLOFF!")
Martin found the sound of soup so funny that in a *Mad* cartoon entitled
"Last Week in a Freensville Diner," we see a man eating soup for three
successive panels, surrounded by those trademark slurping sounds. In the
third panel, the hefty cook asks, "How's the soup, pal?" In the fourth, the
man stops eating and replies "Too noisy!!" while the soup itself continues
to make noises: "GLIP SHPIKKLE GLUP GAPLORK."

We associate soup with poverty and illness—with charity kitchens and sickrooms. When, in a famous early sequence of *Blondie* strips,

Dagwood goes on a hunger strike to protest his millionaire parents' refusal to let him marry lowborn Blondie Boopadoop, the latter suggests squirting soup down his throat with a bicycle pump, and a week later takes the liberty of injecting hot soup into his arm with a hypodermic needle. Toward the end of the strike, when Dagwood's condition is critical, his millionaire parents resort to force-feeding, which involves an elaborate array of tubes and tanks and motors and two nurses bearing giant vats labeled CONCENTRATED CLAM BROTH and CONCENTRATED CHICKEN BROTH.

Some old jokes about bad restaurants emphasized the thinness of the soup du jour, which sometimes contained little more than water and the occasional housefly. In "The Soup Song," a zany 1931 cartoon, Flip the Frog works as a waiter and cook in a cheap eatery. In one scene, we see him make soup by dipping various items briefly in a pot of boiling water—first a bunch of carrots, then a CABBAGE, then a wedge of Swiss, then an old boot, and finally a plucked chicken that is resurrected by immersion just long enough to towel off like a bather (a faintly naughty joke, since after all a plucked chicken is a naked female).

Soup is a funny place to find things that don't belong, whether the thing is a fly, the tip of an old man's beard, the overalls in Mrs. Murphy's chowder, or the camera that Maxwell Smart, posing as a butler, hides in the bowl he serves to a criminal in an episode of *Get Smart*. In an episode of *Leave It to Beaver* ("In the Soup"), the Beav gets trapped in a giant steaming bowl held by a giant Mom after climbing a billboard to see if there's actually soup in the bowl (there isn't). He is rescued, in the end, by the fire department.

Spanking

> *Mothers who raise*
> *A child by the book*
> *Can, if sufficiently vexed,*
> *Hasten results*
> *By applying the book,*
> *As well as the text.*
> —W. E. FARBSTEIN

THE KATZENJAMMER KIDS began in 1897, when its creator, Rudolph Dirks, was nineteen years old. It was the first comic strip to appear regularly in color, and it racked up all sorts of other firsts as well: Dirks, for example, pioneered the saw-in-the-log ideogram to indicate SNORING. He also established most of the conventions regarding corporal punishment in comics—not surprisingly, since almost every day his strip ended with young Hans and Fritz getting spanked. Their long-suffering mother delivered so many spankings that the activity changed her musculature; at least, that's how I explain her presence on the short list of comic-strip characters (the only others who come to mind are Alley Oop and Popeye) with forearms bigger than their upper arms.

We're so used to the conventions established by Dirks that we may fail to notice how stylized the standard comic-strip spanking is. We never see a hand or hairbrush striking a bottom, for instance, but always raised to strike. If there's only one authority figure on the scene to administer two spankings, we are always shown the *second*; the first malefactor is already crying.

Few later comic-strip tots were quite as demonic as Hans and Fritz. Dennis the Menace (1951–present) wreaked just as much havoc, but never maliciously. As with Bill Watterson's Calvin (clearly indebted to Dennis), most of his mischief was due to the dissonance between his worldview and the grownups', as when Dennis soaks his business-suited father with a garden hose because he thinks his dad looks too hot. Like

Fig. 146 *Buster Brown*, 1916

Calvin, Dennis is punished not with spankings but with what we now call "time-outs."

Why is spanking so much more common in old comics than in old movies? Mainly because comic strips allow and encourage all kinds of outrageousness that wouldn't work in any other medium, not even the related one of animated cartoons. Just imagine how many aspects of *Krazy Kat*—the absurdly changing backgrounds, the constant violence against the most lovable character, the carefully maintained uncertainty as to that character's gender and sexual orientation, the Joycean wordplay, the sheer oddness of the humor—would have to be lost or dialed down to convert Herriman's vision into watchable cartoons. Not even *Peanuts* made the leap from comic strip to cartoon specials without signs of strain. As for the constant spankings in early comics, what might be unpleasant on film for all but the fetishists (who admittedly are legion) is merely amusing on the funnies page.

We tend to assume that our objections to real-life spanking never occurred—and would have made no sense—to the parents of a hundred years ago, but in fact the debate about corporal punishment goes way back, further than the hindsight of this book. Strips like *The Katzenjammer Kids* show a world where spanking was taken for granted, but also one where it accomplished nothing, and served no other purpose than sheer retaliation. If it had any deterrent value, why would Hans and Fritz reoffend day after day, every day, for decades? In one strip, as they watch their latest prank unfold, Hans says, "Something tells me we are going to get a licking," and Fritz replies "Vat do we care? We're used to it!" Decades later, Red Skelton made the same point with his "Mean Widdle Kid" routine: "If I dood it, I dit a whippin' . . . I DOOD IT!"

The old phrase "Spare the rod, spoil the child" (which dates back to the 1600s in that form, and ultimately to the Old Testament) shows that some people have always inclined to spare the rod. Dickens pointed out in several of his novels the needless cruelty of school floggings, and a little earlier Wordsworth had gone further, implying that if floggings *aren't* needless in the classroom, so much the worse for classrooms. At least that seems to have been one reason he and his fellow Romantics bore such a grudge against traditional pedagogy: a sense that there must be something unnatural about a learning process that needs to inflict so much bodily pain. A century later, Orwell wrote, "I doubt whether classical education ever has been or can be successfully carried out without corporal punishment," though out of context that could pass for a *pro*-spanking sentiment.

In a 1909 installment of *The Dingbat Family*, a pre–*Krazy Kat* comic strip by George Herriman, Mrs. Dingbat returns from a meeting of her woman's club just as her husband is about to spank their rotten son Cicero for disrupting his nap. Like a governor phoning in a last-minute stay of execution, she tells Mr. Dingbat that "the Mothers' Council have just decided that spanking destroys the sub-conscious spirituality of the child." ("Well," replies her husband, "he had no consideration for *my* sub-conscious spirituality.")

Of all the topics in this guide, spanking was the easiest to research online, because I soon found that a horde of spanking fetishists had already done the spadework, and more lovingly than a mere student of humor ever could. Thanks to this anonymous but public-spirited network of pervs, I can say with confidence that in the 1940s, right around the time that wartime labor shortages were giving women a chance to work in munitions factories, a great change took place in American comics: after decades of standing by sweetly while their brothers were spanked, little girls had their turn. Art, as Cocteau said, is forever looking for the fresh spot on the pillow, and comic artists found one such fresh spot on the bare or panty-clad buttocks of such tykes as Little Audrey, Little Dot, Little Iodine, and Little Lulu (the earliest of the four—she received her first spanking in 1935). Their exploits took place for the most part not in wholesome family papers but in comic books, as befits a fad that often verged on fetish porn. If the daily spankings of Hans and Fritz were primitive morality tales of crime and punishment, the spankings in the little-girl comic books were ends in themselves. There wasn't even always the pretext of misbehavior before the baring of the little girl's buttocks; sometimes a bully would administer a wholly gratuitous spanking, not in loco parentis but rather on behalf of the deviants who clearly made up an important part of the readership.

The fad for little-girl spankings was oddly predated by a fad, in superhero and adventure comics of the 1930s, for big-girl spankings. Manly men like Mandrake the Magician, Price Valiant, and the Phantom often dealt with spoiled socialites and other difficult young women the same way the mother of Hans and Fritz dealt with *their* mischief. Like the little-girl spankings of the 1940s, these retributions often suggested a fetish on the part of cartoonist and reader alike, though sometimes corporal punishment was a simple assertion of male prerogatives, like Ricky Ricardo's spankings of Lucy. Lucy is more spirited and more articulate than her spouse, but Ricky is the man in a world where men are in charge, and when all else fails he can put his wife in her place as surely as a parent does a misbehaving toddler, by spanking. (The same solution is advocated in our own time by stern proponents of the school of wife-rearing called Christian Domestic Discipline.)

Spanking, of course, wasn't the only form of parental or quasi-parental beating practiced in that era (though, for reasons that deserve a closer look, it's the one that fascinates our culture). In *Nize Baby*, Milt Gross's illustrated *hörspiel* of immigrant life in the mid-1920s, little Isidor receives hundreds of carefully transcribed smacks in the course of his father Morry's tirades:

> So, Isidor!!! Benenas you swipe from de pushcar', ha? (SMACK!)
> A Cholly Chepman you'll grow opp, maybe, ha? (SMACK!!) I'll
> give you. (SMACK!) Do I (SMACK!) swipe? (SMACK!!) Does
> de momma (SMACK!!!) swipe? (SMACK!!!) From who you loin
> dis? (SMACK!)

Speaking of Cholly Chepman: in *Tillie's Punctured Romance* (1915), Charlie spanks a tiger rug after it trips him—but considering that earlier in the same film we've seen him throw a brick at Marie Dressler's head, the tiger gets off pretty easy. (In a *Moon Mullins* strip from 1934, Mullins spanks a pet *parrot* after its abusive language earns its owner a black eye from a passerby.) Buster Keaton began his showbiz career as a battered child in the family vaudeville act, the Three Keatons. Billed as "The Little Boy Who Can't Be Damaged," young Buster would provoke his father into throwing him across the stage or even into the audience. To facilitate this rough handling, Buster had a suitcase handle sewn onto his clothing. And people paid to watch.

Spendthrift Wives

AFTER DITZINESS AND bossiness, the trait most often imputed to wives in the mainstream humor of the early and mid-twentieth century was prodigality. The classic emblem of that trait was the wife returning from a shopping expedition with a big stack of parcels, and saying something cute to her shocked or fuming spouse. Invariably one of the boxes was a big round hatbox—because nothing better emblematizes the frivolity of women's spending habits (as seen by their husbands) than women's hats.

In the middle of the last century, binge shopping was depicted as a strictly female addiction. In a gag cartoon from a 1960 compilation called *Thimk*, the whole joke is that the *husband* comes home with the parcels: "Got feeling low—bought a new hat, new suit, couple of ties." Real men didn't care what they wore.

In the racier humor of the era, the most common failing of wives was infidelity. Women were often portrayed as GOLD DIGGERS—as de facto prostitutes auctioning their bodies to the highest bidder. Was the compulsive-shopping gag a cleaned-up, G-rated expression of deeper male anxieties about the unbridled appetites and mercenary nature of the female?

Spinach

One man's poison ivy is another man's spinach.
—GEORGE ADE

*This would be a better world for children
if the parents had to eat the spinach.*
—GROUCHO MARX IN *ANIMAL CRACKERS*, 1930

WILL ROGERS SAID, "An onion can make people cry but there's never been a vegetable that can make people laugh." He was wrong. People have been laughing at veggies for ages, just as they've been laughing at HASH and other unpopular foods. Admittedly, there's no consensus as to which vegetable is funniest. Potatoes are surprisingly funny despite the fact that no one seems to hate them.

Fig. 147 "It's broccoli, dear." "I say it's spinach, and I say the hell with it."

Fig. 148

CABBAGE has inspired enough mirth to merit its own entry, but just barely. Turnips, too, might have merited an entry, if the root-vegetable vote weren't split by parsnips, rutabagas, mangel-wurzels, and beets. For Will Cuppy, beets were funniest:

> I dare say that pickled beets, with their deadly, soul-sapping monotony, have torn more fond hearts asunder, broken up more happy homes and caused more crimes of passion than any other three vegetables chosen at random. . . . pickled beet relish with all its brood of quarrels, flatirons and BRICKS.
> —*HOW TO BE A HERMIT, 1929*

But the vegetable most often maligned by humorists is spinach, largely because it was the one most often forced on reluctant children. Spinach was the wonder food of the early twentieth century, a food believed to be ridiculously healthy, like pomegranate juice in our own time. One reason the Popeye cartoons got away with their unprecedented violence is that they were such effective pro-spinach propaganda. (Spinach never played as big role in *Thimble Theatre*, the Popeye comic strip, which originally attributed his strength not to eating a vegetable but to rubbing the head of an animal, the fabulous Whiffle Hen.)

In 1928, or just a couple of years before Popeye started campaigning for spinach, a *New Yorker* cartoon by Carl Rose showed a mother arguing at dinner with an adorable curly-headed little girl: "It's broccoli, dear," says the mother. "I say it's spinach and I say to hell with it," replies the girl. The answer became proverbial, and for the next twenty years or so, *spinach* was a synonym for *bullshit*. In 1938, a former fashion designer published a tell-all book about the fashion business with a title that no longer makes sense: *Fashion Is Spinach*.

The nationwide obsession with spinach and spinach-bashing seems to have peaked around 1930 (Popeye, whose first deployment of the stuff occurred in 1931, seems to have been as much a symptom as a cause of that obsession). A 1930 installment of a comic strip called *Now You Tell One*—a spoof of *Ripley's Believe It or Not*—features "the wonder child of Cedar Carpets, Iowa. Loves to have his face washed (especially behind the ears), likes to go to school, hates school vacation and is particularly fond of eating SPINACH!"

Since then, spinach has become—like most of the laughingstocks considered in this guide—less and less lafftastic. That it was still a little funny in 1955 may be deduced from the menu at the vegetarian restaurant in *The Seven Year Itch*, which offers Spinach Loaf, along with such dishes as Soybean Sherbet, Dandelion Salad, and Sauerkraut Juice. In a 1958 Sunday episode of *Hi and Lois* where Hi (who was zanier in this youth) decides to do everything backward for one day, we see him at the dinner table happily eating chocolate ice cream while his wife and kids face platefuls of spinach.

Nowadays, people are more likely to joke about broccoli. I've never met anyone who named spinach as his or her least favorite vegetable, but of course it's been a while since parents were zealous about ramming it down children's throats. And Americans—especially the ones most likely to worry about healthy eating—have gotten better at preparing veggies. Eighty years ago, when the first Popeye cartoons appeared, most people got their spinach out of cans, like Popeye himself—and nothing makes a vegetable less appetizing than a stint in a TIN CAN.

Spouse-Killing

When you consider what a chance women have to poison their
husbands, it's a wonder there isn't more of it done.
—KIN HUBBARD

Ricky to Lucy: And as I recall, it was till death do us part.
That event is about to take place right now!!
—I LOVE LUCY

I'VE NEVER BEEN married, and I don't know what to make of all the cartoons, sitcom episodes, and other works of humor involving murderous spouses. Do people joke about uxoricide because it's so unthinkable, or because it's a universal fantasy of long-suffering husbands and wives alike? How many spouses, on an average night, drift off to sleep with a smile on their lips and an ingenious fantasy of murdering the person SNORING next to them in the dark?

If Charles Addams were alive, we could ask him. No one was fonder of spouse-killing gags, though his favorite couple, the oddballs Morticia and Gomez, were too happily married to dream of such a thing. Actually, there is one cartoon from 1943 in which a tall, dark-haired woman who could be Morticia asks a bookstore clerk: "Do you have one in which a wife murders her husband in a very ingenious way?" As a rule, though, the domestic murderers in Addams's famous cartoons were seemingly normal people: the plainly HENPECKED HUSBAND who parks his car and its wife-bearing trailer at the edge of a cliff and says, "Oh, darling, can you step out for a moment?"; the ultrarespectable OPERA-going society lady who emerges from a performance of *Salome* picturing her husband's head on a platter. My favorite example, though, of Addams's deceptively normal murderers is the brand-loyal wife who explains to the police:

. . . and then I disconnected the booster from the Electro-Snuggie blanket and put him in the deep-freeze. In the morning, I defrosted him and ran him through the Handi Home Slicer and then the Jiffy Burger Grind, and after that I fed him down the

Dispose-All. Then I washed my clothes in the Bendix, tidied up the kitchen, and went to see a movie.

It's notable how much spouse-killing humor there is in old sitcoms, since one purpose of those early-evening shows was helping married couples coexist by giving them something besides each other to look at. They can always read, of course, but they'd better stay away from murder mysteries, since—at least on sitcoms—those books have a way of convincing suggestible readers that their spouses are trying to kill them. Or of spooking the reader's spouse. That's what happens on "Dial S for Suspicion," the *Flintstones* episode in which Wilma's fondness of the mystery she's reading, and her sudden eagerness for Fred to get life insurance, convince him that she's about to murder him.

Is that really one of the fundamental comic misunderstandings—the delusion that your spouse is trying to kill you? *I Love Lucy*—an encyclopedia of comedic misunderstandings—had been airing for less than a month before it got around to a spouse-killing episode, "Lucy Thinks Ricky Is Trying to Murder Her." Lucy is already jumpy from reading

The Mockingbird Murder Mystery when she overhears and misunderstands a phone conversation, then finds what proves to be a fake gun in Ricky's desk. She takes to carrying a garbage can lid as a shield, but then becomes convinced that Ricky has poisoned her orange juice, and heads to his club with that gun to shoot him.

Juice also comes under suspicion in "Suspense," the *Honeymooners* episode in which Ralph

Fig. 149 Charles Adams, 1956

becomes convinced—after overhearing Alice and Trixie rehearsing a play about a murderous wife—that Alice plans to kill him. When he then sees her put a vitamin pill in his breakfast juice, Ralph accuses her of trying to poison her, then panics when she drinks the juice herself, as if she were that desperate to escape her marriage one way or another.

More often than not, the suspicion has its origin in a book or play or movie involving spouse-killing—in a character's sudden and endearingly dumb conviction that life is imitating art, or that he or she is involved in the kind of story where people commit murder. Sitcom characters, of course, never do kill their spouses, though sometimes the producers will, when the actor quits the show while it's still going strong. The first such casualty in television history was Margaret, the wife on *The Danny Thomas Show*, who was killed off in 1956 when the actress who played her (Jean Hagen) left the show.

It's a truism that our culture is more comfortable with violence than with sex; in the days when that was even truer—when TV could show a double homicide but not a double bed—spouse-killing was sometimes easier to joke about than infidelity. So when I tell you that "So You Don't Trust Your Wife" is a short comic film from 1955, you won't be surprised to hear that the issue in question is not whether the wife of Joe McDoakes is sleeping with another man, but whether she is planning to murder her suggestible mate, who for no good reason begins to suspect the worst when she innocently asks him if his insurance policy is paid up. He doesn't even want to let her rub his neck.

Squirting

THE FIRST PUBLIC screening of motion pictures was held in 1895 by Louis Lumière, who showed ten very short films directed by him. Most of these were microdocumentaries, but there was also a comic anecdote entitled "L'arroseur arrosé" ("The Sprinkler Sprinkled"). This forty-four-second movie, which has been called the first comic film, involves a middle-aged man and an adolescent boy. The man is watering a lawn when the youth steps on his hose, interrupt-

Fig. 150

ing the flow of water and causing the man to peer into the nozzle with a stupidity that foretells the whole future of film comedy. Then the boy removes his foot from the hose, which squirts the man in the face.

If you think the symbolism Freud saw everywhere was just a figment of his filthy imagination, a good look at the humor of his era—the late nineteenth and early twentieth centuries—will convince you that he wasn't the only one with a dirty mind. We all have dirty minds, in the sense of thinking a lot about sex; and when a culture forbids people to discuss or represent sex directly, they don't think about it any less. They just discuss and represent it *in*directly. There's no other way to account for the bewildering profusion, in old humor, of jokes about squirting and soaking.

Garden hoses, seltzer bottles, squirting flowers, dunking stools, water balloons, plumbing disasters, puddles, brimming buckets above doorways—an intelligent being from a planet with humor but not water might conclude from earthling humor that there is something uniquely funny about that substance. In Snoopy's first appearance, in the third-ever *Peanuts* strip (October 5, 1950), he gets drenched as he walks below Patty's window with a flower affixed to his head just as she is watering the flowers in her window box. Chekhov famously wrote that if you show a gun above a mantelpiece in Act 1, the gun has to go off in Act 3. And it's the same with squirt guns, hoses, and the like: if you show one in the first scene of a slapstick comedy, or the first panel of a comic strip, it has to soak somebody by the last.

If we grant that a train going into a tunnel can stand for intercourse, and a burst of fireworks for orgasm, we should at least be willing to entertain the proposition that the water squirting at people in a zillion comic strips, cartoons, and live-action comedies—and in real life from a zillion trick flowers and other squirting novelties—sometimes stands for urine or semen. Every baby pisses on its parents, and the urchins who squirt grownups in old comics are asking to return to that beatific state when such deeds were allowed because all was allowed. As for semen, men have been ejaculating in other people's faces as long as oral sex has been around, and it's safe to say that in any era where they couldn't joke openly about such things, humorists have joked about them covertly.

Mad's maddest artist, Don Martin, was especially fond of squirting flowers, and used them in many of his *Mad* cartoons. In one, a doctor attending to the owner of Irving's Trick and Novelty Store is squirted in the face—with a "SHKLITZA"—by a vase of flowers at the convalescent's bedside. In another, a man buys a squirting flower from Hal's Novelty Shop and then tries it on a pedestrian, but the rubber bulb bursts messily in his pocket with a "SKLOOSH . . . glik glik glik glik." (Anyone who doubts that the real gag with squirting flowers is about piss should reflect that the water is kept in a rubber bladder in the prankster's pocket, close enough to his penis that if the bladder bursts, it looks like he's wet himself.) In another, two men are walking on a beach when one is squirted in the eye with a "SHKLIKSA!" by something buried in the sand that turns out to be a clam. They stroll on, with the unique double-jointed gait of all Don Martin characters, until the other man gets squirted with a "SHKLIZICH!" by what proves to be a buried squirting flower. Nor should we forget the one where an Old Testament practical joker comes up to Moses and says, "Hey . . . get a load of my new boutonniere." When the joker tries to squirt him, Moses parts the waters with a "GASH-KLITZ."

Flowers are the classic squirting novelty, but by no means the only one. The 1929 Johnson Smith catalog also offered a Squirt Pencil ("It is a good joke to play upon the inquisitive person who insists on looking to see what you are writing"), a Squirt Cigar Case, a Squirt Cigar Cutter, a Squirt Pipe, a Squirt Electric Button (which looks like a doorbell but squirts the caller rash enough to push it), a Squirt Pocket Mirror ("If charged with scent instead of water it will probably prove less objectionable to the ladies"), a Squirt Rubber Heart (imprinted with the words "Wiedersteht jedem Eindruck"—a suspicious number of laff-getters originated in Germany), a Squirt Rubber Snake, and a Squirt Mouse. By the 1940s, the company had added several new squirting gags, and anyone who doubts that the real joke has do with bodily fluids should consider the ad, in the 1942 catalog, for the Squirt Chocolate Bar: "'Say, sweetie, have a piece of chocolate!' This is the one all the girls 'bite' on. The chocolate bar is temptingly peeled open. As they reach for a piece, give the bar a gentle squeeze, and out shoots a stream of water."

Stuffed Shirts

There are people who think that everything one does
with a straight face is sensible.
—GEORG C. LICHTENBERG

There's nothing that starts the adrenaline of a humorist
going faster than a humorless man in power.
—WILLIAM ZINSSER

THE SIMPLEST DEFINITION of "stuffed shirt" might be "the sort of dignitaries made indignant by the Marx Brothers' antics": diplomats, mayors, COLLEGE PROFESSORS, judges, cabinet ministers, OPERA managers, and the like. (Their favorite victim was Margaret Dumont, but when the shirt in question is stuffed with a heaving BOSOM, its wearer is not a stuffed shirt but a DOWAGER.) The essence of Marx Brothers humor is deflating the pompous, shocking the prudish, outraging the respectable, toppling anyone who stands on ceremony, and generally refusing to play the game by other people's rules, thereby revealing the absurdity and artificiality that govern so much of civilized life.

Their movies are famous for nonsensical Alice-in-Wonderland dialogue (Groucho hands Chico a pen to sign the contract they've just negotiated; when Chico admits he can't write, Groucho consoles him: "That's all right—there's no ink in the pen"), but a penchant for funny illogic isn't the only things the Brothers share with Lewis Carroll. Each of the *Alice* books comprises a series of encounters with all kinds of touchy and humorless grownups, whom Alice constantly and helplessly antagonizes just by being herself, and by not understanding the rules of the grownup world. Like the Marx Brothers, she creates chaos wherever she goes, whether by tactlessly telling birds and mice about her lovably carnivorous pet cat, or by growing uncontrollably during a courtroom trial. Unlike the Marx Brothers, Alice doesn't *try* to make mischief, but she appeals to the same mischief-loving tendency in the audience—to the child's sense, which some of us never outgrow, that the rules and rituals of the adult world are absurdly arbitrary.

Those rules and rituals are best embodied by characters who take them, and take themselves, extremely seriously. The Marx Brothers didn't just have it in for stuffed shirts; they *needed* them, lest we come to take the absurdity for granted, as long as it lasts (as we do with musicals, where supposedly real people keep lapsing into song and dance), and cease to measure its distance from real life. The humor is in the incongruity between the Brothers' anarchy and the norms the other characters embody.

Suggestion Boxes

I N A TWO-PANEL cartoon from the *Saturday Evening Post* (later reprinted in a 1954 collection of captionless cartoons called *Too Funny for Words*), an office employee is squirted in the face by an over-energetic water fountain, and reacts by angrily directing its stream into a nearby suggestion box. In another cartoon from the same magazine and era, an employee stands at the suggestion box writing a comically wordy suggestion on a sheet of paper so long it curls into a scroll on the floor. Behind him, in the doorway of an office labeled PRES., the scowling boss tells a subordinate, "Keep an eye on that new man—he looks like a troublemaker." In another cartoon from the 1950s, a scowling boss glowers down so menacingly from a painting hanging above the box that an employee stands before it shaking, afraid to submit his suggestion after all.

Like coffee breaks, suggestion boxes were largely a 1940s development, a consequence of the shortage of civilian manpower during World War II: suddenly there were more jobs than workers, and employers felt the need for cheap and largely symbolic means of increasing worker satisfaction. Fittingly, *The Adventures of Ozzie and Harriet*—one of the quintessential expressions of the Eisenhower era—devoted a whole episode to the suggestion box. Ozzie decides the family needs one, builds it in his basement workshop (naturally hitting his finger with a hammer), and places the finished box in the front hall, where family members can deposit their suggestions anonymously. There follows a montage in which we see four different hands each dropping a suggestion apiece through the slot. "Sounds pretty dangerous to me," says their neighbor Thorny, when Ozzie shows him the box. "You could get some pretty strong stuff in there." Ozzie of course dismisses Thorny's warning, reasoning that "any intelligent person should be willing to accept friendly criticism from other members of his family." It seems clear where we're headed—Ozzie blows his top when someone ventures to criticize *him* via an anonymous suggestion—and we do get there eventually, but not without an interesting detour: the first day, the "suggestions" are all shameless flattery of Ozzie. Thorny, true to his name, suggests that the other Nelsons are too afraid of the head of the household to say what they really think of him.

Unlike many gag-cartoon clichés—miniature casks around the necks of St. Bernards, Boy Scouts helping old ladies cross the street—suggestions boxes are something you also see in real life, though to me they look cartoony even there. It's easy to see why cartoonists find them irresistible: a suggestion box is a special kind of wastebasket for a special kind of trash—ideas and requests from employees too lazy or fearful to propose them in person. There's something farcical, in corporate settings, about the very idea of *suggestions*, about the idealized model of decision-making it implies, in which rational adults, ennobled by mutual respect and a common quest for excellence, swap ideas until a good one emerges, to be embraced by all. Only in those rare cases where no one has power over anybody else are true suggestions possible; most so-called suggestions are really pleas or plaints. Or, when they issue from the boss, veiled commands.

Suicide

> *In New York, people were killing themselves jumping out of*
> *skyscrapers after the stock market crash. In Jackson, Michigan,*
> *where the buildings were much shorter, people were jumping out of*
> *windows and spraining their ankles.*
> —JACK PAAR, 1961

EIGHTY YEARS AGO, Mickey Mouse had his own comic strip, ostensibly the work of Walt Disney himself. If the Disney corporation ever authorizes a reprint of the strip, it's safe to say they'll cut the sequence from October 1930 in which Mickey, despondent after being dumped by Minnie, attempts suicide several days in a row—by gas, by gun, by jumping off a bridge. We tend to think of 1930s humor as pretty tame compared to what comedians get away with today, but it wasn't always tame. We're just more aware of other eras' taboos than of our own, and when something old does shock us by reminding us of our own taboos, we condemn it without ceasing for an instant to pride ourselves on our unshockability.

Suicide gags used to be common on the funnies page, especially in rough-and-tumble strips like *Mutt and Jeff*, which ended one 1919 episode with the cartoonist himself attempting suicide by gas. Snuffy Smith's wife, Loweezy, attempted suicide in 1935—tying a big rock around her neck and diving into a pond—when she thought Snuffy was dead. "Life 'thout Snuffy wud be naught but sorrow 'n' trouble," she says as she leaps. "Farewell, cruel worl'." Li'l Abner contemplated suicide in 1937 when forced into a brief marriage with the repulsive Widow Grubbs, and got as far as the brink of Suicide Cliff before stopping himself. It was, incidentally, due to a long-standing feud with Al Capp, *Li'l Abner*'s creator, that Ham Fisher, creator of *Joe Palooka*, killed himself in 1955. Other cartoonists who have killed themselves include Walt McDougall, Wally Wood, Jack Cole (*Plastic Man*), and C. D. Small (*Salesman Sam*).

One reason comic suicide attempts so often fail is that, in general, failure is funnier than success. The botched attempt is always good for a laugh, especially when a character fails repeatedly due to the same chronic bad luck or ineptitude that has led to the attempts. In "The Wrong Mr. Fox," a short film released in 1917 by Klever Komedies, an unemployed actor in a depressing BOARDINGHOUSE tries to end it all by uncoupling the metered gas line from the camp stove in his rented room and sticking it in his mouth ("not realizing the high price of gas," according to the intertitle). Just in the nick of time, his landlady interrupts with good news from his agent; he shuts off the gas but spends the next scene or two accidentally breathing fire.

In "Haunted Spooks" (1920), Harold Lloyd plays a young man who tries repeatedly to kill himself after losing his girl to a more assertive rival. First he tries to blow his brains out with a pistol he finds on the sidewalk, but when, after considerable balking and wincing, he finally pulls the trigger, he's rewarded with a squirt of water in the side of the head. Next he stands in the path of an oncoming trolley, but he happens to stand near a switch point, and the trolley changes tracks and rushes past without even noticing him. Spotting a footbridge over a river, he ties a big rock around his neck, bids the cruel world farewell, and jumps—into water so shallow it barely wets his ankles. Finding a deeper spot, he prepares to jump off the bridge again but is interrupted first by a man wanting a light, then by a man asking the time. After each interruption, the stranger goes on his way and lets Harold get back to his suicide attempt, but when he finally jumps again, he lands in a canoe. And so on.

But sometimes the attempt succeeded. In old humor, people kill themselves in circumstances where nowadays they'd simply be shown screaming in exasperation. In Jack Benny's yearly Christmas-shopping sketch, the stinginess and wishy-washiness of Benny's radio persona finally drives the salesman to suicide, or sometimes attempted suicide. (One such at-

Fig. 151 Mutt and Jeff enter a suicide pact, 1910.

tempt—a gunshot—is followed by: "Look what you done! You made me so nervous, I missed!") Like the much more recent cinematic cliché of showing someone puking in response to bad news, attempted suicide is a lurid but lazy way of manifesting a character's inner state, something that movies have never been especially good at.

Suicide was a tempting subject for humorists who sought to be a little shocking. Think of "Résumé" (1925), Dorothy Parker's famous little rhyming list of reasons for living:

> *Razors pain you;*
> *Rivers are damp;*
> *Acids stain you;*
> *And drugs cause cramp.*
> *Guns aren't lawful;*
> *Nooses give;*
> *Gas smells awful;*
> *You might as well live.*

Around the same time, Edna St. Vincent Millay wrote a strikingly similar poem:

> *I know a hundred ways to die.*
> *I've often thought I'd try one:*
> *Lie down beneath a motor truck*
> *Some day when standing by one.*
> *Or throw myself from off a bridge—*
> *Except such things must be*
> *So hard upon the scavengers*
> *And men that clean the sea.*
> *I know some poison I could drink.*
> *I've often thought I'd taste it.*
> *But mother bought it for the sink,*
> *And drinking it would waste it.*

Parker's reasons for staying alive are selfish, Millay's altruistic. Both could be accused of trivializing a serious subject—like Nietzsche when he jokes,

"The thought of suicide is a great consolation; it
helped me through many bad nights." What ma
the poems memorable is that they do contain a gra
of truth: many people give reasons equally silly.
The fact is that most of us are ingrates and malcontents (as Parker and Millay both famously
were) who tend to take for granted the things
that make our lives worthwhile—and in any
case, we are so hardwired for survival that our
stated reasons for living are usually rationaliza-

Fig. 152

tions. It would be almost as silly to list reasons for breathing. That's why
even happy people find it hard to say why they remain alive. As for the
rest of us, when our ringing denunciations of life are briefly embarrassed
by the fact that, after all, we do choose to go on living, we're more likely
to joke about the logistics of suicide than to stop and count our blessings.

Depending on your theory of humor, you might expect the stock of
those jokes to have surged after the Great Crash of 1929 and the only real
suicide epidemic our country has had. *The American Chronicle* cites this as
a popular joke from 1930 (the year of Mickey Mouse's suicide attempts):
"Have you heard the one about the two men who jumped hand in hand
because they had a joint account?" Likewise, the Black Thursday suicides
clearly inspired a fake ad for the Suicide Institute that appeared in 1931
in a humor magazine called *Ballyhoo* (a strikingly modern precursor of
Mad): "After you've read the Market Reports . . . discovered you have Pink
Toothbrush, B.O., Halitosis, Lordosis, Athlete's Foot . . . then is the time
you want to jump out of a forty-story window." The Institute makes things
like rubber nooses, mini-parachutes, and guns with twisted barrels for
people who feel obliged to give suicide a try but want to make sure they're
unsuccessful. The Wall Street crash and the suicides it triggered were still a
recent memory, but evidently it wasn't too soon to joke about them.

Overall, though, the threadbare 1930s saw *less* gallows humor than the
Roaring Twenties, though that doesn't prove much about the uses of ad-
versity. In general, the '20s were a better decade for humor. And by 1929,
suicide humor was already in decline. The *first* decade of the twentieth century was a heyday for jokes about small children taking their lives—as in

the postcard (illustrated by Grace Drayton, creator of the Campbell's Kids) showing a ringletted toddler walking away with her arm around a little boy, while a second, sad-eyed little boy—the odd boy out—holds a bottle of CASTOR OIL and says, "Fickle woman farewell, me for the fatal dose."

Those were the days. Suicide humor has been on the wane ever since, though with plenty of holdouts and throwbacks of the sort that make it hard to chart any long-term trend in American humor. In a 1944 *Amos 'n' Andy* episode, Amos seeks to avoid a breach-of-promise suit by faking suicide; his note is signed by two witnesses. In the 1965 film of Evelyn Waugh's novel *The Loved One*—a satire of Hollywood and of the modern funeral industry—aspiring mortician Aimee Thanatogenos takes her life by embalming herself. On the funnies page, Al Capp continued throughout his career to joke savagely about suicide. He especially liked to show greedy businessmen swan-diving out of corner offices or throwing themselves in front of trains after some new phenomenon like the Kigmies or the Shmoos created a utopian abundance of whatever the businessmen had been selling. And the death of Fearless Fosdick—star of the strip-within-a-strip whereby Capp parodied *Dick Tracy*—touched off a nationwide suicide epidemic in the world of *Li'l Abner*. ("Oh mother, please don't take poison!!" "I have nothing to live for but my happy home, my children, and my loving husband, now that Fosdick is g-gone!!")

Not surprisingly, Charles Addams drew a lot of cartoons on the subject, usually involving hanging. (Nooses are funnier than guns or razor blades because they have no *other* purpose.) In one, a desolate swami hangs himself by tying a noose around his neck and throwing the other end of the rope up into the air. In another, we see, through the frosted glass pane of an office door (marked PRIVATE), the silhouette of a hanging businessman. "I know," says his SECRETARY to a coworker without ceasing her typing, "but I don't go in unless he buzzes." A third cartoon shows a group of Boy Scouts tying knots, and one boy is tying a noose—maybe the same boy who, in yet another cartoon, enters his father's room just as the father is about to hang himself from the chandelier, and says "Hey, Pop, that's not a hangman's knot."

Animated cartoons afforded another refuge for suicide jokes, after the Zeitgeist decided their Zeit was past. In "Show Biz Bugs," after repeatedly failing by any other means to upstage Bugs Bunny at the Bijou, where they share the stage, Daffy finally resorts to "the act I've held back for a special occasion," ingesting a can of gasoline, a bottle of nitroglycerine, a powder horn of gunpowder, a bottle of uranium-238, and then a lit match—literally killing himself for applause. Sylvester the cat made his debut in "Life with Feathers," a 1945 cartoon that pitted him not against Tweety Bird but against a lovelorn lovebird bent on suicide by cat. At one point, the bird sandwiches itself between two slices of bread in an effort to get Sylvester to eat him.

Sweet Adeline

> *And when lovely woman stoops to folly,*
> *She does not invariably come in at four* A.M.
> *Singing Sweet Adeline.*
> —PHYLLIS MCGINLEY

THIS IS THE song that chummy DRUNKS and drunken ALLEY CATS are always singing. If there ever was a "barbershop" craze like the one envisioned in a *Simpsons* episode, "Sweet Adeline" (1903) was its "Stairway to Heaven." As with the Zeppelin song, the lyrics aren't the point:

> *Sweet Adeline,*
> *My Adeline,*
> *At night, dear heart,*
> *For you I pine;*
> *In all my dreams,*
> *Your fair face beams.*
> *You're the flower of my heart,*
> *Sweet Adeline.*

As poetry, it makes "Sweet Jane" look like Keats, and "Sweet Georgia Brown" like "Il Penseroso," but it lends itself to four-part harmony, and to the sort of lugubrious groaning that feels so agreeable to the male

Fig. 153

larynx when relaxed by alcohol. (To quote a quip from *Reader's Digest*'s *Book of Fun and Laughter*, "'Sweet Adeline' still sounds best when the basses are loaded.") There are those who insist that the otherwise-mute Harpo joined his brothers in harmonizing to "Sweet Adeline" at the beginning of *Monkey Business*, though it's hard to say for sure, since the four stowaways are hiding in BARRELS.

"All the boys are singing love songs, / They forgot 'Sweet Adeline,'" laments a 1929 song called "Wedding Bells Are Breaking Up That Old Gang of Mine," whose author, Irving Kahal, surely knew that "Sweet Adeline" is itself a love song. By 1929, though, it was so strongly associated with the male bonding of the boys' night out that it would have seemed strange to sing it to a woman, even one named Adeline.

There are other old songs long associated with comedy drunks, such as "The Near Future," written by Irving Berlin in 1919, on the eve of Prohibition, and imagining what life will be like once alcohol is banned. The song is sometimes known as "How Dry I Am" for its famous lines, "How dry I am, how dry I am / It's plain to see just why I am"—which is as much of the song as you ever hear in old cartoons. More recently, Judy Garland made the mistake in *A Star Is Born* (1954) of acceding to a drunk's persistent requests for "My Melancholy Baby," helping to make it the standard song for drunken hecklers to demand in 1960s sitcoms—the "Free Bird" of its era.

T t

Thumbtacks

*It's a sure sign somebody has been thinking about you
when you find a tack on your chair.*
—OLD PROVERB

ON THE CONTINUUM of slapstick violence, poking someone
in the RUMP with a thumbtack is at the opposite end of the
spectrum from dropping a grand PIANO on his head. With
the thumbtack, part of the humor is the incongruity between the tiny
cause and the spectacular effect. Though HEAD INJURIES are more popular with humorists than tail injuries, and though neither part is especially
sensitive to pain, a blow with a blunt instrument usually hurts less than a
jab with a sharp one. A ROLLING PIN to the head is more likely to knock
you out, but a pushpin in the rump will get a better yelp. As for the noise
the pin itself makes, Basil Wolverton asserts, in his treatise on "Acoustics
in the Comics" (1948), that the sound of a man sitting on a short tack is
"SQUINCH!" and that of a man sitting on a long tack is "SQUONCH!"

In a famous limerick, getting poked in the ass is seen as a paradigm
for physical pain—indeed for reality itself, if we use Philip K. Dick's
handy definition of reality as "that which, when you stop believing in it,
doesn't go away":

> *There was a faith healer from Deal*
> *Who said, "Although pain isn't real,*
> *When I sit on a pin*
> *And it ruptures my skin,*
> *I dislike what I fancy I feel."*

That's a funny limerick. Is it, then, an exception to the rule that the only funny limericks are dirty? Not quite. In the sentence preceding the poem, I considered rewording the bit about "getting poked in the ass" to eliminate the grotesque association with anal rape, but that association, however unconscious, is one reason people put thumbtacks on chairs in the first place.

It's an old, old joke. In a silent comedy called "Mr. Flip" (1909), a pair of seamstresses harassed by an obnoxious grabby ladies' man retaliate by sticking the pointy end of a pair of sewing scissors up through the woven cane seat of a chair, then shoving the guy into the chair: in effect, the women punish his quasi-rapist behavior by sodomizing him.

Is there a connection between sitting on a flagpole and sitting on a thumbtack? Flagpoles aren't as pointy—the sittable kind are usually crowned by a spherical finial—but they're certainly more phallic. In both cases, as in all cases where someone sits on something rigid, upright, and rod-shaped, whether a thumbtack or the seat post on a bike, part of the humor is the suggestion of anal penetration.

Tightwads

> *Any man who would walk five miles*
> *through the snow, barefoot, just to return a library book*
> *so he could save three cents—that's my kind of guy.*
> —JACK BENNY ON ABRAHAM LINCOLN

JACK BENNY CALLED his comic persona "a composite of every human weakness," but the foible he worked hardest was stinginess. His most famous joke—said to have provoked the longest laugh in radio history—was a skit in which Jack was accosted by a mugger who demanded, "Your money or your life!" The ensuing pause was enough in itself to get a big laugh from the studio audience, but an even bigger one came when the mugger repeated his demand, causing Jack to grumble, "I'm thinking it over!"

Back in those days, there was a lot more humor at the expense of the stingy. Humorists identified so many different kinds of tightwads that a whole taxonomy evolved: the Bargain Hunter; the Stingy Boss; the Cheapskate Suitor (who dates girls born on February 29, so he only has to buy them birthday presents every four years); the Pennywise Do-It-Yourselfer (always trying, with disastrous results, to save the cost of a PLUMBER); the Miserly Husband; the Undertipper. In 1930s bellboy slang, a *bathroom charlie* was a guest who ducked into the bathroom to avoid tipping.

One favorite target was the Check Fumbler, who liked eating out with friends but always managed not to notice when the check arrived. An old vinegar valentine elaborates: "Scotch is yours, and Scotch is right: / You're the original Sandy MacTight. / Some day you're going to sprain your neck / In trying not to see the check." The Cheapskate License issued by Topps in 1964—one of a series of Nutty Awards trading cards—entitles the bearer to keep his fingernails trimmed extra-short so he's unable to pick up the check.

In the second decade of the twentieth century, E. W. Gale created *Mr. Wad*, a comic strip about a cheapskate named Titus Wad. In one episode, Titus gives a single penny to a woman soliciting for charity, explaining, "I'm for helpin' unfortunate cusses. I always give till it hurts." In another, he refuses to buy a penny pencil from a blind beggar; as he explains to his exasperated cousin, "I didn't have anything smaller'n a nickel and I didn't want to break it—you know how durned fast a five goes after you break it." In another, we learn that Titus stops his watch every night at bedtime—and resets it every morning—to save on wear and tear to the works of a timepiece that set him back a full dollar.

Humorists like coming up with funny ways to evoke the extent of a tightwad's miserdom—no other stock character inspired so many flights of descriptive fancy. Here's a description of the resident tightwad from the inaugural let's-meet-the-characters installment of a short-lived comic strip called *Good-Time Guy* (born and died in 1927): "He's tighter than a sleeve garter, and he squeezes nickels until he bends the buffalo's horns."

Tightwads are often portrayed as elderly, like Ebenezer Scrooge, or Mr. Potter in *It's a Wonderful Life*. Do misers really grow more miserly in old age, or is it just that their penny-pinching is more poignant, and more funny, the more secure they grow financially, and the closer they get to death? They do tend to forget that they can't take it with them. An old insult: "If he drank poison, he'd try to get the deposit back on the bottle before passing away."

Stinginess has inspired some great slang. A *skinflint* is a person with a hide, and heart, as hard as quartz. A wad is a roll of paper money, so a *tightwad* is one from which it's hard to extract a single dollar. As for *cheapskate*, I like to picture someone roller-skating on one foot to save wear and tear on his skates, but in this case *skate* means a contemptible person; it's an alteration of *skite* (as in *blatherskite*) and is etymologically related to *shit*. *Penny-pincher* and *nickel-nurser* need no explanation, though you wonder why the latter is so much less common. Just because the higher denomination makes frugality five times more excusable?

It's puzzling because nickels are funnier than pennies. Or at least funnier-looking. What with its misleading bulkiness, the drabness of its alloy, and the artlessly close cropping of poor Jefferson's glanslike profile, the nickel is the ugliest American coin. "Floor Nickel" is the official name of S. S. Adams novelty #A1700, a real nickel with a nail soldered to its obverse so it can be pounded into the floor. The antiquity of the gag is attested by the low denomination of the coin, harking back to a time when a nickel was worth bending over to pick up. Adams also sells a SQUIRTING nickel, with a flexible metal diaphragm welded to one side: "A real nickel squirts a fine stream of water at anyone examining it closely." (Again the archaic note: has anyone bothered "examining" a nickel since the days when Shoeshine Boy—Underdog's humble alter ego—made a point of biting them to test for counterfeits?) But if you're a nickel-nurser, a fine stream of water is not the worst you have to fear from humorists.

Tin Cans

down with the human soul
and anything else uncanned
for everyone carries canopeners
in Ever-Ever Land
—E. E. CUMMINGS

I told her I wanted to be surprised for dinner,
so she soaked the labels off the cans.
—*BRAUDE'S TREASURY OF WIT AND HUMOR* (1964)

ONE REASON TIN cans are funny is that canned food is bad, and a heavy reliance on it implies bad taste as well as poverty. (In 1955, Altman's department store in New York City sold can openers with mink-covered handles.) Mid-century humorists often used canned food as a symbol of everything wrong with modernity. In the movie *Life Begins at Forty* (1935), Will Rogers unloads a bag of groceries and marvels at all the cans, observing that our country's emblem should not be the bald eagle but the can opener. For a while there, canned food was even seen as an assault on family values, part of the conspiracy to let women leave the kitchen where they belonged. A "tin can housewife" was one who never learned to cook, only to open cans and heat their contents. This view of canned food was actually encouraged by some of its producers, as in the relatively recent Campbell's Soup commercials in which liberated housewives sang "Give me the Campbell's life."

Tin cans were patented in 1810 and have been mass-produced since 1813. They were never made entirely of tin (any more than nickels ever were of nickel), but rather of steel plated with tin to increase resistance to corrosion. The first utensil designed specifically to open cans was patented in 1858 and used by the U.S. military in the Civil War. Unlike bottles, tin cans weren't reusable. Unlike some more recent forms of packaging, they didn't last forever, but they lasted long enough, and were cranked out fast enough, for empties quickly to become a blight on the landscape, especially in neglected spots like vacant lots and back alleys. (One of H. C.

Tin Can Housewife.
CAN you broil a steak for two?
CAN you make a chicken stew?
CAN you cook with your two hands?
or do your meals ALL come from CAN ?

Fig. 154

Earwicker's many monikers in *Finnegans Wake* is "Heinz cans everywhere.") They appear in *Hogan's Alley* strips from the 1890s. Happy Hooligan was already wearing a tin can as a hat when his strip debuted in 1900. If we want to know what the world looked like before this first great plague of throwaway containers, we must turn to older media than comics, which have been littered with cans from the very start.

Old comics would be even more cluttered with tin cans if comic-strip goats didn't keep their numbers down, since that's almost all those goats are ever pictured eating. Empty cans contained traces of food and were common in the dumps and trash heaps where goats foraged. Cans are frequently coupled with goats in the elaborate improbable sequences of cause and effect for which Rube Goldberg's contraptions are famous.

Why do comic-strip cans always have their lids attached and raised like the lid of a toilet? Is it because, in the days before Saran Wrap and Tupperware, the semi-attached lid was the latest thing in reclosable packaging? That seems unlikely, unless we assume that hobos and homeowners alike were too prudent ever to eat more than half a can of pork and beans in one sitting. More likely, the lid stayed on for the sake of recognizability. Without its lid, a tin can could be anything, especially at comic-strip resolution. With its lid agape but still attached, a can could only be a can.

Like barrels, tin cans were an early form of mass-produced container that—though more biodegradable than glass or plastic—tended to stick around long after emptied of their contents. For several decades in the first half of the twentieth century, tin cans were *the* archetypal throwaway object. Even as late as 1960, empty cans were the main kind of garbage pictured in *Mad* magazine's proposal to shoot garbage into space.

This guide almost included an entry on Garbage and its loving depiction by comic artists of the early and mid-twentieth century. Cartoon garbage containers were shown brimming with eggshells, banana peels, apple cores, fish skeletons, and—especially—tin cans. We may surmise that our forefathers didn't recycle, though in Milt Gross's 1924 retelling of "Rumpelstiltskin," the title character is shown feeding tin cans and old shoes into the hopper of a miraculous machine that spits out gold ingots and jewelry.

Another funny thing about canned goods is that, without a special utensil, the food inside the can is almost as maddeningly inaccessible as money in a SAFE. In a 1912 essay on hair, Irvin S. Cobb refers in passing to "the standard joke about your wife's using your best razor to open a can of tomatoes with." Toward the end of *It's a Gift* (1934), Harold Bissonette (W. C. Fields) drives his family to California. They pause en route for a picnic of canned foods, but can't find the opener. Bissonette winds up opening a can with a hatchet, spattering himself and his family with tomatoes. A little later he locates the missing utensil the painful way, by sitting down on it and piercing his own can.

He wasn't the first traveler to misplace the can opener. In Jerome K. Jerome's *Three Men in a Boat* (1889), one of the most successful comic novels ever written, the boaters spend two pages trying to open a can of pineapple. After failing with a knife and then a pair of scissors, injuring themselves in the process, they debark from their boat and start bashing away at the can with the mast:

> We beat it out flat; we beat it back square; we battered it into every form known to geometry—but we could not make a hole in it. Then George went at it, and knocked it into a shape, so strange, so weird, so unearthly in its wild hideousness, that he got frightened and threw away the mast. Then we all three sat round it on the grass and looked at it. There was one great dent

across the top that had the appearance of a mocking grin, and it drove us furious, so that Harris rushed at the thing, and caught it up, and flung it far into the middle of the river, and as it sank we hurled our curses at it. . . .

Toothaches and Dentistry

Stranger, approach this grave with gravity:
Dr. Grey is filling his last cavity.
—OLD EPITAPH

Robin: Holy molars! Am I ever glad I take good care of my teeth!
Batman: True. You owe your life to dental hygiene.
—"THE RIDDLER'S FALSE NOTION," 1966

RUBE GOLDBERG'S TOOTH-PULLING device is as comically elaborate as his other inventions. Its ultimate purpose is to yank a string tied around a loose tooth, and it is set in motion by the owner of that tooth, but between his initial motion (wiggling a foot) and the final yank, there intervene a feather, a laughing bird, a cocktail shaker, a drunken squirrel in a squirrel cage, a hand-cranked phonograph, an insulting record, an insulted dwarf, a flame (when the dwarf gets hot under the collar), a fuse, a cannon, and a cannonball whose flight is what finally pulls the tooth, since the two are tied together.

The contraption looks as crazy as it sounds, and yet its complexity isn't as gratuitous as usual with Rube Goldberg inventions. Anyone is strong enough to yank out any tooth that's ready to be yanked, but to do so directly, you must override a real inhibition. We are not so far from our prehistory as hunters red in tooth and claw, and pulling your own tooth would feel almost as unnatural as severing one of your fingers. In the days before universal dentistry, much of the humor about toothaches involved Goldbergian efforts to yank teeth indirectly.

The standard method, at least in old cartoons (in real life, for all I know, it may have been as rare as strippers bursting out of giant cakes), is to tie one end of a string to the tooth and the other to a door-knob, and then have somebody yank the door open. If you can't find anyone willing to assist, just sit tight until somebody comes along and extracts your tooth unwittingly. A gag cartoon from around 1950 shows a little boy fishing glumly from a pier, a telltale kerchief wrapped around his head, and one end of the fishing line emerging from his mouth: he'll be fine as soon as he gets a bite.

Fig. 155 *Nize Baby*, 1926

There used to be a lot of humor about the incompetent dentists. The one in "I Can Hardly Wait" (1943), a Three Stooges short, admits to having been a butcher before he went to dental school. In "The Tooth Will Out" (1951), the Stooges themselves are dentists—such a terrifying prospect, even for a slapstick film, that the screenwriter sent them straight from their week in dental school to the Wild West, where they can inflict their mayhem on an outlaw rather than the solid citizens they tangle with in so many other shorts.

Like podiatrists and chiropractors, dentists are funny because they're not quite doctors. Or maybe they are—they're allowed to use the "Dr." title, after all—but no one thinks "dentist" when someone says "doctor." (In *Class*, a brilliant if mean-spirited take on class differences in America, Paul Fussell notes that dentists insist on referring to doctors as "physicians," while doctors themselves persist in saying "doctor.")

In any case, dentists are so funny that a company called OnDeck Home Entertainment has released a compilation of classic comic shorts called *Hollywood's Dental Comedy*. Among the painful pleasures on the disk are "Dental Follies" (Pinky Lee), "Laughing Gas" (Charlie Chap-

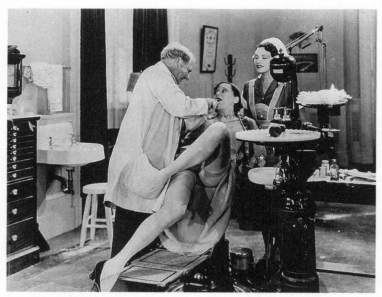

Fig. 156 *The Dentist*, 1932

lin), "Dentist the Menace" (Three Stooges), "Oh! My Achin' Tooth" (Abbott & Costello), "A Man's Teeth Are Not His Own" (an episode of *The Dick Van Dyke Show*), and best of all, a W. C. Fields short called "The Dentist" **(Fig. 156)**," still shocking after eighty years (in part because it appeared in 1932, or just before movies ceased for several decades to be shocking with the enactment in 1934 of the puritanical Motion Picture Production Code). Dr. Fields sees several patients, but the climax of the film is his X-rated interaction with a tall, horse-faced, ominously silent woman who first writhes orgasmically in the dentist chair while her tooth is drilled, then spreads her legs and wraps them around Fields, and her arms around his neck, as he stands facing her. When he backs away she comes with him, so that they appear to be copulating, especially because her skirt has ridden up so that her legs are bare.

Hollywood's Dental Comedy also features a clip from *Little Shop of*

Horrors (1960), in which a young Jack Nicholson plays a masochistic patient who just can't get enough of the evil Dr. Farb's sadistic drill. That, of course, is less a joke about dentistry than a joke about masochism—a condition that, when misrepresented as a simple love of pain rather than a sexual preference, looks comically absurd. But a sadistic dentist is the perfect foil for a comedy masochist, because no other profession (aside from that of medieval torturer) is so strongly associated in the public imagination with the infliction of pain.

Searching for representations of toothaches among old postcards, magazine ads, figurines, and other collectibles, I found more among the sentimental kitsch of the early and mid-twentieth century than among the comic art of that era. The best place to look for the swollen cheek, the pained expression, and the head-encircling bandage is in heartwarming illustrations and mantelpiece tchotchkes designed to appeal less to the sense of humor than to the sense of cuteness. Boy with Toothache, Hummel figurine #217, is a perennial bestseller.

The sense of humor and the sense of cuteness: in some ways they are mutually exclusive. (Think of Charlie Chaplin, and how in his films a surge of sentimentality almost always means at least a brownout in the humor.) What they have in common, the two tastes—or two ways of looking at the world and liking what you see—is sadism. Like the budding serial killers who torment neighbors' pets, the cornballs who buy prints of injured puppies have found a way of getting pleasure from another creature's pain, as surely as the evil dentist in *Little Shop of Horrors*.

The Three Stooges exemplified dental humor at its most sadistic. In "I Can Hardly Wait," Curly's toothache is keeping all three of them awake ("It feels like gremlins are gremling in it," he complains), and so, in what turns out to have been a dream sequence, Moe ties a fishing line to it and tries to reel it in, or reel it out, with a fishing rod, while Curly flops around like a hooked manatee. Moe also tries the doorknob trick, instructing Larry to open the door from the far side, but of course the door swings inward and bangs Curly on the head. When Moe then slams the door shut, the doorknob gives way instead of Curly's tooth. They finally give up and visit a dentist who, in a typically improbable chain of events, pulls Moe's tooth instead of Curly's.

But despite the importance of sadism to humor—to its production and to its consumption—the actual events in the dentist's office are *too* terrible, *too* painful, for most of us to want to contemplate even when somebody else is in the chair. That's why there's more humor about toothaches and fear of dentistry than there is about dentists. After all, as Robert Benchley points out in "The Tooth, the Whole Tooth, and Nothing But the Tooth" (1922) the dread is bad enough:

> As a matter of fact, the actual time and suffering in the chair is only a fraction of the gross expenditure connected with the affair. The preliminary period . . . is much the worse. This dates from the discovery of the wayward tooth and extends to the moment when the dentist places his foot on the automatic hoist which jacks you up into range. Giving gas for tooth-extraction is all very humane in its way, but the time for anaesthetics is when the patient first decides that he must go to the dentist. From then on, until the first excavation is started, should be shrouded in oblivion.

Traveling Salesmen

> *The traveling salesman stared at the farmer's daughter. "Tell me,"*
> *he said, "are you the Chesterfield or the Camel type?" "Meaning*
> *what?" she asked. "Do you satisfy—or do you walk a mile?"*
> —*JOKES FOR SALESMEN,* 1951

IN THE 1940s, the International Mutoscope Reel Company of New York produced a series of arcade cards (the size of postcards, but sold in penny arcades) entitled Your Husband and Family to Be. These were facetious fortune-telling cards (similar but not identical to the series discussed in the entry on SCOTSMEN), and one featured a photograph of a grinning, winking man with a cigar, smaller pictures of four homely children, and a grim prognostication:

Your Husband and Family To Be:---

Your Husband will be a TRAVELING SALESMAN. He will be expert in selling "his line" to "farmers daughter's". After each trip you will have to shake the hay out of his clothes and listen to the latest tall tales he has picked up. He will talk his way out of any situation and you will have a tough time keeping track of him. Between trips you will have 4 little "prospects" to look after.

(w

I. M. R. CO., N. Y.   MADE IN U. S. A.

Fig. 157 Traveling salesman

One reason for the popularity of arcade cards in the 1930s and '40s is that, since they weren't meant to be mailed, they could be racier than postcards, to say nothing of movies. According to H. L. Mencken, the Motion Picture Production Code forbade the very phrase "traveling salesman" in any context "where reference is made to a farmer's daughter." (Nevertheless, between 1910 and 1962, there were eight different films entitled *The Farmer's Daughter*, of which the most successful—it led to a sitcom—was a 1947 feature starring Loretta Young and Joseph Cotten. In 1973, a ninth *Farmer's Daughter* appeared, this one a hardcore pornographic film in which farmhands, farmers' daughters, and escaped convicts—one of them played by Spalding Gray—gang-rape one another.) Farmer's daughters are so inextricably linked with traveling salesmen as not to merit their own entry in this Laffopedia, though those salesmen are also fond of mountain gals. The groom in SHOTGUN WEDDINGS is usually a salesman.

Salesmanship is such a natural seduction metaphor that you wonder why DOOR-TO-DOOR SALESMEN didn't inspire as many prurient jokes as the traveling kind. After all, other men who knock on the door in the middle of the day while the husband is at work—the milkman, the iceman—have given rise to reams of dirty jokes. But the man urging housewives to buy vacuum cleaners or kitchen gadgets is almost as asexual a being, as far as humorists are concerned, as the Avon lady. Only traveling salesmen inspire much "adult" humor. They are more glamorous than door-to-door salesmen, in the same way that itinerant HOBOES are more glamorous than stationary BUMS.

And the jokes about them have been around so long that you wonder if the stereotype isn't self-perpetuating—if some men got into that line of work precisely because of how much action traveling salesmen get in dirty jokes. Certainly it seems like an ideal way of life for a certain kind of irresponsible scumbag: traveling from place to place, selling shoddy goods to hicks and getting their daughters in trouble, then moving on before either misdeed is discovered.

Though it seems like a hopelessly lowbrow cliché, the traveling salesman has appealed to some highbrow humorists. Before he turned into a giant insect, Gregor Samsa was a traveling salesman, and it isn't hard to imagine a prequel to *The Metamorphosis* starring Gregor in that capacity. It wouldn't take too many alterations, in fact, to turn K. in *The Castle* into a salesman—dealing, no doubt, in office supplies—rather than a land surveyor, and so to transform Kafka's last and funniest novel, already full of promiscuous sex, into one gigantic bawdy joke.

Sadly returning from the hypothetical to the actual, we can console ourselves with the knowledge that literature does offer at least one great work of fiction in the form of such a joke: Flannery O'Connor's story "Good Country People." O'Connor's salesman sells Bibles, but his name is Manley Pointer, so we know he's up to no good. The girl in the story isn't strictly speaking a farmer's daughter, but the daughter of a farmer's ex-wife who still owns the farm. Neither is she a girl, but a bookish, homely thirty-two-year-old virgin, with a wooden leg and a doctorate in philosophy. She leads Manley up to the hayloft, expecting him to behave like the salesmen in dirty stories, but he's even more depraved than that: instead of having sex with her, he runs off with her leg.

Trombones

I like people
With swagger in their step
Hot-air people, full
Of popcorn and pep
Four-flushing people
Whose gestures are free . . .
—STODDARD KING, "TROMBONE SOLO"

IN OUR GRANDPARENTS' somewhat less deafening era, trombones seemed even louder than they do now; often in old comedy they function as the ultimate sonic nuisance. In Disney's "Trombone Trouble" (1944), Donald Duck's neighbor Pegleg Pete makes so much noise with his trombone that it annoys not only Donald, whom everything annoys, but the gods themselves: Jupiter and Vulcan give Donald magic powers so he can silence Pete. In Tex Avery's "Sh-h-h-h-h!" (1955), trombones are the cause of the nervous-wreck protagonist's initial jitters and also his final explosion. When the Marx Brothers sabotage a performance of *Il Trovatore* in *A Night at the Opera*, Harpo—going for maximum disruption—plays a trombone instead of a harp.

If they were merely loud, though, trombones wouldn't be as funny. Humorists like the trombone because it is both funny-looking and funny-sounding. The sight gag is a dick joke, the slide thrusting in and out like Elvis Presley's pelvis. The *sound* gag is a fart joke. In 1943, when even vulgarity was devoted to the war effort, Spike Jones and his City Slickers recorded two versions of "Der Fuehrer's Face," a song about farting at Hitler: "When der fuehrer says we is de master race / We heil heil right in der fueher's face." In the original recording, a trombone blat was used to make the rude noise after every "heil." Executives at

Victor thought the trombone blats sounded *too* much like farts, so Jones recorded another take with a rubber razzer that he called a "birdaphone" and that nowadays is sold as a Fart Whistle. And that version passed muster: high-powered executives at a leading record label evidently decided that the Fart Whistle sounded less objectionably flatulent than the trombone.

In *Some Like it Hot*, one saucy member of the all-girl orchestra makes good use of the instrument's timbre, giving a flatulent blat on being told that the newest members, Josephine and Geraldine (Tony Curtis and Jack Lemmon in drag), were classically trained at the prestigious Sheboygan Conservatory. Naturally, the trombonist uses the slide—one of the movie's many dick jokes.

Tubas

The tuba is certainly the most intestinal of instruments,
the very lower bowel of music.
—PETER DE VRIES

A S A RULE, the bigger the musical instrument, the more laughter it provokes. Contrabassoons are hilarious. String basses are less so only because of their cool jazz associations. Within the brass section—and even with TROMBONES to contend with—the funniest instrument is the tuba. In "You're Darn Tootin'" (1928), Laurel and Hardy are cast as bumbling musicians—players of a clarinet and a French horn, respectively. Though the movie begins with a long, anarchic concert scene that leaves no doubt as to who plays what instrument, the original 1928 movie poster shows Hardy playing the clarinet and Laurel playing a *tuba*: either the illustrator couldn't be bothered to watch the twenty-minute film, or else he reasoned—correctly—that a tuba is funnier than a French horn, even in a silent movie, or on a silent poster.

Or in a magazine cartoon. In one that appeared in *Judge* around 1930, Dr. Seuss recommends the tuba to those New York bank presidents (and

Seuss claims to know more than twenty) who
want to eat lollipops as they walk to work but
are prevented by their need to keep up
appearances: "the size of the horn would
divert the public's gaze from the lollipop."

Tubas are funniest, of course, when
you can hear them. As the lowest-
pitched of all the brasses, and indeed
of all the wind instruments, they are
the most flatulent members of the
orchestra. In "The Tuba Tooter," an
animated cartoon from 1932—back
when Cartoonland was more animistic and surreal than it would ever be
again—a momentarily sentient tuba
gives its owner a "raspberry," that traditional nonverbal euphemism for a fart.

Fig. 158

Twenty-Three

QUICK: WHAT'S THE funniest number? I myself have always
favored 37, and I've always had the sense that most people
pick a two-digit number ending in 7—if not 37, then 17, perhaps, or 27. The number 7 itself is never named—its other connotations
command too much respect—but the fact that it's the only two-syllable
digit somehow makes it the funniest to end a larger number with.

Odd numbers—especially primes—are usually funnier, but it's hard
to generalize. According to Douglas Adams, the answer to the riddle
of the universe is "42," though the riddle itself remains a mystery. Adams's joke might not have aged as well if he'd opted for a number more
obviously zany. And as long as we're in the 40s, I should mention the
facetious proof devised in 1964 by Professor Donald Bentley of Pomona
College to demonstrate that all numbers are equal to 47. He could have

INSPECTOR BADGES

They are nickleplated, each bearing a different inscription as illustrated. Flash your Badge at an opportune moment and have lots of fun. They are well made, entirely of metal with safety clasp at the back for attaching to coat or vest. All one **price, 10 Cents Each.** Any 3 for 25 Cents, or 12 (all one kind or assorted) for 75 Cents Post-Paid.

No. 2000. Bathing Suit Inspector. 10c.

No. 2002. Fireman. 10c

No. 2003. Scout. 10c

No. 2005. Moonshine Inspector. 10c

No. 2006. Constable By Heck. 10c.

No. 2008. Indian Chief. 10c.

No. 2009. Captain. 10c.

No. 2001. Charleston Inspector. 10c.

No. 2004. Private Detective. 10c.

No. 2007. Police By Heck. 10c.

No. 2020. Deputy Sheriff. 10c

304   *JOHNSON SMITH & CO.,*   *RACINE, WIS.*

Fig. 159

chosen any number for his "proof"; presumably he picked the number he considered funniest.

Modern tastes in funny numbers go back at least to the 1960s. If we dig a bit deeper, though, we reach a period of several decades when the hands-down winner for funniest number was not 37, 42, or 47, but another two-digit number that no one today would name.

In the second decade of the last century, Frank King (who went on to create *Gasoline Alley*) had a full-page comics feature called "The Rectangle" that consisted of a bunch of unrelated gags. For several weeks in 1915, one of those gags was his Home Study Course on How to Be a Cartoonist. Each week he offered a different tip, like how best to draw ALLEY CATS (on a fence top, silhouetted by the moon) to how to indicate surprise (by means of what I call a HAT TAKE). Lesson #3: "Put the number 23 on all cop's stars, license tags, and hotel rooms, etc. It is the most humorous number we have."

That might sound like a lone cartoonist's whim, but the 1929 Johnson Smith catalog offers thirteen different phony badges ("Garter Inspector"; "Moonshine Inspector"; "Charleston Inspector") featuring the number 23 **(Fig. 159)**. Every time a numeral was needed to make the badge look more official, the numeral was 23—as customary in that context as the 555 prefix to phone numbers in the movies and TV shows of our own era.

In "R-E-M-O-R-S-E," a song by George Ade from 1903, the singer regrets all the cocktails he drank the night before: "Last night I hoisted twenty-three / Of those arrangements into me." The number seems to have become funny around 1900, though you do find earlier instances. In "The Bishop of Rum-ti-Foo," an 1867 poem by W. S. Gilbert, the title character is a colonial bishop whose congregation numbers "twenty-three in sum" (twenty-three headhunters whose diet consists of "scalps served up in rum").

Franz Liebkind, the Nazi playwright in *The Producers* (1968) whose play *Springtime for Hitler* makes such an unexpected hit, lives in apartment 23 of his building, though he prefers to hang out on the roof communing with the pigeons. Vitameatavegamin, the health tonic Lucy promotes in the fan-favorite *I Love Lucy* episode "Lucy Does a TV Commercial," not only contains vitamins, meat, vegetables, and minerals, but is also 23 percent alcohol. Since Lucy ingests only a spoonful of the tonic for each take, her rapidly advancing intoxication would be more plausible if the stuff contained, say, *83* percent alcohol instead, but 83 is not a funny number.

Twenty-three was still funny in 1961 when, in "Too Many Daves" (collected in *The Sneetches and Other Stories*), Dr. Seuss asked, "Did I ever tell you that Mrs. McCave / Had twenty-three sons and she named them all Dave?" It was still good for a laugh in 1966, when S. J. Perelman published *Chicken Inspector No. 23*. In some nooks and crannies of our culture it was still funny as late as 1975, to judge by this exchange from Donald's Barthelme's novel *The Dead Father*:

> How many of them are there?
> Near to a million, at the last census.
> How many of us are there?
> Twenty-three, Thomas said.

The first film to capitalize on the funniness of the number in its title was *Skidoo-23* (1902), an animated short produced and distributed by Thomas Edison himself. Many other comedies followed suit, including *Private Box 23* (1913), *In Taxi 23* (1914), *Apartment 23* (1919), *23 Skidoo* (1930), *23 1/2 Hours Leave* (1937), and *Pier 23* (1951).

The origin of the phrase "23 skidoo" is hotly disputed. According to one theory (see ANKLES for another), the catchphrase dates to 1899, when a dramatization of *A Tale of Two Cities* called *The Only Way* featured an old lady seated by the guillotine and counting the heads as they fell. Her only comment at the beheading of Sidney Carton was "twenty-three." Somehow as a result of that scene, "23" became telegraphese for "bad news"; and *skidoo*, a variant of *skedaddle*, was later added by cartoonist T. A. Dorgan (or TAD), who probably coined more slang than anyone else in the history of the English language. So the closest modern equivalent of "23 skidoo" might be Shaggy's favorite expression when he and Scooby-Doo encounter a ghost: "Zoinks! Let's get out of here."

Of course, that hardly explains why, for a while there, 23 became the funny number par excellence. As so often with the mysteries of our language, we must settle for a semi-explanation. Was that moment in *The Only Way* so much funnier than any other numerical reference in any play of its time? If Sidney Carton had been victim 10, or 25, would *that* have become the funniest number? It seems unlikely.

To those of us who seek to understand the relation between mirth and seriousness—to anyone who's noticed that the two are not mutually exclusive—it's interesting that the same numbers that strike humorists as especially funny tend to strike more earnest writers as especially trustworthy. If I claim to have caught 23 fish, or 27, you're more likely to believe me than if I claim 25. To modern ears, numbers ending in 7 are not only the funniest but the most honest-sounding and trustworthy: their very clumsiness assures us that we're not dealing with a smooth-talking dude out to hoodwink us. That may be why the author of *The Only Way* made poor Sidney Carton number 23 in the first place.

Li'l Abner's favorite comic-strip character, the incorruptible and bullet-ridden Fearless Fosdick, earns $22.50 a week, suspiciously close to $23—Capp must have wanted to emphasize the puniness of Fosdick's salary by not rounding it off to the nearest dollar. (As for *Catch-22*, Joseph Heller may have felt that as of 1961, 23 was *too* obviously funny a number—the numeric equivalent of names like Murgatroyd or Aloysius—and so went with 22 instead.)

In at least one episode, Fearless Fosdick loses his job and must get by on nothing, but it's hard enough to live on $22.50 per week. In "Fosdick and Hyde," we see a detailed breakdown of his weekly budget, which after various kickbacks, deductions, and time-payments, leaves him with exactly 42 cents to eat on for a week. Douglas Adams was by no means the first humorist to see the humor in the number 42; for much of the twentieth century, it ran second to 23 as the favorite funny number.

At one point it may have been the funnier. When Alice starts growing again in the great courtroom scene at the end of *Alice in Wonderland*, the King of Hearts invokes "Rule 42. *All persons more than a mile high to leave the court.*" Alice accuses him of inventing the rule on the spot, but he insists that it's "the oldest rule in the book." "Then it ought to be Number One," says quick-witted Alice. The speakeasy in *Horse Feathers* where college president Groucho goes to recruit ringers for his school's football team is located at 42 Elm Street, and we see a lot of that address because it takes a while for Groucho to bluff his way past the doorkeeper. In a cartoon dating from right around the time of the Great Crash, Dr. Seuss claimed that "in New York, where chaps are forever falling off of high buildings," doctors specialize according to the number of stories fallen. "The doctor above, for example, being an expert in mere forty-two-story falls, is not qualified to take the case of the poor fellow who has just plunged down forty-three," reads the caption below an illustration of a top-hatted man with an "M.D." bag gazing upward and counting "41—42—43—Oh pshaw" as the patient lands at his feet.

S. J. Perelman, in a 1963 *Paris Review* interview, managed to work in two funny numbers in a single answer:

> Q: How many drafts of a story do you do?
> A: Thirty-seven. I once tried doing thirty-three, but something was lacking, a certain—how shall I say?—*je ne sais quoi*. On another occasion, I tried forty-two versions but the final effect was too lapidary.

That Perelman said "thirty-three" instead of "twenty-three" doesn't mean he'd ceased to find that famous number funny, just that it wasn't funny enough to merit sacrificing the larger joke of his answer, that there are predictable differences between a story revised 37 times and one revised a few times more or less.

Uu·Vv·Ww

Ugliness

> *My wife was at the beauty shop for two hours,*
> *and that was only for the estimate.*
> —HENNY YOUNGMAN

> *She's so ugly she has to sleep with her face under the pillow*
> *to keep from scaring the covers off.*
> —RED SKELTON

> *My husband was ugly. He was so ugly he hurt my feelings. He had*
> *to sneak up on a glass of water to get a drink. He used to stand*
> *outside the doctor's office and make people sick.*
> —MOMS MABLEY

HOLLYWOOD HAS ALWAYS been so obsessed with human beauty that the very appearance of a distinctly nonbeautiful actress tends to register as a cruel joke. That was even truer in the early days. In *Tillie's Punctured Romance* (1915), Charlie Chaplin plays a fortune-hunting cad who woos a large and homely farm girl (played by Marie Dressler) strictly for her father's money. Their courtship is unusual. When Charlie shows interest in her, she becomes as coy as the most frivolous coquette; but the joke is not so much her coyness as her deluded belief that someone who looks like her is *entitled* to coyness. At one point she flirtatiously flings a rose in Charlie's face, knocking him on his ass; he retaliates by hurling a large BRICK at her head, causing her to stagger but not to lose her footing. It's a memorable scene, both

Fig. 160 Ugliness. See also HONEYMOONS AND NEWLYWEDS.

for its glimpse of Chaplin before his self-typecasting as the HOBO with the heart of gold, and for its unusually explicit statement of Hollywood's eugenicist policy toward ugly people, and especially ugly women. Usually they are conspicuous by their absence.

But if Movieland tried not to think about the ugly, old-time radio joked about them constantly. On old shows involving a lot of persiflage, "ugly" jokes were inescapable, and usually moronic:

> Bob Hope: Look at my face.
> Colonna: Pass the Tums.
> —*THE BOB HOPE SHOW,* 1947

Zing! Here's another zinger from 1947, this one spoken by Mr. Dithers on the radio sitcom *Blondie*: "My wife is the melancholy type. She has a figure like a melon and a face like a collie."

Cartoonland, too, has always welcomed the ugly with open arms. From Hogarth and Cruikshank to George Booth to Gary Larson, comic artists have always shown a special fondness, almost a fetish, for the misshapen and misbegotten. Ugliness is easier, and probably more fun, to draw. And—face it—funnier. The fad for PRETTY GIRLS in newspaper comics was never about making comics funnier, but about titillating male readers—about what fans of anime and manga call "fan service"—even if it meant putting the humor on hold for a panel or two. Ugliness is an especially heartless thing to laugh at, but it's hard to blame cartoonists if they got sick of always drawing pretty girls, even in strips where no one else was pretty.

No cartoonist had more fun at the expense of ugly people than Al Capp. A yearly feature of *Li'l Abner* was Sadie Hawkins Day, when all the single men in Dogpatch were required to participate in a foot-race with the single women—most of them not merely unattractive but grotesque—and any man who was caught had to marry his captor. The strips were ostensibly jokes about BACHELORS fleeing the responsibilities of marriage, but in fact a lot of the humor was at the expense of ugly women. During the 1964 Sadie Hawkins race, the repulsive Beer Barrel-Olga tries to capture Tiny—Li'l Abner's handsome, gallant, sweet-tempered, perpetually fifteen-and-a-half-year-old brother, who like Abner wears huge clodhopper boots—and Tiny kicks her in the face.

Capp was a brilliant cartoonist but a nasty one, and this yearly spree of schadenfreude—which inspired Sadie Hawkins dances on hundreds of college campuses—wasn't always enough for him. In 1946, he embarked on a plotline about a Lower Slobbovian named Lena the Hyena, the world's ugliest woman. With his usual flair for showmanship, Capp built suspense by not picturing Lena at all for several weeks, claiming that her face was so ugly that to lay eyes on it was to risk insanity. Then he changed his tack and announced a contest inviting readers to submit their own drawings of what they imagined Lena to look like. The winner of the contest was Basil Wolverton, who went on to draw grotesques for *Mad*.

So Capp was not alone in his cruelty to the ugly. The criminals pursued by Dick Tracy in the heyday of his comic strip were so often grotesquely deformed as to suggest a primitive theory of physiognomy: good guys are handsome, bad guys are ugly. Or possibly a theory of developmental psychology. Either way, the equation of ugliness with evil is one that still permeates our culture, as it does old fairy tales. And new ones. "Only bad witches are ugly," says Glinda to Dorothy in *The Wizard of Oz*. George Orwell concurs: "At forty, everyone has the face he deserves." But if Pruneface, Coffyhead, the Brow, Little Face Finney, Ugly Christine, and other *Dick Tracy* villains really deserve their faces, it is because they've gradually become as ugly on the inside—as if in pique at the cosmic joke life has played on them—as they were born on the outside.

Ugly characters look uglier next to pretty ones, and some people find it funny to juxtapose the two. In "Scrambled Brains," a Three Stooges short from 1951, Shemp is discharged from a mental hospital after some unspecified psychotic episode. He is supposedly cured of his hallucinations, and he announces to Larry and Moe that he's madly in love with Nora, "the most beautiful nurse in the world. . . . She's got eyes like stars, a shape like Venus, and teeth like pearls!" A moment later, this vision of loveliness appears, and in fact she has squinty eyes, a shape like a bouncer's, and hardly any teeth at all: Shemp is still hallucinating after all. As he gazes raptly at his beloved (and his fellow Stooges recoil in horror), we briefly see her as Shemp does, as a beautiful young blonde.

Though nowadays such depictions of insanity draw complaints from mental-health advocates, the real cruelty of the scene is aimed not at the crazy but at the ugly. It is certainly funny-peculiar that some of us are beautiful and some of us are not. It is funny-peculiar that, all else being equal, an ugly secretary (nurse, WAC, waitress . . .) and a pretty one will receive glaringly different treatment from employers, coworkers, clients, and the world at large. Is it also funny-haha? Some men have always thought so, though the joke is distinctly lowbrow, found most often in men's magazines, and certainly beneath *The New Yorker*.

Secretaries in particular are likely to be classified as either cute and dumb or smart and ugly, and both types thrive in offices across the land, or at least in movies, TV shows, and comic strips concerning office life across the land. Evidently the average red-blooded executive really needs two secretaries, or two kinds of assets seldom (according to popular culture) combined in a single employee: sensual and secretarial. So, in *Beetle Bailey*, General Halftrack has buxom Miss Buxley and homely Miss Blips, a complementary pair of female stereotypes. In a tongue-in-cheek 1952 "textbook" called *How to Succeed in Business Without Really Trying*, Shepherd Mead advised that any businessman picking a secretary should "take no halfway measures"—that is, should opt for either a Beauty or a Beast. If you choose a Beauty, "your little corner will become a mecca for influential men." If you choose a Beast ("the oldest, fattest, and least attractive woman in the building"), her experience will enable her "to do all your dull, routine work better than you can," and her looks will earn you a reputation as a serious, no-nonsense employee.

The dichotomy could be seen as a version of the virgin/whore dichotomy, but I prefer to see it as a divide-and-conquer strategy to meet the threat posed to male egos by women in the corporate world. As a rule, male humorists depicted those women either as airheads unable to do anything but jiggle and simper or as sexually frustrated hags whose competence is a consolation prize for losers in love.

Sometimes in old cartoons and comic postcards, hottie and nottie are embodied in a single woman, usually a young one with a good bod and an ugly face. Thus the cartoon in *Big Dame Hunters* (a mildly raunchy collection from 1962) that shows a man passing a shapely young woman on the street: the woman is Ugly (big nose and glasses), so he pictures her naked with a bag over her head, mentally veiling what he sees as well as unveiling what he can't. Even by the standards of lowbrow magazine cartooning, this cliché is unusually crass—though maybe not as crass as the one about the fisherman or castaway forced to choose between two mermaids, an ordinary one with a woman's head and torso, and another with the fish half on top joined to a woman's lower half. One possible extenuation of "hot-bod-ugly-mug" cartoons is that some men (such as Dan Clowes, one of the best cartoonists of our era) do find that combination sexy—sexier than the standard head-to-toe hottie idealized by our culture.

Ulcers

ULCERS, LIKE YES-MEN, have always been with us, but emerged as a cultural fixation in the 1950s, around the time that office workers came to see conformity—rather than pluck or hustle or pep—as the ticket to the top. It's hard to say now if the plight of the white-collar worker really did become more hellish in that decade, or if the sudden proliferation (in novels, movies, magazine cartoons, and so on) of ulcers and other white-collar afflictions (commuter trains, cocktail parties, suburban angst) simply reflects the gentrification of American humor. There's no question, though, that American humor did become more genteel—more attuned to middle-class sensibilities and preoccupations—between 1900 and 1950. A comparison of early silent comedies (Chaplin, Fatty Arbuckle, Keystone Kops) and mid-century Hollywood comedies tells the same story as a comparison of newspaper comics from the first and the fifth decades of the last century: a puerile taste for zany violence gave way to a slightly more mature taste for jokes based on the real trials of suburban life. That the older films and comic strips are funnier suggests the drawbacks, for a humorist, both of realism and of maturity.

We tend to think of ulcers as more Jewish than otherwise, thanks in part to Jewish comic novelists like Philip Roth and Bruce Jay Friedman, who liked to give physical form to a character's spiritual crisis by somatizing it. In Friedman's novel *Stern* (1962), the stress of life in a largely gentile and sometimes hostile suburb gives rise to the title character's ulcer—"a hairy, coarse-tufted little animal within him that squawked for nourishment."

Like baldness, ulcers are usually a male affliction, but not always. "I wonder if I have room for another ulcer," says Sweet Sue, the no-nonsense leader of the girl orchestra in *Some Like It Hot* (1959). Later she reflects: "That's one good thing about ulcers—it's like a burglar alarm going off inside you."

It can also be an honorable affliction, like a battle scar, and in certain lines of work the absence of one is positively suspect. In a 1963 Syd

Hoff cartoon, a young employee is reprimanded by his boss: "I have it on good authority, Peebles, that your blood pressure is down and your ulcer is inactive. Am I to conclude that you no longer care about moving up in the firm?"

Underwear

Underwear makes me uncomfortable and besides
my parts have to breathe.
—JEAN HARLOW

FEW PHENOMENA SUM up the blend of innocence and horniness we associate with the 1950s as poignantly as panty raids. There had been panty raids in the 1940s—the term itself dates from 1949—but it was a massive and well-publicized one in early 1952 at the University of Michigan that touched off a nationwide craze; that year alone there were raids on fifty-seven campuses. In a full-blown raid, hundreds or even thousands of male students would storm the women's dormitories and bear off articles of lingerie as trophies, usually with the blessing of the women, though in some cases things got violent. Some accounts of raids make them sound like the rape of the Sabine women, except that the lust-crazed men weren't bearing off actual women, just women's underthings. But panty raids sometimes led to injuries, arrests, suspensions, expulsions, tear gas, property damage (ten thousand dollars' worth in the case of a raid at the University of California, Berkeley in 1956, back before its students channeled that energy into political causes). Sometimes hordes of women returned the favor, raiding and pillaging the men's dorms.

Seen as examples of mob action, the panty raids are—even in retrospect—a little frightening. Seen as instances of mass fetishism, though, they're funny and pathetic, since the raids, and the panties themselves, were of course a substitute for all the sex the students weren't having. Some must have masturbated with their trophies, if that was the closest they could get to a member of the other gender.

Fig. 161 The author considers this 1949 *Blondie* panel the funniest illustration in the book.

The more buttoned-up and repressed a culture is, the funnier and more exciting it finds panties. Children aren't exactly repressed about sex, but they are kept in the dark. They do know that certain body parts—and by extension the garments that cover those parts—are naughty, and much of their transgressive humor features underwear, as in such playground rhymes as "I see London, I see France, / I see Mary's underpants" and

> *Oh Grannie's red drawers,*
> *Oh Grannie's red drawers,*
> *There's a hole in the middle*
> *So Grannie can piddle.*
> *Oh Grannie's red drawers.*

As for adults, some of them never outgrow their infantile fascination with undies; hence the thriving sector of the porn industry catering to men who long to see panties rather than vaginas. The rest of us are like people who outgrow their old hobbies without ever quite repudiating them. Now and then we dust off the old stamp album, or rummage through the closet for the untuned ukulele. *Captain Billy's Whiz Bang*, the raunchy Jazz Age humor magazine, featured plenty of little-boy undie jokes, for example: "Rose's are red / Pearl's are white / I seen 'em on the clothesline / Just the other night" (February 1928).

In a cartoon from *More Over Sexteen* (1953), a sewer worker sits underground, leering up through an open manhole as he keeps a running tally of the types of panties he sees on female pedestrians. So far he's counted two pairs of pink panties, five of white, two of lace, and— improbably, I can't help thinking, but I've never been a sewer worker— fifteen women with no panties at all.

If the entry on BOSOMS AND BREASTS weren't already so long, I'd discuss bras there, since jokes about bras are of course jokes about breasts. In an age of censorship and indirection, though, when in many venues it was forbidden to picture bare breasts or even to name them barely, brassieres were fetishized—and therefore funny—in a way they no longer are. They are also funny-looking: when Ellie Mae Clampett, the tomboy gal on *The Beverly Hillbillies*, receives her first brassiere, she mistakes it for "a store-bought, lace-trimmed, double-barreled slingshot."

In *Operation Petticoat* (1959), the USS *Sea Tiger*, a World War II submarine, is painted pink because there isn't enough red or white to paint it all one or the other, and the Navy prizes uniformity. To feminize things even further, the sub is carrying a horde of army nurses, including the colossally big-breasted Second Lieutenant Crandall (Joan O'Brien). When the *Sea Tiger* is attacked by an American destroyer force assuming that a pink sub can only be a Japanese sub, the captain sets them straight and saves the day by firing the nurses' lingerie from a torpedo tube. As soon as the destroyers get a good look at Lieutenant Crandall's brassiere, they know they're dealing with Americans.

Veeblefetzers

If you have a knickknack with a nick in it,
we'll knock the nick outta the knickknack with Brighto!
—LARRY FINE, "DIZZY DOCTORS," 1937

Laurel: What's a knickknack?
Hardy: Oh, a knickknack is a thing that sits on top of a whatnot.
—*BLOCK-HEADS*, 1938

ENGLISH HAS THE largest vocabulary of any language in the world, and you'd think it would need few words—fewer than any other language—to designate otherwise nameless objects. In fact, it has dozens of such words, most of them jocular: *dealie-bob, dingbat, dingus, doodad, fizgig, frammis, gadget, gilguy, gilhickey, gilhoolie, gizmo, jigamaroo, macguffin, polywhatsit, thingumabob* (cf. the eighteenth-century "jigummbob," which Dr. Johnson defines as "a trinket; a knick-knack; a slight contrivance in machinery"), *thingumagig, whatchamacallit, whatsit, widget.* The most impressive assembly of such words I know of is in Paul Dickson's *Words,* a logophile's paradise that allots a whole chapter to jocular place-fillers, including some I've been unable to find anywhere else, like *kadigan* and *gubbins*—did Dickson make them up?

Maybe he just spells them differently. Few of the whatsit words can be found even in unabridged dictionaries, though they have as much business there, you'd think, as ridiculous formations like *tearablenesses* (which really does appear in *Webster's Third*). But lexicographers, with their heroic dedication to assigning precise meanings to every word they acknowledge at all, may be excused for excluding these boastfully *im*precise words from the gated community of Standard English. All dictionaries are prescriptive as well as descriptive, and if you love words enough to devote your life to the drudgery of lexicography, you have a right to wage war on the sort of creeping imprecision that James Thurber denounced in his 1960 essay "The Spreading 'You Know'": "About five years ago, both men and women were saying things like 'He has a new Cadillac job with a built-in bar deal in the back seat.'"

My inner buffoon persists in applauding words that my inner bow-tied usage curmudgeon deplores. My favorite of these whatchamacallit words—because of the uses to which it's been put—is *veeblefetzer*, thought to come from nineteenth-century Yiddish slang, though most people familiar with the word probably associate it with *Mad* magazine, and especially with the golden age when Harvey Kurtzman was the editor. The word first appeared in Issue 7, October 1953, in a *Smilin' Jack* parody called "Smilin' Melvin": "I will be sucked into the turbine if you press down on the veeble-fetzer switch that starts the motor!" The chilling tale of "Frank N. Stein" (December 1953) is set in "the little European town of Veeblefetzer." In "Gasoline Valley" (September 1964), Skizziks makes a living by fixing cracked veeblefetzers, first as a door-to-door tinker, but finally as the head of a giant corporation that also handles veeble*fee*tzers, feeblezetzers, and potrzebies. In that piece we also learn that veeblefetzers can be right- or left-handed, and that some have a belt in back. We even lay eyes on thing itself, which looks like something assembled from Tinkertoys. We feel we are finally getting to the heart of the veeblefetzer mystery when Skizziks's partner Booble announces, "Note to readers: Naturally, there is no such thing as a veeblefetzer! This grotesque designation is used merely to disguise our real operation. . . ." But then the letters page for the January 1955 issue includes a diagram and assembly instructions for a Type Seven veeblefetzer—the type with the single throttlever, the long elbow, and the pair of zorks, though there is some doubt as to whether the finished product will really fetz veebles.[50]

Vomit and Nausea

I USED TO FANTASIZE about amassing the world's most extensive collection of fake vomit. I would track down vintage specimens from the Gay Nineties, the Great War, the Roaring Twenties, the Depression, World War II. England would contribute Victorian,

---

[50] See also January 1959's "Veeble People," which purports to be the house organ of the North American Veeblefetzer Company.

Fig. 162 Sick passengers

Edwardian, and Georgian examples. And each would be an historical document, reflecting not only the characteristic diet of the phony-vomit-buying demographic of its era (you'd expect Depression-era vomit to be thinner, for example, and wartime vomit to give evidence of food rationing), but also the changing attitudes toward the great issue of realism versus stylization.

In fact, though, fake vomit wasn't invented till 1959, and met with surprising initial resistance. It seems that when its inventor, an employee of the toy company Marvin Glass & Associates, showed it to Glass himself, the mogul of mirth was not amused. In *Cheap Laffs*, a celebration of such things, Mark Newgarden quotes an employee who witnessed the historic event: "A designer (I wish I remembered his name) came up with the totally original idea of fake vomit. He showed it to Marvin and Marvin hated it. 'That's disgusting, you're sick, there is nothing funny about it' shouted Marvin Glass." Phony vomit might have never seen the light of day if not for the chutzpah of that nameless designer, who went over his boss's head and showed it directly to Irving Fishlove, a leading seller of laff-getters:

The presentation with Fishlove was not going anywhere. Several items were met with polite interest but nothing more. The fake vomit designer then burst through the conference room door and slapped the PUKE squarely on the table in front of the client. You can imagine Marvin's face. Fishlove was laughing hysterically and clearly loved it. Marvin immediately piped up: "Yes this is great! That's why we saved it for last. We love it!", and Marvin sold it to the client like it was the greatest thing ever.

But even Fishlove seems to have had misgivings. Like many laff-getters, his phony vomit—dubbed "Whoops"—was packaged for sale on a display card, but in the early days it was mounted on the *back* of the card, as if to preserve some air of propriety about the matter.

That sort of squeamishness was typical of vomit humor for at least the first two-thirds of the last century, and few would claim that movies are better now that the camera is free to zoom right in on the chunky aftermath of a puking fit. *The Bank Dick* (1940), one of the funniest movies of all time, had a lot of fun with Franklin Pangborn's nausea. W. C. Fields has gotten a bartender (played by Shemp Howard) to slip Pangborn a Mickey Finn; the drug doesn't quite knock him out, but it makes the poor man very queasy. We don't see him vomiting, of course (much less see the vomitus), but several times we see him on the point of doing so— see him dashing offscreen whenever Fields sadistically mentions chili con carne or breaded veal cutlets. Nausea is the opposite of hunger, and the very thought of foods that would make a hungry man hungrier can suffice to make a nauseated man remit his most recent meal.

To anyone who has ever suffered it, the sight of nausea is not only funnier but more convincing than the sight of puke. In *Road to Rio* (1947), there's a ridiculous scene in which Bing Crosby and Bob Hope, famished stowaways on an ocean liner, spot a FAT MAN in a deck chair who has just been served a giant breakfast. By standing in front him and swaying back in forth in unison while discussing the choppiness of the ocean, the greasiness of SAUSAGE, and kindred matters, Bing and Bob soon induce the fat man to abandon his breakfast and hasten offscreen to puke. When they sit down to eat his food, though, they find that all that swaying and talk of greasy food has made *them* seasick, too.

Incidentally, dozens of old comic postcards dealt with seasickness—not surprisingly, since two of the main things people do when traveling is send postcards and fight the urge to vomit. Most cards show the sufferer leaning over the rail of a ship, often looking slightly green. (Between about 1870 and 1940, to *feed the fish* was to vomit overboard.) Several cards have the punning caption "Everything going out, nothing coming in"—since one of the main things postcard-writers do is to complain about not receiving mail themselves. On American and British postcards, the puke itself is never pictured, though French postcards sometimes show it spraying out like water from a fountain. Sometimes a crew member stands by with a white enameled basin, but sometimes the joke is that the sick guy *is* a crew member. On May 5, 1945, *The New Yorker*'s cover showed a small, greenish, slope-shouldered naval officer on the deck of a sea-tossed ship, fighting back nausea while reviewing his tall, broad-shouldered, unflappable sailors. The image perfectly captures the horror and isolation of motion sickness when you are the only one who's suffering it, and the borderline sadism of those who flaunt their immunity. It also reflects the widespread contempt of enlisted men toward low-ranking officers (as does the endless feud in *Beetle Bailey* between Sergeant Snorkel and Lieutenant Flap). In honor of my father, who entered the army as second lieutenant after putting himself through college via the ROTC, I've decided not to include an entry on second lieutenants in this guide, but there used to be a fair amount of mirth at their expense.

Winged Money

IN EARLY ANIMATED cartoons, it's not uncommon for the moon to wear a nightcap and wink, for a leering or glowering tree to bend over and grab at passersby with its limbs, for an ocean to congeal into fists and pummel an ocean liner. The results, though almost never funny, can be beautifully surreal, as in some of the stranger Max Fleischer cartoons. It's one type of surrealism that never caught on in newspaper comics. There have been plenty of anthropomorphic animals on the funny pages, but not much in the way of intelligent vegetables or minerals. If animation lends itself to animistic portrayals of reality, the fixity of the comic-strip panel resists such transformations, with a few exceptions. The most notable exception is the flying dollar bill, still used on occasion to indicate worrisome expenses.

I find that particular sight gag both funny and eerie—eerie because, aside from its wings,

Fig. 163 *Smokey Stover*, 1938

the dollar is an ordinary one, with no other attributes of birds or any other sentient beings: no eyes, no mind, no motives. It resembles a living creature in only one particular, its ability to fly. The wings are usually mounted on edges, but sometimes on the front and back instead, making for a more airworthy bill. Sometimes a whole moneybag will be shown flying off to the great beyond.

A sudden unforeseen expense is seldom funny enough in itself to serve as a strip's main joke, but it can set up a joke by driving a tightfisted character to outlandish behavior. In a 1929 *Banana Oil* strip by the great Milt Gross, a young lady in a fancy restaurant orders the priciest things on the menu, forcing her penniless boyfriend to compensate by ordering nothing, insisting that he isn't hungry. In the next panel we see him on all fours in a meadow, eating grass.

It's easy to imagine how the restaurant scene would be played in a sitcom, with the penny-pinching beau flinching every time his date utters a word like *caviar* or *truffle*. Comic strips don't have the resources of sitcoms, though, and must find other ways to show what characters are thinking, in situations where characters can't just say what they think. (The whole premise of *Banana Oil* was that we *don't* say what we think;

instead we spout nonsense, hogwash, applesauce, banana oil.) In the restaurant strip, the young man pictures not a flying dollar but the three hanging globes of a pawnbroker's sign.

Though it has come to seem natural to us, the obvious way for a cartoonist to depict a sudden expense, the winged-money icon was uncommon before the 1930s. (In a 1914 cartoon about the high price of car maintenance—already a common gripe in those days—Frank King shows a man pouring coins and bills through a funnel straight into his gas tank.) By the same token, we shouldn't assume that the winged dollar is here to stay. No doubt some Web cartoonist has already updated the cliché, and brought it online, by having the suddenly penniless character picture a depressing ATM screen or receipt. Cartooning clichés come and go, but money problems will always be with us.

Woman Drivers

Q: Why don't they let Helen Keller drive?
A: Because she's a woman.
—OLD JOKE

If your wife wants to learn to drive, don't stand in her way.
—SAM LEVENSON

IN "WIMMIN' HADN'T Oughta Drive" (1940), Olive Oyl insists that Popeye let her drive his new car, and when the car's horn plays a snatch of Chopin's Funeral March—the "Pray-for-the-dead-and-the-dead-will-pray-for-you" part—we know what to expect. Sure enough, Olive proceeds to exemplify all the time-honored stereotypes about woman drivers: expecting the car to drive itself, reacting blithely to the numerous collisions she causes, driving up onto the sidewalk while RUBBERNECKING at a display of "ducky hats" in a shop window, going the wrong way on a one-way street (and insisting, despite all the oncoming vehicles, that she's in the right and everyone else is going the wrong way), and so on. Though Popeye tries to be supportive ("Am I doing all right?"

THE SATURDAY
EVENING POST

Fig. 164

"You couldn't do better"), by the end it's clear that women hadn't oughta drive. At the climax, only SPINACH enables Popeye to stop Olive from driving off a cliff. In the final scene he's pushing her on a go-cart.

Jump ahead sixteen years, to one of Jimmy Hatlo's "They'll Do It Every Time" cartoons from 1956, and you find that nothing has changed. The cartoon's first panel, captioned "Portrait of a Lady on Her Way Downtown," shows a lady driver in an open car blithely speeding through an intersection, barely missing another car, a mailman, two dogs, a crossing guard, and a group of schoolchildren. The second panel, "Portrait of the Same Lady When She Gets There," shows her lollygagging at a streetlight (where she's been idling so long that a spiderweb stretches between the light post and her side-view mirror), holding up a line of honking motorists as she gazes into the display window of a clothing store. Most of Hatlo's gags were submitted by readers, whom the cartoonist acknowledged by name; that one came from Fred W. Rawlings of 291 E. 12th St., Hialeah, Florida, who included his address (as most contributors did, in that more trusting era) in case any other readers wanted to strike up a correspondence with him on the strength of his droll observation about lady drivers—a pre-Internet form of social networking.

Fred must have heard from a lot of kindred souls, since men have been joking about women's driving for ages. The gag must be almost as old as cars themselves, and by the 1940s it was huge. *Esar's Joke Dictionary* (1945) has ten jokes on the topic, more than for brides or MOTHERS-

IN-LAW or STENOGRAPHERS or OLD MAIDS or even for women in general. Here's #10:

> George had been patiently trying for weeks to teach the little woman how to drive the car, but without much success. They were out one afternoon and she was driving along a quiet country road when suddenly she screamed in fright, "Quick, George, you take the wheel! Here comes a big tree!"

The golden age of woman-driver humor, though, was probably the 1950s and early '60s—due, I've seen it said, to the rise of suburbia, which made it necessary for everyone to drive. Suddenly even the worst male chauvinist had to let his wife use the car unless he wanted to do the grocery shopping himself.

It was a favorite joke on old sitcoms. *I Love Lucy*, *The Beverly Hillbillies*, and *The Andy Griffith Show* each devoted an episode to the premise, and the titles of those episodes—"Lucy Learns to Drive," "Granny Learns to Drive," and "Aunt Bee Learns to Drive"—show that the writers considered the premise too intrinsically funny to require a creative title. On the other hand, the corresponding episode of *Bewitched*—in which Samantha's student driving drives her instructor to a PSYCHIATRIST—was called "Driving Is the Only Way to Fly."

Naturally the theme has been transposed to other forms of transportation. "What's THIS button?" ask a woman in a tiny private plane from which she's just unwittingly ejected her husband or instructor. It's one of the better cartoons, actually, in a weak collection by Dana Fradon called *Breaking the Laugh Barrier* (1961), of which the gimmick is that all the cartoons pertain to air travel. Inevitably the book contains another cartoon about a BACKSEAT DRIVER, female as usual, but hectoring the scowling pilot of an airplane ("Get a little more air speed . . . Watch out for that other plane") rather than an automobile. A 1957 cartoon by Al Kaufman shows two dumpy housewives, next-door NEIGHBORS, whose lawn mowers have just collided violently and stand in a puddle of engine parts and gasoline—a collision all the more ridiculous because the mowers are not ride-'ems but push-'ems.

Xx·Yy·Zz

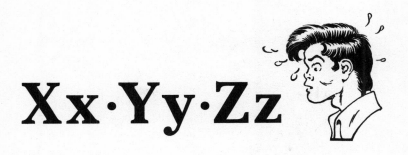

Xylophones

When he strikes this *note, instead of a xylophone,*
he'll be playing a harp!
—DAFFY DUCK, BOOBY-TRAPPING BUGS BUNNY'S
XYLOPHONE IN "SHOW BIZ BUGS"

IN ANY NUMBER of old animated cartoons—and nowhere else that I'm aware of—murderous characters booby-trap a xylophone, or sometimes a PIANO, so that it explodes when someone plays the first five bars of "Believe Me, if All Those Endearing Young Charms," a traditional Irish tune to which Thomas Moore supplied the words in 1808:

> *Believe me, if all those endearing young charms,*
> *Which I gaze on so fondly today,*
> *Were to change by tomorrow and fleet in my arms,*
> *Like fairy gifts fading away*
> *Thou would'st still be adored, as this moment thou art,*
> *Let thy loveliness fade as it will;*
> *And around the dear ruin each wish of my heart*
> *Would entwine itself verdantly still.*

Invariably, it is the repeated high note corresponding to the words "young charms" that triggers the explosion, though it's often the villain who winds up sounding those notes, after the intended victim plays the tune wrong. In "Ballot Box Bunny," when Yosemite Sam challenges Bugs

Fig. 165 "Show Biz Bugs," 1956

to play the tune on a rigged piano and even supplies sheet music, the deadly notes are printed in red instead of black.

Why that particular tune? We may never know, but it's fun to speculate. It couldn't be just any tune; it had to be one whose first phrase ends with a note that hasn't been sounded yet, and ideally with two successive instances of that note, less for logistic than comedic reasons. In fact, it must be *harder* to rig a bomb so that it will explode on being struck *twice* rather than once.

As for the lyrics, "Those Endearing Young Charms" is a sappy sentimental song expressing a sentiment we all wish we all felt but that probably no one ever has. It's a hard song not to laugh at when you know the lyrics. (For one thing, the use of a count noun like *charms* instead of a mass noun like *beauty* or *allure* makes it hard for the dirtier-minded among us not to picture the specific body parts that comprise the addressee's "charms.") When a cartoon uses the song as a murder weapon, the watcher always knows before the victim does that the piano or xylophone is booby-trapped, and it's customary to prolong the suspense, and the humor, by having the intended victim playing the tune wrong the first time through, generally by missing—flatting—the lethal final notes corresponding to "young charms." As usual in sentimental diatonic music, the high notes are supposed to be moments of heightened poignancy, so when the intended victim *flats* them, it's a funny kind of bathos that, I'd argue, affects you subliminally if you've ever heard even the first line of the song. When someone finally plays the tune correctly and the "young charms" note detonates the bomb—well, in my opinion, that's a better musical joke than most of PDQ Bach's.

Do we know how the first animator to use this gag hit on that particular tune? No—we can only speculate. In any case, it's not surprising that later animators who rehashed the joke found it easier to use the same tune than to come up with another. And now that tune—that cliché—is part of the joke.

Yes-Men and Sycophants

> *I don't want any yes-men around me. I want everyone*
> *to tell the truth, even though it costs him his job.*
> —SAMUEL GOLDWYN

THE BACK COVER of the April 1960 issue of *Mad* is a phony advertisement for Aspire Boot-Lick Polish. Under the picture of a sailor who has dropped to hands and knees to lick the shiny black shoes of a pompous commodore, the ad copy informs us that Aspire is a delicious blend of nine ingredients ("licorice, caviar, chocolate, caramel, molasses, borscht, halvah, and Moxie in a base of chicken fat") concocted "after years of research by the skilled Aspire chefs to make boot-licking a little more tasty when you gotta do it."

And you had to do it a lot in those days, if you worked for a big organization and hoped to get ahead. In 1956, William H. Whyte added a term to the language with *The Organization Man*, a critique of corporate culture and the premium it places on conformity. Five years later Richard Yates wrote *Revolutionary Road*, a brilliant novel about a bohemian couple whose marriage falls apart when the husband gets too caught up in a dull corporate job and becomes the kind of clone he used to despise. In an interview, Yates described his book in terms that apply to Whyte's as well:

Fig. 166

I meant it more as an indictment of American life in the 1950s. Because during the Fifties there was a general lust for conformity all over this country, by no means only in the suburbs—a kind of blind, desperate clinging to safety and security at any price.

One price was the stifling of originality even in situations that depend on it. In a multi-panel magazine cartoon by R. O. Blechman from the 1950s or '60s, a group of executives sit in a boardroom, grimly brainstorming. One has an idea indicated by a small LIGHTBULB above his head, and the other executives smile—all except for the CEO at the head of the table. The same thing happens—smiling colleagues, scowling boss—when another executive has a brighter idea (bigger bulb), a third a brighter still (table lamp), and a fourth an idea so dazzling as to merit a chandelier. Then the CEO himself has a very dim, low-wattage idea (tiny Christmas-tree bulb), and of course his underlings react by throwing up their arms in joy at the boss's brilliance.

If today we have less humor at the expense of corporate yes-men, it isn't because they are any less common, but because we take them for granted. And no one who ridicules them openly will last for long in any corporate setting. "Corporate humor" is almost an oxymoron, though the existence of court jesters in the distant past—and, for that matter, of humor consultants in our own time—suggests that the relation between humor and power isn't always one of simple mutual antipathy.

I will go so far as to say, though, that of all the lamentable human types considered in this guide, none is more repugnant to the true humorist than the sycophant. That's why Alexander Pope was forced to support himself with translations instead of dedications, and why Swift never landed the sinecure he craved: they were constitutionally incapable of the sycophancy their age demanded as the price of patronage. One reason the two satirists so often targeted ass-kissers must have been a sense of what their own incapacity for ass-kissing had cost them.

Neither ever used that idiom, though Swift had been dead for only three years when its first known use occurred in 1748 in Smollett's *Roderick Random*, where Mr. Potion is described as "a canting scoundrel, who has crept into business by his hypocrisy, and kissing the arse of every body." To *lick ass* dates from 1864, to *lick boots* from 1929, according to Lighter's *Historic Dictionary of American Slang*, though Lighter dates *bootlick* (as a noun) and *bootlicker* to 1834 and 1848, respectively. As for *brownnose*—probably the single best term for the type of asshole-nuzzling asshole this entry concerns—it has been around since World War II, and is honored in *Webster's Third* with the funniest etymological note I've ever found in that book: "*brown + nose*; from the implication that servility is tantamount to having one's nose in the anus of the person from whom advancement is sought." I also like *in the brown*, which dates from 1938.

Other colorful terms for sycophants—terms suggesting the hatred as well as the mirth that the type has inspired—include *apple-polisher*, *assenter*, *backscratcher*, *backslapper*, *brownie*, *camp follower*, *company man*, *doormat*, *doter*, *fawner*, *flannel-mouth*, *flunky*, *groveler*, *kowtower*, *lackey*, *minion*, *pawn*, *pickthank*, *puppet*, *sheep*, *stooge*, *suck*, *suck-up*, *teacher's pet*, *toadeater*, and *underling*.

Yokels and Hicks

PETTICOAT JUNCTION, THE dumbest of the three moronic rural sitcoms featured on CBS in the 1960s, aired from 1963 to 1970, when it was the first one canceled in the network's "rural purge." (The other two, *Green Acres* and *The Beverly Hillbillies*, ended the following season.) The premise of the show—a train run like a small-town taxicab—was actually clever. Trains are all about rigid routes and rigid timetables, so a train that manages to do its own thing is a triumph of small-town laxity and eccentricity. In the pilot episode, "Spur Line to Shady Rest," a fussy functionary from the parent railroad comes to town to check up on the branch in question, and is comically incensed by the fecklessness of its operators. We're supposed to side with the easygoing townsfolk and not with Homer Bedloe, the tight-assed type-A inspector, but I strongly identify with Bedloe. Or as strongly as you can identify with anyone in a show where there's no middle ground between the im-

Figs. 167 Reuben and
the toilet: A popular
turn-of-the-century gag

becilic hicks and the citified villains—no voice of sanity corresponding to Andy on *The Andy Griffith Show* (which proved for all time that a rural show doesn't *have* to be dumb). Twice in that first episode when Bedloe objects to unscheduled delays (objecting not just as an inspector but as a passenger), the townspeople put it to a vote and of course overrule him. It's an especially ugly caricature of democracy, a tyranny of the majority that verges on mob rule. I was reminded of Nabokov's great story "Cloud, Castle, Lake" (1937), an allegory about Nazi Germany also set on a train and concerning the ordeal of Vasiliy Ivanovich, a traveler ostracized and tortured to the point of suicide by his fellow passengers for simple nonconformity. Shows like *Petticoat Junction* appeal to and celebrate the sort of morons who tortured poor Vasiliy.

Some claim that pop culture per se is a tyranny of the majority that forces everyone to watch the shows—and read the books, and hear the music—that the lowest common denominator favors. But that's not quite true, or we'd have nothing *but* idiocy like *Petticoat Junction* **(Fig.168)**. Luckily, some demographics are more desirable than others (that's why CBS canceled all its rural sitcoms); most major networks, studios, publishers, and so on care about prestige as well as profit; and people aren't as stupid as they're portrayed on *Petticoat Junction*. Just as few grownups elect to eat nothing but junk food day in and day out, few content themselves with a cultural diet of pure junk.

And in fairness to the episode described above, you can't blame country mice for making fun of city mice when city mice have always laughed at their country cousins. Just look at names we call them: *acorn cracker, buckwheat* (hence the Little Rascals character[51]), *bumpkin, chaw-bacon, clodhopper, goober grabber, gully jumper, hayseed, hick, punkin roller, redneck, rube* (short for Reuben, as cartoon embodiments of yokels were frequently named), *Silas* (Reuben's bother), *sodbuster, stump jumper, turnip sucker*, and, of course, *yokel*.

Not all yokels are HILLBILLIES, though all hillbillies—and farmers, and small-town businessmen—are potentially yokels. Like a

---

[51] Hal Roach seems to have made a joke of naming characters after cereals and grasses—cf. Farina and Alfalfa.

Fig. 168 *Petticoat Junction*

party-crasher or a burglar, a yokel is defined by being where he doesn't belong—by his fish-out-of-water status. He is the exact counterpart of the city slicker (who also becomes funny as soon as he ventures out of his element, like Homer Bedloe in *Petticoat Junction*). The instant a farmer sets foot in a big city, he becomes a yokel. He looks ridiculous in city clothes, like a gorilla in a tuxedo. He often wears a straw hat on his unkempt hair and a scraggly billy-goat beard on his chin, and is easily spotted by con men. It's only a matter of time before one sells him a gold brick, if the yokel hasn't already spend his last cent on a deed to the Brooklyn Bridge. As for legitimate transactions, his sense of inferiority causes him to overspend or overtip, but no one admires his wealth or generosity; they refer to him instead, derisively, as a "big butter-and-egg man." He is bewildered by indoor plumbing; I own three different postcards, postmarked 1905, 1908, and 1910, in which a yokel named Reuben uses a toilet bowl as a washbasin.

Al Capp liked to send Li'l Abner—and sometimes the whole Yokum family—to New York City, and must have done so at least a dozen times. No doubt Capp wanted to give himself and his readers a vacation from Dogpatch, the tiny, backward Ozark community where most of *Li'l Abner* occurred, but he also wanted to exploit certain irresistible comic potentials that remained untapped as long as the Yokums stayed in Dogpatch among their own kind—specifically, the comedy of culture clash, of mutual smugness and incomprehension between groups that might as well have been living in different centuries, or indeed in different galaxies.

Zealots

> *Rule 3: The Coyote could stop anytime—if he were not a fanatic.*
> —CHUCK JONES[52]

> *. . . the inexorable logic that reality*
> *applies to the correction of dreams . . .*
> —HENRI BERGSON

TRIX WAS INTRODUCED by General Mills in 1955. Since 1959, it has been marketed with commercials in which a cartoon rabbit tries obsessively to eat a bowl of the cereal, only to be thwarted by children who tell him, "Silly rabbit, Trix are for kids." The idea seems to be that eating Trix will feel like more of a privilege if some are denied it, so it's interesting that on the two occasions (in 1976 and 1990) when the makers let children vote on whether to let the rabbit have a bowl of Trix, the kids of America voted yes by an overwhelming margin.

Some of the most memorable depictions of zealots and enthusiasts

---

[52] From his list of "Rules we obeyed in the Coyote/Road Runner Series." Jones elaborates Rule 3 with a quotation from Santayana: "A fanatic is one who redoubles his effort when he has forgotten his aim."

have been in commercials, which makes sense because commercials are all about convincing us that the sponsors' products are more exciting than they could possibly be. On some old radio sitcoms, characters were required to plug their sponsors' products in the course of the show, endorsements that made the crassest of modern product placements seem not just subtle but subliminal. The writers for *Fibber McGee and Molly*—a show sponsored by Johnson's Wax, and officially known for much of its run as *The Johnson's Wax Program*—made a virtue of necessity by writing the show's announcer into every episode as a Johnson's Wax salesman whose inability to think about anything else verges on the pathological.

We all have things we care about more than other people do. I can't imagine wanting Trix as much as the Trix rabbit does, but there are things I want just as intensely, and some of them, like writing an encyclopedia of stale humor, would strike many people as every bit as silly as the rabbit's all-consuming pursuit of Trix.

In the entry on PREDICTABILITY, my list of one-note comic strips grew so long that I omitted strips in which the running gag is not a character trait but an obsession. *Snapshot Bill* (1914–18) concerned the misadventures of a compulsive shutterbug. *Otto Auto* (1920–21), a not-so-great strip by the great Gene Ahern, featured an obsessive motorist and mustn't be confused with *Otto Watt* (1925), one of several would-be-funny 1920s features about radio addicts, anticipating much of our own era's lame humor about Internet addicts. *Physical Culture Phil* (1907–1908) starred an early fitness buff who was always lecturing his fellow men about healthy living. *Major Ozone's Fresh Air Crusade* (1904), by the great George Herriman, starred the funny pages' first environmentalist. In one scene, Major Ozone gets jumped in Chinatown by a bunch of Chinese after extinguishing their joss sticks; in another, he gets pelted with BRICKS by urchins after offering to pay for them to visit the countryside (since he wants fresh air for everyone, not only himself); in a third, the major visits the countryside himself only to be toppled by a pig, chased by a ram and a swarm of bees, kicked by a mule, and treed by a dog.

Nowadays, the major's obsession seems more prophetic than funny, like that of another comic-strip zealot from the same era, Fizzboomski the Anarchist, who in a series of 1905 strips (inspired by news of the October Manifesto) tries repeatedly to assassinate the Czar and the "Prime Minister-a-vitch" with his homemade bombs, and meets with as much success as the Coyote when he tries to catch the Road Runner, or Charlie Brown when he tries to kick the football. Zealots are funny only when they fail.

And seldom very funny even then. I'd venture to say that neither the Johnson's Wax salesman nor the Trix rabbit ever made anyone laugh. Perhaps it serves me right that my own zeal for encyclopedic scope and alphabetical order forces me to end this guide, as I began it, with one of the feebler comic archetypes. Like the ABSENTMINDED PROFESSOR, the zealot is too selfless to be much fun to laugh at. You can't be really laughable unless you care more about what people think of you than about wax or Trix or even fresh air.

Afterword

Some drink deeply from the river of knowledge. Others only gargle.
—WOODY ALLEN

And here, poor fool! With all my lore
I stand! no wiser than before.
—GOETHE

HAVING GARGLED FOR so long with the tangy mouthwash of the formerly funny, I will probably find it hard for several years to talk about anything else. My book is finished, but there's always more to say. I said nothing about sculptors, for example, though they have always been funnier than painters. No square of canvas, no matter how vast, can suggest artistic grandiosity and grandiose bad taste like an enormous cube of marble.

I didn't say a word about the whole vexed question of which sitcom first treated viewers to the shocking sight of a full-sized bed in the master bedroom. I dodged that question not because it doesn't interest me, but because it interests me too much. I fear my own capacity for nerdy expertise—for masochistic narrowing of my intellectual horizons, such as they are.

It would be so easy to spend the rest of my life writing about the history of married sex as seen (or rather not seen) on TV.

It would be so fun to make oneself an authority on itching powder, crying towels, squirting nickels, self-relighting candles, chattering teeth, exploding cigars, disappearing ink, and all the other classic laff-getters still sold as "novelties" because they were new once, and though they haven't changed since the days when our grandfathers ordered them from ads in comic books and inflicted them on siblings. The classic whoopee cushion, for example, is still crudely printed with the same crude illustration of a FAT LADY looking alarmed as she sits down on one, and still claims to emit "A REAL BRONX CHEER," though not even New Yorkers use that phrase much in our ruder era, when *The New Yorker* itself is free to call a fart a fart.

American Cornball could have been longer than *Infinite Jest*. Not only is there more to say on each of its 195 topics (even FLATULENCE—which demanded and received the longest entry—remains to be exhausted), but there are at least another 195 topics that would have been fun to expatiate on. There was even going to be an entry on root vegetables.

Here are a few of the other fine laughables that didn't make the final cut:

Aardvarks. Funny because of the word's lonely isolation at the beginning of the alphabet, at the edge of the forest of symbols, exposed to the predations of humor in a way that *hedgehog* and even *titmouse* are not. Also because an aardvark is "a burrowing nocturnal African mammal about five feet long that feeds on ants and termites [and] has a long snout, a snakelike tongue, large ears, and a heavy tapering tail."

Academia. Funny for all, but almost unbearably funny if you stay there past your early twenties. In my days as a professor, my tics were notably worse from the strain of keeping a straight face whenever anybody was in a solemn mood. Someone always is.

Adenoids. All glands are funny, but few have such funny names.

Adult Games. The prepackaged kind you used to see in the X-rated alcove at Spencer's Gifts. Maybe you still do. "Funny" in a mirthless *Happy Hooker* way, painfully stupid to anyone not momentarily lobotomized by alcohol and lust. The only funny part is that—with spin-the-bottle and strip poker playable for free—ambitious swingers used to shell out for boxy games with names like Office Party (1969), Let's F*ck (1969), and Strip Checkers (1972).

Aprons. Funniest on men, especially when frilly or pink. As for the mid-century fad for cookout aprons printed with jocular slogans like KISS THE COOK or GENIUS AT WORK, was that a concession to male anxiety about wearing an apron of any kind? Or was it rather that even then, in that less exhibitionistic era, when few males would have wanted to spend a full day in a wearable joke like the I'M WITH STU-PID T-shirts of a later, even dumber decade, just as few would have wanted to cook every day—was it possible that even back in those gray-flannel, no-comment days, a lot of manly men liked wearing a joke for the time it takes to burn a meal?

Armchairs. One reason armchair quarterbacks are funny is that armchairs are funny. Even ones that don't recline. Sitting itself is a little funny.

Barbecue Pits. Only as funny as the men who use them, but back in the 1950s that was funny enough. Men used to lose their tempers when they tied on funny aprons and faced the primeval male task of roasting meat.

Bathtubs. How could bathtubs not be funny, when nudity, hygiene, and getting wet are all comedy gold?

Bees. If you're ever chased by a swarm of bees, the only—and funny—thing to do is to run like crazy till you reach a swimming hole.

Beets. Insufficiently funny, like the other vegetables with which they split the root-vegetable vote: parsnips, turnips, rutabagas, mangel-wurzels . . .

Bicycles. Never hilarious, or not since the day of the velocipedes. But always slightly funny, even now.

Blabbermouths. Funniest where silence is golden, as in church or on the golf course.

Black Eyes. The funny punishment for getting fresh.

Blind Dates. And it must mean something that Mystery Date, the Milton Bradley board game, was designed by the same genius (Marvin Glass) who gave the world Toss Across and Rock 'Em Sock 'Em Robots.

Bookworms. One of the rare pejoratives that don't evoke a consensus of associations with one gender or the other. As with other worms, the sex of the bookworm is hard to determine.

Bras. Funny to this day, but there are already separate entries for BOSOMS AND BREASTS, and I don't want the happenstance of alphabetical order to make me look like too much of a lecher too early in the alphabet.

(I envision people using my encyclopedia as a work of reference, a Zagat's Guide to the Land of Liver-Spotted Laffs, but I also like to picture people reading it from A to Z.) I thought the better, likewise, of a later entry on three-breasted women, though a case can be made that sixty to eighty years ago, men found the idea of three breasts distinctly—if not quite 50 percent—funnier than the idea of two.

Bulldogs. Funny peculiar. If the standard cartoon cat a hundred years ago was a scraggy black stray, the standard cartoon dog was a white bulldog, plump and well groomed, because those are the perks of letting the Man put a collar on you.

Cake. Funnier than pie? Funnier than pie theft, anyhow.

Cannibals. The sight gag of the giant cauldron used for missionary soup has been around—and funny—since 1871.

Cavemen. Even funnier because we don't think of *them* as having a sense of humor: they let their caveman truncheons do the laffing for them. Back in the surly adolescence of our species (if infancy was ape-hood), humor—or what later evolved into humor—was probably no more than schadenfreude. As it still is, most of the time, either because the mutant gene for real humor is recessive, or because the funny have never been very good about propagating themselves. And any caveman who laughed much *without* schadenfreude would have been considered insane and ostracized.

Cigars. Timelessly funny, though as a rule—and whether the joke is on its foulness or on its tendency to explode in the smoker's face after a few sucks—a cigar joke is a dick joke. Groucho Marx's cocky cigar is a dick joke—a running dick joke—and so therefore is the compulsive carrot-nibbling of Groucho's cartoon avatar Bugs Bunny. I'm not calling anybody gay, but those *are* dick jokes. I submit that Groucho was so demonically possessed by the spirit of mirth that he couldn't be in the same room with a cigar—or any other object—without every possible joke about that object instantly suggesting itself to him, like so many Arnold Horshacks soliciting Mr. Kotter's attention. All good comedians, even the G-rated ones, have dirty minds. Question: What do P. G. Wodehouse, Flip Wilson, Erma Bombeck, Dr. Seuss, Andy Rooney, Gracie Allen, Charles Schulz, Charles Addams, Harpo Marx, and Will Rogers have in common? Aside from the fact that all were funny, all are dead, and none was publicly notable for bawdiness (à la Milton Berle or Moms Mabley)? Answer: Each and every one could have brought down the house with a shockingly filthy version of the "Aristocrats" joke. Any sense of humor worthy of the name has a mind of its own (it really *is* like demonic possession), and all sorts of ways to circumvent the censorship by which the solemn keep their minds out of the gutter.

Dandruff. The quintessential trivial affliction, harmless but embarrassing, and wholly unheroic. Most old dandruff humor features people taking the affliction too seriously. In "Dizzy Doctors," a Three Stooges short from 1937, one of the bedridden patients has been *hospitalized* for dandruff.

Deodorants. And were you aware that Ban Roll-On, which debuted in 1952, was purportedly inspired by the wizardry of the then-newfangled ball-point pens?

The Dutch. Once proverbial for comic stinginess, as the Scottish are to this day. The stereotype endures in fossil form in expressions like "Dutch auction," "Dutch treat," and "Dutch oven." The last phrase at least is still funny, or funny again, due to its recent enlistment as a name for a sexual practice that strikes most of us as disgustingly funny. If you don't know about that practice you can find out with great ease online. While you're at it, read up on the Flying Dutchman wedgie, further evidence that our culture—or its collective unconscious, as embodied by sadistic middle schoolers—continues to laugh about the Dutch.

Elopement. Funny only if a ladder is involved.

Flagpole Sitting. Funny because it was the most improbable of fads, but also because it's always funny when someone sits on something rigid and pointy, be it a thumbtack or a minaret. The chorus girl in *42nd Street* turns down a patron's offer to sit in his lap by saying "I ain't no flagpole sitter."

Goats. Still funny, but nowhere near as funny as they used to be. In 1905, there were at least two comic strips (*The Goat Family* and *Panhandle Pete*) whose daily punch line was somebody being butted by a billy goat.

Goethe. At least four kinds of funny, since he was poet ("I sing as the bird sings"), a German ("Mehr Licht!"), a lover ("A poem is a kiss bestowed on the world, but mere kisses do not produce children"), and a sage ("The man of understanding finds everything laughable").

Gravy. One of the funniest substances omitted from this book.

Halitosis. Like dipsomania or diarrhea, an everyday condition rendered funnier with a Greco-Roman name.

Horny Doctors. You don't think horny doctors are funny? Try to picture Rilke writing a poem about one.

Horny Patients. Especially the ones in full-body casts. Where there's lust, there's life.

Incompletion. As no less an expert than W. C. Fields once observed, "The funniest thing a comedian can do is not do it."

Acknowledgments

The author would like to thank Kathryn Francavilla, Sarah McAbee, Cal Morgan, Eric Simonoff, and Bradford Verter. I'd also like to thank the many bloggers who share my old-humor obsessions, and especially two who helped me track down images, L. F. Appel of Postcardy.com and Steven Stwalley of Crumbling Paper.